READIN
D0890401

in Managed Health Care

A Companion to
Essentials of Managed Health Care, Second Edition

Editor
Peter R. Kongstvedt, MD, FACP

Partner
Ernst & Young LLP
Washington, DC

AN ASPEN PUBLICATION®
Aspen Publishers, Inc.
Gaithersburg, Maryland
1997

This publication is designed to provide accurate and authoritative information in regard to the Subject Matter covered. It is sold with the understanding that the publisher is not engaged in rendering legal, accounting, or other professional service. If legal advice or other expert assistance is required, the service of a competent professional person should be sought. *(From a Declaration of Principles jointly adopted by a Committee of the American Bar Association and a Committee of Publishers and Associations.)*

Library of Congress Cataloging-in-Publication Data

Readings in managed health care: a companion to the Essentials of managed health care, second edition/Peter R. Kongstvedt, [editor].
p.   cm.
Includes bibliographical references and index.
1. Managed care plans (Medical care)—United States.
I. Kongstvedt, Peter R. (Peter Reid)   II. Essentials of managed health care.
[DNLM: 1. Managed Care Programs—organization & administration—United States—collected works.   2. Delivery of Health Care—economics—United States—collected works.   W 130 AA1 R2 1997]
RA413.5.U5R43   1997
362.1'04258—dc21
DNLM/DLC
for Library of Congress
97-7980
CIP

Orders: (800) 638-8437
Customer Service: (800) 234-1660

About Aspen Publishers • For more than 35 years, Aspen has been a leading professional publisher in a variety of disciplines. Aspen's vast information resources are available in both print and electronic formats. We are committed to providing the highest quality information available in the most appropriate format for our customers. Visit Aspen's Internet site for more information resources, directories, articles, and a searchable version of Aspen's full catalog, including the most recent publications: **http://www.aspenpub.com**
Aspen Publishers, Inc. • The hallmark of quality in publishing
Member of the worldwide Wolters Kluwer group.

Editorial Resources: Lenda Hill
Library of Congress Catalog Card Number:
ISBN: 0-8342-0963-2

Printed in the United States of America

1 2 3 4 5

Table of Contents

Contributors

David Aquilina
Director
Business Development
O'PIN Systems, Inc.
Bloomington, MN

Paul B. Batalden, MD
Vice President for Medical Care and Head of
  the Quality Resource Group
Hospital Corporation of America
Nashville, TN

Charlette L. Beyerl
Executive Director and CEO
Wisconsin Independent Physicians Group, Inc.
Milwaukee, WI

John D. Blum, JD, MHS
Associate Dean and Professor of Law
Loyola University Chicago, School of Law
Institute for Health Law
Chicago, IL

Caron Primas Brennan, RN, BSN
Director of Marketing
Health Network Ventures
Westchester, IL

Montague Brown, MBA, Dr PH, JD
Editor of *Health Care Management Review*
Chairman
Strategic Management Services, Inc.
Tucson, AZ

Lawton R. Burns, MBA, PhD
Department of Management and Policy and the
  School of Public Administration and Policy
College of Business and Public Administration
University of Arizona
Tucson, AZ

James Chase
Director of Purchasing and Service Delivery
Minnesota Department of Human Services
St. Paul, MN

Stephen F. Coady, MS
Consultant
Value Health Information Group
Avon, CT

Russell C. Coile, Jr., MBA
Editor of *Russ Coile's Health Trends*
President
Health Forecasting Group
Santa Clarita, CA

Christopher W. Counihan, MSW
Regional Manager
Network Management
Boston, MA

Andrea de Vries
Research Assistant
Institute for Health Services Research
University of Minnesota
Minneapolis, MN

Gloria J. Deckard, PhD
Assistant Professor and Broward Program
   Coordinator
Health Services Administration
Florida International University
Miami, FL

Bryan Dowd, PhD
Professor
Institute for Health Services Research
University of Minnesota
Minneapolis, MN

Robert J. Dymowski, FSA
(Retired) Former Consulting Actuary
Milliman & Robertson, Inc.
Radnor, PA

Suzanne Felt-Lisk, MPA
Senior Health Researcher
Mathematica Policy Research, Inc.
Washington, DC

Steven A. Finkler, PhD, CPA
Professor of Health Administration,
   Accounting, and Financial Management
The Robert F. Wagner Graduate School of
   Public Service
New York University
New York, NY

Nancy B. Fisher, MSW, MBA
Planning Analyst
Presbyterian Healthcare Services
Albuquerque, NM

Robert Giffin, PhD
President
Health Care Strategy Associates, Inc.
Washington, DC

Thomas D. Gotowka
Assistant Vice President
Medical Policy and Programs
Aetna Health Plans
Middletown, CT

Nicholas A. Hanchak, MD
Medical Director of U.S. Quality Algorithms
   and Vice President of Research and
   Development
U.S. Healthcare, Inc.
Blue Bell, PA

Sandra R. Harmon-Weiss, MD
Vice President and Medical Director
U.S. Healthcare, Inc.
Blue Bell, PA

Philip M. Hawley, Jr., MD
President
Pace Healthcare Management, Inc.
Los Angeles, CA

David W. Hilgers, JD
Managing Director
Hilgers & Watkins, P.C.
Austin, TX

Alex Hirsch
MIS
Clinical Studies and Analysis
U.S. Quality Algorithms, Inc.
U.S. Healthcare, Inc.
Blue Bell, PA

Melville H. Hodge, BSEE
Principal
Melville Hodge-Consulting
Saratoga, CA

Mark Jackson
Senior Systems Consultant
Aetna Health Plans
Middletown, CT

Sheila Jacobs
Senior Consultant
The HSM Group, Ltd
Scottsdale, AZ

John D. Klein
Vice President
Health Strategies Group, Inc.
St. Paul, MM

John E. Kralewski, PhD
Professor and Director
Institute for Health Services Research
University of Minnesota
Minneapolis, MN

Joyce A. Lanning, PhD
Health Care Consultant
Schools of Public Health and Health-Related
   Professions
University of Alabama at Birmingham

Patricia D. McDermott, RN
Member
Research and Development
U.S. Quality Algorithms, Inc.
U.S. Healthcare, Inc.
Blue Bell, PA

S. Spence Meighan, MD, FACP, FRCP
President
Spence Meighan and Associates
Portland, OR

Dale Mickey, MBA
Consultant, Quality Research
Health Services Quality Management
Aetna Health Plans
Hartford, CT

Wayne J. Miller, Esq.
Attorney
Weissburg and Aronson, Inc.
Los Angeles, CA

Philip Nathanson
Vice President
Health Services Quality Management
Aetna Health Plans
Hartford, CT

Roger C. Nauert, JD, MBA
President
RCN Associates
White Plains, NY

Anne-Marie Nelson
Vice President
The HSM Group, Ltd
Scottsdale, AZ

Deborah Nelson, PhD
Director of Quality Management
Network Management
Boston, MA

Eugene C. Nelson, DSc, MPH
Director of Quality Education, Measurement
   and Research
Dartmouth-Hitchcock Medical Center
Lebanon, NH

Monica Noether, PhD
Vice President
Abt Associates
Cambridge, MA

Stephen J. O'Connor, PhD
Assistant Professor of Health Care Management
School of Business Administration
University of Wisconsin-Milwaukee

James F. Owens, JD
Counsel
McCrutchen, Doyle, Brown & Enersen
Los Angeles, CA

Ronald J. Ozminkowski, PhD
Senior Economist
Abt Associates
Bethesda, MD

Derick P. Pasternak, MD, MBA
President
Lovelace, Inc.
Albuquerque, NM

Elizabeth Pattullo, MEd
Executive Director
Network Management
Boston, MA

Sandra Potthoff, PhD
Assistant Professor
Division of Health Management and Policy
University of Minnesota
Minneapolis, MN

Reinhard Priester, JD
Associate for Health Policy at the Minnesota
    Center for Health Care Ethics
Minneapolis, MN

Brendan E. Raney, MD
Managed Care Consultant
Pace Healthcare Management, Inc.
Los Angeles, CA

Robyn Rontal
Product Specialist
Development Center
MEDSTAT Systems, Inc.
Ann Arbor, MI

Leslie J. Scallet, JD
Founder and Executive Director
Mental Health Policy Resource Center
Washington, DC

Neil Schlackman, MD, FAAP
President
U.S. Quality Algorithms
Chairman of Corporate Quality Improvement
U.S. Healthcare, Inc.
Blue Bell, PA

Howard L. Smith, PhD
Professor and Associate Dean
Anderson Schools of Management
University of New Mexico
Albuquerque, NM

Kevin M. Smith, MD
Managed Care Consultant
Pace Healthcare Management, Inc.
Los Angeles, CA

Ellen E. Stewart, MSHA, JD, FHFMA
Gorsuch Kirgis L.L.C.
Denver, CO

Darrell P. Thorpe, MD, MPH
Senior Vice-President for Strategic Services
Tucson Medical Center
Tucson, AZ

James J. Unland, MBA
Editor of the *Journal of Health Care Finance*
President
The Health Capital Group
Chicago, IL

Steven D. Wood, PhD
Chairman
The HSM Group, Ltd
Scottsdale, AZ

Preface

This collection of readings is a companion to *The Essentials of Managed Health Care, 2nd Edition.* That text, while providing a broad view of the managed health care industry (though not a comprehensive view; for that reader is referred to the *Essential's* parent text—*The Managed Health Care Handbook, 3rd Edition*), is necessarily limited in scope simply due to the fact that it is a single text. To address that issue, this companion collection of readings has been assembled. The readings are articles on managed health care culled from the following Aspen journals:

- *Managed Care Quarterly,*
- *Health Care Management Review,*
- *Journal of Health Care Finance* (formerly *Topics in Health Care Financing*), and
- *Quality Management in Health Care.*

There are several reasons an article may have been selected for inclusion. In some cases, the article presents a next level of depth on a subject that is worth further discussion. In other cases, the article presents a point of view not found in the *Essentials* (or possibly a point of view not shared by another author). Some articles are included primarily to provoke discussion in the classroom, not necessarily because I agree with the point the author is making, but in order to expose the reader to an alternate point of view, or at least an alternate interpretation.

The readings roughly parallel the parts in the textbook. The exception to this is the inclusion of an additional part: Integrated Delivery Systems. This part has been placed in the readings to provide the reader with more information and viewpoints regarding organized provider systems than is found in the *Essentials* in the second section of that book.

These readings are by no means exhaustive nor do they represent more than a sampling of available literature on the topic of managed health care. Most chapters in the *Essentials* contain references and suggested readings that may also be of value. These readings and those suggestions combined still represent only a fraction of the available literature. Therefore, the serious student of this topic will use these readings as a springboard only, and will find additional sources to enrich their knowledge of the field.

On a final note, I am delighted to report that the level of professionalism and quality of published articles on managed health care has been steadily increasing over the past decade. It is my sincerest hope that these companion texts, as adjuncts to the academic courses on managed health care, will inspire additional high quality research and publications by those who are reading these words right now.

Peter R. Kongstvedt
Editor

Part I
Introduction to Managed Care

1

Does Managed Care Offer Value to Society?

Reinhard Priester

A Promising Health Reform Strategy

The rapid adoption of managed care is the most significant development in America's health care system over the past decade. Despite the federal government's failure in 1994 to arrive at a comprehensive strategy for national health reform, the health care system in many regions of the country is being transformed, usually around managed care. This transformation is driven principally by market forces, and in some states reinforced by government action. Managed care is now also widely embraced in Congress as the means to help curb the soaring costs threatening the Medicare and Medicaid programs. Thus, managed care is viewed as the most promising health reform strategy in both the private and public sectors. With or without comprehensive national reform, managed care is likely to become the dominant model for health care delivery and financing for the foreseeable future.

Large employers and other purchasers are now exploring value-based formulas for purchasing managed care products. Other articles in this issue address this development from various stakeholder perspectives; for example, by evaluating alternative mechanisms for measuring the "value" of a managed care product to the purchaser. This article takes a broader view and considers whether managed care offers value to our society. This question is important for assessing both the overall growth of managed care as well as changes within the managed care industry including, for example, the shift from staff and group model HMOs to less tightly managed health plans.

Five essential goals can be used as benchmarks for evaluating managed care:

1. promote efficiency
2. expand access
3. improve quality
4. preserve freedom of choice
5. protect patient advocacy.

These goals are not pulled from thin air; rather, there is widespread agreement on their central role in shaping our health care system.[1,2] After briefly outlining the five goals, the article presents a preliminary assessment of how well managed care advances each of them. Such an assessment can help us determine whether managed care is, all things considered, a good investment. This assessment is only a first step; much work remains before we will be able to definitively conclude that managed care does or does not offer value to our society.

Recent Trends and Projections

The term *managed care* has two distinct meanings. Though sometimes used to refer to discrete initiatives that seek to combine financial and medical decisions (e.g., utilization management), managed care is most often used to refer to the continually adapting and developing alternative health care plans that, in varying degrees, integrate the financing and delivery of medical care. Despite the variations, all managed care plans "manage" physician and patient behavior through a host of financial and administrative mechanisms, reverse the economic incentives of traditional fee-for-service practice, and require physicians to assume some of the financial risk of their decisions.[3] To reflect contemporary usage, this article will use managed care as shorthand to refer to all types of managed care plans.

Over the past two decades, managed care has shifted from not-for-profit, relatively tightly managed (staff, group, or network) independent HMOs to for-profit, independent practice associations or mixed models affiliated with a national managed care firm. For example, while not-for-profit HMOs outnumbered

Managed Care Quarterly 1997; 5(1): 57–63

for-profit HMOs by 2 to 1 in 1985, by 1994 this ratio was reversed. The shift toward for-profit plans has been accompanied by a trend toward ownership by insurance companies and investors, instead of hospitals and other health care providers.[4]

Targeted growth areas for managed care include Medicare and Medicaid and the small employer market, particularly among employers who offer only one plan. The looming financial crisis for Medicare has fueled interest in both government and the private sector to dramatically increase managed care's role in the program. Medicaid managed care enrollment more than doubled between 1987 and 1992 to 3.6 million beneficiaries and had risen to 11.6 million by June 1995—nearly one of every three Medicaid beneficiaries. Among small employers, managed care plans that offer greater choice of physicians are now gaining acceptance. Such plans give these employers the opportunity to achieve the potential cost savings of managed care and yet provide their employees a health plan with substantial freedom of choice.

The types of changes in the makeup of the managed care industry observed over the past decade are likely to continue. Thus, national managed care firms are expected to dominate the managed care market and to continue to account for the majority of enrollees. Managed care's involvement in Medicare and Medicaid will likely increase significantly. Renewed enthusiasm, particularly among congressional leaders, for the free market as the appropriate framework for health care means that investor-owned managed care is likely to flourish. And, the less tightly managed plans that offer greater choice and flexibility, such as IPAs and POS plans, will continue to gain market share as their popularity grows among enrollees, providers, and purchasers of managed care. These changes, even more so than the growth of managed care itself, will affect the assessment of managed care's value to society.

Goals for Assessing Managed Care's Value

Managed care is championed by many as the best strategy to control costs as well as to improve the efficiency and quality of care. To achieve these objectives, however, managed care profoundly alters the roles, responsibilities, and relationships of physicians, purchasers, patients, and society. Most notably, managed care enters into decisions that have tradi-

tionally been confined to the clinician/patient relationship, historically, the most important relationship in our health care system.[5] To assess whether managed care—and the changes it has wrought— provide value to our society, we can measure its performance relative to five essential health care goals. These goals, which have shaped and continue to shape health care policy at both the national and state levels, define what is important to us in our health care system; in short, they reflect what we, as a society, value in our health care system.[6,7]

Promote efficiency

Efficiency has two important dimensions: minimizing the cost of whatever services are provided, and choosing the set of services that leads to the maximum excess of benefits over costs.[8] An efficient health care system is thus not necessarily the least expensive, but it obtains the greatest benefit (defined in terms of desired outcomes) for the lowest cost. So defined, efficiency has only recently been recognized as important to our health care system. When all health care needs cannot be met because financial resources are limited, as is true today, it is inappropriate to simply try to hold down costs, which was the focus of cost containment initiatives in the 1970s and 1980s. Instead, we must also pay attention to what works in health care, seeking to achieve desired outcomes with the least expenditure.

Expand access

Health care is of special importance in promoting personal well-being; relieving pain, suffering, and disability; and preventing premature death.[9] Without access to beneficial services, an individual is at risk of significant, perhaps irreversible harm, and the individual's potential for participating in the "array of life plans" that are reasonable to pursue within a given society (for example, various education or career paths) is seriously impeded. In one commentator's words, "an individual's range of opportunities is reduced when disease or disability impairs normal functioning. Since we have obligations to protect equal opportunity, we also have obligations to provide access, without financial or discriminatory barriers, to services that adequately protect and restore normal functioning."[10] Accordingly, expanding access to the health care services that individuals need to cure or prevent illnesses, mitigate symptoms, and ease pain and suffering is a priority goal for our health care system.

Two distinguishable objectives are to expand access to needed health care services for individuals who already have insurance and to expand access for individuals without insurance. A variety of strategies, from 24-hour nurse hotlines to case management programs to assure appropriate care for persons with chronic illnesses,[11] can reduce barriers to care for health plan enrollees. The principal strategy for expanding access to persons without insurance is to reduce the number of uninsured individuals. However, though providing health insurance coverage provides individuals with the financial means to obtain needed care, language handicaps, cultural barriers, and other nonfinancial barriers to care must also be overcome before access can be assured.[12]

Improve quality

Quality care maximizes the likelihood of desired health outcomes for individuals and populations, is consistent with current and emerging professional knowledge, and is humanely and respectfully provided.[13] The appropriate focus for quality is on health outcomes, as opposed to the structure and process of care, or even on intermediate outcomes, such as changes in a blood cell count. It is important to note that quality health care is an ideal; maximizing the likelihood of desired outcomes is a goal to strive for. Finally, the preferences and values of individual patients should help determine which health interventions and associated outcomes are desired.

Preserve freedom of choice

Consumer's freedom of choice is important in both the market for providers (and services) and the market for health care coverage. Theoretically, a market for particular goods or services responds to, and thus ultimately reflects, the choices of individual buyers or consumers: they, not the sellers or some third party, determine the shape of the market. In this way, freedom of choice functions as a check on the health care system, making it more responsive to consumer preferences regarding the times, places, and quality of care. A system unresponsive to consumer preferences would lack accountability to patients. Unfortunately, the vast majority of privately insured Americans have group (usually employer-provided) health insurance.

These plans reflect directly the purchasing decisions made by employers, and only indirectly the decisions of individual consumers themselves.

Protect patient advocacy

Patient advocacy, a central tenet of medical ethics, requires physicians to single-mindedly pursue individual patient's best interests, regardless of others' interests.[14] As one doctor forcefully stated, "Physicians are required to do everything that they believe may benefit each patient without regard to costs or other societal considerations."[15] Physicians, it is often said, cannot serve two masters, and circumstances that present potential conflicts of interest should always be resolved in favor of the patient. This traditional conception of advocacy has also been a cornerstone of patients' trust in their physicians: "The patient-physician relationship flourishes and patient care is improved when patients trust their physicians and that trust is promoted when patients recognize that their physicians are their advocates" and not the agents of a health plan, some other third party, or society in general.[16]

Record and Potential of Managed Care for Advancing These Goals

How well does managed care advance these goals? How well does it accomplish what we—collectively, as a society—want it to? Despite the enthusiasm for managed care, and despite its rapid and projected continued growth, its impact on our health care system is not well understood. Information on the effect of managed care plans on cost, quality, and other performance indicators, for example, is mixed, with many questions still unanswered. Furthermore, studies evaluating the performance of managed care plans have focused on HMOs, especially staff and group models, which no longer dominate the managed care market. Relatively little information exists for other types of HMOs, even less for PPOs and POS plans, which now exhibit the fastest growth. Managed care's potential effects on physicians' advocacy role and on patients' confidence in their doctors (perceived as a real threat by many[17]) have also not been adequately researched.[18] The following analysis thus provides only a preliminary assessment of managed care's value to society.

Record to promote efficiency unclear, but potential high

In a recent comprehensive review of the literature on managed care's performance, Miller and Luft found that the widespread belief in managed care's ability to save costs relative to the traditional nonmanaged health care system is not substantiated. Based on the author's findings that "published information on hospital charges per stay, hospital expenditures per enrollee, ambulatory charges and expenditures per enrollee, and total expenditures per enrollee is scant and limited in usefulness," they conclude that "adequate bottom-line estimates of expenditure differences per enrollee" of managed care compared with indemnity plans are not yet possible.[19] (Nevertheless, Miller and Luft argue that in light of differences between HMO and indemnity plans, such as more comprehensive coverage in HMOs plans, "HMOs provide care at lower cost than do indemnity plans.") Similarly, with only a few exceptions, managed care has not yet been found to produce significant savings for Medicaid programs.[20]

Information on the efficiency of managed care is even more limited. Needed are studies of managed care that link costs with outcomes, especially functional health-related quality of care outcomes. Presently, any conclusions regarding managed care's relative efficiency are premature. However, there are strong theoretical reasons to believe that managed care plans have a greater potential to promote efficiency than traditional indemnity insurance. Because of their organizational structure, managed care plans are better equipped to measure the outcome of care, identify quality problems, and implement strategies for improvement, such as adopting clinical guidelines to reduce unjustified variations in medical practice. Managed care plans also have a unique opportunity to intervene at the system level, and thus have the potential to overcome the fragmentation that underlies much of the inefficiency of the poorly organized fee-for-service sector.[21]

Record in expanding access mixed and potential limited

Through both organizational structures and financial incentives, managed care plans can restrict enrollee access to needed services. The potential for harm is particularly acute for certain vulnerable populations. Some fear that managed care disrupts long-standing physician-patient relationships and restricts access for patients in need of specialty care such as mental health care and services for chronic illnesses. The extent to which managed care plans in fact restrict such access is unclear, however. Others note that even if evidence suggests that managed care limits access to mental health care, "the question of whether it ought to do so [for instance, for strong social or therapeutic reasons] would still need to be addressed."[22] Also, relatively few managed care plans have experience in providing care for Medicaid enrollees—a poor, culturally diverse, and poorly educated population whose health care needs are often more complex than those of the plans' traditional privately insured enrollees. As a result, managed care has sometimes compromised access for Medicaid enrollees, whose needs often stretch the boundaries of traditional health care.[23] On the other hand, managed care plan enrollees generally have greater access to preventive services and health promotion activities.[24]

Managed care's record on reducing the number of uninsured individuals is also unclear. The recent rapid growth of managed care has been accompanied by a steady rise in the number of Americans without health insurance; yet the relation between these two developments has not been sufficiently studied. However, the growth of managed care clearly has the potential to further restrict access for people without insurance: capitation and similar risk-sharing arrangements, which are common to managed care plans, provide incentives to avoid costly (that is, sick) patients, and managed care plans have benefitted from such favorable selection in the past.[25] Again, vulnerable populations appear to be at greatest risk.

Record in improving quality meager, potential ambiguous

Studies measuring patient satisfaction and other features such as the continuity, comprehensiveness, and coordination of care show some differences on these indicators of quality between fee-for-service and managed care settings. Managed care enrollees are generally less satisfied with their quality of care and physician/patient interactions, and less likely to rate access (e.g., to specialty care and emergency services) as excellent. However, they are more satisfied with the costs of their health plans.[26,27]

Studies measuring health outcomes show little or no measurable differences between managed care and traditional fee-for-services care. For example, one large study found no meaningful differences in changes in overall health status among Medicare enrollees between 10 communities with Medicare managed care options and 10 communities without such options.[28] Studies comparing outcomes for care of specific conditions in managed care and fee-for-service for Medicaid enrollees also show no or only modest differences.[29] In their literature review, Miller and Luft conclude that based on current studies, HMO and indemnity plans provide roughly equal quality of care as measured for a wide range of conditions, diseases, and interventions.[30] Notable exceptions to these outcome findings are studies that show poorer outcomes for patients with mental health problems in managed care relative to fee-for-service settings.[31,32]

The potential for managed care to improve, rather than simply preserve, the quality of care is ambiguous. As previously noted, managed care plans can use their clinical information systems and administrative databases to monitor patient care and, as a result, are better equipped to identify quality problems and implement strategies for improvement. Some conjecture, however, that the quality of care in managed care may in fact suffer, for example if gatekeeping and other features encourage or require primary care clinicians to practice outside their areas of competency.[33]

Record and potential to protect freedom of choice unclear

Restricting choice of provider is a central element of most managed care plans. It is often "enforced" through significant financial penalties incurred if individuals choose to obtain care outside of the plan's identified group of providers. Generally, however, freedom of choice among health plans subsumes choice among providers. That is, while some plans restrict choice among providers, others do not; thus, the voice of consumers will remain strong even if the freedom to choose among providers is (somewhat) restricted—so long as choices exist among plans that offer a choice (among providers) and those that do not.[34]

It is not clear if freedom of choice in the market for health insurance has become more restricted, despite the proliferation of managed care plans. Clearly, many employees (particularly in smaller firms) do not have a choice of health plans. Such lack of choice has now been found to be strongly related to satisfaction. In a 1994 study, twice as many managed care enrollees with no choice of plans rated their plan fair or poor than managed care enrollees who had a choice and those in fee-for-service plans. Freedom to change plans is also "likely to facilitate more effective care, [by safeguarding] against poor quality or nonresponsiveness to patient needs."[35]

Record in protecting patient advocacy problematic and potential slim

Managed care challenges the essential tenets of the patient-centered ethic that has been the foundation of our health care system. The economic incentives of managed care conflict with the physician's duty of fidelity to the individual patient, "transforming the physician's role from advocacy to allocating."[36] The gatekeeper role in managed care presents perhaps the clearest challenge to the traditional articulation of the advocacy role. Gatekeepers in a managed care plan, typically the enrollee's primary care physician, are expected to serve the patient's best interests, while simultaneously being cognizant of and complying with the plan's cost control efforts. The potential conflict is clear: to serve the patient, the physician may offer additional services; to serve the organization, the physician may err on the side of economy by restricting patient access to costly services.

The traditional conception of advocacy is challenged by other changes in the health care system as well. Physicians' undivided fidelity to individual patients is appropriate only if two conditions are met: (1) everyone has a physician-advocate; and (2) resources are limitless. Yet neither condition is met today: many people (primarily people without insurance) do not have an advocate, and health care resources *are* limited, for the health care system generally as well as for individual health plans.[37] Requiring physicians to do everything of medical benefit for their patients, to make treatment decisions *as if* resources were limitless, leads to irrational allocation of resources. An alternative conception of advocacy is therefore needed to resolve the conflict physicians face today. This conception would explicitly recognize scarcity, pointing out that treatment choices for an individual patient will affect the resources available for others and that money used to care for this patient means money not spent to care for another—who may, in fact, benefit more. Physicians' concern would not be limited to the care of a particular patient, but also encompass the particular patient's needs in relationship to the needs of others and in light of available resources. Physicians would have obligations not only to their patients, but also to others, recognizing that "behind each presenting patient awaits another patient in need of services."[38] This clearly conflicts with the traditional view since here physicians may do less than the maximum for some patients in order to conserve resources for the greater benefit of other patients.

Though these changes in the health care system call for a modification of the concept of advocacy, managed care presents the most direct challenge. Because of their obligations to use a fixed budget to provide health care services to a defined population, managed care plans make trade-offs between patients more explicit. In managed care plans, the key is not for physicians to ignore the consequences of their treatment decisions on the amount of resources available for the benefit of the population (e.g., the health plan enrollees), but for them "to strive to ensure that those decisions do not adversely impact the health of patients."[39]

Often, however, competition, market forces, and other economic considerations can present just such a threat to patients' health. For many managed care plans, especially investor-owned, for-profit, cost containment is the primary purpose, rather than an unexpected benefit.[40] Such plans may subordinate health care values to marketplace values, thereby undermining clinicians' roles as patient advocates.[41] Moving Medicare and Medicaid enrollees into managed care raises particular concern about double agency and loss of appropriate advocacy for an already vulnerable population.

●   ●   ●

As this preliminary assessment shows, we know surprisingly little about the impact of managed care. While managed care obviously has the capacity to improve our health care system (for example, by creating the mechanisms to measure and hold providers accountable for the outcome of care), it also has the potential to interfere with our ability to achieve important health care goals. The concerns about managed care's ability to advance these goals and thus to offer value are heightened if recently observed trends continue. The accelerating push to enroll more Medicare and Medicaid recipients in managed care plans has resulted in a rapid influx of high-risk persons into such plans. Yet managed care may not be ready for the unique challenges these persons pose—especially Medicaid enrollees with severe mental illnesses.[42] The growth in the for-profit sector is similarly troubling since the values of the marketplace are fundamentally at odds with the values and goals of health care professionals and institutions. Market-driven health care places the interests of shareholders above the interests of patients and is thereby "likely to alienate physicians, undermine patient's trust in physicians' motives . . . and expand the population of patients without health care coverage."[43] In sum, the jury is still out for determining whether managed care offers value to our society.

REFERENCES

1. Priester, R. "A Values Framework for Health Reform." *Health Affairs* 11(1) (1992): 84–107.
2. Brock, D.W., and Daniels, N. "Ethical Foundations of the Clinton Administration's Proposed Health Care System." *Journal of the American Medical Association* 271(15) (1994): 1189–1196.
3. Fletcher, J.C., and Englehard, C. L. "Ethical Issues in Managed Care." *Virginia Medical Quarterly* 122(3) (1995): 162–167.
4. Davis, K., Collins, K.S., and Morris, C. "Managed Care: Promises and Concerns." *Health Affairs* 13(3) (1994): 178–185.
5. Angell, M. "Cost Containment and the Physician." *Journal of the American Medical Association* 254 (1985): 1203–1207.
6. Brock and Daniels, "Ethical Foundations."
7. Fletcher and Englehard, "Ethical Issues."
8. Pauly, M.V., et al. "A Plan for 'Responsible Health Insurance.'" *Health Affairs* 10(1) (1991): 5–25.
9. President's Commission for the Study of Ethical Problems in Medicine and Biomedical and Behavioral Research. *Securing Access to Health Care.* vol. 1, report. Washington, D.C.: Government Printing Office, 1983.
10. Daniels, N. "Health Care and Distributive Justice." *Philosophy and Public Affairs* 10 (1981): 146–179.
11. Sandy, L.G., and Gibson, R. "Managed Care and Chronic Care: Challenges and Opportunities." *Managed Care Quarterly* 4(2) (1996): 5–11.
12. Ginzberg, E., and Ostow, M. "Beyond Universal Health Insurance to Effective Care." *Journal of the American Medical Association* 265 (1991): 2559–2562.
13. Institute of Medicine, Committee to Design a Strategy for Quality Review and Assurance in Medicare. *Medicare: A Strategy for Quality Assurance.* Washington, D.C.: National Academy Press, 1990.

14. Council on Ethical and Judicial Affairs, American Medical Association. "Ethical Issues in Managed Care." *Journal of the American Medical Association* 273(4) (1995): 330–335.

15. Levinsky, N. "The Doctors Master." *The New England Journal of Medicine* 311 (1984): 1573–1575.

16. Brody, H. "The Physician-Patient Relationship: Models and Criticisms." *Theoretical Medicine* 8 (1987): 205–220.

17. Kassirer, J.P. "Managed Care and the Morality of the Marketplace." *New England Journal of Medicine* 333(1) (1995): 50–52.

18. Blumenthal, D. "Effects of Market Reforms on Doctors and Their Patients." *Health Affairs* 15(2) (1996): 170–184.

19. Miller, R.H., and Luft, H.S. "Managed Care Plan Performance Since 1980: A Literature Analysis." *Journal of the American Medical Association* 271(19) (1994): 1512–1519.

20. The Kaiser Commission on the Future of Medicaid. *Medicaid and Managed Care: Lessons from the Literature.* Menlo Park, CA: Henry K. Kaiser Family Foundation, 1995.

21. Sandy and Gibson, "Managed Care and Chronic Care."

22. Boyle, P.J., and Callahan, D. "Managed Care and Mental Health: The Ethical Issues." *Health Affairs* 14(4) (1995): 7–22.

23. Kaiser Commission, *Medicaid and Managed Care.*

24. Udvarhelyi, I.S., et al. "Comparison of the Quality of Ambulatory Care for Fee-For-Service and Prepaid Patient." *Internal Medicine* 327 (1991): 424–429.

25. Blumenthal, "Effects of Market Reforms."

26. Rubin, H.R., et al. "Patients' Ratings of Outpatient Visits in Different Practice Settings: Results from the Medical Outcomes Study." *Journal of the American Medical Association* 270 (1993): 835–840.

27. Davis, K., et al. "Choice Matters: Enrollees' Views of Their Health Plans." *Health Affairs* 14(2) (1995): 99–112.

28. Retchin, S.M., et al. "How the Elderly Fare in HMOs: Outcomes from the Medicare Competition Demonstration." *Health Services Research* 27 (1992): 651–670.

29. Carey, T.S., Weis, K., and Homer, C. "Prepaid versus Traditional Medicaid Plans: Lack of Effect on Pregnancy Outcomes and Prenatal Care." *Health Services Research* 26 (1991): 165–181.

30. Miller and Luft, "Managed Care Plan Performance."

31. Rogers, W.H., et al. "Outcomes for Adult Outpatients with Depression Under Prepaid or Fee-For-Service Financing." *Archives of General Psychiatry* 50 (1993): 517–525.

32. Wells, K.B., et al. "Detection of Depressive Disorder for Patients Receiving Prepaid or Fee-For-Service Care: Results from the Medical Outcomes Study." *Journal of the American Medical Association* 262 (1989): 3298–3302.

33. Blumenthal, "Effects of Market Reforms."

34. Priester, "A Values Framework for Health Reform."

35. Davis, et al, "Choice Matters?"

36. Mechanic, D. "The Transformation of Health Providers." *Health Affairs* 3(1) (1984): 65–72.

37. Aaron, H., and Schwartz, W. "Rationing Health Care: The Choice Before Us." *Science* 247 (1990): 418–424.

38. Jonsen, A.L. *The New Medicine and the Old Ethics.* Cambridge, MA: Harvard University Press, 1990.

39. Clancy, C.M., and Brody, H. "Managed Care: Jeckyl or Hyde?" *Journal of the American Medical Association* 273(4) (1995): 338–339.

40. Ibid.

41. Woolhandler, S., and Himmelstein, D.U. "Extreme Risk—The New Corporate Proposition for Physicians." *New England Journal of Medicine* 333(25) (1995): 1706–1709.

42. Durham, M.L. "Can HMOs Manage the Mental Health Benefit?" *Health Affairs* 14(3) (1995): 117–123.

43. Kassirer, "Managed Care and the Mortality of the Marketplace."

2

The Quest for Value in Health Care

Roger C. Nauert

It is a fundamental law of economics that those firms that offer the best value to the marketplace will generally survive the longest. As the health care industry integrates and becomes more competitive, this rule will increasingly determine the winners and losers in the tough new era of managed care.

Whether it is the purchase of a wristwatch, a car, or health care services, buyers will inevitably consider the quality received in light of the price paid. Value, therefore, can be defined as the beneficial relationship of quality divided by cost:

$$\text{Value} = \frac{\text{Quality}}{\text{Cost}}$$

In health care, these concepts have some fundamental aspects that distinguish them from other service industries. This is largely the result of the duality that separates purchasers of benefit plans from consumers who may have less sensitivity to cost because they are generally not responsible for full payment. Consumers, therefore, tend to consider service levels and economic costs (like waiting time) in their determination of "value." Purchasers are much more focused on treatment outcomes and the financial costs of care weighed against the benefits.

Providers of health care add yet another perspective. Motivated by life-saving objectives and compelling ethical mandates, their perspectives on value are different still. They also are driven by the need to maintain financial integrity. They weigh the human costs of care against the risks of rationing and denial.

Each of the stakeholders in health care delivery has different biases and vested interests. If pressured, however, most reasonable constituents could agree on some balancing point where additional resource consumption and costs do not improve quality and do not add

value. This is demonstrated in Figure 2–1 in the graph representing a typical hospital stay. The question is: How do we come up with a common definition of "value" that represents sound health care policy while recognizing the realities of supply and demand?

A Working Definition of Value

Although all three entities are driven by the same quest for value, their definitions and terms vary on the basis of their own enlightened self-interest. Figure 2–2 offers a working definition of value and the focal points maintained by purchasers, consumers, and providers.

Purchaser Dominance

Although all these perspectives influence value determination, the role played by purchasers has become increasingly dominant. Organized business and government exert enormous purchasing power on behalf of employees, dependents, and entitled recipients.

Freedom of choice will become severely restricted in the years ahead. Whether the discussions take place in a boardroom on Park Avenue or under a statehouse dome in the Midwest, purchasers will have much to say about who receives what kind of care and at what price.

As health benefits and entitlements are compared and weighed, they are considered in the context of an agenda that has value at the top of the list. The purchaser's agenda is as follows:

- value for each dollar spent,
- reliable information on cost and quality,
- control and budget power over future health care expenditures,
- improved health status for beneficiaries,
- creative solutions for problem health care areas,

J Health Care Financ 1996; 22(3): 52–61

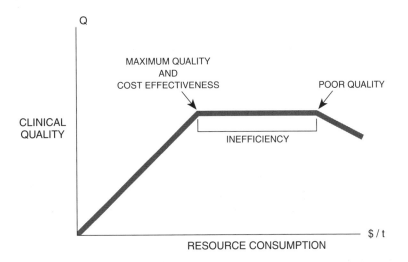

Figure 2–1. Value in a typical hospital stay.

- influence on health policy as stakeholders, and
- economic leverage as major purchasers of health care.

Large, highly experienced purchasers add even greater dimensionality to health plan selection. American Express, for example, conducts extensive interviews and field audits to evaluate a plan's given commitment to preventive medicine and wellness. Similarly, the company also wants to determine the ability of the plan to manage manifestly sick members in terms of resource consumption and measured outcomes.

Well-organized purchasers will also consider a plan's commitment to continuous quality improvement (CQI) and its willingness to respond to quality assurance inquiries. Minimum qualifying scores are typically required for plan selection based on National Committee for Quality Assurance (NCQA) and Health Employer Data & Information Set (HEDIS) standards.

Even after there selection, chosen health plans must demonstrate high levels of accountability to maintain membership. American Express conducts regular on-site reviews focusing on areas such as the following:

- credentialing,
- utilization review case reviews,
- medical records,
- outcome analyses,
- quality assurance minutes, and
- clinical algorithms.

Independent studies are regularly done to assess patient satisfaction. These focus on access and waiting time as well as specific physicians.

Market Evolution

The quest for value is tied to the concept of market evolution. Most health care markets in the United States are heating up in terms of purchaser demands, managed care growth, provider integration, and physician organization. It is a pivotal assumption that these trends will intensify in the years ahead.

Some markets, like Pittsburgh and New Orleans, are still relatively unstructured and noncompetitive. Most are like New York, where large regional systems are developing and competition is becoming more perva-

Figure 2–2. A working definition of value and the focal points maintained by purchasers, consumers, and providers.

sive. A few, like Minneapolis, have evolved into full-scale competition among an oligopoly of a few dominant systems.

Exhibit 2–1 offers a four-stage model of market evolution based on the behavior of purchasers, providers, and physicians in a growing managed care environment.

Some Further Assumptions

As markets mature, competition will increasingly be based on value. Providers and consumers will have their say about health care delivery—and they will exert important influences. But it will be the purchas-ers who will determine the relative market strength of evolving systems.

At this point we can make several further assumptions about the future. First, we can assume that purchasers want to develop high-quality plans at reasonable costs. They will seek providers who can deliver quality care at a competitive cost (i.e., the best value).

Purchasers will prefer comprehensive systemic solutions to their problems and will make most of their choices based on value (although politics, social activism, union whining, and other extraneous factors may occasionally produce some anomalies). Acting alone and in groups, purchasers will assume the role

Exhibit 2–1 Market Evolution

	I **Quiet Village** Unstructured, noncompetitive	II **Perkville** Loose framework, alliance formation	III **Change City** Consolidation, system development	IV **Hell Town** Managed competition, dominant systems
Employers	• Care purchased from major indemnity insurers	• Coalitions forming to evaluate providers	• Strong incentives for managed care • Market influence by business	• Direct employer/ provider contracting
Managed care	• 0%–10% penetration by HMOs • Emergence of plans	• 11%–30% HMO penetration • Leaders emerge • Proliferation of plans	• 31%–50% penetration • Shakeout of marginal players • Emergence of dominant HMOs	• >50% penetration • Strong surviving HMOs in each regional market • Plans act like HMOs
Providers	• Independent free-standing hospitals • Focus on inpatient care	• Bed demand declining • Formation of provider alliances	• Formalized systems developing • Provider/payer alliances forming	• Competing regional provider systems • Solidified provider/ payer alliances • Oligopoly
Physicians	• Independent practices • Free choice referrals • Specialists dominate	• Independent physicians association (IPAs) without utilization management (UM) • Prepaid groups develop to serve HMOs	• IPAs with UM • Groups rapidly form and grow • Linkages with hospitals develop	• Physician-hospital organizations • Large groups • Generalists control

of stakeholders and will exert a growing influence over health policy.

In order to exert greater leverage over providers, purchasers will broker patient volumes among a select group of physicians and hospitals. As such, their volume will represent a greater proportion of the providers' business, thus producing stronger bargaining power.

Under these guide rules, purchasers will shift thousands of individuals from one provider system to another based on demonstrated value. The result will be that competition will increase among providers based on value.

The Consumer Standpoint

Health benefit plan selection by purchasers is subject to significant pressures by consumers and providers. One might think of the demand expressed by consumers as a "push." The supply side offerings of providers constitute a "pull."

The consumer, like the purchaser, also assesses value in terms of quality and cost. But the variables are somewhat different. Quality considerations such as provider image, service, amenities, and outcome data are important. But more controlling in plan selection are the range of programs available, physician quality, and hospital reputation.

Cost is measured in both financial and economic terms. The most important considerations are the out-of-pocket cash impact and the ease of access and convenience offered by the provider(s).

The Health System Standpoint

Integrated health systems and networks are playing a developing role in the marketing and selection of benefit plans. Because they are on the supply side, providers must effectively demonstrate value to purchasers. Again, their offerings are stated in the context of value and measured by quality and cost.

The most important component of patient care in the integrated health system is the doctor. Unfortunately, the physician's perspective on quality and value may, in some cases, be very narrow. It may, for example, be limited to a determination that there was an appropriate diagnosis followed by his or her best efforts to provide care and an outcome within an acceptable range of expectations.

In a fee-for-service arrangement, where the physician's personal income is a function of the level and volume of care, some doctors may choose to recommend more procedures and visits rather than fewer. This lends itself to a seductive definition of quality; that is, more care must always be better than less care.

As physicians become a part of integrated health delivery in a system, and in a managed care environment, they become more aware of broader perspectives and a different paradigm of health care. They begin to realize that clinical pathways and patient satisfaction are also relevant to quality and true value.

Quality in the provider setting lends itself to documentation and comparison. Currently the focus is on outcome defined in terms of mortality and morbidity adjusted for case mix severity. The managed care industry has taken the lead in continually refining useful data approaches that provide assessments of health plan performance results such as HEDIS 2.5 and report card formats that lend themselves to comparisons of physicians and hospitals. Ultimately these will be standardized to enhance measurement and reporting. NCQA is the principal accrediting body for health maintenance organizations (HMOs). It has taken a leading position in assessing health plan capabilities and control over processes. It is also a leader in the search for better ways to document quality assessments of technology for safety and effectiveness.

Increasingly, however, emphasis is being given to more human considerations such as the patient's return to full functionality in his or her occupation and family. Paul Ellwood has designed a simple form of 36 questions (SF36) to address these fundamentally important issues. Patient satisfaction is now widely measured and gives the prospective purchaser insights on service levels, convenience, and overall ambience.

Quality can also be demonstrated, albeit less quantitatively, in terms of effective process. In an administrative environment, "process" is an essential key to quality. This translates into the timeliness and appropriateness of decisions, the efficiency and effectiveness of care, and the professionalism and sensitivity shown to patients and their support groups. For example, health systems can factually present information on their quality assurance and utilization review programs and their commitments to managed care.

Similarly, they can show a commitment of resources to wellness programs and an ability to render care in the least expensive (optimal) settings.

Systems and networks have become increasingly cost conscious as markets have become more competitive and payers have become more parsimonious. Integrated delivery systems are taking advantage of their inherent "systemness" by offering low-cost packages and carveouts for entire segments of care such as behavioral medicine and for major tertiary procedures such as transplants. Systems are inherently positioned to respond to market demands for global pricing and capitation because of the comprehensiveness of their services and their control over all delivery components.

At the heart of these system strategies is the concept of a continuum of care. Integrated systems provide interconnecting programs of care that emphasize prevention, early detection, and ambulatory treatment. They also feature an array of hospital settings tailored to various levels of acute illness and a range of long-term care services to reduce lengths of stay and treat chronic diseases.

Figure 2–3 shows a continuum of care set against a vertical axis of cost and units of service.

Integrated delivery systems exist to serve the full health care needs of large regional markets. Additional hospitals, physicians, and alternative delivery sites are added to capture patients and produce volume.

Perhaps the best standard of proof of the economic effectiveness of systems is in reduced hospital days per thousand population—one of the most expensive measures of health care costs (see Figure 2–4). Immature markets such as New York City are relatively unstructured and lack integration. Indemnity/fee-for-service arrangements still dominate. As a result, utilization remains very high compared with national averages and extraordinarily high relative to California's integrated systems.

Arguably the quality of hospital care in New York City is very good. But so is the care in California—and the per capita costs are far less. As a result, many believe that purchasers and consumers receive better value in California.

Fully integrated regional delivery systems have an inherent capability to reduce costs and produce effi-

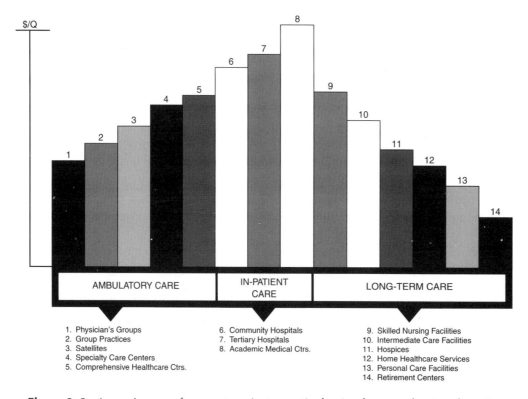

Figure 2–3. A continuum of care set against a vertical axis of cost and units of service.

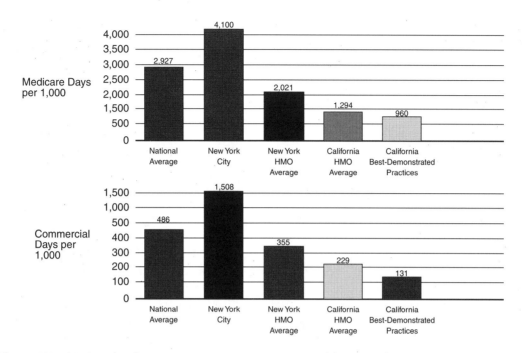

Figure 2–4. National utilization comparisons. Source: Health Care Advisory Board, 1992 data.

ciencies by eliminating redundant systems and fragmentation. This can result in more simplified health care delivery and greater continuity of care. Advances in information technology allow the integration of medical and financial information to further demonstrate cost effectiveness.

Thus there is a "natural" ability of integrated delivery systems to add value to the communities they serve through enhanced quality and reduced costs. Exhibit 2–2 lists the key factors that systems use in exerting influences on health purchasing.

Payment Methodologies

During the past 20 years, payment methodologies have been evolving away from fee-for-service and full-cost reimbursement. A variety of prospective payment systems are at various stages of development. This evolution has the effect of enhancing value.

Fee-for-service methodologies are based on reimbursement for procedures, tests, and other units of service. Because "more is better" from the providers' perspective, they tend to create incentives for high utilization. There is also a built-in bias against low-margin primary care services and preventive medi-

Exhibit 2–2 Value from the Health System Standpoint

Integrated health systems provide a "pull" to purchasers' selections of health plans based on value

Quality
- Outcome measurement
- Documentation of quality
- Focus on managed care (quality assurance/utilization review)
- Emphasis on wellness
- Wide range of benefits
- Service/convenience/flexibility
- Coordination across entire continuum of care

Cost
- Low-cost packages
- Global pricing
- Carveouts
- Capitation
- Ease of administration
- Elimination of redundant systems and fragmentation
- Comprehensive medical and financial information

cine. Quality control is not a major priority. Care is rendered on an episodic basis and inflation costs are passed through to the purchaser. For these reasons, fee-for-service arrangements do not allow long-term budgeting and do not consistently produce value.

Budgeted payments based on diagnoses, defined populations, and resource-based relative value scales (RBRVS) represent a more cognitive approach. Because providers know in advance what the rules and limits are, it behooves them to monitor utilization and quality. Most arrangements create incentives for primary care because of its preventive nature and less expensive settings. The results are improved budgetary control, moderating costs, and better value.

The ultimate plateau in the current cycle of payment methodologies is full-risk capitation. In this arena providers receive set annual fees for a specified range of care. It is incumbent on them to provide whatever care is required to maintain or improve the health status of covered beneficiaries.

In this environment there is a strong focus on prevention and wellness. Utilization and quality are carefully monitored to protect margins and market share. Economic incentives are aligned between providers and purchasers. Revenue and expense budgets become much more predictable and optimal cost control is achieved. The end result is greater value for purchasers and consumers.

Exhibit 2–3 shows the evolution of payment methodologies and enhancement of value.

Challenges for the Future

As markets mature and payment methodologies evolve, the quest for value will accelerate. Patients will learn to assess quality from a consumer perspective and they will become increasingly more price sensitive as they become responsible for first-dollar coverage and higher copayments.

Large purchasers will devote more resources to quantitatively evaluate quality versus costs. Smaller purchasers will increasingly bond together into cooperatives to make the same determinations. A growing number of outside vendors will enter the market to assist in this analysis.

Organized purchasers and consumers will develop consistent definitions and measures of "value." Providers will document their performance against these parameters and will add appropriate supplementary information to showcase their unique capabilities. Organized selection processes and data requirements will become much more structured. The term "spin doctor" will achieve a new, higher meaning.

Across the country perhaps 500 or more major systems and local area networks will evolve to address this demand. They will aggressively compete for market share by demonstrating value and assuming risk. When that day dawns, health care will have completed a 100-year metamorphosis as a service industry and will have taken its place solidly in the mainstream of business. The quest for value will be fully underway.

Exhibit 2–3 Payment Methodologies and Value

As payment methodologies evolve from fee for service to full capitation, value is enhanced		
Fee for service	**RBRVS/budgeted payments**	**Full risk capitation**
• Procedure/test orientation • High utilization incentive • Bias against primary care • Poor budgeting vehicle • High cost	• Cognitive focus • Monitored utilization • Higher volume for primary care • Improved budget control • Moderating cost	• Focus on prevention and wellness • Controlled utilization • Incentives aligned between provider and purchaser • Predictable budgets • Optimal cost control

Source: Based on 1992 Foster Higgins survey comparing FFS utilization with HMO capitation plans

3

Health Care and America's Rolling Depression

Melville H. Hodge

Health care delivery is entering a depression in the United States. While most physicians and health care executives are aware of fundamental change taking place, most have yet to see so dramatic an economic impact. But many physicians in California, Oregon, Minnesota, Maryland, and Massachusetts can attest to a significant loss of patients and the witnessing of newly trained specialists struggling to find any work at all. Numerous hospitals in these areas are experiencing distress. It is important to understand what is causing this depression to gain insight into what policies will hasten its end.

The perceived change—labeled "managed care"—is seen as the enemy, and the medical profession is seeking a variety of rear guard defenses: enactment of "any willing provider" laws, antitrust revision to permit resistance in concert, and laws placing a burden of justification on organizations seeking to discontinue a physician's services.

But managed care has several meanings. To many physicians it implies an organization run by overcompensated nonphysicians who control both the flow of patients and payers' dollars. To others, managed care suggests alternative financing plans—preferred provider, point-of-service, or health maintenance organizations (HMOs)—with near-endless variations and complexities.

It is most useful to understand managed care as *any arrangement where a contractual relationship for services and payment is created between a payer— usually an employer or government (or their agent)— and a provider—physician, hospital, and so forth.* This is a fundamental reversal of the traditional contractual relationship between a patient seeking and agreeing to pay for services and a provider. Providers knew that patients often sought reimbursement from their indemnity insurer, their employer or government, but they, themselves, had no relationship with the ultimate payer.

American Business and the Failure of Reform

What caused payers to abandon their passive role and actively seek to engage providers on the terms and conditions of their services? It happened because health care costs of American employers rose until they not only became their largest non–payroll cost but also by 1986 equalled the entire profit of American business, its raison d'être! At the same time, communications and transportation advances and declining tariffs placed American companies into global competition with firms with far lower health care costs that hence were able to underprice them. That business had become the principal payer for health care in the U.S. was an historical accident arising from World War II evasion of wage controls by offering noncontrolled health care benefits to lure scarce workers, a trend not mirrored in other countries where health care financing was spread over a much broader base.

Businesses responded in several ways. Many forced employees to pay a higher share of premiums and accept larger deductibles and copayments, hoping they would become more frugal health care buyers, but this provided only limited respite. Employers began to seek price control agreements from physicians and hospitals and in a few cases to enter into capitation agreements shifting risk from payer to provider—managed care! Finally, some larger companies sought a governmental solution to shift health care costs from the narrower base of employers to the broader base of all taxpayers, which had helped hold down health care costs for their foreign competitors. Finding common purpose with groups concerned

Health Care Manage Rev, 1996; 21(3): 7–12

about uninsured Americans, a political base for the health reform drive was born, which culminated in 1994 in failure.[1]

Most employers had sat on the sidelines waiting for a federal health care system to be enacted. Now, business sees only one solution—managed care in the free market. And belatedly, government is coming to the same conclusion—with increasing enthusiasm for Medicaid and caution for Medicare. The failure of reform also has brought with it a political sensitivity ensuring the failure is more than temporary.

Arguably, the principal virtue of the free market—capitalism—is the freedom to fail. The absence of freedom to fail is the Achilles heel of government solutions—that hundreds of thousands of farmers continue dependent on subsidies long after the need for their services has been made obsolete by technology serves as a single example. But failure is a near-indispensable factor in any successful economy because it serves to reallocate resources away from where they are no longer needed absent political interference and toward more productive uses.

Overcapacity—The Central Problem

Why is the failure attribute of the free market so important here? Because it offers the *only* real solution to the central problem of American health care—gross overcapacity. Estimates of excess physicians and hospitals may be argued because they invariably rest on a series of assumptions, but data supporting a vast surplus abounds. Winer assumed modest growth in managed care and projected a surplus of 163,000 physicians by the year 2000, including 139,000 specialists.[2] Florida Medical Management Consultants reported Florida has 322 physicians per 100,000, 18 percent of whom are primary care physicians, but needs only 191 physicians per 100,000, half delivering primary care.[3] Kaiser uses 8 cardiologists to care for 365,000 enrollees in San Diego—one for each 45,600; the remaining 150 cardiologists in San Diego care for an average of 13,300 each. According to Alan H. Rosenstein, M.D., Regional Medical Director, Benefit Plan Services, the standard for managed care is 100 physicians per 100,000[4] (or about 300,000 for the U.S.). Yet, there were 670,336 physicians in the U.S. at the end of 1993, 34.4 percent in primary care and *up* 17,274 from the prior year extending an unbroken

growth in physician supply.[5] It appears that our physician supply may be double our real needs. And this surplus is almost entirely in the medical specialties.

A similar conclusion emerges from an examination of hospital capacity. While the differentiating criterion between a town and a city in medieval Europe was the existence of a cathedral, the modern American equivalent has become the existence of a hospital! Exacerbated by decades of federal subsidization, hospitals nearly everywhere are now focusing on downsizing, hoping to avoid insolvency and outright closure (ironically, closures have declined from a 1988 peak at least through 1993).[6] U.S. hospital occupancy is now about 61 percent. An estimate of U.S. requirements under 100 percent managed care by the Sachs Group is only 43 percent of today's 1.2 million beds.[7] The executive director of the United Medical Group Association reports one managed care organization has its commercial (non-Medicare) length of stay (LOS) down to 130 days per year per 1,000 members and its Medicare LOS down to 600 days; if that rate were achieved nationally, the U.S. would require only 18 percent of its current hospital beds.[8] In hospitals also, we appear to have at least twice the capacity we need; we no longer require perhaps 2,500 out of 5,000 short-term hospitals. Using the U.S. mean of 3.4 workers per bed, this suggests a hospital worker surplus of about 1.5–2.0 million.

Most physicians and health care executives are at least intuitively aware of the substantial surplus of both physicians and hospitals even if they have no basis to quantify it. Yet it received surprisingly little attention in the health care reform debate. Common sense suggests, however, that while changes in financing or organization that might have resulted from various reform proposals could have some positive or negative effects on health care costs, real progress will not be made so long as the incomes of perhaps 300,000 unneeded physicians and 1.5 million unneeded hospital workers must continue to be met.

Buyers' Market and Rise of the "Nonprovider Provider"

The consequence of this enormous overcapacity has been to create a classical buyers' market—and given rise to the "nonprovider provider," the managed care organization. Publicly financed entrepreneurial organizations, former indemnity insurers, and

Blue Cross/Blue Shield groups all have seen the opportunity inherent in a buyers' market, the opportunity to buy below the cost of production by contracting on one hand with payers—employers and governments—and on the other with providers—physicians and hospitals. The distinction between *managed care*—a contractual relationship between payers and providers, a repercussion of unacceptably escalating costs—and a *managed care organization* (MCO)—middlemen finding opportunity in a buyers' market—is a crucial one.

The cost models for a managed care HMO contrasted with traditional indemnity financing shown in Table 3–1 reveal the MCO business strategy.[9] The HMO is able to offer a price to the payer only 80 percent of the traditional price, yet achieve a bottom line profit that is 50 percent greater than the traditional indemnity insurer. Note that the price reduction comes principally from three sources—reductions of about one-third each in payments to specialists, drug suppliers, and hospitals. The model suggests a typical HMO medical loss ratio—the portion of the premium dollar expended to purchase health care services—of 80 percent. That the HMO is able to buy such services below the cost of production is suggested by the fact that Kaiser, perhaps the prototypical HMO with a medical loss ratio of more than 95 percent, has been unable to grow since 1990 because it must cover 100 cents on the dollar of its inhouse physician and hospital costs rather than exploit a buyers' market while non-

provider providers have been growing at a rate of 10 percent or more each year.[10]

Response of Providers

Many hospitals and medical groups have responded to the managed care trend by seeking to organize themselves as risk-assuming integrated delivery systems to compete directly with the MCOs for contracts with payers. They must, however, compete with organizations able to buy services below cost. Moreover, they face other formidable difficulties. As they are perceived by MCOs as emerging competitors rather than suppliers they may be cut off from MCO contracts. Logically, they should be organized around primary care practice to control the premium dollar and specialist and hospital referrals in order to optimally balance resources. Yet, most medical groups and hospital medical staffs are specialist-dominated and hospital managers are inpatient-oriented; the requirement that they purge much of their traditional leadership as well as their ranks to achieve the essential skill and facility balance may be too much to expect. Broadening geographic coverage beyond the area traditionally served by a single hospital to achieve sustainable, competitive scale (perhaps a million or more members)[11]—requires true multihospital and group practice mergers, eliminating no longer needed executives, boards, and medical staff leaders. Finally, access to significant capital must be achieved to sup-

Table 3–1

Economics of Managed Care[9]

	Traditional	**HMO**	**$**	**Percent**
Premium	$100	$80	(20)	(20.0)
Delivery system	85	64	(21)	(24.7)
Primary care physicians	10	13	3	30.0
Specialist physicians	30	19	(11)	(36.7)
Drugs	6	4	(2)	(33.3)
Other	2	4	2	100.0
Hospital	37	24	(13)	(35.1)
Payer	15	16	1	6.7
Risk management	6	5	(1)	(16.7)
Administration	5	5		
Profit	4	6	2	50.0

port assumption of risk associated with capitated contracts at a time when hospital balance sheets are deteriorating.

As long as physician and hospital overcapacity persists, providers will face serious difficulties in forming vertically integrated regional health care delivery organizations. Not all of these efforts will succeed. It seems certain that only widespread failures—the working of Adam Smith's "invisible hand"—will actually accomplish the needed capacity reduction. Yet, when surplus capacity is eventually eliminated and supply and demand for health care services from physicians and hospitals is restored to equilibrium, integrated provider organizations should emerge with a competitive advantage over the MCOs, which must continue to support a middleman's overhead and profit requirement after having lost their former buyers' market advantage. Many MCOs will respond by transforming themselves into provider organizations. The first step, acquisition of primary care practices, has already begun.

It seems in the interest of the medical profession to identify and support actions that will hasten the end of the surplus and attendant buyers' market. Reducing the number of medical school positions, closing some medical schools, reducing residencies and closing some graduate medical education programs, reducing licensing of foreign medical graduates, transforming incentives in favor of primary care, encouraging and facilitating migration to underserved areas, and encouraging early retirement all seem worth pursuing. Moreover, cooperating with the hospital community to close unneeded hospitals—not just downsize them with the attendant retention of fixed costs—seems imperative. Conversely, the rear guard actions cited earlier seem likely to only draw out the period of overcapacity and delay the emergence of successful integrated provider organizations able to eliminate middlemen.

To have a real chance for survival as an integrated delivery system, hospitals and physicians must avoid half measures. Cave has pointed out that only the equity, staff, and perhaps foundation models of integrated delivery system organization are likely to be sustainable.[12] This suggests that physicians will be required to forego private practice in favor of salaried status, primary care must become the organizing principle, and numerous facilities must be closed and their executives and employees laid off.

Some have argued that the quality of care resulting from cost reduction imposed by MCOs will cause a public backlash and a demand to return to "the good old days." There is evidence, however, that quality is unrelated to resource consumption.[13] The consequences of undertreatment may not be more serious than those of overtreatment. Experience also suggests that patients' assessment of their care is more related to perceived caring, responsiveness, and communications than to any underlying objective measure of quality.

Others reason that once the excess cost is wrung out by imposition of managed care practices health care costs will once again resume their inexorable double digit climb. Perhaps—but perhaps not. Health care is unique in that there is no "right" amount of health care. The health care dilemma is that new modalities of diagnosis and treatment will continue to result from application of our brightest minds, yet everyone dies.[14] Unlike, say, feeding the hungry, which is bounded by full stomachs, there is no intrinsic bound on health care. Therefore it must be, and is, bounded from without by resource constraints. Under the free market, employers and governments will provide the necessary external constraint based on availability of resources and alternative demands for their uses.

It is important to understand that health care participants cannot reasonably expect to successfully resist the onslaught whose root cause is overcapacity. Either they find and implement a successful organizing principle under which health care resources are reduced to a sustainable level and rationally balanced, or they must expect the market to accomplish a similar result by forcing failures. Unfortunately, wishful thinking remains rampant. In a recent article decrying that "nine of the largest publicly traded HMOs have squirreled away $9.5 billion in cash and marketable securities"[15(p.51)] and the lofty compensation of managed care's 10 highest paid executives, one observer is quoted, "Once hospitals and doctors reach a financial breaking point and demand a bigger portion of the managed care premium dollar, market sensibilities will return without any government intervention."[15(p.54)] Unfortunately for many, market sensibilities will return only after the financial breaking point has been exceeded for a sufficient number of participants to restore equilibrium between provider supply and demand.

Health Care Depression in Context

Recalling the definition of a recession as when your neighbor loses his or her job and a depression as when you lose your job, it is likely that many within health care delivery will experience a depression during much of the next 10 years. *Depression* is a strong word, but its characteristics—falling prices, restriction of credit, reduced production, numerous bankruptcies, and high unemployment[16]—are beginning to be seen or at least voiced here and there. At a meeting of the Philadelphia Industrial Relations Research Association on March 14, 1995, leaders of several of Philadelphia's major health care systems and the local president of National Hospital and Health Care Employees Union predicted that within 5 years one of three Philadelphia hospitals will disappear along with 40 percent of existing health care jobs.[17]

While it may offer scant relief to those who will be affected, it is useful to place this health care depression in the context of the rolling depression experienced in America over the past quarter century and illustrated in Figure 3–1. The debacle of the auto industry in the 1970s along with much of heavy industry as a consequence of 25 years of excess and the Japanese invasion was perhaps the first wave. There was little to distinguish Flint, Michigan in the 1970s from the 1930s. After the "rust belt," the "farm belt" experienced depression as a consequence of skyrocketing interest rates and petroleum prices, and farm foreclosures swept the Midwest. Depression in the "oil patch" soon followed as Texas, Oklahoma, Colorado, and Louisiana economies built on $30 oil prices and $60 oil price projections collapsed with

OPEC. The tornado cloud of depression next touched down on financial services as the savings and loans (S&L) succumbed to the mix of guaranteed deposits and unregulated lending, the October 1987 stock market crash, and the demise of the leveraged buy-out craze. Construction, especially commercial construction, entered a near decade-long depression triggered by massive overbuilding with cheap S&L money and the Tax Reform Act of 1986, which drastically reduced the attractiveness of real estate investment. The still continuing shakeout in aerospace and defense began with the fall of the Berlin Wall and was irrevocably confirmed by the demise of the Soviet Union, ending the careers of hundreds of thousands of aerospace and defense scientists, engineers, and workers. Now it is health care's turn, perhaps to be soon followed by government and academia.

End of Depression

Painful as it might be, a rolling depression ends in a given sector as the excesses or extrinsic factors that caused it diminish. Since underlying health care demand seems biologically and demographically guaranteed, the length of the depression among health care providers will be determined by policy responses to the causative factors governing the excess. Just as the rust belt, farm belt, and other formerly depressed sectors have emerged as vibrant economies, there is no reason why health care cannot be expected to once again thrive. Managed care seems sure to remain with us since it is unlikely that U.S. businesses will ever again be sheltered from the rest of the world nor governments able to avoid rising health care entitlement costs as the baby boomers move inexorably toward their health-care–intensive years. But most pure managed care organizations—nonprovider providers that fail to become providers—should disappear. Health care jobs and incomes should stabilize as supply–demand equilibrium is reached.

Secondary effects will need to be addressed. No longer is it likely that patient care revenues will be available to divert to research—more direct federal support will be required if we are to maintain our medical research momentum. Medical services by fewer interns and residents will necessitate alternatives. But ending these traditional cross-subsidies should render the public health care resource alloca-

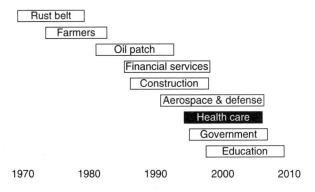

Figure 3–1. Health care and America's rolling depression.

tion process much more explicit and thereby facilitate more rational public debate.

Finally, adjusting our health care costs to a new, lower cost trajectory by eliminating the present burden of enormous overcapacity should improve our ability to care for our uninsured poor. With the promise of ending, or at least reducing, cost shifting both business and government should have an economic stake in achieving this result so that it need not be dependent on compassion alone.

REFERENCES

1. Blumenthal, D. " Health Care Reform—Past and Future." *New England Journal of Medicine* 332 (1995): 465–68.
2. Winer, J.P. "Forecasting the Effects of Health Reform on U.S. Physician Workforce Requirements from HMO Staffing Patterns." *Journal of the American Medical Association* 272 (1994): 222–30.
3. "Too Many Doctors in the Florida Managed Care Scenario." *Managed Care Week—Managed Care Stats & Facts* 4, no. 45 (1994): 2.
4. "Listen for Horses, not Zebras, Says Rosenstein." *CCH Monitor* 12, no. 23 (1994): 7.
5. American Medical Association. *Physician Characteristics and Distribution in the U.S.* Chicago, IL: AMA, 1994.
6. Office of the Inspector General. *Hospital Closure 1993.* Washington, DC: OIG, 1995.
7. "Quick Takes—if the U.S. were a 100% Managed Care Country." *Health Care Reform Week* 24, no. 1 (1995): 6.
8. Sardinha, C. "MCOs Scramble to Cut Hospital Usage as LOS Rates Hit New Low." *Managed Care Outlook* 8, no. 1 (1995): 1–2.
9. Kaufman, N. "Power Notebook." *Hospitals & Health Networks* 69, no. 3 (1995): 58–62.
10. Anders, G. "Aches and Pains—in the Age of the HMO Pioneer of Species Has Hit a Rough Patch—Kaiser Permanente Can't Cut Prices as Much as Rivals that Lack Its Fixed Costs." *The Wall Street Journal*, December 1, 1994.
11. Anders, G., and Winslow, R. "The HMO Trend: Big, Bigger, Biggest." *The Wall Street Journal*, March 30, 1995.
12. Cave, D.G. "Vertical Integration Models to Prepare Health Systems for Capitation." *Health Care Management Review* 20, no. 1 (1995): 26–39.
13. Starfield, B., Powe, N.R., Weiner, J.R., Stuart, M., Steinwachs, D., Hudson Scholle, S., and Gerstenberger, A. "Costs vs. Quality in Different Types of Primary Care Settings." *Journal of the American Medical Association* 272 (1994): 1903–08.
14. Hodge, M.H. "New Perspectives on Our National Health Care Dilemma." *Health Care Management Review* 16, no. 3 (1991): 63–71.
15. Cerne, F. "Cash Kings—HMOs' Big War Chests Raise Questions about Their Pricing Policies and How They Intend to Spend Billions in Reserves." *Hospitals & Health Networks* (April 5, 1995): 51–54.
16. *The Concise Columbia Encyclopedia.* New York, NY: Columbia University Press, 1991.
17. DeWolf, R. "Health Care Officials Predict Philadelphia Hospital Consolidation." *Philadelphia Daily News* March 16, 1995.

Part II
Integrated Delivery Systems

4

Managed Care Contracting Issues in Integrated Delivery Systems

Ellen E. Stewart

Every managed care agreement is unique and has different legal, financial, and operational issues that need to be addressed in the agreement to protect the provider. However, with the expansion of managed care in this country, many nonattorneys are reviewing agreements for their organizations. In an effort to assist in the process, the following checklist for managed care agreements is provided for use by health care providers in reviewing proposed agreements. This checklist is by no means exhaustive and should be used by the organization as a framework for review.

Managed Care Contract Checklist

1. Representation and warranties
    a. Corporate status
        (1) Each party should identify its corporate status in the contract. Nonprofits should indicate such.
        (2) Notification of change in corporate status to other party.
    b. Licenses
        (1) Indication of licensing authority (health maintenance organization (HMO), insurance, hospital, etc.)
        (2) Proof of license
        (3) Notification of change in license status
    c. Compliance with law
    Agreement to comply with all applicable federal, state, and local laws and regulations.
    d. Access to financial statements
    Providers should have access to payer's financial statements to determine financial viability.
    e. Prior authorization

All prior authorization required by federal, state, or local laws has been obtained and if the board of directors of the organization requires agreements to be authorized, that authorization should be obtained.

2. Definitions
    Agreements should contain a definition section that outlines such terms as utilization review, emergency, member/enrollee/insured, medically necessary and reasonable, appeal, provider panel, and so on.

3. Description of covered services
    a. Specifically enumerate covered and excluded services
        (1) Services provided by the provider pursuant to the contract should be indicated either in the contract or in an appendix.
        (2) The provider should indicate which services are explicitly excluded from coverage under the contractual arrangement.
    b. Third party subscriber agreements
        (1) If third party subscriber plans determine coverage, the provider should be able to obtain copies of the coverage under the benefit plans and description of services covered given to members/enrollees.
        (2) Any new services or classes of members or enrollees should be added only with the consent of the provider.
    c. Limitations on coverage
        (1) The agreement should provide for those cases in which the provider is unable to assume the responsibility for furnishing services under the agreement, such as when a referral is needed or when services cannot be provided by the provider.

J Health Care Financ 1996; 22(3): 75–83

   d. No guarantees to provide service

      (1) The contract should state whether the provider has the discretion to refuse to accept members/enrollees/subscribers for treatment.

      (2) The agreement should provide that the provider may refuse to provide care to subscribers or enrollees where facilities or services are not available.

   e. Specialty services

      (1) The agreement should specifically indicate whether the provider is responsible for providing or contracting for specialty services.

      (2) If specialty services are not provided, specific statements as to those services not provided should be made in the contract.

   f. Religious and ethical constraints

If certain services are inconsistent with the provider's religious or ethical principles, they should not be required to provide such services, and the agreement should so state (i.d. elective abortions).

   g. Arrangements for covered services not provided by the provider

      (1) The agreement should permit the provider to transfer patients, or delegated covered services to other providers, in situations where the provider is incapable of providing such services.

      (2) The provider should receive payments for all services rendered prior to any transfer.

   h. Arrangement for noncovered services

Any services that are not covered under the agreement, and that are provided to member/enrollees/insureds, should be paid for pending any transfer of the patient.

  4. Third party membership/enrollment

   a. Patient identification/eligibility

      (1) The third party should notify the provider of all members/enrollees and any changes to such lists (HMOs, preferred provider organizations (PPOs)).

      (2) There should be a structure for notification and verification of eligibility such as membership cards and telephone calls

to the third party. Verification should be done promptly.

      (3) The provider should be guaranteed payment for services provided to patients who are identified or verified by the third party as members or enrollees even if the information provided by the third party is erroneous until the following occurs: (a) notification of a noncovered service is provided by the third party, or (b) alternative coverage has been arranged for a medically acceptable transfer or disposition of the patient.

      (4) Members/enrollees who are later found to be eligible should be covered.

      (5) Emergency services should be paid based on the medical opinion of the provider and not the third party.

   b. The third party should inform its patients of the terms of the provider contract.

   c. The contract should not apply in the following situations:

      (1) Where services are provided to a patient who is in treatment at the time the contract is executed, and

      (2) If a patient's membership/enrollment status terminates during the course of treatment, the contract should not apply with respect to services performed after the termination of enrollment status.

5. Medical records and confidentiality

   a. Maintenance of records

      (1) The provider should assume responsibility for maintaining patient medical records.

      (2) The contract should state that the medical records are to be retained by the provider, but may be inspected by the third party pursuant to specific arrangements negotiated between the parties.

   b. Confidentiality

      (1) The agreement should provide that the provider will disclose information contained in the enrollee/subscriber's medical records only if disclosure is consistent with law,

(2) The third party should be responsible for obtaining any patient releases that may be necessary for disclosure,

(3) The third party should not be permitted to disclose medical information to other third parties without the approval from the provider, and

(4) The provider should be permitted to disclose medical information where disclosure is consistent with law.

c. Medical staff committee reports

The third party should not be permitted to review or obtain copies of the proceedings of any medical staff committees.

6. Patient care audit/access to records

a. The agreement may provide that audits and review of records by the third party should be made consistent with considerations on confidentiality, in a reasonable manner within the proper scope of the third party's review authority, and consistent with other applicable law.

b. Audits and all record review should be as follows:

(1) Performed at only reasonable times,

(2) Performed only after prior notice to provider,

(3) Limited to the third party's authorized scope of inquiries, and

(4) Performed at the third party's expense (photocopying).

(5) Information obtained by the third party through audit or review should not be released to third parties absent provider's consent.

7. Utilization review

a. The third party's utilization review plan should be fully described in the contract (or an exhibit).

b. The utilization review plan of the third party should discuss at a minimum the following:

(1) Whether review is delegated to a hospital or some other entity,

(2) The methods of review (preadmission, concurrent, retrospective, etc.),

(3) The standard of review (i.e., patterns of treatment, medically necessary and reasonable, etc.), and

(4) Whether review will be conducted on-site or by telephone. If telephone review, a procedure needs to be established for the identification of appropriate third party personnel who may conduct the telephone review.

c. The third party should bear photocopying and other costs incurred in complying with the utilization review plan.

d. Provider should maintain existing internal utilization review procedures.

e. The contract should address patient rights in the utilization review process.

f. The contract should clearly delineate an effective appeals process to contest denials, which may include the following:

(1) Provider may challenge the standards of review,

(2) Confidentiality of peer review process,

(3) Notice of denial to patient and providers from the third party.

8. Payment

a. Payment rate—overview

(1) The provider should identify the proposed payment rate, which can include discount from charges, diagnosis related group (DRG), resource-based relative value scale (RBRVS), capitation, or a combination of any of the above.

(2) Payment rates should be carefully analyzed in conjunction with anticipated utilization patterns.

(3) Capitated or "at-risk" arrangements should be analyzed by the provider, and to the extent possible, should include utilization patterns, case mix, percentage premium retention, and plan benefits. At-risk arrangements may result in the inclusion of additional provisions such as incentives, rebates, or withholds.

b. Upside/downside risks

(1) Discounts. *Upside:* Volume of new patients. *Downside:* Current business

discounted; marginal contributions target not met; discount demanded by other payers.

(2) DRG/RBRVS. *Upside:* Volume of new patients; intensity down. *Downside:* Intensity up; improper costs weights.

(3) Capitation. *Upside:* Volume of new patients; frequency of use down. *Downside:* Intensity up; frequency of use up; catastrophic under projected losses; improper capitation levels; out-of-service area losses; administrative expenses.

c. Billing, payment, and collection procedures

(1) The agreement should describe the billing payment and collection procedures and each party's responsibilities.

(2) The provider's existing billing form should be utilized. (Multiple billing forms can cause multiple problems.)

(3) Provision of patient care summaries should be carefully analyzed, along with the related costs of providing such summaries.

(4) Payment by third party should be made promptly.

(5) An analysis regarding interest to be charged and provision therefor, should be made.

(6) Absent statutory provisions to the contrary, the physician should have the authority to bill the patient directly should the third party fail to make payment.

(7) Provisions in the agreement should be made for authorization to bill patients for applicable deductibles and copayments.

(8) The agreement should clearly set forth who is responsible for collection of delinquent accounts.

(9) The agreement should provide that the provider may bill the patient directly for "unnecessary" and noncovered services, and there should be no requirements that the provider obtain the patient's prior consent before billing the patient directly.

d. Assurance of payment

(1) The provider may want to include a provision whereby the third party guarantees a minimum income to the provider for the term of the contract, especially where deep discounts are given.

(2) If the provider is concerned about the financial viability of the third party, the provider may wish to require the third party to post a performance bond, guarantee, or deposit.

9. Coordination of benefits

a. The agreement should specify how benefits from primary payment sources will be coordinated with payments made by the third party to the provider. For example:

(1) Will the third party make full payment at the contract rate and receive a credit for any primary payments later received by the provider, or will the third party be entitled to reduce its payment to the provider in the amount of any primary payments previously made the provider; and

(2) If the contract rate is less than the provider's actual charges, will primary payments be credited to the provider's account (for the difference between the contract rate and actual charges) or to the third party for amounts paid by the third party under the contract.

b. The provider should be permitted to collect from the third party if primary payment is available and the third party should ultimately be responsible for collections.

10. Insurance

a. The provider should assure that the third party meets certain requirements as appropriate:

(1) That the third party maintains comprehensive general liability and professional liability coverage,

(2) That the limits of the liability coverage are subject to the provider's approval,

(3) That the third party provides the provider evidence of coverage upon request, and

(4) That the third party notifies the provider immediately upon any significant changes and insurance.

b. The provider should ascertain whether the types and amounts of any insurance required under the contract are reasonable and are not subject to the discretion of the third party.

c. The parties should agree to cooperate in the legal defense of a lawsuit brought against one party.

d. Preferably, the contract, especially those involving capitated or at-risk arrangements, should provide for stop loss or catastrophic insurance. Generally, the coverage will provide:

    (1) For the contract rate to revert to billed charges for the entire stay or from the time the excess level is met, in the event usual and customary charges exceed a certain level for any individual patient; and

    (2) A similar reversion to a more favorable rate in the event the differences between the aggregate contract rates charged and billed charges exceed an agreed upon amount.

11. Indemnification

a. There should be a mutual indemnification of the parties. *Lois J. Wickline v. State of California*[1] is a case involving a medical reviewer who authorized only four additional days of hospitalization in spite of a request from the attending physician for an eight-day extension. The physician discharged the patient based upon the nurse reviewer's failure to grant an extension, thereby causing damage to the patient. The physician was held liable.

12. Dispute resolution and arbitration

a. The contract should establish and describe a dispute resolution or grievance procedure for resolving disputes between the parties.

b. Alternatives

    (1) Informal process

The contract should establish and describe an informal grievance mechanism.

    (2) Arbitration: binding or nonbinding

Disputes not satisfactorily resolved through the informal grievance mechanism may be referred to the American Arbitration Association (AAA) or to some other arbitration group or firm. Costs of any arbitration should be shared by the parties.

    (3) Mediation

    (4) Rent-a-judge program

    (5) Summary jury trial

    (6) Mini-trial

    (7) Variations and hybrids

c. Keys to success

    (1) Commitment

    (2) Relationship

    (3) Privacy

    (4) Urgency

    (5) Finances

    (6) Principle

    (7) Complexity

    (8) Stakes

13. Third Party Advertising

a. To the extent that third parties direct their patients to certain providers, the providers should be provided a copy of all advertising and marketing materials.

b. Any materials containing references to the provider should be subject to the provider's prior approval before dissemination.

14. Exclusivity

The parties may want to consider an exclusivity arrangement (antitrust concerns).

15. Interruption: cause beyond control of provider

a. The provisions of the contract should be suspended during any period in which the provider's operations are substantially interrupted beyond the events of the provider's control such as natural disaster or labor disputes.

b. The provider should be permitted to terminate the contract upon sufficient prior notice and in the event such interruption continues beyond a prescribed time such as 30 days.

16. Termination

a. The contract should specify an initial term (one or two years). Automatic renewals should be avoided.

b. Grounds for termination

   (1) Material breach by either party; termination upon 30 days' notice unless the other party cures breech within 20 days after receipt of notice to terminate.

   (2) Third party's default in payment; termination effective upon 5 days' notice if payment has been delinquent for a prescribed period of time.

   (3) Contract violates law; the party should attempt to renegotiate upon such termination.

   (4) Either party should be permitted to terminate without cause with sufficient notice such as 60 or 90 days.

c. Effect of termination

Upon termination, the contract shall cease to apply except as follows:

   (1) The contract should state that each party will remain responsible for the obligations or liabilities arising from its actions or inactions prior to termination,

   (2) The third party should remain responsible to make payment at the contract rate for services provided by the provider until subsequent determination regarding a suitable transfer can be arranged, and

   (3) The contract should clarify that a member/enrollee's physician may have access to medical records within a prescribed period of time after termination of the contract.

17. General

  a. No assignment

The third party should not be permitted to assign any rights or obligations under the agreement without the prior written consent of the provider. Ideally, the provider should be permitted to assign its interest under the contract to any corporate parent, affiliate, or subsidiary upon prior notice to the third party, but without having to obtain prior written consent.

  b. Binding successors-in-interest

The party's successors-in-interest should be bound by the terms of the agreement.

  c. Severability

The contract should state that in the event any of its individual provisions become unlawful, invalid, or unenforceable, the remaining provision shall continue to apply.

  d. Notices

There should be a provision establishing the method whereby notices are given to each party and identifying a designee for receipt of such notices.

  e. A provision should set forth that the agreement is the entire agreement between the parties and supersedes any prior agreement either oral or in writing.

  f. The choice of law should be the state where the provider conducts business.

  g. No third party beneficiaries

The contract should state that it does not create any right in third parties.

  h. Captions

This provision should state that captions and headings for the sections of the contract should not be considered as part of the contract itself or otherwise aided interruption of the contract.

REFERENCE

1. *Wickline v. State of California*, 192 Cal. App. 3d 1630, 239 Cal. Rptr. 810 (Cal App 1986).

5

Trends and Models in Physician–Hospital Organization

Lawton R. Burns and Darrell P. Thorpe

There has been a great deal of interest in physician–hospital relationships over the past few years. Surveys to assess the attitudinal climate, governance involvement, and employment relationship between hospitals and their medical staffs have been conducted by academics, professional societies, and consultants.[1-5] Most recently, the Prospective Payment Assessment Commission initiated a survey of hospitals' ability to influence cost-effective practice behavior on the part of their physicians. All these studies focus on internal relationships between a hospital and members of its medical staff.

Competitive economic forces are driving the health care industry to develop new models of physician–hospital relationships, however. These relationships are different in that they are formally organized, contractual, and/or corporate in character and include physicians outside the boundaries of the medical staff. Such relationships are known as physician–hospital organizations (PHOs), management service organizations (MSOs), foundation models, and integrated health organizations (IHOs). These relationships have been described frequently in the medical group management and group practice literatures. With few exceptions, however, the new organizational models have not received much attention in the hospital administration literature.[6,7]

This article outlines the new competitive forces that are encouraging the formation of these new models from the perspectives of the parties involved: physicians and hospitals. It also describes the competitive strengths and competences of the parties that are harnessed in these new arrangements. The article next describes the structural features of these new organizational models. It concludes with a discussion of the issues and implications that these models pose.

Competitive Forces Fostering the New Models

Competitive forces facing physicians

The health care marketplace has become an increasingly unfamiliar, uncertain, and unfriendly environment for physicians. Changes in physician reimbursement in both the public and the private sectors and other environmental changes have significantly affected the ability of physicians to set and maintain their own levels of annual income.

Reimbursement under Medicare is increasingly fixed, and the implementation of the Resource-Based Relative Value Schedule (RBRVS) is lowering levels of payment for specialists while raising levels for primary care physicians (PCPs) in relative, but not absolute, terms. Medicaid payments in most states have become so meager as to discourage many physicians from participating in that program at all. Private payers are limiting the ability of physicians to shift the cost of public programs onto the private sector by expanding the use of managed care and other discounted and/or fixed-fee arrangements for their beneficiaries.

Efforts by physicians to make up for reductions in payment per unit of service by increasing the number of units of service provided are being inhibited (and prohibited) in both the public and the private sectors

This article was written while the first author was supported by the Hospital Research and Educational Trust and the Edwin L. Crosby Memorial Fellowship. The views expressed here are those of the authors. The authors wish to thank Geoffrey Baker and Ross Stromberg for their assistance in compiling some of the information contained in this article as well as Monty Brown and Alexandra Polydefkis for their consultation on the legal elements of the physician–hospital models. The authors also thank Jim Begun, Henry Golembesky, and Bob Hurley for their comments on an earlier draft.

Health Care Manage Rev, 1993; 18(4): 7–20

through utilization review and other monitoring programs. Finally, attempts by physicians to tap alternative sources of revenue through the establishment of in-office ancillary services are discouraged by tighter licensing and other regulatory restrictions and by managed care companies that specify in their contracts where such services are to be provided.

At the same time that physicians are experiencing these limitations on their practice revenues, they are also facing increased costs of operating their practices. The costs of medical malpractice insurance, medical supplies, office occupancy, and nonphysician personnel are all increasing at a rate greater than the increase in practice revenues, resulting in a flattening out of professional net income.[8] The net effect of these new economic realities for many physicians is that financial expectations are not being met and long-term economic security is of increasing importance.

The economics of medical practice is only one source of consternation for today's physicians. The impact of managed care on the practice of medicine itself is perhaps even more important. The physician is no longer the exclusive agent of the patient, determining where the patient should be treated and how much care should be ordered.[9] Instead, the physician is confronted by managed care imperatives such as prior certification for hospital admission and surgery, continued stay review, and case management.

PCPs are being asked to be gatekeepers, that is, to provide care themselves for a broader range of medical conditions and to refer to specialists less and then only when absolutely necessary. Patterns of referral are increasingly dictated by managed care contracts, causing many PCPs to switch from specialists to whom they have historically referred. Some specialists consequently may get fewer referrals and often must seek permission from the gatekeeper or from a utilization management person before performing diagnostic and/or therapeutic procedures or scheduling follow-up visits. Selective contracting arrangements with hospitals may further curb their autonomy.

Finally, physicians are confronted by increasing administrative complexity (popularly known as the hassle factor) in dealing with multiple plans and insurers, each with its own unique administrative and paperwork requirements. In addition to creating the discomfort that comes with significant change, all these factors contribute to the increased cost of operating a medical practice.

The forces and stresses described above have special impact on solo practitioners and small groups. Today's practice environment requires more sophisticated systems, including information systems and in-office medical technology, as well as personnel with managed care contracting, marketing, and other more advanced management expertise. Solo and small group practices do not have the financial wherewithal to acquire and maintain these capabilities. They may also lack the capital needed to recruit partners and expand services. Consequently, physicians increasingly favor group practice settings, as gauged by the number of groups (16,500 in 1988), the percentage of active nonfederal physicians within them (one third in 1988), and their increasingly large average size.[10] Of course, the growing size of group practices also reflects their growing attractiveness to physicians. Groups appeal to the increasing percentage of female physicians who want to balance family and career goals. Groups also appeal to younger physicians who want to balance their personal and professional lives.[11]

Group practices, although better able to deal with many of the challenges facing physicians than their solo colleagues, have a number of unique concerns. Because of growing size, group practices face barriers to entry and exit. Larger size means a greater valuation of the group's tangible and intangible assets and thus a prohibitive cost for prospective members to buy into the group. The greater valuation of intangible assets makes it more difficult to sell them off piecemeal for members who wish to depart the group.[12]

Groups also wish to minimize or share the financial risks incurred in their capitated arrangements with managed care plans. In such arrangements, the physicians may be capitated while the hospital receives a negotiated per diem. Not wishing to assume risk for variables beyond their full control (such as case management, discharge planning, test and procedure scheduling, etc.), all of which can increase patient stays and costs, physicians often prefer hospitals to share the risk associated with these arrangements.

Finally, groups are typically unwilling and/or unable to invest greater internally generated resources into needed administrative and information systems. For example, group physicians may be skeptical of the need to pay higher administrative salaries or to fund greater administrative expenses. There may be considerable pressure to pay out the group's earnings in the form of higher physician salaries and bonuses than in the form of capital or administrative investments.[12,13] Similarly, group members are unable to qualify for tax-exempt financing and frequently are unwilling to access needed capital through personally guaranteed bank loans.

Competitive forces facing hospitals and hospital-based specialists

Like physicians, hospitals face more uncertain revenue streams as a result of the prospective payment system (PPS) and managed care. Hospitals are feeling the long-term effects of PPS, such as a decrease in inpatient volume and a shift to outpatient settings, and are concerned about maintaining and building census. In particular, hospitals need to protect their internal medicine and surgical specialists and thus stabilize their medical staffs. These specialists are concerned about the hospital's PCP base and adequate clinical work to support their hospital practice and to protect their earnings. To protect their specialists, hospitals need to protect and broaden their physician referral base, which acts as a feeder system to the institution.

Hospitals are thus seeking to design structures and ventures that reward loyal physicians on staff yet do not anger other physicians but allow them to participate in other mechanisms. They also seek ways to shore up the practices of aging solo practitioners on staff, which may be deteriorating in both size and value. Finally, hospitals recognize that managed care plans use PCPs as gatekeepers to the hospital system and thus the need to establish linkages with them. This issue is particularly important for urban and suburban hospitals that are heavily laden with specialists and have relatively little inpatient contact with PCPs.

Hospitals, like physicians, also face growing competitive threats to their market share and profitable product lines. This competition comes not only from other hospitals but also from large multispecialty group practices and physicians on staff who set up diagnostic and therapeutic facilities outside the hospital to escape from the RBRVS and hospital control.

The PPS and competition threaten to dismantle the hospital's traditional profit centers, transfer them to the ambulatory care market, and thereby curb the hospital's capacity to cross-subsidize services.[14] Hospitals facing this threat seek to gain some measure of control over physicians' ambulatory care business and to preempt competitive initiatives from outsiders.

Finally, hospitals are confronted by the imperatives of managed care contracting: Cut costs, control utilization, and document/improve quality of care. Hospitals are also being pushed to assume more risk in these arrangements, such as the use of single pricing contracts for hospital and medical services. Hospitals wish to educate their physicians about managed care and to share with them the financial risks of managed care. They also want to increase their leverage over managed care firms. One strategy is to pool their contracting activities with other providers to achieve economies and efficiencies. Another strategy is to create alternative contracting vehicles to attract employers directly.

Strengths and Competencies for Developing These Models

Solo physicians

According to the latest American Medical Association statistics, solo practice still represents the single largest practice setting among U.S. physicians. By virtue of their numbers and the fact that many are practitioners of primary care, solo physicians constitute an important, although fragmented, block of providers to include in any new model of physician–hospital relationships. The most popular way of organizing them during the past decade has been through independent practice association (IPA) model health maintenance organizations (HMOs). IPA-HMOs have experienced the most rapid growth among all HMO types in terms of numbers of plans, enrolled members, and participating physicians.[15] Their popularity stems from their relatively inexpensive start-up costs, the ability of physicians to remain in private practice in their own offices, their protection of fee-for-service reimbursement, and the ability of patients to retain their customary physicians.[16] Most hospital administrators unfortunately lack information about the practices of solo physicians who work primarily in their own offices; such information is needed to harness quickly the IPA-HMO potential.

Group practice physicians

Group practices offer different competitive strengths in the development of new physician–hospital models. An obvious advantage is their strength in numbers.[11,17] The growing number and average size of group practices increase their salience to hospitals as attractive coalition partners and their voice in the governance structures of these arrangements. By virtue of their larger size, groups of physicians can offer a more comprehensive range of services at multiple sites and thus can increase their attractiveness to managed care organizations (MCOs). Their size may also appeal to HMOs and preferred provider organizations (PPOs) that look for provider groups with sufficient numbers to assume risk. At the same time, groups of physicians can present an organized front to managed care organizations and third party payers, thereby augmenting their bargaining position in contract negotiations. As a final advantage of size, groups can band together and meet the competitive threat posed by large networks and systems of other providers, such as Kaiser Health Plan in California.

In addition to their size, group practices enjoy competitive advantages in attracting patients. Groups are better situated than solo practitioners to meet patient demands and preferences for care that is centralized in one site, convenient to access, and comprehensive in the scope of services provided.[11] Groups also enjoy brand recognition (e.g., the Mayo Clinic and the Cleveland Clinic) and a marketplace perception of quality. Research suggests that quality of care may be higher in group settings as a result of greater professional interaction and surveillance.[16,18] Indeed, some analysts suggest that purchasers prefer contracting with groups because of their ability to manage quality and cost.[9]

Finally, in contrast to solo physicians, group practices have sufficient patient volume to permit diversification into ancillary services and ambulatory care businesses.[9] As a result, they may be capable of generating a much higher return on investment. They may also be better situated to take on more risk as well as to self-insure.

Hospitals

Hospitals contribute a different set of strengths to new physician–hospital arrangements. In contrast to physicians, hospitals have greater access to capital because of their nonprofit status and larger scale. Such capital is required to expand service offerings and delivery sites. Hospitals also possess the administrative leadership necessary to develop and guide these new arrangements as well as the required technical capabilities such as management information systems, data processing, finance, and marketing.

Hospitals may possess another critical advantage over other providers as a result of their prior experience with managed care contracting. As a result, hospitals have greater experience with utilization review, practice profiles, contract negotiation, and pricing. Some hospitals are already offering contract review and advisory services to their medical staffs. They also have greater knowledge of competitors' strategies/offerings and physician referral patterns.

Summary

Physicians and hospitals face an increasingly competitive and uncertain environment. They are confronted with a series of challenges, some common to both parties and some unique to each. Perhaps the greatest common challenge is posed by the shift from a non–managed care to a managed care environment, in which they are at greater financial risk. Physicians and hospitals recognize their mutual interdependence in managing these risks as well as their mutual advantage in combining forces to operate within a managed care marketplace. The two parties thus have the incentive to seek closer cooperation. They also have the opportunity. Physicians and hospitals each possess competitive strengths that make them mutually attractive as partners in a coalition that pools their resources to gain greater leverage in a managed care environment. The new models of physician–hospital organization described below constitute different formats for organizing these coalitions.

New Models of Physician–Hospital Organizations

There are at least four different models of new physician–hospital arrangements that have been described in case studies in the group practice literature. These include the PHO, the MSO, the foundation model, and the integrated health organization (IHO). Because each model has a number of variants, this classification should be considered a rough typology. There is some indication that physician–hospital arrangements develop from one model to the next. In this process of development, the arrangements foster much higher integration between the two parties. According to the Leadership Institute, such integration involves shared risk through common ownership, governance, revenue/capital, planning, and/or management.[19] The four basic models are described below.

Physician–hospital organization

A PHO is a joint venture between one or more hospitals and physicians. The physicians may participate in the joint venture as individuals or, more often, as members of a physician organization such as an IPA or professional corporation (PC).

The PHO may be organized for a single purpose, such as acting as a single agent for managed care contracting. More often, the PHO is organized for multiple purposes. It serves as the single agent for contracting with multiple HMOs and/or PPOs as well as directly with employers. It may also own a managed care plan (HMO or PPO), own and operate ambulatory care centers or ancillary services projects, and provide administrative or other services to physician members.

If the PHO is used for contracting, the two parties can present a united front and exert greater bargaining leverage as well as respond to purchaser preferences for a single, bundled price. To be effective, however, this coalition must be viewed by purchasers as a potential cost-control strategy. The PHO therefore requires active utilization management, sophisticated utilization information systems, and intensive involvement of physicians in developing standards of care and monitoring utilization. Given the contentiousness and complexity of economic credentialing, it should be evident that the PHO offers distinct advantages over the hospital medical staff structure as a lean, mean, contracting machine.

To avoid concerns of antitrust, the PHO cannot exist solely to negotiate contracts but must also contain significant elements of risk sharing between the two parties and the integration of operations for some legitimate purpose. Depending upon that legitimate business purpose, the PHO may also need to comply with safe harbors regulations (see below). These regulations are especially pertinent to potential PHO projects involving ancillary medical services, where physician members of the PHO can also be a major source of its patient referrals.

In addition to contracting, PHO responsibilities typically include utilization review and quality assurance, physician credentialing and claims processing, marketing, and the development of fee schedules. The PHO may also serve as an educational vehicle to teach practitioners about the economics of managed care and the economic needs of the hospital.

The PHO model allows alignment of the interests of the hospital(s) and important physicians and provides for the sharing of risk between the parties. That risk is shared, however, only as it relates to those projects/activities that are conducted through the PHO. Each party continues to conduct and carry the risk for the remainder of its non-PHO activities.

Management services organization

The MSO is a corporation (for profit or nonprofit) that may be freestanding or, for purposes of this discussion, owned by a hospital or a physician–hospital joint venture. It provides management services to one or more medical practices (usually sizeable group practices) and serves as a framework for joint planning and decision making in the business affairs of the practice. If forming a new relationship with an existing PC, the MSO purchases the tangible assets of the PC at fair market value to avoid concerns of private inurement (Figure 5–1). These assets are then leased back to the PC as part of a full-service management agreement, under which the MSO employs all nonphysician staff and provides all supplies and administrative systems required by the group in exchange for either a flat fee or a set percentage of group revenues. The practice continues to be owned by the PC and the provider number used is that of the PC. In California, some MSO examples include Alta Bates and Mercy–San Diego.

This brief description conveys three of the main attractions of the MSO to physicians. First, the MSO serves as a vehicle to transfer hospital capital to the group of physicians, which can be used to develop a group as well as to expand existing clinical services, staff, and/or operations. Second, the MSO provides administrative systems that may not be affordable by the individual physicians in the PC. Third, the MSO

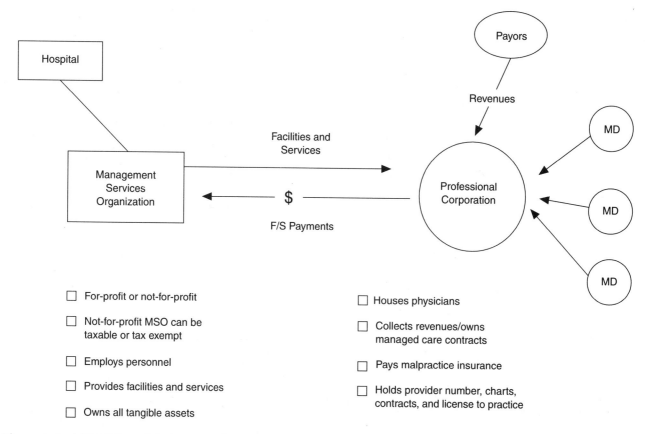

Figure 5–1. MSO/PC model: Common features. Reprinted with permission from BDC Advisors. Copyright © 1992.

may provide comprehensive ambulatory and inpatient services through an integrated business entity that manages that care and assumes financial risk.

The MSO resembles the PHO in several respects. The physicians' PC retains its autonomy and acts as the provider of patient care services. The MSO may also provide for shared governance between the hospital and the PC. Finally, the hospital must comply with antifraud and safe harbors regulations, for example, by granting only limited subsidies to the MSO if it operates at a loss and thus avoiding private inurement of physicians, by demonstrating that the MSO furthers the hospital's charitable purpose and benefits the community, and by negotiating the purchase of the PC's tangible assets at arms' length.

Unlike the situation in PHOs, in MSOs the PC is typically the entity that executes contracts with payers and MCOs. Thus all managed care revenues flow to the PC, not the MSO. Another difference between the PHO and the MSO is the amount of risk shared between the hospital and physicians. In the PHO risk

is shared only for those activities in which the PHO is engaged, generally a limited part of any physician's practice. In the MSO, the full risk of the practice is shared between the PC and the owners of the MSO. Alignment of interests and incentives is thus more complete in the MSO than in the PHO.

The foundation model

The foundation is a corporation, usually nonprofit, that is organized either as an affiliate of a hospital with a common parent organization or as a subsidiary of a hospital. In this model the foundation owns and operates one or more practices, including their facilities, equipment, and supplies. The foundation employs all nonphysician personnel and contracts with a physician-owned entity (usually a PC) to provide the medical services for the practice (Figure 5–2). Some of the more prominent examples of existing foundations in California include UniHealth America, Mercy Medical Foundation, Sharp Rees–Stealy, Palo Alto Medi-

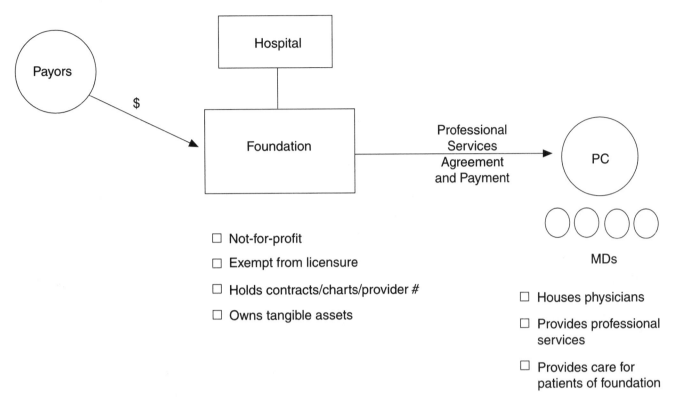

Figure 5–2. Foundation model: Common features. Reprinted with permission from BDC Advisors. Copyright © 1992.

cal Foundation, Sutter Health, and, most recently, Friendly Hills Healthcare Foundation.

Foundations can qualify for tax-exempt status under 501(c)(3) of the Internal Revenue Code by adhering to two main statutory requirements[20]:

1. *Organizational/operational tests:* The foundation must primarily engage in activities that serve charitable purposes, such as promotion of health and provision of health care services to the broader community with no limitations based on ability to pay, educational activities, or medical research. The foundation must also be able to demonstrate that it is not organized and operated for the benefit of private interests (i.e., its board and the board of the medical group do not substantially overlap).

2. *Private inurement proscription:* The foundation's net earnings may not inure to the benefit of any private shareholder, member, or other interested person (i.e., a physician). This requires that all compensation payable by the foundation to physicians be reasonable in amount, be the result of arms' length negotiation, and not be a device to distribute the foundation's operating surplus. Similarly, the acquisition of physician assets by the foundation must bear a reasonable relationship to the foundation's exempt purposes, be purchased at fair market value, be negotiated at arms' length, and not result in more than an insubstantial private economic benefit to physicians in relation to the public benefit that will be conferred from the foundation's activities.

In some states, a medical foundation requires exemption from clinic licensing and application of the corporate practice of medicine rule. In California, for example, where they originated, foundations are explicitly exempt from the former and implicitly exempt from the latter if they contract with a group of physicians (a PC) that numbers at least forty, whose members practice in at least ten specialties, where two thirds of the physicians practice within foundation facilities, and that conducts medical research and health education.[20,21]

In this model, the physician group owns no assets, either tangible or intangible. This makes it much easier for new physicians to buy into the group and for retiring physicians to leave. Moreover, as in the MSO, the transfer of assets from the group to the foundation enables the group to expand services and to recruit additional providers, both PCPs and specialists.

Under this model, the foundation becomes the formal provider of health care but negotiates a professional services agreement with physicians to provide services to foundation patients. As payment, the PC receives either a percentage of the foundation's revenues/collections or a lump sum. The PC retains its autonomy and remains self-governing. It employs or compensates all physicians, conducts all credentialing, and performs utilization review activities.

For its part, the foundation provides the clinic premises, provides all administrative/financial/marketing services, employs all nonmedical personnel, and serves as a vehicle to accumulate and retain surpluses that can be used to finance new equipment, facilities, and operations. In the tax-exempt nonprofit foundation, unlike the MSO, such surpluses are not taxed.[22] In addition, unlike the MSO, the foundation may qualify for tax-exempt financing under certain conditions. These include limitations on the number of contracting physicians who may serve on the foundation's board of directors to one of every five members (the 80–20 rule) and restrictions on the length, compensation features, and termination clause in physician service contracts.[20] Tax-exemption enhances the foundation's access to capital. Tax-exempt foundations, with sufficient cash flow and assets, can get rated by bond rating agencies. These agencies may give higher ratings to more integrative physician–hospital arrangements. Foundations can thus obtain substantial amounts of capital in the form of tax-exempt debt on favorable terms as well as avoid sales and income taxes.[23] As a tax-exempt affiliate of the nonprofit hospital, the foundation may also be able to access additional (hospital) capital via transfers of funds from one hospital affiliate to another with less risk of private inurement.[24]

The foundation also engages in all contracts with payers and managed care firms. This model allows the hospital and physicians to present themselves as a combined contracting unit. Usually both the physicians and the hospital will be capitated in these arrangements. The capitation rate paid by the managed care organization will be divided into a physician capitation pool (cap pool) and a hospital cap pool. In addition, the physicians and the hospital will negotiate a per diem to be charged to the hospital cap pool that should cover monthly expenses on a break-even basis. Both parties have an incentive to conserve resource utilization to ensure that the hospital cap pool shows a surplus that can then be shared. The risks of capitation (i.e., instances where the hospital cap pool shows a deficit) are likewise shared. Other shared incentives to promote efficiency stem from marketplace demands to reduce costs and managerial controls exerted by both the hospital and the medical leadership of the PC.

For hospitals, the foundation constitutes one method for developing the network of providers essential for a vertically integrated system. Hospitals also engage in such arrangements to develop new sources of admissions, to increase market share and their primary care base of patients, to protect their specialists' incomes, and to generate referrals to other parts of the system. Physicians view the foundation as relief from the administrative hassles of practice and freedom to focus on clinical considerations.[24] Physician groups also view the foundation as a means to access capital—whether borrowed externally through tax-exempt debt, transferred from the hospital, or generated internally through operations—without having to borrow it themselves. Such capital can be used to expand to meet growing outpatient demand. Physicians may also view the model as their entree to the managed care market controlled by the hospital or as an accommodation with a potential competitor in a turbulent ambulatory care market.

Organizationally, the foundation and the hospital are on a level plane. Each is free to concentrate on its own special projects or operating issues. The foundation is governed by a combination of representatives from the PC, the hospital, and/or the community. Physician representation in foundation governance is limited by Internal Revenue Service (IRS) regulations to no more than 49 percent of practitioners in the medical group because of IRS reluctance to exempt physician-controlled entities from taxation.[22] The majority of board members are required by the IRS to be nonpaid community leaders and/or nonphysician hospital representatives.

Of course, not every foundation exhibits all the above features. Foundation models vary in terms of state regulations governing the corporate practice of medicine, the existence of a separate legal entity, the managerial and legal commitment made by hospitals and the PC, and the degree of risk assumed by the two parties.[25]

The foundation model offers most of the advantages over PHO arrangements that are offered by MSOs and results in a high degree of alignment of incentives and sharing of risk. It offers a potential additional advantage over the MSO model in the availability of tax exemption and thus access to cheaper capital and avoidance of taxation on foundation surpluses and property values. It carries with it, however, a major disadvantage for physicians compared with the MSO, particularly if tax exemption is sought. Because physician participation in governance is limited in the foundation and not in the MSO, there is a relative loss of physician control. Even so, physicians can maintain significant influence over the foundation's operation through the terms of the professional services agreement between the foundation and the PC.

Integrated health organization

The IHO model involves the development of a separate legal entity (a parent corporation) that typically controls three main subsidiaries: a hospital corporation, a medical services corporation, and an educational and research foundation. Conceptually, the IHO could be either for profit or nonprofit. From a practical point of view, IHOs are usually organized such that the parent and its subsidiaries are all tax-exempt, nonprofit corporations. Some prominent examples of IHOs include Virginia Mason in Seattle (Figure 5–3) and Ramsey HealthCare in St. Paul.

The parent board of the IHO comprises representatives of the subsidiary boards along with lay members from the community. The hospital corporation is generally a community hospital organization with a board of directors. The medical services corporation is unique in that it is a tax-exempt, nonprofit entity with a physician-controlled board and employed phy-

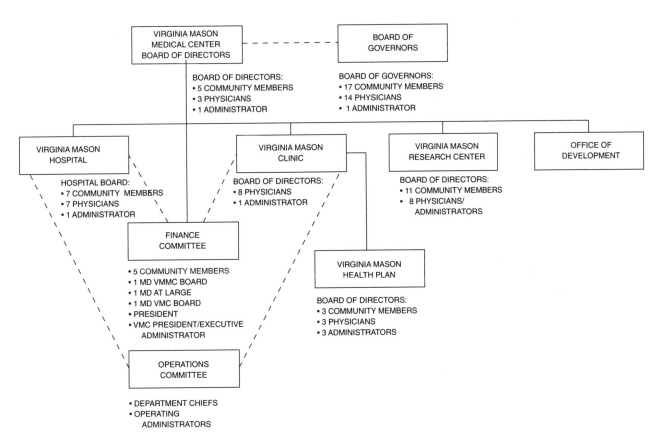

Figure 5–3. Virginia Mason Medical Center Governance Structure, 1992. Reprinted with permission from Virginia Mason Medical Center. Copyright © 1992.

sicians who provide services to patients of the parent. Because physicians are salaried, the nonprofit medical corporation does not face the same IRS constraints regarding physician representation in governance. To qualify for tax-exempt financing, however, the IHO must conform to the 80–20 rule.

In terms of the division of labor, the parent governing board ratifies the budgets of the subsidiaries, reviews their strategic plans, and acts as arbiter in the event of disputes. The medical subsidiary employs all physicians, provides adequate specialty and geographic coverage across the network of delivery sites (satellite clinics), and performs quality assurance, utilization review, and peer review functions.[25] The hospital subsidiary performs most administrative services (e.g., marketing, finance, and management information systems), provides capital for expansion, and provides the systems to integrate administrative with utilization data. It also relieves physicians of the administrative hassle of medical practice.

The IHO can, and frequently does, sponsor its own managed care activities such as an HMO or PPO. It can do this through the parent, but more typically it does this through a joint venture of the medical services and hospital organizations. These managed care companies can be either for profit or nonprofit in their legal form. In this manner, the IHO develops a set of insurance products that enable it to merge the financing and delivery of health care.

There are several advantages to this model of physician–hospital linkage. First, it enables the corporation to design and control its own delivery systems, benefit programs, and contracts. Coordination among hospital, physician, and especially insurance activities is handled through internal transfer pricing rather than through market transactions. Second, it enables providers to compete with existing integrated systems, such as Kaiser and the Mayo Clinic. Third, it enjoys greater leverage over managed care contracts external to the system. Increased leverage over payers is facilitated by the system's extensive network of providers (e.g., satellite clinics), the enhanced collection and integration of operating statistics, the resulting enhancement of utilization review activities and cost-control capability, and the new image of united, coordinated providers resulting from their joint marketing effort.

Finally, the IHO provides the highest degree of alignment of interests and incentives between physicians and hospital. It therefore enjoys the potential to develop a comprehensive, community-based system of health care services that is integrated in design and absent of duplication, what some analysts describe as the seamless delivery of care.[26] Through its network of hospitals and physician groups, the IHO can develop a single strategic plan to deliver comprehensive services to the community. Instead of duplicating expensive services and facilities to compete with other providers, the system can focus on needed services and channel patients to the appropriate service provider in this network. Some systems are currently developing a common patient registration system and computerized medical record that will permit the system to track patients across its multiple provider sites.[27] Such community-based networks form a cornerstone of the National Health Care Reform plan proposed by the American Hospital Association.[28] They are also compatible with the Certified Health Plans proposed by the Washington state legislature and with the Accountable Health Plans described in the managed competition proposal currently being drafted by the Clinton administration.[29]

This movement has several important implications for national health reform. As its health care and insurance services become more comprehensive, the system will collect a premium for each patient and then manage that patient's care, and the risks for that care, along a broad continuum of services. The system will assume the guise of a large supermarket of health care services in which employers shop for their employees. The traditional third party insurer/broker role will be pared down or eliminated. Capital outlays in the system may then be allocated more freely to areas of community need, health promotion, and prevention. In such a system, the managerial emphasis will shift from revenue generation to the conservative management of premium dollars collected. The ideal IHO sketched here, however, will come to fruition only with greater rationality and integration on the purchaser side (such as contained in the Washington state reforms).

Other models

In the interest of brevity, we have omitted mention of two other physician–hospital models that have grown in number over the past few years. One is physician ownership of hospitals. Such a model is certainly not novel. Physicians established and owned many hospitals in the late nineteenth century and have been quite prominent in the ownership and control of several proprietary hospital chains. Since the 1960s, groups of physicians have assumed equity positions in hospitals, at first on a piecemeal basis by leasing radiology and laboratory departments and later developing joint ventures involving surgical suites, specialty operations, and finally the entire facility. A common vehicle is for a hospital corporation to purchase the assets of another facility as a general partner; physician investors serve as limited partners.[30] Physicians may also purchase the hospital's assets themselves and lease back the operations.

Such ventures are more attractive to physicians than other businesses that proved either unprofitable or undercapitalized. They also enable physicians to gain control over hospital management. Hospital corporations expect that such strategies will foster greater physician utilization of the facilities.

The second model is the establishment of hospital-affiliated or hospital-owned group practices. The hospital may contract with a group through a professional services agreement to operate a group practice program as the outpatient department, or it may incorporate the group as a group practice division of the hospital, in which physicians are employees of the division. The advantages to the hospital include enhanced market image, improved quality assurance and utilization review for outpatient care, improved recruitment of new PCPs and improved leadership development among the medical staff. These groups may also compete with external groups in the community, promote physician loyalty to the hospital, permit expansion into new markets, and strengthen practice management and development activities in physician offices.

Issues for Hospitals and Physicians in Developing These New Organizational Models

Legal issues

There are two sets of legal issues that hospitals must consider before developing these new relationships

with physicians. One set revolves around the IRS's General Counsel Memorandum 39862, which deals with problems surrounding joint ventures.[31] Put simply, the IRS look disapprovingly on ventures that entail no public benefits. Problematic ventures, for example, do not further the hospital's charitable mission, expand existing health care resources, create new providers, or result in improved treatments or reduced costs.[32] New physician–hospital models must be capable of documenting their community benefit in terms of access, cost, and/or quality. These models must also distribute risk equally across hospitals and physicians and tie rewards to the level of risk assumed. Finally, these models should structure in safeguards to keep at arms' length any transactions involving the purchase of physician practices or revenue flows.[32]

A second set of legal issues revolves around fraud and abuse problems.[33] These issues stem from the Medicare and Medicaid statute that prohibits payments for referrals (the antikickback statute). In July 1991, the Department of Health and Human Services released its safe harbors regulations, which exempted eleven activities from this statute. One such activity involves the famous 60–40 rule for investments of less than $50 million of net tangible assets related to Medicare and Medicaid services. According to the rule, this investment activity falls within the safe harbor, and thus is exempt from fraud and abuse problems, if no more than 40 percent of the investment is made by those in a position to refer patients to it and if no more than 40 percent of revenues come from referrals generated by the investors. Other safe harbors that are germane to new physician–hospital models involve space and equipment rentals and the sale of practices.

According to legal analysts, the safe harbors are quite narrow in definition and leave much gray area separating exempt activities from fraudulent ones. They therefore recommend several guidelines to reduce the risk of violating the fraud and abuse statute through physician–hospital joint ventures.[34] These include recruiting physician investors regardless of their potential to make referrals, avoiding any linkage between investment and referral obligations, making risk and reward commensurate with investment, incorporating quality assurance and utilization review components, and documenting any agreements in writing. For other types of arrangements, hospitals are advised not to guarantee physician income levels or to provide services, loans, or space to physicians at below market rates. Because the statute exempts any payments made to individuals under a bona fide employment relationship, hospitals are encouraged to hire new physicians and employees.

Organizational issues

The new physician–hospital models generate a host of managerial issues that need resolution. First, the closer integration of the two parties involves the merger of quite different cultures. The physician group and hospital typically have different organizational and political structures, different legal structures, different incentive systems, different types of governance, and different time horizons that require harmonization. Even more important, perhaps, the people involved in these new relationships have different personalities and ways of doing things based upon differences in their training and experience. Physicians characteristically have been taught to function independently in problem solving and to be action oriented. Hospital people, on the other hand, are trained to function in a collaborative and more deliberate manner. Thus a key success factor will be a common vision and shared goals between the physicians and the hospital. A related success factor will be strong physician and administrative leadership to promote the shared vision and goals.

Second, the formation of a unified contracting unit of physicians and hospitals to negotiate with managed care firms involves the merger of their revenue streams. The unified contracting unit receives a capitated payment that must then be split between the two parties. The organization must determine the proper mix of fees, incentives, and/or penalties to ensure that both parties receive fair compensation and manage utilization effectively. In so doing, the organization (not the purchaser) has a greater opportunity to develop new payment methods for physicians and the hospital.

Third, the new organization must develop business plans and negotiate agreements that are attractive to all members.[35] There must be not only adequate phy-

sician representation in the governance of the new organization to foster collaborative decision making but also flexibility to allow each side to engage in ventures that may benefit only one of the parties but will make that party stronger as a partner for the other.

Finally, the management of these new forms of health care organizations requires administrators that have different educational backgrounds, sets of skills, and attitudes than those of most administrators who are currently in the field. Executives of PHOs, MSOs, medical foundations, and IHOs must have a broader understanding of the health care enterprise, must be expert in their knowledge of managed care, and must be skilled in facilitating collaboration between physicians and hospital personnel. These executives are liable to come from the ranks of hospital, medical group, and managed care administration as well as from among physicians. In each case, formal preparation beyond that previously experienced will be needed for them to be successful in this new area of management. Additionally, the managed care focus of these entities will demand other people skilled in the administration of utilization and quality management programs. These managers will usually be health care providers, physicians and nurses who have special interest and capability in these management activities. Most important, executives must be attitudinally prepared to cede real power to physicians in these arrangements. Rather than view such models as potential opportunities for administrative control and victory over the medical staff, executives should be prepared to accept supporting and facilitating roles in systems built around new collectivities of physicians.[36]

Professional issues

The new physician–hospital models must be sensitive to the issue of professional autonomy at both aggregate and individual levels. Considering the aggregate of physicians, the new models should be sensitive to and respect the medical group's control over medical practice and quality assurance activities.[37] Participating physicians may also be concerned about the degree to which their practice is locked in by their contract with the new organization.[35] For their part, hospitals wish to develop closer bonds with participating physicians but may need to avoid the appearance of imposing restrictive covenants that prohibit activities that compete with the new venture. Thus the new models should carefully document the roles and expectations of both parties. Hospitals that seek to restrict the practices of participating physicians may need to work indirectly through the PC to have such covenants imposed.

At the individual physician level, the new models should be sensitive to physician suspicions regarding bureaucratic control, fears over declining autonomy, and apprehension regarding practice in unfamiliar, organized settings. Physicians may need considerable time, significant involvement, and strong medical leadership to get acclimated to the new arrangements.[36] Such arrangements should not be simply imposed from above. Slightly less caution may be needed with younger generations of physicians, who appear to be more mentally prepared to practice in managed care environments.[38,39]

In addition to the issue of autonomy, the new models will need to confront the professional issue of collegiality. In our atomized and competitive health care system, collegiality has become a forgotten term both among physicians and between physicians and administrators. Goldsmith defines collegiality as shared professional values, trust, and collaboration among all parties.[36] He suggests that collegiality will serve as the primary organizing principle in these new arrangements. Such collegiality will enable physicians and hospitals successfully to share financial risks and achieve integration.

Finally, nonparticipating physicians on the hospital's medical staff may be concerned about their exclusion from the new arrangement. They may perceive that the hospital is favoring some physicians over others, helping some of their competitors to succeed, and/or taking away some of their patients.[21] This issue can be resolved by involving the excluded physicians in other arrangements, such as a medical staff IPA.

Indeed, most of the advanced health care systems are actively engaged in linking independent physicians to their integrated physician networks. For example, Health Dimensions, Inc., with its Good Samaritan Medical Foundation incorporates a medical group and an IPA under the foundation with both sets of physicians on the board. Similarly, UniHealth and Sharp have vehicles to tie independent physicians

closely with the system and its medical groups via managed care contracts.

Implications for Educators and Researchers

These trends in PHOs also have important implications for education and research in health care management. For educators, greater emphasis must be placed in the classroom on understanding the professional activities of physicians: their training and socialization, their interests and incentives, and their practice concerns. Attention should be paid to the life cycle of medical practice and how physician practice needs change over time.[40] Heavy emphasis must also be placed on managed care contracting, utilization and quality management, the development of systems and networks, the formation of groups, and the legal barriers in such arrangements. To facilitate this training, health programs may wish to consider structuring part of their curricula around entrepreneurship issues and new venture formation.

In the near term, many, if not most, administrators of the new integrated health care organizations will be individuals with diverse backgrounds who are currently in the health care field and who need additional education and training not previously received. Programs in health administration may need to think about structuring offerings for part-time students, meeting in the evening and on weekends, and becoming more flexible in their content to meet the needs of these individuals.

For researchers, the task is not only to understand the structure and formation of these new models but also to document their process and outcomes. Physician–hospital models have enormous potential not only for aligning provider incentives to control health care costs but also for fostering the development of integrated systems to provide comprehensive care at the community level. It is important to determine which of the various models are most successful in this regard and to identify those specific characteristics of the most successful models that contribute to that success. Researchers from several universities associated with the Western Network Health Management Research Consortium are currently developing a project to study these issues.

REFERENCES

1. Alexander, J.A., et al. "Effects of Competition, Regulation, and Corporatization on Hospital–Physician Relationships." *Journal of Health and Social Behavior* 27 (1986): 220–235.
2. Burns, L.R., et al. "The Effect of Hospital Control Strategies on Physician Satisfaction and Physician–Hospital Conflict." *Health Services Research* 25 (1990): 527–560.
3. Shortell, S.M. *Effective Hospital–Physician Relationships.* Ann Arbor, Mich.: Health Administration Press, 1991.
4. Joint Commission on Accreditation of Healthcare Organizations (Joint Commission). *Report of the Joint Commission Survey of Relationships among Governing Bodies, Management, and Medical Staffs in U.S. Hospitals.* Chicago, Ill.: Joint Commission, 1988.
5. Touche Ross. *U.S. Hospitals: The Future of Health Care—A Survey of U.S. Hospital Executives and Presidents of Medical Staffs on the Challenges They Face in an Environment of Enormous Change.* New York, N.Y.: Touche Ross, 1988.
6. Shortell, S.M. "The Medical Staff of the Future: Replanting the Garden." *Frontiers of Health Services Management* 1 (1985): 3–48.
7. Shortell, S.M. "Revisiting the Garden: Medicine and Management in the 1990s." *Frontiers of Health Services Management* 7 (1990): 3–32.
8. American Medical Association (AMA). *Socioeconomic Characteristics of Medical Practice 1990/91.* Chicago, Ill.: AMA Center for Health Policy Research, 1991.
9. Benvenuto, J., et al. "From 12 Solo Practices to a Hospital-Based LSMG in 100 Easy Steps." *Medical Group Management Journal* 38 (1991): 84–92.
10. Havlicek, P. *Medical Groups in the U.S.* Chicago, Ill.: American Medical Association, 1990.
11. Schryver, D. "Group Practice/Hospital Relations." *Medical Group Management Journal* 38 (1991): 20–23.
12. Korenchuk, K. "Making the Choice: A Close Look at the Joint Venture Option." *Medical Group Management Journal* 38 (1991): 12–22.
13. Peters, G. "Integrated Delivery Can Ally Physician and Hospital Plans." *Healthcare Financial Management* 45 (1991): 21–22, 24, 26, 28, 30, 32.
14. Barnett, A. "The Integration of Health Care as a Model for the Future." *Medical Group Management Journal* 38 (1991): 16, 18.
15. Christianson, J., et al. "The HMO Industry: Evolution in Population Demographics and Market Structures." *Medical Care Review* 48 (1991): 3–46.
16. Wholey, D., and Burns, L. "Organizational Transitions: Form Changes by Health Maintenance Organizations." In *Research in the Sociology of Organizations*, edited by S. Bacharach. Greenwich, Conn.: JAI Press, 1993.
17. McCarthy, G. "Strength in Numbers." *Health Progress* 72 (1991): 50–53.
18. Burns, L., and Wholey, D. "Differences in Access and Quality of Care Across HMO Types." *Health Services Management Research* 4 (1991): 32–45.
19. BDC Advisors. *Physician/Hospital Integration Models.* San Francisco, Calif.: BDC, 1993.
20. Stromberg, R.E. *Medical Foundation and Management Service Organizations: Legal and Regulatory Issues.* Irvine, Calif.: Jones, Day, Reavis & Pogue, 1991.
21. Perry, L. "California Hospital Systems Use Not-for-Profit Foundations in Pursuit of Physician Practices." *Modern Healthcare* 21 (1991): 32.
22. Golembesky, H., et al. "Physician/Hospital Medical Foundations: A Future Model for Integrated Health Care." *Medical Group Management Journal* 39 (1992): 96–104.
23. Lindeke, J. "The 'Foundation Model' as a Hospital–Physician Organizational Structure: Panacea, Fad, or . . . ?" *Health Care Law Newsletter* 7 (1992): 9–12.
24. Stromberg, R.E. *Hospital-Affiliated Medical Group Practice: The Use of Medical Foundations and Management Service Organizations.* Irvine, Calif.: Jones, Day, Reavis & Pogue, 1991.
25. Baker, G. "Hospital Physician Organizations: Models for Success." *Group Practice Journal* 39 (1990): 4–22.
26. Burda, D. "Seamless Delivery." *Modern Healthcare* 22 (1992): 38, 40, 42.
27. Gardner, E. "Shared Information Could Revolutionize Healthcare." *Modern Healthcare* 22 (1992): 30–36.
28. American Hospital Association (AHA). *National Health Care Reform: Refining and Advancing the Vision.* Chicago, Ill.: AHA, 1992.
29. Shortell, S.M. "State Health Policy Reform: A Basis for National Reform." Paper presented to Irving B. Harris Graduate School of Public Policy Studies, University of Chicago, March 1993.
30. Hudson, T. "Hospital–MD Joint Ventures Move Forward Despite Hurdles." *Hospitals* 65 (1991): 22–26, 28.
31. Bromberg, R. "Hospital–Physician Joint Ventures: New, Menacing IRS Stance." *HealthSpan* 9 (1992): 3–12.
32. Herman, A. "IRS Memorandum Limits Joint Ventures." *Healthcare Financial Management* 46 (1992): 49, 51–52.
33. MacKelvie, C. "Fraud, Abuse, and Inurement." *Topics in Health Care Financing* 16 (1990): 49–57.
34. MacKelvie, C., et al. "The Impact of Fraud and Abuse Regulations." *Healthcare Financial Management* 46 (1992): 26–33.
35. O'Gara, N. "Charging Forward: Hospital–Physician Relations in Managed Care." *Healthcare Executive* 7 (1992): 22–25.
36. Goldsmith, J.C. "Driving the Nitroglycerin Truck." *Healthcare Forum Journal* 36 (1993): 36–44.
37. Johnsson, J. "Dynamic Diversification: Hospitals Pursue Physician Alliances, 'Seamless' Care." *Hospitals* 66 (1992): 20–26.
38. Baker, L.C., and Cantor, J.C. "Physician Satisfaction under Managed Care." *Health Affairs* 12 (1993): 258–270.
39. Huonker, J., and Burns, L.R. "Factors Affecting Physician Choice between Managed Care and Fee-for-Service Settings, and the Effect of that Choice on Physician Autonomy and Satisfaction." Paper presented at the annual meeting of the Association of University Programs of Health Administration, Atlanta, April 1993.
40. Super, K.E. "Services Should Be Linked to Practices' Life Cycles." *Modern Healthcare* 17 (1987): 57–58.

6

The Development of Integrated Service Networks in Minnesota

John E. Kralewski, Andrea de Vries, Bryan Dowd, and Sandra Potthoff

This article presents an analysis of the integrated service networks (ISNs) that are developing in Minnesota and provides alternate conceptual models of these new forms of health care delivery. The article is intended as a preliminary analysis of the ISN concept as described by key informants who are developing those organizations and as a baseline document that can be used to evaluate the evolution of these structures.

While several of the current proposals for health care reform, including the legislation enacted in Minnesota during 1993, encourage and in some cases mandate the development of integrated provider systems, the structures developing in Minnesota are largely in response to private sector pressures rather than public policy initiatives. The demand side of the health care market in Minnesota is being restructured by the formation of well-organized purchasing groups. Two of these have had a profound effect on the provider system. The first was formed by the State of Minnesota Employees Health Benefit Program during 1985.[1] It now purchases health care for 144,000 enrollees throughout Minnesota. The second and perhaps the most influential was initiated during 1991 by 14 large employers. This coalition, called the Business Health Care Action Group, now buys health services for about 85,000 enrollees.[2-5]

These two purchasing alliances had an effect on health care providers that went far beyond their relatively small number of enrollees. Physicians, hospitals, and health insurance plans viewed these purchasing groups as the future direction of managed competition in the Twin Cities health care market and, accordingly, began forming networks to bid on contracts to provide services for their enrollees.

ISNs have been defined by the Minnesota State Health Insurance legislation (MinnesotaCare) as "organizations that are accountable for the costs and outcomes associated with delivering a full continuum of health care services to a defined population."[6] Under an ISN arrangement, a network of hospitals, physicians, and other health care providers furnish all needed health services for a fixed payment. In the Clinton proposal for national health care reform, these proposed organizations are called regional health alliances.[7] In these and other managed competition legislation initiatives, such as the Breaux–Cooper bill,[8] these structures are a main component of health care reform. It is proposed that they will create an integrated network of physicians, hospitals, pharmacists, and other health care professionals and institutions capable of providing high quality, cost-effective health care. Although ISNs are built on the health maintenance organization (HMO) concept, they are intended to be more flexible in terms of the organizational relationships with providers and more sophisticated in the management of patient care. In essence, these structures are based on the concepts pioneered by the most innovative HMOs and, in many ways, represent the next generation of this approach to health care delivery. In fact, some respondents expressed their belief that HMOs would have evolved into ISN-type organizations regardless of national or state initiatives for health care reform.

Methods

Data were obtained from eight health care organizations that describe themselves as being in the process of developing ISNs. The case study method was used to acquire, classify, and analyze the data. The study was conducted during November and December 1993 and included two phases. First, two potential ISN organizations were interviewed to identify the issues

Health Care Manage Rev, 1995; 20(4): 42–56

45

that should be addressed and the components of ISNs that should be explored. A case study protocol was then developed to guide the research.

Sites were selected from a list of likely ISN sponsors compiled from discussions with health care provider, health association, and health insurance executives in the Twin Cities. Twenty potential ISNs were identified. Telephone calls were then made to the administrators of those sites to confirm their intent to develop a program. Two sites were only considering sponsorship of ISNs and, consequently, they were dropped from the list. Eight were then selected for inclusion in the study. Only one potential case study organization refused to cooperate, and it was replaced by a similar organization. The case studies were selected to represent urban and rural ISNs and a broad range of sponsoring organizations.

Organizational Structure

The organizational structures of the evolving ISNs are quite similar even though they have a variety of sponsors. The corporate structure brings physicians, hospitals, and an insurance component together in some type of organizational arrangement. In some cases, all of these components are owned by the ISN or the ISN is cosponsored by organizations with these capabilities. For example, a medical group practice, a hospital system, and a health insurance company join forces to sponsor an ISN. In most of these cases, the sponsors have equal ownership and the governing board is made up of representatives from each organization. It is interesting to note, however, that one of the sponsoring organizations usually plays the lead role in the formation of the ISN. This often occurs because of the special administrative capabilities of that organization. Large hospitals or hospital systems, for example, have extensive administrative capabilities and can use those resources to organize an ISN. In these cases, the physician and insurance components are less involved in the developmental phases of the program. If the physicians are not well organized in a large group practice, the developmental phase of an ISN also includes the formation of some type of physician umbrella organization to represent the physician's interest. These organizations are often owned by the participating physicians, although, at times, they may be sponsored and owned by a hospital system or a group practice. In either event, the network organization provides the physician component for the ISN and usually has an ownership position in the firm. The physician component can also be created by acquiring medical clinics. Both hospital systems and large health insurance plans are acquiring clinics to create medical components for their ISNs. While these clinics will provide the core nucleus for the medical component, additional physicians will also be linked to that core through contracts. The health insurance plans that are pursuing this strategy are taking the lead role in sponsoring ISNs and are bringing hospitals into the program through contracts or by giving them a limited ownership position.

Large multispecialty medical groups with substantial administrative capacity also are taking lead roles in developing ISNs. The structure of these plans varies considerably, with some medical groups planning to retain a majority ownership position and with others forming equal partnerships with hospitals or health insurance companies.

In essence, three major stakeholders are emerging: hospitals, physicians, and health insurance companies. Each, in some cases, is playing the lead role in the development of an ISN. The other components are being brought into the program through contracts for services, acquisitions, or as cosponsors. In the case of physicians, a network or umbrella organization often is formed to bring small group practices together to contract with the ISN or to help form the ISN. These umbrella organizations are not always owned by the physicians. In some cases, they are formed and owned by hospitals.

The majority of the respondents interviewed in this study noted that consumer or community representation on the governing board of an ISN would be a positive factor and that they planned to have such representation. It doesn't appear that the ownership of the ISNs or the nature of the lead role organizations has an effect on the type of program being planned. All of those interviewed plan to offer a relatively comprehensive benefit package and are comfortable with offering their plan to both public and private sector enrollees. Some of the proposed ISNs will be limited to specific geographic areas now served by the sponsors, but this doesn't relate to the type of sponsoring organization. Projected administrative costs are also quite similar among the proposed ISNs: about 6 percent to 8 percent of revenues.

We identified 18 organizations or combinations of organizations that now are planning to develop ISNs in Minnesota. Nine are medical group practices or combinations of medical groups and one or two hospitals. Three are hospital systems that own a significant number of medical clinics or have formed physician network organizations. Three are being planned by large successful health insurance plans, one of which is acquiring 20 to 30 medical clinics, and three are being planned by existing HMOs. We identified only one community-based plan for an ISN, but that effort is largely being organized by a medical group practice.

While the ownership of these ISNs varies according to the sponsorship, and the size and geographic focus vary by location and mission, the structures and benefit plans being developed are quite similar. There is clearly a lead agency that takes responsibility for nurturing the idea into good currency and gaining support for the plan. That organization may then play a dominant role in administering the ISN, but not always. The other major stakeholders are being brought into the planning at an early stage and, at times, end up with an equal ownership position. At other times, some providers may not have an ownership position, but furnish services through long-term contracts. While large hospitals (or hospital systems) and large medical group practices have some in-house insurance capabilities or could develop that capacity, it appears that most are planning to obtain those services from an outside agency either through contracts or by bringing that agency into an equal or minority ownership position. The exceptions are the HMOs or hospital systems that now sponsor HMOs.

Insurance Component

Most of those planning to develop ISNs note that it probably will be less expensive to buy the insurance component from an existing health insurance company than to develop that capacity in-house. However, as noted previously, some of the potential ISNs already have this capacity since they now function as HMOs or have an ownership position in an HMO. It, therefore, appears that some organizations that now have health insurance capabilities will both sponsor ISNs and sell their insurance services to other ISNs. Depending on the final structure of MinnesotaCare,

the insurance component may be less important in the future than it is currently. For example, there will be no need for extensive actuarial services or rate-setting capabilities under a community rating system. Moreover, some of the current health insurance functions, such as claims and utilization reviews, will likely be shifted to the information/quality improvement/clinical guidelines departments envisioned by most of the ISNs. The major function that remains is the benefit structure.

There is widespread agreement among the respondents that ISNs should offer some choices in benefit plans but that both the interests of the enrollees and the ISN are best served by a benefit package that includes coverage of a wide range of services. The case for a very inclusive benefits plan is twofold. First, it is argued that physicians are better able to provide cost-effective health care if they are not constrained by the types of services covered. In other words, they need access to a full range of choices in order to mix resources in a cost-effective manner. Second, enrollees will not maximize preventive services or use services in a cost-effective way if they have a disincentive to do so. Consequently, they need coverage of a full range of services so that they will use the system appropriately and will partner with their physician in maintaining their health.

Some ISNs plan to offer more than one benefit plan, but this largely is a hedge against an uncertain market. They simply want to be prepared if consumers (or purchasing groups) demand a low-cost, low-benefit plan, or a plan with point of service coverage. Most of the respondents expect state or national mandated health care benefit packages, and most believe that they will cover a broad range of services. A typical benefit plan that has broad support among the ISNs is shown in Table 6–1.

While there is considerable agreement that ISN benefit packages should cover a wide range of services, there is less agreement on enrollee cost sharing for those services. Some of the respondents argue that cost sharing should be kept to a minimum and should be used only as a means of keeping enrollees in touch with health care costs. Others argue that it is an important mechanism to provide alternate, less costly benefit packages while maintaining the range of services covered. They propose that cost-sharing provisions, choice of provider (including the location of

Table 6–1

Model Health Benefits Plan

Health services	Coverage provided
Preventive Care and Physician Services	Plan pays 100 percent for these services: • Routine preventive exams • Routine hearing exams • Diagnostic radiographs • Newborn baby care • Immunizations • Routine hospital services • Well-child care • Allergy injections • Outpatient surgery • Routine vision exams • Diagnostic laboratory tests Member pays $10 per visit for these services: • Office visits • Physical therapy • Speech therapy • Occupational therapy
Maternity Care*	Plan pays 100 percent for these services: • Physician and hospital services for prenatal care, delivery, and postnatal care * Immediate coverage for infant if enrolled in the Plan
Inpatient Hospital Services	Plan pays 100 percent for these services: • Semi-private room and board • Diagnostic and therapeutic radiographs • General nursing care • Medications, blood, and blood plasma • Surgery and surgical assistance • Physical therapy • Anesthesia and pathology • Physician services
Emergency Services*	Local emergencies: • Member pays $15 per visit for urgent care center services • Member pays $40 per visit for emergency department services (Copayment waived if visit results in admission) • Plan pays 80 percent for emergency ambulance service * Emergency department use must be preauthorized by a Plan physician, except when a medical condition is life threatening Worldwide emergencies: • Member pays $40 per visit, then 20 percent of first $2,500 of covered charges (Copayment waived if visit results in admission) • Plan pays 80 percent of emergency ambulance service * Refer to Certificate of Coverage for notification requirements
Home Health Care	• Member pays $10 per visit for non-custodial care, with proper approval
Prescription Drugs*	• Member pays $9 for up to a 30-day supply of prescription drugs, a 3-month supply of birth control pills, or one vial of insulin * Prescription drugs must be dispensed through a Plan pharmacy
Preventive Dental Services	• Plan pays 100 percent for dental exams, cleaning and scaling, radiographs and fluoride treatments for dependent children ages 2–19
Mental Health and Chemical Dependency Services*	Outpatient services: • Individual, family, or biofeedback therapy . . . Member pays $20 per session, $25 per session after 10th session • Group therapy . . . Member pays $10 per session, $12 per session after 10th session * Outpatient services limited to a combined total of 40 sessions per benefit year, but no fewer than 40 mental health sessions if determined medically necessary; preauthorized required after 10th session

continues

Table 6–1

Continued

Health services	Coverage provided
	Inpatient services: • Plan pays 80 percent for semiprivate room, board, general nursing care, and other eligible expenses * Inpatient care limited to 50 days for mental health; 75 days for chemical dependency
Miscellaneous Benefits	Plan pays 80 percent of the following expenses when prescribed by a Plan physician and purchased from a contract provider: • Prosthetic devices, $5,000 maximum per prosthesis, per benefit year • Durable medical equipment used strictly for medical purposes, $2,000 maximum per piece, $5,000 maximum per benefit year • Reconstructive surgery, physician, dentist, and hospital services • Dental care to restore damage from an accident or injury • Growth hormone solution and supplies • Infertility treatment and artificial insemination for hospital, physician services, supplies, and drug therapy
Special Benefits	• Eyeglasses or contact lenses . . . Special credit toward purchase through selected vendors • Hearing aids . . . 15 percent discount available through selected vendors
What Is Not Covered	In general, any service not provided by or under the direction of a Plan physician. Also, but not limited to the following: • Procedures or treatments that are investigative, experimental, or are not generally accepted by the medical profession • Procedures or services that are not medically necessary and/or are primarily for vocation, comfort, convenience, appearance, or are educational in nature • Dental care and oral surgery, except in limited circumstances • Experimental organ transplants (see Certificate of Coverage for clarification) • Prescription eyewear and the measurement, fitting, or adjustment of contact lenses or hearing aids • Cosmetic surgery except under certain limited circumstances • Physical and mental examinations done for third parties • Custodial care, private duty nursing, and home care for chronic conditions • Reversal or voluntary sterilization or artificial conception process such as in vitro fertilization (except artificial insemination as provided in the Certificate of Coverage), sperm acquisition, and sperm storage • Over-the-counter drugs and equivalents, including enteral feedings and other electrolyte supplements except as required to treat PKU • Religious counseling, marital/relationship counseling, or sex therapy rendered in the absence of a mental disorder

*Out-of-pocket costs cannot exceed $3,000 per member, per benefit year.

technologies), and coverage of services are all part of a series of options that should be offered to enrollees at various premium prices.

Probably the most widely agreed upon argument for selected cost sharing relates to the use of high-cost elective services. Some cosmetic surgeries, mammoplasty, and infertility studies are examples of those services. The underlying philosophy is to include the services in the benefits package but have cost-sharing provisions or caps on expenditures. For example, the first cycle of infertility services might be fully covered but, if unsuccessful, the cost of further services would be shared on a 50/50 basis or capped at $10,000. This approach has a great deal of support among the ISNs because it maintains the integrity of the broad-range benefit philosophy, yet discourages overuse of these discretionary services and keeps premium costs down. It also maintains a basic level of access to health care while enabling those with more resources to purchase discretionary services.

While the benefit plan shown in Table 6–1 appears to have the support of many of those interviewed, it is important to note that some of the respondents believe that a less generous package should be offered as the principal package or as an option. One respondent noted the need for more copay provisions for physician services and radiograph and laboratory procedures to keep enrollees abreast of costs and to gain their commitment to cost-effective practice styles. Another respondent indicated concern over prescription drug costs and recommended less coverage or more controls on the source of drugs, possibly using mail order pharmacy services for maintenance drug products.

Financial Risk-Sharing Arrangements

The respondents described a wide variety of financial risk-sharing agreements with physicians and hospitals. These agreements include various capitation arrangements, reinsurance options, and negotiated or discounted fee-for-service payments. In general, physicians and hospitals are provided the option to assume more financial risk or comply with extensive patient care management guidelines and policies administered by the ISN. For example, a primary care medical group practice could accept capitation payment for *all* primary care and referral services including hospital care and, because they assume that level of risk, they would have a great deal of freedom to practice in accordance with their desired style. At the other end of the spectrum, physicians who want to be paid on a fee-for-service basis would be required to adhere to strict guidelines and policies established by the ISN. Those physicians would be required to request permission from the ISN before hospitalizing a patient, initiating a high-cost treatment regimen, or ordering a high-cost diagnostic procedure such as magnetic resonance imaging (MRI).

The following is a list of alternate financial risk-sharing arrangements being proposed for physician payment by the ISNs. The list begins with the most

extensive risk sharing and progresses to the least risk on the physician's part:

1. primary care medical group practices capitated for all health care services (primary and referral services and hospital care) for a defined population.
2. primary care medical group practices capitated for all physician services, but hospital care paid directly by the ISN on a discounted billed charges or per diem basis.
3. primary care medical group practices capitated for their services only, and all physician specialty care and hospital care paid directly by the ISN. Specialists may be capitated or paid on a negotiated fee-for-service basis. Hospitals may be paid on a discounted billed charges or a per diem basis.
4. same as one, two, or three above, but the ISN offers a reinsurance program for the primary and/or specialty physician groups covering all patients requiring care that exceeds a stated dollar amount (i.e., $20,000 per year).
5. primary care medical group practices paid on a negotiated fee-for-service basis but must comply with practice guidelines established by the ISN. May include a 20 percent holdback, which is paid at the end of the year if costs are controlled. Specialist physicians capitated or paid a negotiated fee for service (with or without holdback) and hospitals paid on a discounted billed charges or per diem basis.
6. all physicians paid on a negotiated fee-for-service basis and must comply with ISN patient care policies and guidelines. May include a 20 percent holdback as in number five above. Hospitals are paid on a discounted billed charges or a per diem basis.
7. salary with some form of bonus system.

Patient care guidelines and policies that are being proposed by the ISNs include:

- development of guidelines for hospitalization of patients (permission required from ISN).
- development of practice guidelines for illnesses that account for a substantial amount of resources. The most frequent illnesses noted include the following:
  Simple cystitis
  Active management of labor
  Low back pain

Pediatric asthma
Depression
Hypertension in adults
Breast cancer detection
Fetal distress during labor
Preterm birth prevention
Common cold in adults
Common cold in children
Pediatric immunization
Cervical cancer screening
Chronic stable angina

- development of pharmacy drug formulary.
- calculation of a physician's resource use for patients with a certain diagnosis compared to all similar physicians' resource use for those patients and then an adjustment of fee if outside some boundaries.
- limitation of the use of high-cost technologies to centers of excellence. The risk-sharing arrangements described above are shown in Figures 6–1 and 6–2.

This spectrum of financial arrangements provides a great deal of flexibility for both the ISNs and physicians. Physicians have less ISN control over their practice styles as long as they are willing to assume the financial risks associated with capitation payment. Consequently, while capitated physicians will be

furnished practice guidelines as a resource to help them improve the cost effectiveness of their services, physicians who elect to be paid on a fee-for-service basis will be required to comply with these guidelines as well as additional policies such as when and where patients can be hospitalized, what drug brands can be used, and where patients must go to obtain high-cost technologies. Physicians in small group practices or in rural areas will be able to participate in ISNs without assuming undue financial risk as long as they are willing to comply with what probably will be rather extensive management of the physician's practice decisions. In almost all cases, this likely will be accompanied by some type of fee holdback provisions (probably as high as 20 percent) with end of the year payout in accordance with resource use compared to other similar physicians treating similar patients.

Information Systems

All of the ISNs plan to develop extensive information infrastructures in both the clinical and administrative areas. However, only one has an information system in place that supports both of these areas. That ISN, cosponsored by a multispecialty group practice and a large community hospital, has an information system that links their 18 clinics to a centralized

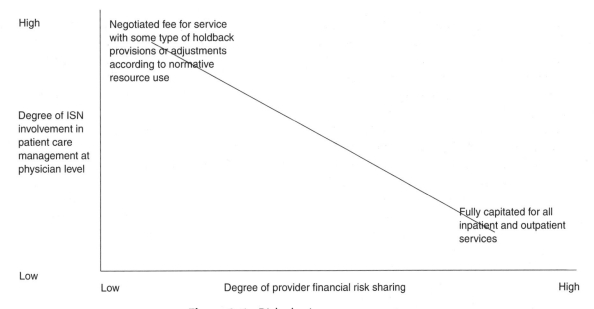

Figure 6–1. Risk-sharing arrangements.

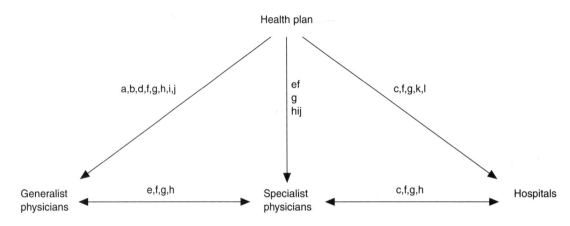

Options
a. Full capitation for all hospital and physician services.
b. Full capitation for all generalist and specialist physicians.
c. Full capitation for all hospital services only.
d. Full capitation for all generalist physicians only.
e. Full capitation for all specialist physicians only.
f. Target rate and corridor for risk sharing for each of the provider groups described in a through e.*
g. Stop loss provisions (usually 10,000 per case) added to any of the above options.
h. Salary.
i. Fee for service with holdback (various formulas for distribution at year end).
j. Fee for service with target per capita rate and corridor for risk sharing.
k. Discounted billed charges.

*For example, a medical group may have a target rate of $50 per member per month for the enrollees selecting their practice and a corridor of $40 to $60 per member per month. If costs are above the $50 target but lower than $60, they are shared according to an agreed upon formula (50/50, etc.). Savings accrued if costs are lower than the $50 target but higher than $40 similarly are shared.

Figure 6–2. Alternate financial risk-sharing arrangements between health plans and health care providers.

patient database and accounting system. This enables staff at any clinic to access patient records from other sites, schedule appointments with other physicians, and schedule laboratory and radiographic procedures at the central facility. Consequently, from the patient's perspective, there is a unified clinic system delivering their care.

Access to care also is tracked using this information and communications network. The system enables staff to record such things as how many times the telephone rings before being answered when a patient calls to make an appointment, and how long the patient is on hold during the call. The scheduling system provides management information such as the time lapse between a patient's call for an appointment and available openings. Patient-to-staff ratios, patient encounters by clinic site, and key quality indicators also are monitored by the system. Data from this system enable the medical directors to evaluate the cost effectiveness of alternate treatment modalities for

some illnesses and then create practice guidelines specifying the preferred approach. Treatment for urinary tract infections (UTI) was cited as an example. The clinical and financial data were integrated to determine the cost per UTI case. The usual treatment modality was then broken into components, and the cost and benefit of each component was assessed. As a result, treatment protocols were modified to improve the cost effectiveness of the services and guidelines were established to help identify patients who could best be treated by the less intensive approach.

Probably the most sophisticated part of this information system is that it enables the medical directors to monitor population-based data regarding health status, illness patterns, preventive practices, and utilization rates. These data are being used to assess the performance of the clinics and for program planning and budgeting.

In the future, the clinic plans to increase the speed of the system by providing more computer capacity at the clinic sites. This will allow staff throughout the organization to analyze data and generate reports at the local sites. In the future, they are envisioning notebook-based data entry by physicians, and computer terminals at the nursing stations for input of clinical data. They also plan to link the ambulatory care system to their hospital. Both the hospital and clinic systems are well developed, but they are not linked together. This is the next phase of development.

Customer Relations

All those interviewed for this study noted that a customer service orientation is extremely important for the success of an ISN in a managed competition environment. There are three dimensions to this issue. First, in order to control costs, ISNs need to reduce the use of some services that are not cost effective but may seem essential to patients. The inappropriate use of some technologies, such as computed tomography (CT) scans, is an example. Consequently, the ISN needs to have a close working relationship with enrollees to maintain their support for these judgments. Programs being planned to build these relationships include newsletters, interactive videos at the clinics, and more time scheduled for nurses to explain treatment plans to patients.

The second dimension focuses on improving patient involvement in the maintenance of their health and in treatment decisions. Working with enrollees to prevent illnesses is a high-level priority. This includes both educational programs and the development of self-treatment protocols for conditions such as hypertension. Our interviews indicate that disease prevention and health maintenance will be major areas of emphasis for ISNs. The data also indicate, however, that preventive measures will be subjected to the same cost-effectiveness analysis as curative services. Although some of these services may be provided based on their contribution to the quality of life, the costs and benefits will be carefully evaluated.

The third part of the customer relations component of ISNs relates to marketing and the competition for enrollees under managed competition. The primary focus of this component is to gain a better understanding of consumer views regarding health and health care, and their decision-making process related to selection of health plans. This largely follows a marketing paradigm but focuses more attention on individual values than do the commercial marketing efforts. This dimension of ISNs also includes consumer satisfaction surveys conducted to gain insights into how the services are perceived from the patients' viewpoint. Most of the ISNs are planning to use these surveys to keep their customer service commitment at the forefront and to ensure that their services are user friendly.

Two of the HMOs that are planning to offer ISNs propose to develop extensive capabilities for patients to interact with computer-based information systems designed to involve them in treatment decisions. The most frequently cited example of such a program is the Trans Urethral Resection Procedure (TURP) for benign prostatic hypertrophy. According to the respondents, the involvement of consumers in decisions regarding their health and health care will receive a great deal more attention under the ISN approach.

Alternate Organizational Models

Figures 6–3, 6–4, and 6–5 show alternate conceptual models of the ISNs being developed in Minnesota. These models show the wide variety of structural arrangements among providers and the financial risk-sharing agreements that are being negotiated to pay for services.

Some Distinguishing Characteristics of ISNs

Although it is far too early in the development of these new organizational forms of health care delivery to explicate a model, several features appear to be common to virtually all of the initiatives. In many ways, these features reflect those of the most advanced HMOs and, indeed, some respondents in this study consider ISNs to be the next generation of the HMO concept. These features include both structural and philosophic considerations. First, the ISNs appear to be developing a much closer working relationship between providers and the insurance component than has been traditional in most HMOs. The provider systems being planned differ from those of the past in that they are highly integrated vertically as well as horizontally to ensure reasonable geographic access to primary care and a close working relationship between those physicians and specialists. The insur-

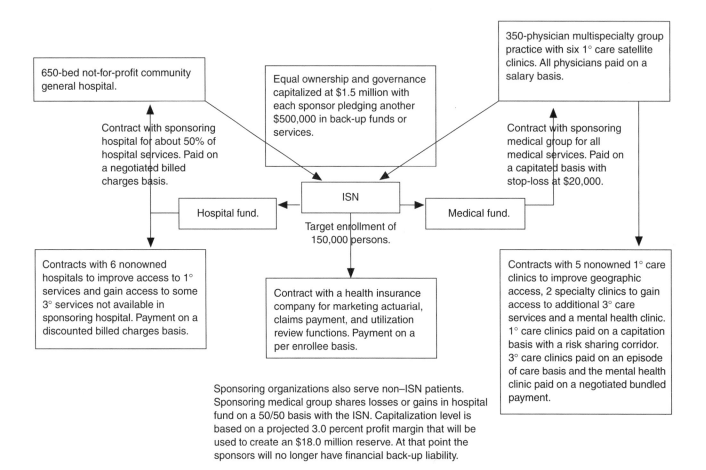

Figure 6–3. ISN—Model I.

ance component also is highly integrated into the organization and is linked to providers through a complex system of financial risk-sharing agreements. The goal is to achieve a tightly coupled organization where physicians take the initiative to provide cost-effective services, the facilities are structured in a manner that enables them to do so, and the insurance component rewards good patient care outcomes.

Some of the respondents believe that the success of these structures largely will depend on the degree to which the physicians share a tight common practice culture and take a leadership role in developing cost-effective practice styles. Consequently, the development of mechanisms to achieve higher levels of physician integration and commitment to cost-effective practices are high-level priorities. Others note the importance of structuring facilities so that they fully support cost-effective practices. The traditional models of clinics and hospitals with few bridging organi-

zations do not provide the mix of services needed to support ISN goals. HMOs have made progress in developing or stimulating the development of alternate structures, such as surgi-centers, but the ISN leadership views this as just the beginning. They believe that inpatient hospital days per 1,000 enrollees will drop below 200 (now about 240 in the Twin Cities HMOs) and that several new organizations will be developed to provide services that fall between hospital and clinic care. Whether or not this restructuring can be accomplished through incentives provided by the ISNs is still a question. One of the respondents indicated that while some gains can be made through incentives and contracts, the major gains in restructuring provider organizations will only be achieved if the ISN owns all the production components and has salaried physicians. If this is true, the small ISN may be seriously disadvantaged, and small provider groups may not be able to survive.

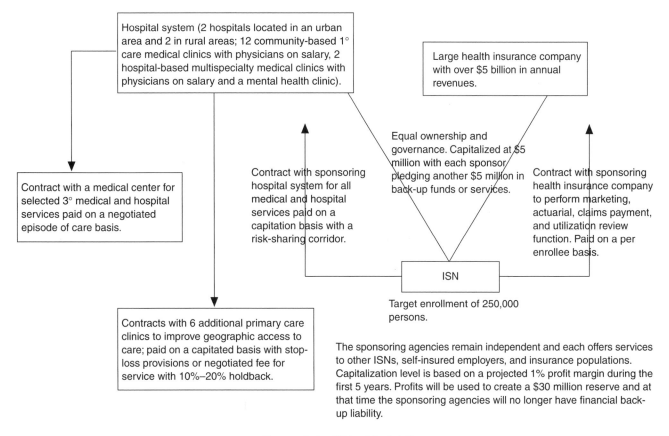

Figure 6–4. ISN—Model II.

The second major feature that appears to differentiate ISNs from other health care delivery systems is that they operate from a population perspective and focus a great deal of attention on patient outcomes. In the more well-developed ISNs, this philosophy seems to permeate the entire organization. Extensive plans are being developed for preventive services. Patient care outcomes measures are being developed and patient satisfaction surveys are being planned. This philosophy also influences the business operations. While business plans for new facilities or technologies largely were based on projections of revenues and expenses, they are now being based on population needs and the potential contribution to the improvement of cost-effective practices. While some of these programs and parts of the philosophy are direct descendants of HMOs, it appears that ISNs are taking a much more aggressive role in shifting to a population-based health care philosophy and developing innovative programs to achieve those goals.

The third important feature is the involvement of enrollees in decisions related to their health and health care. At one level, this involves an expanded health education program, but the total program goes far beyond this effort. Some of the developing ISNs are planning extensive programs to acquaint patients with the probabilities of various adverse as well as positive outcomes of a procedure and are encouraging the patients to take an active role in the decision-making process with their physicians. The goal, as expressed by one respondent, is to create an environment that encourages patients to take an active role in their health and health care and to provide the support services they need to do so. This, he noted, is a significant change in philosophy and often requires extensive retraining of clinicians.

A fourth characteristic that seems to be evidenced in the more well-developed ISNs relates to the changes in the way health care is provided. Medical directors of the highly integrated ISNs describe a vision of a

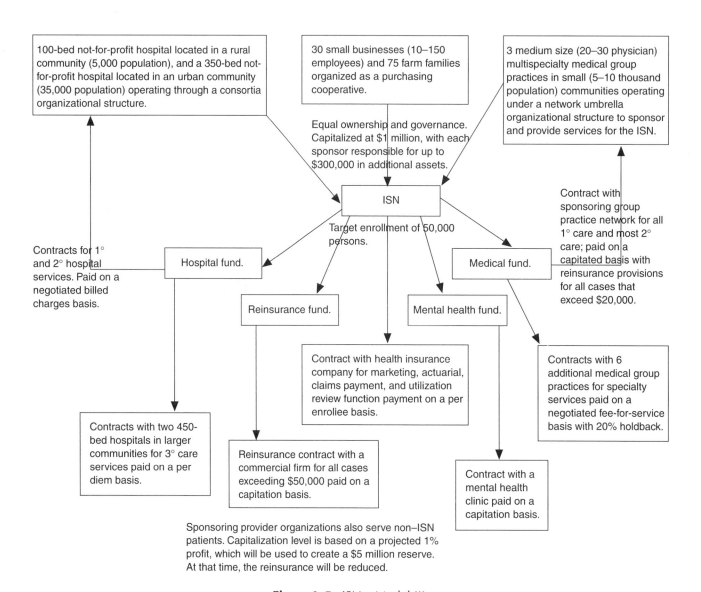

Figure 6–5. ISN—Model III.

health care system with multiple points of entry facilitated by an extensive communication network that enables enrollees to interact with clinicians by videophone, transmit clinical information to the clinics, and access information about their illnesses without leaving home. At least one medical director expects clinic visits to be cut in half as these improved communication systems are put in place. These programs are also restructuring the clinical staff. Nurse practitioners are going to play prominent roles in the provision of primary care, backed up by generalist physicians. In the specialty areas, the role of technicians also is being expanded. Some of the respondents believe that the restructuring of clinical services will

reduce the current specialty physician staff by about 40 percent. However, they project a need for three to four times the number of nurse practitioners now being employed. Since these practitioners are in relatively short supply, some of the larger ISNs are considering the development of programs to retrain their current nursing staff.

As noted previously, it appears that the preventive side of health care is receiving much more attention from the ISNs than in any previous health care delivery system. Plans are in place for data systems that will track the provision of preventive services on a population basis, and incentive systems are being developed to reward clinicians with good performances in the prevention of as well as in the resolution of health problems. One medical director stated that he plans to base part of the physician's income on how well he or she solves patients' problems using the resources available through the ISN in a cost-effective manner.

Another unique characteristic, which we identified in the ISNs, is the high degree of commitment to finding better (more cost-effective) ways to treat illnesses. Those developing ISNs acknowledge that their success in achieving high levels of cost-effective care largely depends on the degree to which the clinical staff takes an ownership role in creating cost-effective practice styles and a practice culture that supports that approach. A single multispecialty group practice with a tight practice culture often was noted as the ideal way of achieving this goal. Continuous physician-directed improvements in the effectiveness and efficiency of services was noted by many of the respondents as the key to ISN success in a highly competitive market. The success in reducing the costs and improving the quality of treating urinary infections and benign prostatic hypertrophy were given as examples of the effectiveness of this approach. Gaining the commitment of clinicians to continued improvement in the cost effectiveness of care and providing them with the information and support services needed to do so was noted as the basic philosophy of the most innovative ISNs.

Although this approach may prove to be quite successful, the ISN leadership recognizes that it tends to limit geographic access to care, especially in rural areas. The respondents offered two potential solutions to this problem. The first is that since several relatively large medical group practices exist in rural Minnesota, those organizations can and should develop ISNs covering small communities through their existing satellites or through the development of satellites. They may be in competition with urban-based ISNs in some cases and in other cases may be part of an urban ISN through contracts. In either event, it is argued that those rural group practices, along with their satellite clinics, should be able to develop very effective health care programs for rural areas. The second solution offered by the ISN leadership is that the payment of physicians in small rural practices can be tailored to reflect the degree to which he or she wants to become part of an ISN's culture. Physicians

who are unwilling or unable to adopt the ISN practice culture can be paid on a negotiated fee-for-service basis (or a fee-with-holdback provision) while those who want to become part of the culture can be paid on a risk-sharing or salary basis. Fee-for-service physicians will be subjected to more intense micromanagement of their patient care practices while risk-sharing physicians will have greater freedom to determine how to bring their practice styles into line with the ISN standards. Micromanagement in this context includes both the utilization of services (through practice guidelines) and the specification of the location of high-cost technologies and specialty physicians. The respondents with the most experience in HMO development believe that these alternate structural models will enable ISNs to serve all of rural Minnesota effectively. They add, however that the incentives to do so will depend on the development of effective purchasing groups that adequately represent the needs of rural residents.

Discussion

Minnesota has had a long history of innovations in health care delivery. Some of the first hospital systems were developed in the Minneapolis/St. Paul metro area and the HMO concept was initiated here. ISNs reflect this innovative climate. While flexible in the way they organize and pay for services, the ISNs that are up and running are highly integrated vertically and horizontally to provide a full continuum of care ranging from preventive services to highly complex tertiary services. Access to services and the involvement of enrollees in the maintenance of their health, as well as in health care decisions, is emphasized. All of those interviewed stressed the need to develop a strong practice culture that emphasizes cost-effective care and minimizes the traditional adversarial relationship between clinicians and those attempting to control costs. The focus is on the creation of environments that enable clinicians to practice cost-effective medicine and provide incentives to do so. This includes the development of highly integrated hospital and clinic systems that support the provision of appropriate care at the appropriate location in a cost-effective manner. It also includes information systems that provide clinicians the data needed to practice cost-effective medicine within these structures. Those forming the ISNs note that, in order to maximize the effectiveness of these organizational structures, the physicians' role must be reconfigured. This includes the expanded use of clinical nurse practitioners, a shift from gatekeeping to more accessible services through telemedicine, and development of a population perspective. This they note often requires significant physician retraining. They also believe that a shift to some form of salary remuneration of physicians is essential in order to provide the incentives needed to achieve cost-effective care.

In the metropolitan Twin Cities area, the creation of ISNs has resulted in several mergers of hospitals (or hospital systems), HMOs, and medical clinics. These merged structures have much more political and economic power than any of the previous HMOs. Consequently, they are able to address patient care issues that go far beyond traditional concerns about resource utilization. Some of the most sacred traditions of medicine are being challenged. More importantly, the most sophisticated ISNs are developing structures and incentive systems that encourage their physicians to challenge these traditions rather than attempting to dictate top-down change. This probably is the most important difference between the emerging ISNs and the HMOs that have been providing services in Minnesota. While the HMOs largely concentrated on changing the behavior of providers and consumers who were high utilizers of services, the ISNs appear to be concentrating on providing incentives and the organizational support for their physicians to restructure clinical practices in a manner that provides the appropriate services at the appropriate time by the most appropriate health professional. Clearly, not all ISNs will achieve this level of organizational sophistication. However, even at a lower level, it still promises to be a very dramatic reorganization of the health care delivery system.

REFERENCES

1. Klein, J., and Cooley, R. "Managed Competition in Minnesota." *Managed Care Quarterly* 1, no. 4 (1993): 58–67.
2. Feldman, R., Jensen, G., and Dowd, B.E. "What Are Employees Doing to Create a Competitive Market for Health Care in the Twin Cities?" *Contemporary Policy Issues* 3, no. 2 (1984–85): 69–88.
3. Sullivan, C., Miller, M., Feldman, R., and Dowd, B. "Employer-Sponsored Health Insurance in 1991." *Health Affairs* 11, no. 4 (1992): 172–85.
4. U.S. Congress, Office of Technology Assessment. *Managed Care and Competitive Health Care Markets: The Twin Cities Experience.* OTA-BP-H-130. Washington, D.C.: U.S. Government Printing Office, July 1994.
5. Business Health Care Action Group. *1993 Annual Report.* 3639 Elmo Road, Minnetonka, MN 55305; 612-854-7066.
6. Laws of Minnesota 1993, chapter 345, House File, 1178.
7. American Health Security Act of 1993.
8. Managed Competition Act of 1994, Breaux/Cooper (S. 1579, H.R. 3222).

7

Mergers, Networking, and Vertical Integration: Managed Care and Investor-Owned Hospitals

Montague Brown

Hospitals, physicians, insurers, and managed care firms are networking, merging, and forming horizontally and vertically integrated organizations to finance and deliver health care. Organizations, investors, health professionals, governments, and others are positioning themselves to gain or preserve market share, income, revenue, and power in a radically agitated marketplace. Power and control of the health care enterprise is shifting, threatening to topple traditional institutions even as traditional institutions try to reinvent themselves into what the leaders of those institutions think will be the most logical inheritor of power in the future. (Power is used here to mean control, authority, and ability to make things happen in the way those in control of the organization want these things to happen. Physicians, hospitals, managed care firms, traditional insurers, and those controlling such organizations are pursuing strategies they each hope will position them to have substantial power. That not all can occupy the same space simultaneously accounts for much of the attempts to establish networks and other loose forms of affiliation.)

Where is the field going and what does all of this shifting herald? Are we seeing the elaboration of the next generation of organizations, which are going to solve the riddle of affordable, accessible, quality health services for all Americans? Or are we in the middle of a transition that holds yet other surprises just up the road? What ideas are driving the field toward integration and consolidation?

A central thesis of this article is that ideas have power. People who lead institutions are doing things that they think will position themselves for success in a changed world of health care. What they think are the major changes necessary to make health care more affordable is what will drive them to reposition their organizations. Much of the change of the past 30 years has been driven in large part by expectations of how managed care will evolve and how competing provider institutions will compete. Ideas help to explain why people pursue networks and alliance building. For many volunteer hospitals the ideas of networking, alliance building, mergers, and vertical integration are further conditioned by expectations of what investor-owned institutions can and will do with their access to equity market capital. (Over the years the author has noted that investor-owned institutions have done many things well but they come only recently to regional integration of their units. But now that they have moved in this direction, they are moving aggressively, with Columbia/HCA going for tertiary referral hospitals to complement its networks in all regions in which it aspires to have a major presence.)

Managed care and investor-owned institutions with presumed unlimited access to new equity capital have been powerful motivators for voluntary and many governmental hospitals to find competitive strategies for coping. Those strategies have ranged from loose affiliation to total consolidation under single ownership. The most recent strategy has involved the merging of physicians with the hospital. Ultimate ideas include putting managed care, hospitals, and physicians under one corporate control. Naturally, each competitor envisions its group leading this new integrated entity. This struggle for power and control accounts for many of the failures to create successful alliances, networks, and mergers.

In summary, this review of trends, prognostications, and recent writings on the subject is approached from the perspective of how the ideas of managed care and competition with investor-owned operation of hospitals and other elements of health care delivery have impacted the trends and events noted so well in

Health Care Manage Rev, 1996; 21(1): 29–37

the many reviews of the subject presented in *Health Care Management Review*. (A collection of earlier papers on this subject is contained in *Strategy and Structures in Health Care Management*, a best-of-HCMR publication, Aspen Publishers, Inc., 1992, Montague Brown, Editor.)

Background

As Medicare and Medicaid passed in the mid-1960s, the health care industry geared up for heady growth. For many, this heralded the promise of health care as a right, with the government picking up the tab for the elderly and poor. New York and California each exceeded the Johnson administration's estimates for the nation. The new plans with their mandate to continue fee-for-service payment to physicians and cost plus for hospitals looked like a steady increase in money and a practical federal guarantee for whatever it would take to make an investment in health services pay off.

As this promise for cost plus reimbursement for hospitals and universal coverage came into play, entrepreneurial physicians and others were able to convince equity market players that the industry would be a gold mine for investor capital. Medicare standards required many hospitals to be rebuilt, making it attractive for individual physician-owned institutions to join this new use of equity market financed modern corporations, the investor-owned hospital chain. The South, Southeast, and West, where for-profit hospitals already existed in fair numbers, soon became the regions with greatest chain growth. Many small hospitals built with federal funds sold out to the new chains, which then scrapped obsolete plants and built modern hospitals in small towns and second or third hospitals in many larger cities. Many large, well-established not-for-profit hospitals began to find these firms coming to town, taking over marginal hospitals, replacing them with first class facilities, and trying to recruit some of their physicians.

By the early 1970s the need for cost containment was becoming screamingly evident, putting pressure on providers to find ways to contain cost. Shared services, especially purchasing programs, became popular mechanisms to deflect criticism from rising cost. Health planning attempted to curtail duplication of costly technologies. With new capital flooding into

the market and competition growing, solutions were being sought but nothing seemed to be working well. It was during this period that the idea of using health maintenance organizations (HMOs) to contain cost evolved. Modeled basically on an older idea of prepaid group practice, adoption was slow but many agreed that it would take something like this with strong economic incentives for physicians to keep cost down and for patients to accept the discipline of such regimes. By the 1980s both managed care and investor-owned hospitals appeared, with their built-in scale advantages for national purchasing and the use of standardized approaches to building and operating hospitals. (By talking here about their purported advantages of scale for purchasing, the author does not believe that the chains actually benefited from trying to use this power until nearer the mid-1980s. Many authors have noted that these chains benefited greatly from their ability, like all hospitals, to price their product to produce the profits they required for their business. This is changing now but provided a solid basis for growth throughout the 1970s and 1980s.)

In the 1970s, the nation tried price controls, voluntary efforts, and other slogans to contain cost. (Any starting point for consideration of a subject as broad as networking and alliances is somewhat arbitrary. Hospital associations grew after the first world war and got another big boost during the days of Hill–Burton facilities financing. Many of these associations built additional shared services. The rationale for cutting the time reviewed around early 1970 is that the big national alliances getting so much attention today were built to give one group of hospitals a competitive advantage vis a vis their neighboring hospitals. Earlier and most current hospital association efforts included all hospitals. These were called shared service programs. All could benefit. Today's alliances, for the most part, consider competitive advantage as a major deciding factor in admitting members and designing programs.) Shared purchasing grew from hospital association efforts to construct national alliances built outside the political structure of hospital associations. A number of these national alliances merged; indeed the merger of these giant purchasing organizations continues today. (In this merger of buying organizations, American Healthcare System's 500 million annual purchases from Johnson and Johnson make them J&J's biggest customer. Look out little niche companies, when elephants dance they can be dangerous.[1]) A comprehensive assessment of alliances is presented by Zuckerman, Kaluzny and Ricketts.[2]

Hospital mergers and consolidations held out the promise that if the number of owners were reduced, then hospitals could plan more rationally and reduce the duplication of high cost technologies in individual markets. This was the promise. Shortell has studied many of the systems that built upon mergers and concluded that many of the promises of such systems have not been realized.[3] The potential exists but has not been realized.

Many reasons for these unrealized aspirations have been asserted and speculated upon. Getting a larger market share in adjacent markets locks in sufficient scale to justify the more complex procedures that require access to large population bases and it provides primary care sites to attract managed care. If the market does not have strong competitors, which leads to price and cost reductions, it would seem that many systems have gained major advantages from mergers and system building without having to go through the harder job of rationing programs and services among several owned hospitals.

Before the nation's antitrust laws were applied, hospitals planned "voluntarily" and each hospital sorted out what it would do and what others would do. Much of this behavior was encouraged by health planning agencies, based on a long history of voluntary planning. During this era, collaboration, sharing, and other adjectives aptly described much hospital behavior vis a vis neighboring hospitals. Everyone got the programs they wanted so voluntary collaboration worked fairly well. Even when not everyone got everything they wanted, there was usually an explicit or implicit quid pro quo for the "losing" organizations.

Dividing markets through agreement became a verboten topic once the antitrust laws were applied directly to medicine.[4] Since agreements to fix price or divide markets[5] became illegal, it became necessary to look at whether or not more total integration might be necessary to achieve collective, regional action. (The author would not, of course, argue that everyone was satisfied with voluntary dividing up of markets. Those who got the heart programs from such past divisions have done very well, much to the chagrin of those who got behavioral units.) While multihospital systems grew during the 1970s[6], after the antitrust moves dampened

the ability of hospitals to voluntarily assign markets and roles, local and regional mergers grew.

The growth of managed care during the 1980s and its further acceleration in the 1990s became driving forces behind physician alliances, hospital mergers, and national and regional hospital alliances. The idea driving providers was the thought that managed care firms would eventually narrow their provider list to those most efficient in their delivery of a comprehensive range of services. That the reality might not have caught up with the theory did little to stop attempts by providers to form their own networks so that they could collectively bargain with insurers. From the beginning of the formation of the large voluntary hospital alliances, competitive advantage in local competing networks was a prime factor in building these alliances. (Having studied one of the early multihospital systems in the late 1960s and early 1970s for my doctoral work in public health, I personally met with and had discussions regarding such matters with many of the chief executive officers [CEOs] running such systems. Later I served as consultant and conceptualizer for the CEOs who started many of the national alliances. So much of this history reflects personal involvement as well as following and contributing to the literature of the period.) Even in the 1970s there was an expectation of managed care networks that would be exclusive to selected groups of providers, and providers have been positioning for this eventuality. Ideas have power. Ideas can drive the field even when marketplace realities have not caught up.

Of course, managed care firms have the theoretical possibility of signing up just the best providers and leaving the rest off their preferred list. While the idea of managed care was popular and anticipated, many physicians and hospitals dreaded its introduction to the market. Many of the concepts of networking, mergers, alliances, and the like, often touted for their likelihood of bringing economic and other advantages, often obscured the underlying fact that such linkages also made it more difficult for managed care to emerge or if it did emerge, such networks had some inherent advantages because of their geographic dispersion of members and the comprehensives of their services.

Managed care firms only recently have gained sufficient expertise and market penetration to begin to put the kind of pressure on providers for more efficient care that was anticipated by the pioneers in networks, alliances, and regional hospital systems. Those who prepared early and moved expeditiously are in a position today to benefit from their early efforts to build regional systems. Many single hospitals that ignored these trends often have found themselves closed out or severely handicapped in their marketplace.

Alliances

Earlier efforts to develop joint purchasing programs, training, and industrial engineering were carried out by trade associations and catered to all hospitals, not some subset. When asked for public evidence of what was being done to contain the rising cost of health care, these programs were trotted out and displayed for all to see. The industry was responding to cost through collective programs to contain the cost of purchases and improve the efficiency of individual operations. (There are many other activities of the major alliances, but their central dollar impact and the source of funding for such alliances comes in large part from imposed group purchasing activities.) By the late 1970s hospitals were organizing national cooperative enterprises like the Voluntary Hospitals of America, SunHealth, Premier Alliance, and American Healthcare Systems to carry out collective enterprises, most notably purchasing. The major national alliances strategies were begun after HMOs were identified more clearly as a likely winning strategic concept and the investor-owned hospital groups had gained substantial stature in the marketplace.

Were these purchasing efforts successful? All claim great advantages from such buying cooperatives. If one assumes that such programs impact 10 percent or so of hospital budgets and that group buying gets a 10 percent or more better price, this would moderate hospital costs only 1 percent. While not yielding much on a yearly basis, compounding such savings would show a sizable amount of money ultimately saved.

However, it is difficult to assess the overall impact of such buying practices. As the hospitals developed oligopolistic buying behavior, the companies able to respond grew increasingly few and more powerful. Since there is no discernible lowering of the growth in health care cost during the period, it is not easy to point to any discernible consumer benefit coming

from this new level of aggregation in the industry. Rebates and price discounts make good public relations copy, however, and thus one hears little or no complaints about the efficacy of these programs. At a minimum, hospitals probably gained some clout vis a vis powerful national suppliers and moderated their pricing policies. It would seem that these programs represent a modest success in dealing with a modest share of the hospital budget.

Suppliers may have lost a bit of margin in their dealings early on but probably recouped those losses later as smaller competitors found it difficult to compete with the integrated buyer alliances doing business with the integrated supplier firm. Also, with more comprehensive, committed volume contracts, economic savings can be achieved and are probably shared between buyer and seller. Savings of this sort make good economic sense. Will these advantages offset the squeeze on the small supplier, the entrepreneur with a better idea but no access to the large, overarching contracts? The studies of this aspect of alliances are yet to be told.

The trading of profits and business volumes among firms within the industry has little positive meaning ultimately for the consumer. Providers do not necessarily pass on purchasing savings to consumers. Some of the savings are retained in the alliance organizations while much are used for ancillary needs of the members and the alliance. For the buyer of health services it makes little difference who profits from the vast purchasing power unless the benefits are passed on to consumers. Of course with savings there is a potential for consumer benefit, but one would expect that benefit to be conferred only after buyers for health care services make price demands on competing provider groups. With substantial aggregation occurring on the provider side and still little buyer pressure for deep price concessions, there is a possibility that by the time buyers get well organized to purchase, sellers may already have reached a critical mass, making it possible for them to exert pressure to keep prices up.

Managed Care

Being positioned for survival in a managed care marketplace was and is the crown jewel of purpose of the major national alliances. (This is not to argue that other purposes were and are not now important. Once institutions are developed, it is a well-known phenomenon that they take on a life of their own and that the "profits" from most such entities, especially those that are "not for profit," are the benefits that participants derive through participation. Although many of the not-for-profits and cooperatives have developed spin-off operations into for-profit formats, allowing executives and members to benefit personally from their success, for the most part the alliances remain a not-for-profit type of enterprise. Executives and compensation experts have long since found many ways to extend equity types of rewards to these executives so they too can be expected to operate with many of the same incentives in place that permeate big business in the nation.) Managed care makes it theoretically possible for the most efficient, highest quality places to win the competition for dedicated blocks of patients and thus become the survivors. Remember in the mid-1970s when these national alliances were being built, managed care as we know it today did not exist. In fact, managed care, as it was envisioned in those days, has yet to emerge in most markets. Every professional in the field knew that the nation had too many hospitals and too many beds. And, in a fragmented marketplace, managed care firms could induce hospitals and physicians to give discounts to get business. But if hospitals were merged or "held together" in regional networks, few buyers would be able to resist buying from such networks. Even today, tight, exclusive networks with full capitation are still a small part of managed care. Yet most of the national and regional alliances represented steps along the path toward that end when they were formed in the late 1970s.

Managed care enterprises promise to offer greater opportunity to achieve consumer benefit but they require great investment and strong discipline to make them work. They also require incentives that strike at the heart of medical decision making: the medical staff. To make such an enterprise work requires a highly disciplined medical staff and one of two other things: either a very efficient system that could offer lower prices because of its lower utilization, and/or a regional monopoly or superior concentration and range of services. In short, success requires a highly disciplined medical staff (or panel of physicians) who are committed to actually reducing the use of resources (including their own activities) to get cost down so that prices can be lowered for customers!

A number of the alliances have tried national managed care ventures with insurers. Most dropped the national efforts after years trying to get members prepared for something for which the market was not yet ready. Readiness was and is not merely one of provider nor insurer preference. It is as much or more individual consumer preference and the ability of corporations to channel their employees into a narrow set of choices. Managed care is moving slowly in this direction. Everyone has a steep learning curve ahead. Even the traditional Kaiser-Permanente staff model has problems competing for populations that want a bit more choice. Still, provider opinion and the models providers continue to build and elaborate upon anticipate this kind of change.

Alliances have worked hard to aid individual and regional collections of members to build managed care alliances. Preferred provider organizations (PPOs) abound, many regional alliances seek contracts, and a number have chosen to fund and operate regional HMOs that accept risk. Being positioned to offer a geographically dispersed, comprehensive range of service networks is probably one of the greatest positioning benefits of the major national alliances. Unlike trade association efforts at purchasing, the national alliances have pushed to segregate out hospitals into competitive clusters to prepare for a managed care world of the future, a future still on the way.

The record around the country in building managed care networks is mixed. For those regional networks built on ownership, it is relatively easy for a cluster of hospitals to deal with managed care firms. For those networks built on contracts and jointly owned organizations, it is necessary to bargain on discounts off of charges that are set independently by the separate institutions. Since most managed care organizations seek large networks and discounts off charges, this early form of network works fairly well. But when the choices need to be made about what smaller subset of physicians and hospitals get the capitation contract, such networks will likely fail from a provider perspective although insurers will find it to their benefit. (In theory one expects that the more tightly managed care under capitation will involve procedures that require using fewer physicians who themselves work more and more exclusively for patients in this type of plan. No one expects to get both the tight management and low resource use from physicians and other providers when they are moving from patients where they make more money for more work to patients where they make money by using fewer resources. Those involved in this kind of split environment report difficulty in their practice.) When such networks have a hard time getting committed volume purchasing contracts because hospitals cannot exert sufficient control over personnel and physicians to buy one brand versus others, it challenges credibility to believe that these voluntary alliances can make the hard choices of dropping some physicians and hospitals from the existing networks. Even in networks owned by one hospital system, it is nearly impossible to limit networks to select groups of physicians. (At a larger system level, legislation to allow any willing provider to participate reflects this underlying battle to be included in any networks. As this article is written, this epic battle to limit networks to allow for competition among tightly managed networks is being waged.) Much of the difficulty in building owned or contractual networks stems from the natural and pervasive desire by professionals to keep their practices intact, avoid change until it becomes essential, and modify the change if possible to accommodate their preferred form of practice. These major fault lines underlie most networks—keeping them in a fragile state—while managed care firms are relatively free to exploit this weakness in such alliances.

Pointing out this difficulty in overcoming the large odds against making tight, limited networks is no criticism toward hospitals per se since many managed care firms have failed, others have merged to survive, and many have had many owners before strong profitability emerged. Employers have difficulty getting employees to accept limited networks. Building managed care organizations, recruiting providers, selling to buyers, and making it work are real challenges since providers resist the constraints of managed care just as do many consumers.

Hospital organizations operating successful regional managed care organizations often find that the success of the operation actually outgrows the needs of the hospital owner. In some cases this inappropriateness has stemmed from the fact that other managed care organizations would resent and react negatively to contracting with hospitals who were in fact their competitors in providing managed care products and services. Second, hospitals often have partnered with physicians who during the process have sought op-

portunities to maximize the return on their investment, an expectation that requires selling out at some point. This factor makes it likely that a competitive bid would be used to make a sale, often to competing organizations that could gain market share advantages in the regional market involved. (A colleague related a story that highlights some of the difficulties with the buying and selling of physician practices and managed care firms. A local physician group built a successful HMO. The group reportedly saw themselves as offering a community benefit. They made many contributions to the community. Then they sold the firm and rapidly found that by getting a generous price for the firm the new owner was mostly interested in keeping cost down and prices up.) Third, other successful ventures simply have outrun their usefulness and appropriateness for a local hospital. These organizations simply needed new capital and a much broader scope to best use their talents and organizational infrastructure. Fourth, still other successful organizations have been merged into other managed care operations in the region, leading to dilution and broadening of ownership and operation of the managed care operation. So, even with success, the size, scope and nature of the managed care operation often does not fit with the owners' capability of using, supporting, or growing it.

Walston, et al. (see this issue of HCMR, pages 83–92) raise serious questions as to whether hospitals use ownership as the better mode of relating; instead, they recommend contracting. The requirements for making an integrated network ultimately will be manifested when the incentives of the various parties are aligned and owning does not overcome the ability of persons and organizations that are part of the owned network from resisting or keeping the organization from functioning smoothly.

Overall, single hospitals and regional hospital systems with the greatest success with managed care have been those organizations that had a strong share in their market, making it possible for them to compete with other managed care organizations without at the same time losing their business. This ability normally requires substantial market share and a reputation among consumers that make it necessary for all or most managed care organizations to contract with them in order for them to attract major business clients for their products.

National chain organizations had a different kind of experience with managed care. Hospital Corporation of America (HCA) was engaged in a major joint venture with a major insurance company. That venture failed to become a major force in the field. HCA hospitals were unable to give the joint venture any major advantage in markets where the hospitals themselves were less than market leaders. Humana (then a hospital company) started its own managed care firm but encountered major resistance to their insurance products from physicians and hospital administrators who saw their profitability drained away to promote the managed care product. These kinds of difficulties ultimately led Humana to split off the insurance firm from the hospital company; later, they sold the hospital company to another firm, Columbia, which still later merged further with HCA and Health Trust. By 1995 none of the major hospital chains had a significant interest in managed care firms. Their current strategy seems to be to gain sufficient market share in each regional market and sufficient cost effectiveness to become the provider of choice for managed care firms. It is important to note that announced strategies, while true, can also mask fallback strategies, which are also true. Provider groups that cannot be ignored by managed care firms because of substantial market presence (size, geographic dispersion, comprehensiveness) can, when the market is ready, sell direct to employers.

Future Trends

Given the forces driving the current waves of integration, what seems likely in the next five or so years?

Physicians

The question of how physicians will fit into the overall scenarios envisioned by hospitals and many managed care firms remains open. Physicians see the trends and expectations as well as anyone else. Managed care and investor-owned health services are somewhat less frightening to physicians than executives of not-for-profit hospitals. But they too see the consolidation trend and are finding ways to join the trend and to resist it.

Several trends seem likely to continue. Physicians will continue to form networks for managed care. Many of these will be in conjunction with hospitals.

However, these forms of affiliation are relatively weak, with each party continuing to protect individual interests. More group practices will form. Groups represent a more firm commitment among physicians as to how they will govern and how revenue will be split. Groups also have a hefty advantage over alliances and networks. They are one economic unit, sharing risk, and can deal with the whole world as a unit without the antitrust strictures that are applied to independent economic units acting collectively.

As physicians seek capital to expand and managerial expertise they will increasingly turn to firms like Caremark, InPhyNet, PhyCor, and Coastal Physician Group, which bring capital and management expertise to the table.[7] The appeal of these groups is that neither *at this point* represents hospitals and managed care. Physicians retain more input into decisions and operate as free agents and/or corporate partners when dealing with hospitals and managed care firms.

Insurers

Some of the most dramatic changes in health care have come in the insurance side of the business. Major insurers have been in and out of managed care, with many venerable insurers ultimately getting out of managed care and leaving it more to the firms dealing with it exclusively. The Blue Cross and Blue Shield firms have made the most impressive turnaround, converting their business from service and indemnity contracts to managed care. The Blues have been going through a consolidation phase and now appear fully poised to become equity market firms, which frees them to merge with many others as well as to tap Wall Street for more equity. The Blues are experimenting with all kinds of integrative moves.

Insurers must build a niche for themselves that fends off or negates the effort by providers to gain sufficient market clout to deal directly with buyers. One way to do that will be for the insurers to merge with or buy out the providers. (For a more detailed examination of some of the issues involved here, see, "Getting To Go in Managed Care" in *Health Care Management Review* 18, no. 1 [1993]: 7–20, by Rodney Wolford, Montague Brown, and Barbara McCool.) A key issue when speculating about the concept of full merger is the question of whether or not it is driven by a vision of market protection or a brave new age of efficient care. As with any of these massively integrated firms, the cost of internal transactions can go down, but human frailty and the tendency to build fiefdoms when the market allows it can frustrate such hopes and actually lead to higher cost. Furthermore, there is the question of competition and monopoly behavior. With fewer entities in the market, there will be a great danger that provider–insurer entities will use their power to benefit the sellers and rip off consumers. Getting providers and insurers to be more efficient and price competitive has been a tough job for buyers even when the field was relatively fragmented. Will it get better with consolidation or worse? (For a more complete discussion of some of these issues see "Hospital Markets and Competition: Implications for Antitrust Policy," in *HCMR* 19, no. 1 [1994]: 34–43, by Nguen Xuan Nguyen. For a candid description of how price fixing and market allocation works, see "My Life as a Corporate Mole for the FBI," in *Fortune* [4 September 1995]: 52–62. In this view, sellers agree on market share and price and then move to bid work in order to achieve these goals. Customers are described as enemies who must be made to pay to keep up prices and profits to sellers.) As providers seek legislative approval for market consolidations that go beyond current antitrust guidelines, providers are seeking approval to be the communities' guardians of supply and price. If they had done a better job of reforming in the past, then giving them such powers would be less risky than it is when we know from recent history that the industry resists mightily any attempts to change its ways. Most likely this type of move will be resisted by managed care firms and insurers . . . unless they are part of the deal in some assured manner.

Academic medical centers

Academic medical centers have been the last to join the parade. Now we see many investor-owned chains looking for economic ties to such centers of excellence. If one seeks to play the regional provider of choice card and go for a major portion of any market, then these institutions need to be part of the package. The Mayo Clinic recognized this necessity early on and moved to develop national and regional satellites. Nationally, teaching centers are reaching out in ways unheard of 5 years ago. Some are joining Columbia/HCA in markets where the academic medical center completes a regional, full-service package of services. In the future we can expect more of these alliances.

And, we can expect the not-for-profit hospital systems to seek to link up as a competitive response to a real threat of investor-owned market dominance.

Community hospitals

Community hospitals will continue to merge with regional players including selling out to investor-owned chains. No hospital will believe that it can remain outside and independent when the dominant belief is that buyers will choose networks. And, network hospitals will choose to send business to owned hospitals over affiliated hospitals. A very sophisticated buyer group might select such hospitals if they were the most efficient but providers have 10 years of system building under their belt and buyers are just beginning to consider major buying coalitions. Sellers of service are bundling product while buyers, including managed care firms, will seek to unbundle. That tug of war will continue for the near term.

Regional multihospital health systems

Regional multihospital health systems are the best positioned organizations to become the providers of choice for managed care or direct contracting. They will continue their push to bring more and more physicians, especially in primary care, into the fold through a variety of devices. The most extensive elaboration of this model is playing out in Minneapolis and environs where three or four systems are integrated with physicians and managed care. One might also examine this area for issues raised regarding concentration and pricing. Employers in that region seem to be concerned with how to break through this control by provider–insurer conglomerate to get even greater efficiencies than currently are available.

In Missouri the regional hospital system to watch is BJC, an entity formed from Barnes, Jewish, Christian, Baptist and a variety of other hospitals in the region.

Unfortunately many of these systems have managed to get ownership consolidated but have themselves become captive to the status quo and have not achieved anywhere near the economies anticipated by the theorists. Many have troubles incorporating different cultures. And, no doubt, some merged to reduce consumer choice, which might have forced their independent units to compete and change.

In the near term we can anticipate that more single hospitals will merge with systems, systems will merge, and a growing number will forge strong bonds—even merge or sell—to insurers. However, we can also expect insurers to continue their use of contracts to build virtual networks and avoid asset acquisition until the price for such operations comes down. And the price will come down as hospitals are forced to compete. The mergers being sought by hospitals in smaller markets do promise to lower some hospital costs for technology and overhead but they simultaneously promise to eliminate price competition.

Overall Prognosis

The health care field's anticipation of managed care and fear of investor-owned hospital chains continue to drive the consolidation effort. This will continue into the indefinite future. Physicians will join the trend. Before physicians become fully integrated they will go through some intermediary forms including group practice, becoming units of national firms, employees of managed care firms, and employees of hospitals. By going through the intermediary forms of ownership it will be possible for physicians to raise the value of their business. Why? A well-oiled group with a good balance of primary and specialty is worth more than a herd of cats!

As components of the field consolidate, future consolidations will be even more complex. Like the Disney–NBC consolidation, we will see some even bigger and more complex deals ahead in health care. There is a real possibility that a handful of national firms will dominate health care but the route to that end is two steps forward, three back, and forward again. The dance goes on.

REFERENCES

1. "AmHS, Premier Alliances to Merge." *Modern Healthcare* 2–3 (7 August 1995): 2–3.
2. Zuckerman, H., Kaluzny, A.D., and Ricketts, T.C. "Alliances in Health Care: What We Know, What We Think We Know, and What We Should Know." *Health Care Management Review* 20, no. 1 (1995): 54–64.
3. Shortell, S.M. "The Evolution of Hospital Systems: Unfulfilled Promises and Self-Fulfilling Prophesies." *Medical Care Review* 45, no. 2 (1988): 177–214.
4. Brown, M., and Nichelos, P. "Court Shoots Down Antitrust Immunity." *Modern Healthcare* 12 (August 1982):164–68.
5. Brown, M., and Nichelos, P. " Analysis Probes Risk of Antitrust Suit." *Modern Healthcare* (December 1982): 104–09.
6. Brown, M., Warner, M., and Steinberg, J. "Trends in Multihospital Systems: A Multiyear Comparison." *Health Care Management Review* 5, no. 4 (1980).
7. "Doc Practice Management Set to Explode." *Modern Healthcare* 25 (14 August 1995): 26–31.

8

Managing Conflict in an Integrated System

S. Spence Meighan

THE CULTURE IN which health care is delivered is in the process of tumultuous change. In the past, people who worked in health care were regarded as caring and compassionate. In today's world, physicians often are regarded as greedy; they are seen as more interested in their own financial condition than in their patient's welfare. Hospitals are seen as corporate behemoths, centers of technology, where science predominates and caring is secondary to invasive techniques and the ability to pay.

Among physicians there is fear of the future and anger that they are being blamed for the rise in health care costs while at the same time they are enduring loss of control over their patients and reduction of income. Physicians are being forced to abandon their cherished autonomy for financial security. Major shifts of power are taking place between specialists and generalists. Specialists fear that they may be left out of the new systems, and while generalists have no such fears, they are concerned about their increasing responsibilities.

Hospital managers see themselves as architects of new health care services at the local level. Accompanying these positive emotions, however, are enormous stress and tension about their capacity to survive in their executive roles.

Board members, the most diverse and idiosyncratic members of the hospital leadership, are angry about the amount of work that now falls to them and the amount of time they must devote to hospital business.

Nurses continue to be dissatisfied with their role and their relationships with physicians.

In summary, therefore, people in health care fear for the future and are angry that forces have conspired to change their personal prospects from being advantageous or prosperous into situations of perceived financial insecurity. With these negative feelings, there is also a history of adverse relationships with each other, lack of trust, inability to identify common ground, and failure to agree upon a collective vision of the future. It is hardly surprising that the health care culture is one in which system changes are likely to provoke intense personal and group conflicts.

Conflict

Conflict occurs when a person experiences that his or her initiatives are being threatened or are about to be threatened; conflict may be real or perceived. Conflict is not necessarily a dysfunctional event; a desire to achieve excellence may create conflict but can stimulate creative work. But when conflicts are dysfunctional, they drain energy and reduce the chances of achieving useful outcomes. Conflict can ruin the effectiveness of groups. Unless conflicts are resolved, groups may seem to work together but will fail to achieve any meaningful outcomes.

Here are 12 antecedent conditions that are associated with conflict:

1. When survival is in question.
2. When allocation of scarce resources is competitive.
3. When there is concern for personal rather than group welfare.
4. When I or my group may be excluded from an initiative.
5. When power or control is uncertain—jurisdictions are ambiguous.
6. When personal goals are diverse.
7. When ideologies clash.
8. When there are barriers to communication.

Top Health Care Finance 1994; 20(4): 39–47

9. When emotions are high.
10. When conflict is expected.
11. When I have not decided that working together is more important than preserving my independence.
12. When there is a history of unresolved conflicts.

From these 12 points derived from general concepts of human behavior, it must be apparent that the health care culture has enormous capacity for serious conflict. This forest is tinder dry and just waiting to burst into flame. This environment is an arsonist's dream.

The relationship of conflict to sponsorship of a project

Under conditions where the various parties are involved in integration, the question of sponsorship is highly significant.

When the hospital is the agency that institutes the concept, it will do so to protect the market for its services and for the services of its physicians. It will claim to have the welfare of the community at heart. In sponsoring the integration, the hospital will import many sources of conflict, such as physician selection, utilization review, patient management, and so on.

When physician groups initiate the integration, they will do so to preserve the market of their physician members and will claim to have the welfare of patients at heart. Physician groups have a history of not being particularly strong or stable when faced with financial pressures and have a tendency to break apart.

When the sponsoring organization is a financial agency such as an insurance company, then both physicians and hospitals will view with suspicion the motives of the sponsor and will allege that the goal of the project is to make money for the company and that the hospital and physicians will become the tools of capitalism. Insurance or financial groups have long and sophisticated experience with money management and in dealing with physicians and hospitals in relation to costs of care. They lack experience in how to develop creative and community-based plans with health care providers.

Whoever is the sponsor, the formation and development of the group of physicians who are interested in and see the benefits of the integration are essential. Many stress the importance of a strong driving force within the physician group.

Recognizing Conflict

How do you recognize that conflict exists? In its most flagrant form, conflict exists when people disagree vehemently, shout and yell, or even indulge in fisticuffs. Such behaviors, fortunately, are the exception rather than the rule. Conflicts much more often find expression in more sophisticated subversive behaviors designed to thwart the goals of the other party. The nature of these behaviors is limited only by the imagination but includes proposing entirely inappropriate individuals for leadership; seeming to cooperate while finding all sorts of mechanisms to block progress; finding fault with current leaders and leadership strategies; and pointing out the great opposition to the plan and the dire consequences that would follow implementation, while perhaps protesting mildly that they are all in favor of the project. Such actions frequently are subconscious expressions of opposition to the plan. Many, while exhibiting these behaviors, would vehemently deny negative intentions if the matter were brought to their attention.

Locations of conflict in an integrated system

Conflict can, of course, happen anywhere within an integrated system. The nature and seriousness of the conflict are dependent to a considerable extent upon the sponsorship of the integrated system and the stage of development of the system.

When the integrated system is developed by a hospital, then all of the well-worn pathways by which conflicts have been expressed in the past can be opened up. Enormous pressures can be exerted by physicians upon the hospital board and management of the hospital. Either or both may be unequal to their task. The board will have to make sure that its members have the necessary financial expertise and general understanding of the new relationships involved in integration. The board must understand and be committed to the plans for integration and have the courage to stand its ground in the face of opposition.

Management will need to be very clear about their goals and avoid being caught and pulled into competitive and exclusionary issues between physicians while yet maintaining a serious leadership role—no easy task.

Physician members of the board will have to examine their competing and conflicting interests and when appropriate abstain from the decision-making process. It may be impossible for actively practicing physicians to participate in many of the fundamental decisions without being involved in conflicts of interest.

It is among physicians that the most severe conflicts seem likely to occur. To understand the genesis of these interphysician conflicts, it is necessary to examine the stages of the integration process because relationships are very different at different stages.

Stages of integration in relationship to conflict

Stage 1

The setting is a loosely arranged independent practice association (IPA) or physician-hospital organization (PHO).

At this stage, where nothing much has happened to change patterns of care, there can be a rosy vision of a new and preferred future but accompanied by often dire and dark predictions about the true significance of the integration process and any range of feelings between these two extremes.

Conflicts will tend to follow the patterns established in previous times. The physicians, although suspicious of each other and of everybody else, probably will have formed a loosely coordinated group. The integrity of the group will require that all physicians except the most incompetent, egregious, or expensive ones be included. The physicians will look to management, the hospital board, and to outside consultants to get their group together. There may well be good feelings among the majority of the physicians about protecting their market.

Stage 2

Capitation is the mode of payment to primary physicians in this stage. There is selective contracting with specialists, and referral patterns change. Patient management committees are instituted.

New referral patterns emerge. The primary care physicians emerge as controllers or gatekeepers and are monitored regarding cost and quality. The primary care physicians endure new stresses and tensions as a consequence of enhanced responsibilities

but by and large appreciate that they are at the center of the system. Their security is little threatened, but they are expected to perform well.

Conflicts may arise among the physicians and the patient management committee, especially when their recommendations are not accepted or are modified. Conflict may occur with committee staff but they will quickly pass such matters along to the medical director who not only is likely to be experienced in dealing with angry physicians but also is a figure whom the primary care physicians see as having some authority and therefore likely to be somewhat reasonable.

Among the specialists, the conflict is likely to be the most extreme. The attraction for the specialist to sign with the integrated system involves a promise of greater volume to offset discounted fees. To obtain the increased volume, the system must either obtain a greater number of members or else reduce the number of specialists who compete for the same numbers of members. Although the former is everybody's preference, the latter is the more likely eventuality.

Those specialists excluded in the selection process experience fear for the future of their practices and anger at those who have dared to leave them out. They may well write letters to the plan, to their patients in which they run down the plan, and to other sources of authority. They will try to gain an interview with the president of the plan or intrude into the bureaucracy of the system. They may threaten to sue.

Their relationships with those specialists who have received contracts with the plan are likely to be constrained.

Those specialists who received contracts, while glad to be favored, may have second thoughts about the extent of the discounted fees that allowed them to be successful in the bidding process. Did they give away too much? They also may experience some discomfort such as embarrassment and even guilt. They are aware that erstwhile colleagues have now become envious or unfriendly. The level of conflict among the specialists who have been successful in contracting, however, is much less than those who have been left out!

As a tailpiece, here it seems appropriate to comment that between specialists there has nearly always been a sense of competition for patients but at the same time efforts were made to maintain a facade of collegial relationships. It is as if the contracting process has taken away the mask of good fellowship and has allowed the real spirit of rivalry to show through.

Stage 3

In this stage the delivery of health care is changed by the integrated plan in a fundamental manner. Real economies are achieved. Monitoring of physician performance is enhanced and intrusive.

In Stage 2 in the vast majority of instances, referral patterns have changed, the number of providers has been reduced, but the actual delivery system is little altered. In Stage 3, the changes that the future may bring and the alteration in professional relationships that will follow are limited only by the imagination. It will be wise to continue to watch keenly and deal with new relationship changes as they occur.

Anticipation of conflict

At the beginning of the integration process, particularly in Stage 1, the strategies that follow may enable the various parties to come together.

Emphasize collaboration and team building

To reduce the breeding ground for conflict, it is highly desirable that everybody be included in the initial stages of the planning process. Later, representative groups will be formed to carry the project forward.

Some physicians will want to proceed with forming a physician organization while others will decide that they do not wish to join. It should be emphasized that the decision to join or not to join is an expression of free choice. Attempts to prevent or obstruct formation of the group, therefore, should be regarded as interference with this freedom and should not be tolerated.

Seek trust relationships

In many hospitals, levels of trust are low. When asked why this is so, people often respond, "It is our history." While it may not be possible to rewrite history, it may be possible to remember it differently. Exploration of old wounds, who caused them, and how they were inflicted is not an effective method of building trusting relationships. Instead, there should be an attempt to develop mutual respect, understand

the stresses and strains upon the potential partners, be willing to forgive one another for past perceived injustices, and be willing to recognize that the world is full of shifting alliances in which from time to time we may be on the same and then on different sides of an issue.

It also is important to remember that how we handle conflict is directly related to how trustworthy we are seen to be. If, in a situation of conflict, parties become overtly hostile and act out anger in destructive ways, people learn that they would be wise to repose limited trust with such individuals. If, on the other hand, parties respond to a negative incident by seeking solutions and by showing concern for the other person's point of view, then they will be seen to be trustworthy. Trusting relationships grow from positive experiences with conflict and its resolution.

Be open and honest

Hidden agendas are antithetical to trust building and, in most instances, are obvious to all. In developing discussion around an issue likely to cause conflict, it is appropriate to indicate that open, honest, tough, disciplined, and principled conversation is what is required.

Set the climate

A great deal can be accomplished by the person who has responsibility for leading or facilitating the work of a group. At the first meeting, considerable time should be taken up with such matters as how conflicts will be resolved, the desire that members of the group be "hard on the problems and soft on the people," that ultimatums be avoided, and that "timeouts" are a legitimate mechanism.

The group leader will recognize that there are competing interests around the table and that they are respected although they may have to be examined and even discarded in terms of the greater goal.

Reduce negative mindsets

When conflict occurs among people who have different ideologies, there is a strong tendency to develop negative mindsets. In this way, hospital managers become power-hungry individuals bent on controlling physicians; physicians become greedy, uncaring individuals seeking only materialistic rewards; and board members become irrelevant and uneducated citizens determined to dabble in matters that they do not understand. People in insurance or financial executives and groups become hardhearted, flinty individuals only interested in making a profit and who work in a luxurious office on the top floor of a large downtown building remote from the concerns of real people.

These negative stereotypes must be reduced and disposed of. Some first steps are recognizing the negative mindsets existing within ourselves, developing a personal relationship with these individuals, and learning to respect them for their skills and attributes. As R.D. Laing observed:

> As long as we cannot up-level our "thinking" beyond Us and Them, the goodies and baddies, it will go on and on. The only possible end will be when all the goodies have killed all the baddies, and all the baddies all the goodies, which does not seem so difficult or unlikely since, to Us, we are the goodies and They are the baddies, while to Them, we are the baddies and they are the goodies.
>
> It seems a comparatively simple knot, but it is tied very, very tight—round the throat, as it were, of the whole human species.
>
> But don't believe me because I say so, look in the mirror and see for yourselves.[1(p.124)]

If we are to work together effectively, we must unfreeze our negative stereotypes of each other. We must develop empathy for others by sharing their concerns and aspirations, because in this manner we are able to gain new insight about them and about ourselves.

Search for common goals

It may be too much to expect to identify common goals quickly. Initially, it may be helpful to look for common themes and expectations and to use these as building blocks to identifying common goals and understandings. In the process of searching, it is important to develop alternative solutions or proposals, because through commitment to this process many people can make a contribution and the plan that ultimately emerges is one to which they can make a substantial commitment.

Develop process skill

The process by which any group comes together to do useful work is a very complex matter. When deal-

ing with complex issues, it is desirable for the group leader or facilitator to have had some experience and training in the management of groups. Managing the process of the group—how the members work together—is in many instances critical to the development of effective outcomes.

Build the record

A group that is working with important and complex issues must be sure that an accurate record of the points of agreement is preserved.

Commit the whole group

The last phase is to have the whole group accept a solution or plan. After the various ideas are examined thoroughly, commitment is sought from group members regarding reducing the alternative proposals and, eventually, to accepting a plan of action.

Avoid a win-loss solution

"Win-win" solutions are very attractive and should be sought whenever possible. There are times when win-win solutions seem inaccessible. Under such a circumstance, the idea of principled negotiation as a way of mutual problem solving is a highly desirable goal for the process of the group.

In later stages of integration (Stages 2 and 3), several of the issues around which conflict is likely to develop have been described previously. In circumstances where individuals who want to be included are left out, or where the patient management committee refuses to go along with a projected course of action, the conflict seems much more likely to be interpersonal, whereas in the earlier stages the conflict is more likely to be between groups.

Also, in the later stages of integration, the die is cast, the plan is formulated, and the rules and regulations are written and accepted. There is little chance that the rules will be changed in response to acting out behaviors by a dissident physician.

Dealing with conflict

When integrating physicians and other services together, it is inevitable that conflict will arise. It is recommended that everything be done to anticipate it. It is almost certain, too, that initially efforts will be made to deny or gloss over its significance. Eventually, however, the work necessary to deny the reality of conflict becomes so burdensome that the existence of conflict will be recognized and accepted, and efforts will be made to deal with it.

A helpful schema for dealing with conflict has been developed by Pareek, who suggests that if attempts to defuse the problem fail, then the conflict will be managed sometimes by avoidance and sometimes by approaching it and attempting to reach a solution.[2] The method selected for conflict resolution can be chosen from among the eight alternatives offered in Figure 8–1.

The quartet of alternatives listed under avoidance can be invoked when the individual or the group as a whole decides that the conflict is best not confronted. It may be that it is relatively insignificant or that the time is not right to deal with it.

The quartet listed under approach represents ways of seeking a solution. If the opposed groups are belligerent and unreasonable, *fighting* to resolve the issue in favor of one side may occur and set up a highly unfavorable win-lose situation. Such episodes of fight-ing are very destructive. If the opposed groups are belligerent but reasonable, then some form of *arbitration* or some intervention by a neutral third party may be effective.

If the opposed groups are interested in peace but still unreasonable, then *compromise* may be attempted. In compromise, each group may gain but in general compromise has a lose-lose configuration. Each group gives up things to achieve some unity.

When the groups are interested in peace and are reasonable, then *negotiation* is possible. Negotiation offers the best chance of solving problems in a creative and satisfying way.

Entire books have been written about the process of negotiation. Among the best of these are *Getting to Yes*,[3] *Getting Past No*,[4] and *Beyond Machiavelli*.[5] These books are particularly valuable because they regard negotiation as a process through which problems and conflicts can be solved. These methods avoid the win-lose methods espoused in many other publications and which, though attractive in the short run, often serve to store up problems for the future.

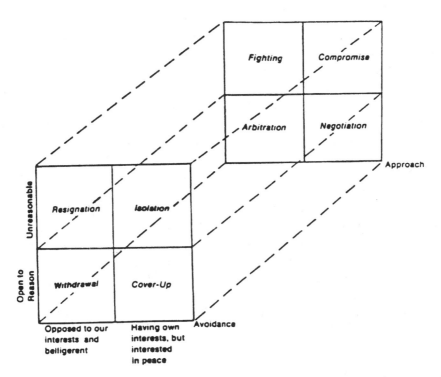

Figure 8–1. Styles of conflict management. Reprinted with permission from U. Pareek, Preventing and Resolving Conflict, in *The 1983 Annual for Facilitators, Trainers, and Consultants,* L.D. Goodstein and J.W. Pfeiffer, eds., p. 166, © 1983, Pfeiffer.

In an integrative process in which groups with individual values and traditions come together, conflicts are inevitable. The best investment is in prevention. When this fails, then resolution of the conflicts is necessary. The manner in which the conflicts are resolved has enormous implications regarding the climate of working relationships for the future. When conflicts are dealt with openly and fairly, the process of resolution can be a very positive experience and will go a long way toward building trust and commitment to the venture.

REFERENCES

1. Laing, R.D. *The Politics of the Family.* New York, N.Y.: Vintage Books, 1972.
2. Pareek, U. "Preventing and Resolving Conflict." In *The 1983 Annual for Facilitators, Trainers, and Consultants,* edited by L.D. Goodstein and J.W. Pfeiffer. San Diego, Calif.: Pfeiffer & Co., 1983.
3. Fisher, R., and Ury, W. *Getting to Yes.* 2d ed. New York, N.Y.: Viking Penguin, 1991.
4. Ury, W. *Getting Past No.* New York, N.Y.: Bantam Books, 1993.
5. Fisher, R., Kopelman, E., and Schneider, A.K. *Beyond Machiavelli.* Cambridge, Mass.: Harvard University Press, 1994.

9

Year 2000 Scenario for Physician–Hospital Organizations

Russell C. Coile, Jr.

A HIGH PROFILE of physician involvement is the key factor in this "year 2000" scenario of physician-hospital integration:

- Many hospitals and health systems (10–15%) will be headed by physician executives, especially larger (250+ beds) institutions.
- Physicians will comprise 35 to 50 percent of hospital boards and health system trustees.
- Most hospital–health system senior management teams will include at least two to three physicians.
- Paid physician managers will manage the cost and quality of medical care at the department level.
- Every hospital will own at least one large physician group practice.
- One third to half (35–45%) of hospital-based specialists (radiologists, anesthesiologists, pathologists, emergency) will be directly hospital-employed.
- Hospital-owned multispecialty group practices will employ one physician in three (35%).
- Managed care contracts will "bind" most physicians (more than 75%) to practice exclusively with a single hospital–health system.
- The "medical clinic" physician staff model (Mayo, Cleveland, Oschner, Virginia Mason) will be recognized as providing the highest quality of care for the most efficient cost, which the market will recognize as "value."

Purchasing Practices

The trend to physician group acquisition or merger is broadening, involving 35 percent of U.S. hospitals in a recent national survey. A wave of announcements will be coming in the 1990s, as the movement toward hospital-physician partnerships and mergers accelerates.

Purchasing or building practices is only part of a broader array of strategies by hospitals to support physicians. The most frequently provided assistance to physicians includes the following:

- set up a new office practice (78%),
- add a partner (71%),
- physician referral service (59%),
- marketing of office practice (50%), and
- medical waste disposal service (47%).

Fewer than 20 percent of hospitals reported providing retirement planning assistance. This may be a missed opportunity and an underutilized strategy for identifying physicians who need associates or would potentially join groups and pool their patients.

Corporate Medicine

Trade in the primary physician's "little black bag" for a briefcase. Tomorrow's primary care specialists are flocking to group practices to practice corporate medicine. This change has come swiftly.

Why groups? Because physicians in groups make more money—15 to 35 percent more income per specialty. Primary care group physicians make 10 to 25 percent more than their colleagues in solo settings. The reason is that groups see more patients, in about the same proportion as the income gap between group-based physicians and physicians in solo practice.[1]

Primary care medical groups will grow strongly in the 1990s, with more groups and more physicians. Low levels of reimbursement held primary care groups down in the 1980s. The proportion of general or family practice groups stayed about the same, at approximately 11 percent, until the early 1990s.[2] Fueled by the demand by health maintenance organizations (HMOs) and managed care plans, organized

Top Health Care Finance 1994; 20(4): 75–83

primary care groups and primary-based multispecialty groups began to achieve new market power as gatekeepers. The size of primary care groups is growing proportionately. Tomorrow's primary care groups will be larger—6 to 15 physicians in mid-size groups, 25 or more primary physicians in large practices, often with multiple office sites.

Physician types most likely to affiliate

What kind of physicians should hospitals target for affiliation? Start with the "YIPs" and "PIPs," recommends health care consultant Daniel Beckham of Quorom Health Resources in Whitefish Bay, Wisconsin. Beckham identifies four groups of physicians, each with its own set of needs:

1. young physicians interested in personal security (YIPs),
2. physicians exiting practice (PEPs),
3. physicians interested in practice support (PIPs), and
4. physicians independent until they die (PIDs).[3]

YIPs are interested in employment opportunities. Some 80 percent of young physicians in residency programs are only interested in working for groups or staff model HMOs.[1] PEPs are also interested in employment, full- or part-time, but they are even more concerned about retirement security. PIPs are committed to maintaining their independence, but they would like to have some help with the nonclinical business pressures (e.g., reducing overhead). PIDs will maintain their autonomy at any cost; many are successful entrepreneurs.

In the past, most physicians could be characterized as PIDs. Hospitals had to respect this demand for autonomy; any intrusion on PID territory could be dangerous to a hospital chief executive officer's health! But today, physicians are demanding different sorts of accommodations, each according to his or her needs. Tomorrow's successful hospitals and health systems will be designed primarily around the needs of YIPs and PIPs. For the YIPs, hospitals will need to encourage group practice development, through support, formation, or acquisition. PIPs need a broader array of support programs (e.g., office practice marketing and managed care contracting). Ultimately, the PIPs may also see their future in group practice. Hospitals can be helpful in bringing PIPs together to form groups, or

creating new models for integration such as the "group practice without walls."

San Diego's Sharp HealthCare: Case study in physician-hospital organizations

Look at the payoff from building physician-hospital organizations (PHOs). In San Diego, California, the Sharp HealthCare System acquired the Rees-Stealy Medical Clinic in 1985, a 200-physician medical group practice. Sharp HealthCare is emerging as one of three dominant health systems in the San Diego area, with 5 hospitals totaling 1,355 beds, 7 physician group practices, 14 clinics, and 5 skilled nursing facilities. With 25 percent of the market, Sharp is responsible for 325,000 "covered lives" under its 60 to 70 managed care contracts (8–10 contracts are capitated).

A key factor in the Sharp system's success in this heavily managed care marketplace is its "partnership" relations with the seven physician groups who are involved in risk-sharing (capitated) contracts. But the Sharp system takes a pluralistic relationship with its 2,000 physicians. Some physicians are employed by group practices or independent practice associations (IPAs), some physicians are salaried by Sharp, and others are independent members of the hospitals' medical staffs.

A collaborative approach with physicians is now being taken in development of practice guidelines and clinical protocols. Sharp is making a $30 million commitment to integration over the next four years to develop and install a regional information system that will centralize financial and clinical data in a single "electronic medical record."

Caution: Creating PHOs can be a "CLA"

Hospital executives beware! Creating PHOs can be a "career-limiting act" (CLA). At Good Samaritan Regional Medical Center in Phoenix, a hospital-initiated group practice startup led to a major shakeout in the hospital's management team. The situation triggered an investigation by the Federal Trade Commission of alleged attempts by physicians to block growth of the group.

In San Diego, acquisition of the 100+ physician group, the Rees-Stealy Medical Clinic, by the Sharp hospital system was considered a strategic masterstroke that would make Sharp and the Clinic a magnet for managed care contracts. But the administrators underestimated the reaction by Sharp physicians. The acquisition led to a major confrontation with disgruntled members of the medical staff, who feared the Clinic would get special treatment by the hospitals. In the aftermath, the system CEO and a key hospital administrator were fired, and a member of the board became the chief executive. Six years later, the deal looks much better. As hoped, the Clinic has been a major asset in managed care contracting, and the Sharp system is rapidly becoming one of the three dominant integrated health systems in the region, with Kaiser and Scripps.

In San Jose, California, controversy flared in 1992 over Health Dimensions' strategic alliance with Medical Dimensions, a 700-physician medical practice. Health Dimensions, a three-hospital system with a reputation for leadership, thought it was building a strategic alternative to the Kaiser system in the "Silicon Valley." But community physicians were rankled by the deal with Medical Dimensions. A key multispecialty group located adjacent to one of the Health Dimension hospitals was so miffed that it shifted strategic alliances to Stanford and two other community hospitals. The predictable result was the departure of two key Health Dimensions executives who had orchestrated the Medical Dimensions affiliation.

Supergroups

The consolidation of these supergroups is accelerating. The Mulliken Medical Center acquired almost one group practice per month in Los Angeles in 1992, including Hawthorne, Moore-White, and Burbank medical groups, some with more than 100 physicians. Now Mulliken's more than 400 physicians networked across 30-plus offices have contracted responsibility for 260,000 covered lives.

Both Mulliken and Pacific Physician Services (PPS) are expanding statewide, purchasing medical groups in northern California. PPS has capital for growth. It is a publicly traded stock company whose investors are betting on the growth of supergroups of primary care physicians to control hundreds of thousands of "covered lives" and dominate the future health care marketplace.

More consolidation (and growth!) is coming. Merger of California Primary Physicians with the Huntington Medical Group in mid-1992 created a 100-plus physician group with more than a dozen offices controlling central Los Angeles and the San Gabriel Valley.

Overcoming physician alienation

Deteriorating physician relationships are a shortcut to disaster for tomorrow's hospitals. It is easy to spot "troubled hospitals," those institutions that are struggling to keep their beds full and finances in order. Turnaround-management specialists David Hunter and Marrilee Gerew of the Tampa, Florida–based Hunter Group, identify three key symptoms of worsening medical staff relations:

1. decreasing admissions,
2. rising length of stay and ancillary utilization, and
3. increasing physician hostility toward management.[4]

These problems are not due to "the environment." Too often, they are the direct result of a medical staff that is uninvolved, unmanaged, undeveloped, and uninspired. Physicians are left out of the planning proc-ess and not involved in key managed care contract decisions. In these distressed hospital situations, little information has been shared about hospital strategies, activities, and current status. Dialogue between physicians and administration is curtailed to formal medical staff committee meetings.

The Hunter Group recommends these six strategies to overcome physician alienation:

1. full-time medical director,
2. physician "sales" and service by the hospital,
3. seeking and listening to physician advice,
4. frequent communication,
5. physician leadership in "care management" (costs and quality), and
6. physician involvement in strategic decisions.[4]

Not all physicians ready for "integration" future

Citing the "hassles" of medical practice, a growing number of physicians are disgruntled with the current system and not hopeful about the future. Some physicians are retiring early, cutting down their practice time, or switching to jobs such as "medical director" that do not involve patient care, according to a recent *New York Times* article by Belkin, "Sensing a Loss of Control, More Doctors Call It Quits."[5] Early retirement is a signal of more widespread malaise among the medical profession, from studies cited in Belkin's article:

- If given a second chance, a reported 40 percent of physicians would not enter medicine, according to a recent *New York Times* poll.
- Of physicians who had soured on the medical profession, 42 percent cited outside interference and regulation in a 1990 study by the American Medical Association.
- Some 30 percent of internists said they would forego part of their income in a tradeoff for fewer administrative requirements, in a study published in the *Annals of Internal Medicine.*

Physicians feel their power slipping away. Power in the health system is a function of who controls the flow of patients. In the past physicians held the most power. Their perception was—and often still is—that the hospital exists to serve the physicians. Physicians admitted patients and controlled their care with little external oversight or hospital interference. With the intrusion of managed care, physicians are rapidly losing clinical autonomy as they simultaneously lose income. Medicare's physician payment reform worsens the impact of discounted fees from insurance plans and HMOs.

Much of the frustration with managed care stems from the physicians' loss of clinical autonomy in conducting tests, doing procedures, and admitting patients. The feeling that they are working harder for less money is frequently heard in physicians' anecdotes. Adding to the mental fatigue factor is the resentment by physicians that their efforts are unappreciated: "Patients view the doctor as the 'enemy'— that gets tiresome," notes Dr. A. Burton White, an orthopaedist from Great Neck, New York, who stopped doing surgery in 1987 and cut his office hours in half two years ago. At Dr. White's hospital, the oldest surgeon is now age 53. "They burn out faster," reports Dr. White in Belkin's *New York Times* article.[5]

Two "trigger events" are cited in the decision of some physicians to quit. New federal regulations governing physician office laboratories from the Oc-

cupational Safety and Health Administration (OSHA) were a nightmare, regulating even the details of how employees' uniforms were to be laundered. Medicare's new resource-based relative value scale (RBRVS) for physician payment was the other major catalyst of physician unrest. Specialists' fees under Medicare were downgraded by 10 to 25 percent in the federal effort to reform physician payment and establish a uniform set of physician prices.

Models for PHOs

Model #1—medical foundation

The medical foundation model potentially represents a closer integration of hospital and physician services with a resulting stronger interdependence between participating providers. The Kaiser Permanente Medical Foundation is the largest and best known example of a medical foundation. There are several options with the medical foundation model. Consider the following three:

1. *Free-standing medical foundation.* The freestanding medical foundation is not hospital or health system owned, although it may have close clinical and contractual links with a hospital or system. Free-standing medical foundations are tax-exempt 501(c)(3) organizations that often have a strong research and education purpose. There is limited board overlap with their physician corporation, called MD Inc.
2. *Hospital-affiliated tax-exempt clinic.* In this model, the medical foundation is an affiliate of the hospital or health system. Affiliation may be for managed care contracting or other shared purposes, e.g., to provide a primary care base or operate an ambulatory care center.
3. *Hospital-owned medical foundation.* The hospital or health system may directly own the medical foundation (subsidiary), a model that provides for greater control of the medical group practice through the professional services arrangement.

Model #2—management services organization

The management services organization (MSO) can be an important vehicle to bring capital and other management expertise to medical group practices. The MSO compares favorably in many respects with the medical foundation model, and yet allows physicians to retain direct ownership of the group practice. The MSO model provides many of the business and business support services to medical groups, but may be perceived as less of a threat to physician independence. The MSO model also presents less of a corporate practice of medicine issue in that it does not provide services to patients, but only to the physicians in the contracting group (MD Inc.).

Two options for MSOs are possible. The free-standing MSO is an independent, taxable business corporation whose ownership may be lay (entrepreneur/investor) and/or physician. The MSO furnishes all sites, facilities, equipment and supplies, personnel, and administrative services to a physician corporation (MD Inc.). Terms of services and responsibilities are defined in a "turnkey management services agreement." The MSO bills in the name and on behalf of MD Inc., and may also manage other groups and entities. MD Inc., the professional corporation, may have a single owner (e.g., physician owner of the MSO) or multiple owners (e.g., physician participants). The group may be primary care or multispecialty, employing individual physicians to provide services to patients and payers. MD Inc. owns and operates all clinical aspects of group practice. It also "owns" the charts and patients.

The second option, the hospital-affiliated MSO, may be separately incorporated or operated as a division of the hospital or health system. The hospital-affiliated MSO may qualify for 501(c)(3) tax-exempt status, unlike the free-standing MSO. The hospital-affiliated MSO provides all sites, facilities, equipment and supplies, personnel, and support services required by the physicians in the professional corporation (MD Inc.). The MSO bills on behalf and in the name of MD Inc., and may manage other groups and entities. MD Inc. is a professional corporation wholly owned by physicians, and either primary or multispecialty. The practice provides services to patients and payers, and may be affiliated with an IPA. MD Inc. owns and operates clinical aspects of the group practice, "owns" the charts and patients, and employs individual physicians.

Medical foundation or MSO: is one better?

Capital is a major factor in creating either a medical foundation or an MSO. Both the medical foundation

and MSO hold the assets and reserves, not the physician corporation (MD Inc.). The medical foundation provides a mechanism by which a hospital can purchase a physician group, with the purchase price thereby providing a return to the physician owners. That capital (purchase price) can also "cash out" retiring physicians, or provide an incentive pool to remaining physicians. The MSO model provides a structure for investors (lay, physician, or hospital) to capitalize future growth and development of the physician organization.

Medical foundations may qualify for tax-exempt financing, subject to meeting restrictions regarding terms of any agreements with the physicians, as well as limitations on physician participation in governance. It is relatively more difficult to secure tax-exempt status for the MSO, even if it is affiliated with a tax-exempt hospital or health system.

"Inurement" (financial conflict of interest) is another issue. Not for the medical foundation, which is a tax-exempt affiliate of the hospital and directly involved in the provision of health care services. But the MSO alternative potentially presents a greater private inurement risk to the hospital. Issues of concern would be the level of consideration received by the hospital for services provided (fair market value), the magnitude of any income guarantees, and aggregate subsidies to the group practice by the hospital. Even with these concerns, there is considerable latitude for a tax-exempt hospital to support group practices through MSO arrangements.

Model #3—physician service bureaus

Commonly provided services of physician service bureaus include:
- billing,
- collections,
- accounting,
- administration of pension/benefit plans,
- staff leasing,
- diagnostic testing (lab/radiology),
- practice management,
- information systems,
- office leasing,
- shared office arrangements,
- recruitment, and
- "bridge" agreements (loans in lieu of practice guarantees).

Model #4—IPA

To add complexity to this distinction, however, the MSO could also manage the IPA, and MD Inc. could participate in managed care contracting as a component of the IPA. The IPA could also have a sponsorship function or otherwise affiliate with a hospital/health system's group practice program. For example, the IPA may have the right to designate seats on the medical foundation/MSO and MD Inc. governing boards. The IPA and MD Inc. may develop protocols on appropriate utilization of specialists affiliated with the IPA, not only for managed care but also for other patients seen within the group practice program.

PHOs under national health reform

The American Hospital Association's (AHA) national health care reform plan, "Community Care Networks," is missing a critical building block—the medical component. Support by the American Medical Association (AMA) has been withheld. Physicians fear the community care networks would be hospital dominated. Somehow the AHA and AMA must find common ground. The development of community care networks by America's hospitals must be done with true physician partnering strategies.

The AHA reform proposal calls for universal access to health care, to be provided through local integrated delivery systems called "community care networks." Each local system will be different, but they will share common elements:

- *Financial risk.* Community care networks will take on significant financial risk to provide care to a defined population for a fixed premium (capitation).
- *Continuum of care.* A comprehensive array of services and facilities will be organized across the system, with routine services provided by a primary care network.
- *Integration.* All care offered will be coordinated so patients move through the system efficiently.
- *Outcomes data.* Data will be collected on the system's impact on community health, for which the system will be held publicly accountable.
- *Clinical protocols.* Community care networks will develop critical paths and care algorithms to promote quality and clinical efficiency.

Looking forward

The coming of "managed competition" cannot happen without strong partnering relationships between physicians and hospitals. Physicians are critical to the management of quality and efficiency. What is missing at present are the medical organizations on which to build the community care networks of tomorrow.

In the coming era of managed competition and health care reform, hospitals and health systems will need a portfolio of approaches and services including the following:

- A medical clinic foundation for acquiring and merging physician practices,
- Two to three IPAs, at least one of which is capable of taking risk (capitation),
- A primary care network of affiliated primary care physicians and groups for managed care contracts,
- A "group practice without walls" as a vehicle for solo physicians and small groups to gain the benefits of group practice,
- An on-campus primary care–family practice group,
- A multispecialty clinic located on campus or adjacent to the hospital, which is primarily committed to the hospital,
- Long-term exclusive contracts with key specialists for hospital-provided services (pathology, radiology, anesthesiology, emergency),
- A physician management/support organization dedicated to promoting successful physician practice,
- An integrated information system linking the hospital, ambulatory care settings, medical office buildings, and physician practices,
- A utilization review–quality assurance management function, and
- A vice president for medical services (full-time physician executive).

National health care reform will only accelerate changes in the health care marketplace being driven by managed care. Converging strategies of national health reform (public policy) and managed care (market economics) will speed the development of these relationships in the next 3 to 5 years. Whatever the scenario for national health care reform in the future, hospitals must begin to develop community care networks with their physician partners.

REFERENCES

1. Cohen, A.B. "Young Physicians and the Future of the Medical Profession." *Health Affairs* (Winter 1990): 138–48.
2. Grant, P.N. "Dramatic Developments in IPA, Medical Group Practice, and HMO–Hospital–Medical Group Relations in California." *California Physician* (September 1991): 32–38.
3. Beckham, J.D. "Remaking the Medical Staff." *Healthcare Forum Journal* 34, No. 5 (1991): 27–29.
4. Hunter, D.P., and Geren, M. "Physician Relationships in Troubled Hospitals." *Healthcare Forum Journal* 33, no. 5 (1990): 14–17.
5. Belkin, L. "Sensing a Loss of Control, More Doctors Call It Quits." *New York Times,* 9 March 1993, pp. A1, C2.

10

Physician-Hospital Organizations: The "Training Wheels" of Tomorrow's Provider-Sponsored Networks?

James J. Unland

Promise Gives Way to Criticism

The concept underlying the emergence of the physician-hospital organization (PHO) a few years ago—that a hospital and its medical staff should become a "unified provider" for the purpose of negotiating managed care contracts—originally sounded so logical and worthwhile as to be unarguable, and there is hardly a hospital in Illinois that has not attempted to put together a PHO. Multihospital networks are putting together "super" or regional PHOs, and these kinds of efforts are even being attempted by various kinds of hospital confederations with some common interest, such as religious affiliation à la the Catholic hospitals in the greater Chicago area.

Following the first wave of PHO formation a couple of years ago, however, various criticisms began to emerge—not just in the Chicago area, but nationally. The criticisms have generally followed one of two lines of argument:

- The structural characteristics of PHOs are untenable.
- The theory underlying the PHO concept is itself fundamentally unsound.

Faultfinding regarding the structure of PHOs has most often revolved around issues of organization and implementation. PHOs have been condemned for being too inclusive of physicians, not inclusive enough, too dominated by specialists, too tilted toward hospitals, lacking in infrastructure, self-competitive, and possessing various other faults. The ownership and governance of PHOs—and even whether they should be for-profit or not-for-profit entities—have been debated. The ability of hospitals to competently manage PHOs and provide the underlying "infrastructure" has

J Health Care Financ 1996; 22(4): 29–32

been questioned.

A lot of criticism of PHOs has come from physicians. Physician criticism has boiled down to a control issue, with many physicians reminding us all that they did not go to medical school to work—directly or indirectly—for hospital administrators, much less give hospitals control of the money in master contracts when, after all, physicians themselves are the ones being asked to "manage" care.

Despite the sound and fury, all of these structural, organizational, and implementational criticisms of PHOs can be solved, and a number of progressive hospitals and their medical staffs have, indeed, sat down and worked out these issues, including a number of hospitals in the greater Chicago area. The early models of PHO structure that gave hospitals a great deal of control have given way to "partnership" models in which a hospital and physicians own and govern the PHO on a 50/50 basis. In addition, a number of PHOs have been assembled after a critical mass of physicians is already in place in the form of either an independent physicians association (IPA) or a physician organization (PO). Some hospitals are even encouraging physicians to first form a PO that will then become a member of the PHO, thereby hoping to mitigate some potential logistical as well as governance problems.

Is the PHO Concept Viable?

The second major area of criticism—that the PHO is untenable to begin with—is actually a more difficult issue to dispel.

Arguments that PHOs are untenable per se revolve around the fact that single-hospital PHOs are, by definition, restricted to the hospital's market "catchment area." In rural areas where one hospital frequently covers a large geographic area this may not be a problem. In competitive urban areas, however, it is a serious problem, especially with respect to employer-based insurance: even though a company may be located in a hospital's service area, many of its employees may live outside the service area. Managed care is a business of covering defined populations over as wide a geographic area as possible, especially with commercial populations who are almost universally employer-insured.

When managed care comes to Medicare, the single-hospital PHO may appear, on the surface, to be more viable because the Medicare population is not obtaining insurance from one place and obtaining health care in another place. Because most Medicare recipients are retired, a single-hospital PHO can reach out to its own market catchment area and, at least theoretically, capture covered lives. In practice, however, even Medicare-covered lives will most likely be bid upon by provider networks, not by individual, single-hospital PHOs. Providing health care services to Medicare populations will require more than one hospital, both because of the need to provide comprehensive services and the need to provide services cost effectively with appropriate economies of scale and infrastructure.

The Regional PHO: A More Potent Contracting Entity

A multi-hospital PHO ("regional" PHO or "super" PHO) can be more viable than the single-hospital PHO if (1) the hospitals have overlapping service areas with no gaps; (2) they cover a relatively large total geographic area; (3) they have a large number of physicians who, on a combined basis, cover all of the major specialties in each sector of the total geographic area; and (4) the hospitals and physicians are cost-competitive—individually and as a whole—permitting the super-PHO to offer competitive rates.

It is important to point out that a regional or "super" PHO can take many organizational forms, including a fully merged hospital network, a looser affiliated hospital consortium, or hospitals that are unaffiliated except through PHO-to-PHO joint marketing and contracting. Regardless of the specific organizational form, the important features of the regional PHO are (1) its ability to cover a wide area and population, (2) its cost-

competitiveness, and (3) its capability to contract as a "unified provider," including both the hospitals and the physicians, through one means or another.

The regional or "super" PHO begins to assume some interesting characteristics if it is properly structured. The term "properly structured" cannot be overemphasized. The organization will not be effective unless it has, among other things, the enthusiastic support of a large number of physicians who cross all the specialties and who cover the contiguous area. If the properly structured regional PHO is large enough—regardless of whether it is assembled through a true hospital network or through a looser consortium of individual PHOs linked by contractual agreements—the organization is positioned to make the eventual leap to become a "provider/insurer" or what has often been called a provider-sponsored network (PSN).

The leap from PHO to PSN is not easy and should in no way be underestimated. There are four main hurdles: (1) restructuring the ownership and governance of the organization, most likely to a for-profit model with significant physician ownership; (2) assembling—directly or indirectly—a threshold level of capital; (3) dealing with insurance and regulatory issues which, it is hoped, Congress will make easier in this or its next session; and (4) launching the marketing program quickly and effectively so as to replace existing payers with the PSN—by no means an easy task.

It should be noted that as an alternative to forming a totally independent provider/insurer, it is possible for providers to form a joint venture of some sort with an existing payer who handles the "insurance" functions of the PSN. This may permit the PSN to be jump started; on the other hand, a joint venture with an insurance company could result in higher costs by inserting another level of profit-taking—nearly all payers are in business to make money for their executives and stockholders.

Regardless of the exact form that PSNs take (and they will probably take many different forms in the coming years), many experts and a not insignificant number of legislators believe that PSNs are the next logical evolutionary step beyond today's fragmented, layered, expensive system of payer "middlemen." Thus, the individual hospital PHO may give way to a regional PHO which, in turn, may represent the critical stage of evolution preceding the provider/insurer.

Appendix 10–1

Hearing It from the Horse's Mouth: A Payer Speaks Out About PHOs

At the January 11, 1996, program sponsored by the First Illinois Chapter's Managed Care Committee, "Succeeding in Managed Care," Frank Nicholson was one of the panelists. Nicholson is Vice President of Managed Care at Blue Cross/Blue Shield of Illinois and, in addition to his other responsibilities, manages HMO Illinois. Following are some key points from Nicholson's presentation:

* The inherent structure of many PHOs renders them "programmed for failure." Blue Cross looks for win-win partnerships between the hospital participants and the physician participants in a PHO.
* 50/50 governance between the physicians and the hospital is desirable; it is also vital that the parties share the same philosophy and recognize the facts of life in highly evolved managed care.
* A major market shakeout is inevitable due to oversupply. Thus, not everyone will be a winner among hospitals or physicians.

* Physicians should be required to contribute some of their own money to help capitalize the PHO. In this way, there is a greater likelihood that they will behave as true partners with a vested interest in the organization's success.
* Parties considering a PHO should talk to the four or five big payers in the Chicago market to get their ideas prior to establishing the PHO.
* A 70/30 ratio of primary care physicians to specialists is desired, but probably unrealistic at this time; a 50/50 split is acceptable.
* Attempt to enter into capitated contracts as soon as possible. The state of the art will become the HMO with opt-out provisions.
* Geographic and population coverage are vital to the success of a PHO. Patient convenience and customer service are considered high priorities by Blue Cross.

Part III
The Health Care Delivery System

11

Critical Factors in Recruiting Health Maintenance Organization Physicians

Nancy B. Fisher, Howard L. Smith, and Derick P. Pasternak

What are the critical factors that facilitate successful recruitment of medical staff members? This question is very important to many health care organizations. Over 80 percent of hospitals with up to 399 beds report recent physician recruitment activity, while over 76 percent of hospitals with 400 or more beds are actively recruiting staff members.[1] Health maintenance organizations (HMOs) are expanding rapidly and as a result are recruiting physicians at unprecedented rates.[2] The situation may be most challenging for rural areas, which continue to have problems in attracting physicians despite changes in the national physician supply.[3] In sum, most health care organizations are vitally interested in recruiting high-quality medical staff members. Nonetheless, there is limited information available on effective recruitment practices. Health care executives face a difficult problem for which few innovative strategies have been proposed.

Physician recruitment is an especially perplexing challenge confronting HMOs. Although recent medical school graduates are more likely to pursue practice opportunities with HMOs than before, a recruitment problem remains.[4] Family practitioners, internists, pediatricians, obstetrician-gynecologists, and general surgeons are in high demand due to HMO enrollment growth.[5] Primary care practitioners normally provide a case management function essential to utilization and cost controls.[6] In the past, these physicians were difficult to recruit because of negative attitudes associated with HMOs and their tendency to view HMO care delivery as inferior to that in other practice settings.[7,8] Additionally, physicians have perceived a significant loss of autonomy and independence in HMOs.[9] Possibly as a result of the above factors, there

is a tendency for HMO physicians to be younger, concerned about practice location and off-hour coverage, and less interested in income issues.[10]

The purpose of this article is to address the issue of physician recruitment in HMOs by clarifying critical factors involved in the recruitment process. A study of medical staff members associated with the Lovelace Health Plan, an HMO comprised of approximately 300 physicians in Albuquerque, New Mexico, is used to define salient concerns in recruitment. The study also examines medical practice attributes important to Lovelace physicians, and to physicians who declined medical staff positions with Lovelace. The implications of this investigation for physician recruitment in HMOs and other health delivery settings are discussed.

Background

Limited research is available on physician recruitment. Most of the literature is experientially based and reported in professional journals. Some authorities indicate that physicians make practice location decisions based on income potential, geographic factors, perceived quality of medical care at the prospective site, quality of potential colleagues, and institutional reputation.[11,12] These criteria are similar to those used by physicians in ranking hospital attributes.[13] While these decision criteria influence whether a physician joins a health care organization, the recruitment process itself also may become an obstacle. Health care organizations may fail to adequately plan for the physician visit and subsequently create a poor impression that undermines recruitment.[14] Normally overlooked are invitations for family members and a concluding session to market the distinctive qualities of the organization.[15]

Although more than a decade old, a study by Fink[16] of 69 HMOs in the United States suggests that many of

Health Care Manage Rev 1993; 18(1): 51–61
© 1993 Aspen Publishers, Inc.

the recruitment issues noted above apply to HMOs. Fink's findings indicate that almost 75 percent of all HMOs studied recruit physicians who have just completed their residencies. More than one-third of the HMOs studied expressed concern that physicians were biased against group practice arrangements, an attribute that inhibited the recruitment process. However, new data do not necessarily support this finding.[17] Additionally, the HMOs indicated that they were at a distinct advantage in meeting salary and compensation offered by fee-for-service practices. The HMOs target new physicians who may be more amenable to group settings and may have lower salary expectations.

Fink's investigation confirmed the efficacy of personal contacts as well as advertisements in periodicals when recruiting physicians. Physician recruiters were not specifically mentioned as a prevalent strategy. It was also observed that 27 percent of the HMOs reported unsolicited inquiries from physicians. Fink concluded that this reflected greater acceptance of HMOs by physicians in general.

Potential resistance to group and managed care plans is a salient recruiting issue that has changed significantly in recent years. Formerly, physicians anticipated limitations on earning potential, lower quality of care, and decreased autonomy relative to HMOs. However, a study of 850 HMO physicians in Wisconsin discovered that physicians' expectations for lower earnings and quality of care were not realized.[18] The HMO physicians reported that their autonomy had decreased, which could lead to dissatisfaction and hesitancy to embrace systems designed to achieve efficiencies.[19] The implication for recruitment is significant. HMOs must work to keep medical staff members satisfied in order to prevent them from conveying negative messages to medical staff candidates.

An Investigation into Physician Recruiting

The Lovelace Health Plan (LHP) is New Mexico's largest HMO with over 128,000 enrollees. The LHP is an integral element of a complex health delivery system. Health plan members receive primary care at a main medical center and 12 satellite clinics in Albuquerque, New Mexico. Two clinics serve Santa Fe. The clinics are staffed by the physicians employed by Lovelace, Inc., a 300-physician-member medical

staff offering multispecialty care. Lovelace, Inc. includes LHP as well as a for-profit hospital, clinical facilities, equipment, and all necessary personnel supports. The hospital facility consists of 235 inpatient beds and generally maintains an occupancy rate greater than 85 percent.

The market for managed care in Albuquerque has approximately doubled in the last five years. Total enrollment in 1986 was over 107,000 and by 1990 exceeded 193,000. In 1990, LHP's market share was 56 percent of all HMO enrollees. LHP's strategy is to maintain quality of care as well as economic viability. It is not particularly concerned about being the largest HMO solely because it has enrolled the highest number of members.

With 300 physicians assigned directly to the LHP medical staff, it is inevitable that annual recruiting must be undertaken. Turnover is very low—in the range of 5 percent—when considering retirements and those who have left for other professional opportunities. Nonetheless, when turnover is added to growth, LHP inevitably seeks to fill several medical staff positions yearly. Having historically maintained a strong reputation for high quality of care, LHP is interested in attracting the finest candidates. Consequently, LHP has recently reviewed its physician recruitment process. This article assesses the current recruitment process and suggests several recommendations for other providers to consider when developing recruitment strategies.

From a methodological perspective, the study began with a review of the literature and telephone interviews with five other nationally visible multispecialty group practices to obtain information on their recruitment processes. On the basis of this information, a physician recruitment survey questionnaire was designed with the input of key medical and administrative personnel at Lovelace. (Copies of the questionnaire are available from the authors.) The questionnaire was then mailed to all physicians who interviewed for positions at Lovelace during 1989 and 1990. The responses included 76 physicians who were subsequently hired at Lovelace and 29 physicians who were offered positions at Lovelace but declined them. The response rate for the survey was 84 percent among physicians subsequently hired and 51 percent for physicians not hired by Lovelace. All data were collected over a one-month period.

Findings

Physicians were asked to indicate their specialty, means of learning about Lovelace, the Lovelace representative who made the first recruiting contact, and length of time that passed until a final hiring decision was made. Respondents indicated their perceptions of eight critical factors in the recruitment process (Table 11–1). Additionally, the physicians were asked to rate the overall coordination of the recruitment process. Finally, a five-interval rating scale (1=not important; 5=extremely important) was used to assess various practice attributes (e.g., salary, location, quality of care). In rating practice attributes, physicians were requested to indicate how important each attribute is to them (as physicians). They also indicated on a five-interval scale (1=very poor; 5=excellent) their perceptions of how Lovelace rates on each attribute.

Recruitment process perceptions by physicians employed at Lovelace

Table 11–1 presents perceptions of the recruitment process by the 76 physicians employed by Lovelace. The data indicate a wide variety of clinical specialties among the respondents; no single clinical orientation dominates. Given the rapid growth of the LHP, this finding is anticipated. Both primary and specialty care received attention in physician recruiting. The predominant method of learning about the opportunities at Lovelace was through a colleague. Forty percent of the physicians hired at Lovelace indicate the importance of word of mouth in identifying placement opportunities. It should also be noted that only 11 percent learned about Lovelace through a recruitment firm. Thus, a good reputation remains a key basis for effective physician recruitment.

Clinical department chairpersons, division chairpersons, or administrators were the representatives most likely to make initial contact with a prospective recruit in 66 percent of the cases. Again, a physician recruiter was less likely to be the representative making the initial contact. These data underscore the relative value of professional networking and socialization in the recruitment process. Table 11–1 also confirms the importance of decision making at the completion of the interview. Forty-five percent of the physicians indicate that Lovelace contacted them within 1 to 7 days with a final decision, 29 percent

indicated the decision took 8 to 14 days after the interview, and 13 percent indicated that a decision was made on the spot. In only 13 percent of the cases did it take more than 2 weeks to make a decision. Ability to deliver a quick decision appears to have some importance in retaining candidates.

The physicians hired by Lovelace were asked to express their perceptions of the recruitment process. As Table 11–1 suggests, almost 90 percent of the respondents answered affirmatively relative to the following:

- adequate information being provided in the first recruiting contact,
- accessibility to the department chairperson within a reasonable amount of time,
- provision of adequate information about the practice opportunity during the on-site interview,
- adequate information being provided on salary and benefits during the on-site interview, and
- adequate information on when Lovelace would contact the candidate with a final decision.

These data suggest that Lovelace has effectively managed physician recruiting by presenting important information to candidates at key points over the course of the process. In this manner, Lovelace is not only able to communicate its strengths, but it also establishes confidence that there is nothing to hide.

Lovelace's recruiting process did not produce similar results on two recruiting issues. Only 54 percent of the physicians agree that they received a recruitment packet prior to on-site interviews. This failure is of limited practical significance to this particular group of respondents because they eventually were hired. However, the same conclusion may not hold true for other candidates. A recruitment packet may be valuable to both physician candidates and to Lovelace. It can establish a basis for further discussion and identify an inappropriate match. Effective recruiting takes time and effort from existing staff. Therefore, the ability to identify a poor match early in the process (either by Lovelace or by the candidate) may prevent unnecessary expenditures.

Only 47 percent of physicians indicated that Lovelace invited decision makers such as a spouse, significant others, and children to accompany the candidate on first interviews. It must be remembered that an institution is often recruiting the entire ensemble. Obviously, transportation and housing costs associated with recruitment can escalate rapidly if a

Table 11–1

Perception of issues surrounding the recruitment process by physicians employed at Lovelace*

Specialty	%
Other	21
Family practice	16
Other surgical specialty	14
Internal medicine	12
Other medical specialty	12
Urgent care	9
Obstetrics-gynecology	8
Pediatrics	8

Means of learning about the Lovelace Medical Center	%
Colleague	40
Other	32
Professional journal	12
Recruitment firm	11
Residency program	5
Professional meeting	1

Lovelace representative who made first recruiting contact	%
Lovelace department chairperson	35
Lovelace division chairperson	18
Lovelace physician	17
Lovelace administrator	13
Other	12
Physician recruitment firm	5

At completion of the interview, how many days did it take until Lovelace contacted you with the final decision?	%
1–7 days	45
8–14 days	29
Immediate	13
2–4 weeks	7
More than 4 weeks	6

Perceptions of recruitment process	Yes %	No %	No response %
Was adequate information provided by the Lovelace representative who made the first recruiting contact?	91	9	0
Were you able to speak with the department chairperson within a reasonable amount of time?	95	1	4
Did you receive a recruitment packet prior to your on-site interview?	54	45	1
Were all decision makers (spouse, significant other, children) invited to accompany you on the interview?	47	36	17
During the on-site interview were you provided adequate information on the practice opportunities?	94	5	1
During the on-site interview were you provided adequate information on salary and benefits?	93	7	0
At the completion of your interview were you provided adequate information on when Lovelace would contact you about a final decision?	89	7	4
Was the contact on a final decision made by the department chairperson?	75	20	5

How do you rate the overall coordination of the physician recruitment process at Lovelace?	%
Good	67
Excellent	21
Fair	9
Very poor	0
Poor	0
No response	3

*n=76

candidate is accompanied by a large entourage. Therefore, there must be prudent decisions on who should be invited, but such decisions should be relatively easy when recruiting for positions that are traditionally difficult to fill. If there is uncertainty about the suitability of the candidate or the prognosis for a good fit, then an invitation to others associated with the physician can also be extended after the initial recruiting visit.

Finally, the physicians rated the overall coordination of the physician recruitment process at Lovelace. Eighty-eight percent rated the process as good or excellent. None of the physicians rated the process as poor or very poor. However, it must be remembered that these respondents were eventually employed by Lovelace, which is the optimal measure of recruiting success.

Recruitment process perceptions by physicians declining employment

Table 11–2 displays the perceptions of physicians who were recruited and made an offer but who did not accept the offer. Similar to the physicians who were hired (Table 11–1), there is no specific pattern by specialty. Primary care specialists appear to be more prevalent in this group than physicians who actually were employed by Lovelace. Twenty-nine percent of the physicians who did not accept a job offer are family practitioners and 17 percent are internists. A wide variety of clinical specialties are represented among the respondents.

Similar to the comparison group of physicians hired at Lovelace (Table 11–1), those declining an offer also indicate that they primarily learned about Lovelace from colleagues. Forty-one percent became acquainted with Lovelace's opportunities from colleagues, and 17 percent learned about Lovelace through professional journals. Again, only a small percent (i.e., 10 percent) became familiar with Lovelace through professional recruiters. Another similarity between the comparative groups is found in Lovelace representatives who made the first recruiting contact. Fifty-two percent of the physicians who did not accept a job offer by Lovelace indicate that a department chairperson, division chairperson, or administrator made the first contact regarding the position. This is similar to the results for Lovelace medical staff in Table 11–1. However, there appears to be greater initial contact

made by professional recruiters in the case of physicians who did not accept Lovelace's job offer. It may be that recruiters are less able to identify and forge a match to the same extent as Lovelace staff.

A final similarity is found in the length of time required before being contacted about a decision. Forty-eight percent of the physicians who did not accept the job offer indicate that Lovelace contacted them within 1 to 7 days with a decision, 28 percent indicated the decision took 8 to 14 days, and 14 percent report the decision was immediate. In conclusion, Lovelace is able to reach a quick decision on a potential affiliation.

The physicians who did not accept a job offer perceive that the recruitment process was effective in

- providing adequate information in the first recruiting contact,
- enabling candidates to speak with the department chairperson in a reasonable amount of time during the recruitment process,
- providing adequate information on practice opportunities, and
- having the department chairperson contact the candidate about a final decision.

Lovelace's physician recruitment process also appears to deliver in a timely manner a recruitment packet prior to an on-site visit, to provide adequate information on salary and benefits, and to provide an indication at the end of the interview as to when a final decision will be made. In sum, there are only minor differences between response levels in Tables 11–1 and 11–2. This suggests that variations in Lovelace's recruitment process are not the primary determining factor relative to whether a physician is employed or not at Lovelace. This conclusion is further supported by the fact that 83 percent (compared with 88 percent in Table 11–1) of the physicians who did not accept the job offer by Lovelace rate the overall coordination of recruitment as good or excellent.

Practice ratings by physicians employed at Lovelace

Table 11–3 reports ratings of the practice attributes at Lovelace. The physicians employed by Lovelace were asked to rate the attributes' importance to physicians (1=not important; 5=extremely important) and to rate the attributes as present at Lovelace (1=very poor; 5=excellent). The results indicate that (on aver-

Table 11–2

Perception of issues surrounding the recruitment process by physicians declining employment*

Specialty	%	Perceptions of recruitment process	Yes %	No %	No response %
Family practice	29	Was adequate information provided by the Lovelace representative who made the first recruiting contact?	93	7	0
Internal medicine	17				
Other	17				
Pediatrics	10	Were you able to speak with the department chairperson within a reasonable amount of time?	97	3	0
Other medical specialty	10				
Other surgical specialty	10				
Obstetrics-gynecology	7	Did you receive a recruitment packet prior to your on-site interview?	72	24	3
Urgent care	0				
Means of learning about the Lovelace Medical Center		Were all decision makers (spouse, significant other, children) invited to accompany you on the interview?	62	34	3
Colleague	41	During the on-site interview were you provided adequate information on the practice opportunities?	100	0	0
Other	29				
Professional journal	17				
Recruitment firm	10	During the on-site interview were you provided adequate information on salary and benefits?	83	14	3
Professional meeting	3				
Residency program	0				
Lovelace representative who made first recruiting contact		At the completion of your interview were you provided adequate information on when Lovelace would contact you about a final decision?	79	17	3
Lovelace physician	35	Was the contact on a final decision made by the department chairperson?	93	4	3
Lovelace department chairperson	24				
Lovelace administrator	14				
Lovelace division chairperson	14				
Physician recruitment firm	10				
Other	3				
At completion of the interview, how many days did it take until Lovelace contacted you with the final decision?		**How do you rate the overall coordination of the physician recruitment process at Lovelace?%**			
1–7 days	48	Good	52		
8–14 days	28	Excellent	31		
Immediate	14	Fair	10		
2–4 weeks	7	Very poor	3		
More than 4 weeks	3	Poor	4		
		No response	0		

*n=29

Table 11–3

Practice attribute ratings by physicians employed at Lovelace*

Practice attribute	$\bar{X}$†	S.D.	% Rating attribute as very or extremely important to them as physicians
Quality of care provided	4.66	0.58	95
Amount of clinical time spent on patients	4.19	0.68	84
Number of hours worked per week	4.18	0.78	80
Interaction with colleagues	4.14	0.69	80
Professional autonomy	4.00	0.79	77
Salary	4.01	0.77	76
Geographic location	4.04	0.84	75
Call schedule	4.08	0.87	74
Nonsalary fringe benefits	3.87	0.75	71
Input into managerial decisions	3.70	0.87	55
Amount of administrative time	3.07	1.04	32

Practice attribute	$\bar{X}$‡	S.D.	% Rating practice conditions at Lovelace as good or excellent relative to attribute
Geographic location	4.25	0.81	79
Quality of care provided	3.97	0.73	74
Nonsalary fringe benefits	3.92	0.86	74
Number of hours worked per week	3.93	0.78	71
Call schedule	3.86	0.92	70
Interaction with colleagues	3.83	0.81	66
Amount of clinical time	3.76	0.78	62
Professional autonomy	3.68	0.75	59
Salary	3.43	0.85	51
Amount of administrative time	2.97	0.90	28
Input into managerial decisions	2.65	0.88	18

*n=76

†Scaling: 1=not important; 5=extremely important

‡Scaling: 1=very poor; 5=excellent

age) all of the practice attributes were rated as at least fairly important (i.e., $\bar{X}$=3.00) to the physicians. Furthermore, 72.7 percent (i.e., 8 out of 11) of the practice attributes are rated as very important by the physicians. The most important practice attributes are quality of care ($\bar{X}$=4.66), amount of clinical time spent on patients per week ($\bar{X}$=4.19), number of hours worked per week ($\bar{X}$=4.18), and interaction with colleagues ($\bar{X}$=4.14). At least 80 percent of the physicians retained by Lovelace rate these attributes as very or extremely important.

Professional autonomy ($\bar{X}$=4.00), salary ($\bar{X}$=4.01), geographic location ($\bar{X}$=4.04), and call schedule

($\bar{X}$=4.08) are also important practice attributes listed by the physicians. At least 74 percent of the respondents indicate that these attributes are very or extremely important. Less important are nonsalary fringe benefits and input into managerial decisions. However, more than half of the physicians still view these attributes as fairly important on average. Only the amount of administrative time is rated relatively low by the physicians hired at Lovelace. Thirty-two percent view this as an important practice attribute.

The physicians hired by Lovelace were also asked to rate the practice attributes as they apply to Lovelace. Some differences in perspective emerge in this comparison. Only geographic location is rated as good ($\bar{X}$=4.25) relative to Lovelace's practice conditions. The other practice attributes are rated as fair. Quality of care ($\bar{X}$=3.97), nonsalary fringe benefits ($\bar{X}$=3.92), number of hours worked per week ($\bar{X}$=3.93), and call schedule ($\bar{X}$=3.86) are rated as good by at least 70 percent of the physicians. Interaction with colleagues ($\bar{X}$=3.83), amount of clinical time spent with patients ($\bar{X}$=3.76), professional autonomy ($\bar{X}$=3.68), and salary ($\bar{X}$=3.43) are also rated as good at Lovelace by at least half of the physicians. Again, amount of administrative time ($\bar{X}$=2.97) and input into managerial decisions ($\bar{X}$=2.65) are rated low by the physicians.

The overall impression from these findings is that many of the practice attribute factors that are rated as very or extremely important to physicians are, for the most part, present at Lovelace. Lovelace does offer good quality of care, geographic location, nonsalary fringe benefits, number of hours worked per week, call schedule, and interaction with colleagues. It appears that Lovelace could do a better job relative to clinical time spent with patients, professional autonomy, and salary.

Practice ratings by physicians declining employment

Table 11–4 presents ratings of practice attributes by physicians who did not accept the job offer by Lovelace. There are many parallels with the results in Table 11–3. This set of physicians rate quality of care ($\bar{X}$=4.79), geographic location ($\bar{X}$=4.39), interaction with colleagues ($\bar{X}$=4.32), and amount of clinical time spent on patients ($\bar{X}$=4.08) as the most important practice attributes. Nonetheless, all of the other practice attributes are rated as at least fairly important. Salary, input into managerial decisions, professional autonomy, call schedule, nonsalary fringe benefits, and number of hours worked per week are rated as important by almost 60 percent of the respondents. Only the amount of administrative time required by a practice is not consistently rated as important by the physicians.

For the most part, there is substantial consistency between practice attributes rated as important by physicians hired at Lovelace and those who did not accept the job offer by Lovelace. Quality of care, interaction with colleagues, and amount of clinical time spent with patients are the prominent common denominators be-

tween the two groups. The physicians employed by Lovelace do indicate a greater number of very important or extremely important attributes; notably, number of hours worked per week, professional autonomy, salary, geographic location, and call schedule. However, high percentages of the physicians who did not accept the Lovelace job offer also rate these factors as important. The differences in mean scores are not statistically or practically different.

Furthermore, the physicians who did not accept Lovelace's job offer rate Lovelace quite positively on many of the practice attributes. Over 70 percent of these physicians view Lovelace's practice environment as good or excellent on geographic location, number of hours worked per week, quality of care provided, amount of clinical time, nonsalary fringe benefits, and interaction with colleagues. These findings suggest that Lovelace has done a very good job in cultivating an attractive practice setting. Again, there are many favorable comparisons with the evaluations of physicians employed by Lovelace (Table 11–3).

Call schedule, salary, professional autonomy, and input into managerial decisions are rated as good by 55 percent of the physicians who did not accept the job offer at Lovelace. Comparison of these results with Table 11–3 suggests that the physicians employed by Lovelace also believe that the practice attributes could be more fully developed. Input into managerial decisions is the only attribute not rated highly by the two groups of physicians. The overall view of Lovelace's practice setting by physicians who have visited Lovelace and those who ultimately were employed is quite comparable.

In view of the similarities between the response sets, it is appropriate to ask why some physicians decided to join the staff at Lovelace and others did not. The physicians who did not accept Lovelace's job offer were asked to clarify their reasons for their decision. A variety of reasons surfaced (see Exhibit 11–1). Interestingly, many (20 percent) of the physicians discovered that after visiting Lovelace their desire to relocate had changed. This implies that they could not perceive sufficient comparative advantage to undertake a move. Eighteen percent cited inadequate or noncompetitive salary, while 14 percent listed a desire to remain in their present position. These results suggest that on further examination, the physicians remained in their present practices. The

Table 11–4

Practice attribute ratings by physicians declining employment*

Practice attribute	$\bar{X}^\dagger$	S.D.	% Rating attribute as very or extremely important to them as physicians
Quality of care provided	4.79	0.50	93
Geographic location	4.39	0.57	93
Interaction with colleagues	4.32	0.67	86
Amount of clinical time spent on patients	4.08	0.63	76
Salary	3.89	0.63	72
Input into managerial decisions	3.86	0.93	72
Professional autonomy	3.89	0.59	69
Call schedule	3.74	0.94	62
Nonsalary fringe benefits	3.74	0.66	59
Number of hours worked per week	3.71	0.76	59
Amount of administrative time	3.07	0.83	24

Practice attribute	$\bar{X}^\ddagger$	S.D.	% Rating practice conditions at Lovelace as good or excellent relative to attribute
Geographic location	4.32	0.72	83
Number of hours worked per week	4.07	0.60	83
Quality of care provided	4.11	0.69	79
Amount of clinical time	3.96	0.69	79
Nonsalary fringe benefits	4.07	0.72	76
Interaction with colleagues	3.89	0.74	72
Amount of administrative time	3.67	0.68	59
Call schedule	4.00	0.65	55
Salary	3.39	0.92	48
Professional autonomy	3.41	0.84	45
Input into managerial decisions	3.33	0.87	34

*n=29

†Scaling: 1=not important; 5=extremely important

‡Scaling: 1=very poor; 5=excellent

"grass is greener" phenomenon may have been operating in these cases.

Implications

What factors facilitate successful recruiting of medical staff members? Worthwhile answers to this question have surfaced in the course of examining the LHP's efforts to attract and retain physicians. In considering the implications of these findings for other HMOs and providers it should be remembered that Lovelace's experience may not be completely transferable to other settings. Clearly, Lovelace has carefully cultivated an HMO practice setting conducive to

attracting physicians of the highest caliber. The practice opportunities themselves play an important role in recruitment. In short, simply following well-designed recruitment strategies will not always guarantee success. The nature of an organization, personal rewards, practice climate, linkages with teaching and research institutions, location, and other factors affect recruitment success. Lovelace has carefully attended to these practice attributes, which, in turn, has reinforced recruitment efforts.

Lovelace's experience suggests that when recruiting, health care organizations should consider several strategies. First, potential physician candidates are likely to learn about an opportunity from colleagues,

Exhibit 11–1 Primary Reasons for Not Accepting a Position at Lovelace

	%
No response given by physician.	28
Discrepancy between Lovelace position and desired position.	20
Inadequate, noncompetitive salary.	18
Wish to remain in present position.	14
Personal (family, location).	10
Another opportunity was better.	10

professional journals, and other sources, but less often from professional recruiters (Tables 11–1 and 11–2). For difficult-to-recruit positions it may be essential to tap the professional network of the medical staff. For example, if an organization has trouble attracting a surgical specialty, it may be useful for all medical staff members to write several colleagues alerting them to the position. Word-of-mouth advertising seems to work in the case of Lovelace. It may work for other organizations if the professional network is exercised.

Second, Lovelace's experience suggests that candidates should be contacted with a final decision within 14 days (Tables 11–1 and 11–2). Exceptions to this strategy may arise where a clinical department is sensitive to a particular personality or where physician availability allows some slack in the hiring decision. Nonetheless, it appears that organizations should establish a recruitment process that can deliver a decision within two weeks. This approach capitalizes on the strengths of the visit and reinforces the clarity of thinking by the provider relative to potential candidates and the requirements of the position.

Third, Lovelace has found that an effective recruitment process is highly capable of communicating critical information (Tables 11–1 and 11–2). Specific ingredients of this process include the following:

- providing adequate information during the first recruiting contact,
- communicating between the clinical department chairperson and candidate within a reasonable amount of time,
- providing a recruitment packet before the on-site interview,
- communicating adequate information on practice opportunities during the interview,
- clarifying specifics regarding salary and benefits, and
- indicating when a final decision will be made.

It is unlikely that these elements of effective recruiting are germane solely to Lovelace. Other organizations should consider incorporating these ingredients in their recruiting process if they wish to establish a basis from which successful recruiting can evolve.

Finally, Lovelace has discovered that some practice attributes are more important to physicians than others (Tables 11–3 and 11–4). Reputation for quality care, ability to spend time in delivering patient care, and collegial interaction appear to be the most important practice attributes to physicians. In order to achieve successful physician recruitment, it is necessary to cultivate those attributes. This may not be an easy task because quality care reputation and collegial interaction are professional issues that seldom are developed overnight. However, emphasis on visible organizational commitment to quality and team-building efforts may grow the sort of climate that supports recruitment.

In the case of Lovelace, it rates fairly well on these key practice attributes. Nonetheless, like most organizations, progress can still be made. Several strategies are already being implemented to improve the prospects of delivering a better practice environment relative to collegial interaction and patient care delivery. Meanwhile, Lovelace can capitalize on its other distinctive features such as geographic location, practice hours required per week, nonsalary fringe benefits, and call schedule. These attributes have provided Lovelace a strong measure of success in physician recruitment.

•   •   •

Health care organizations that face the challenge of recruiting physicians can reconfigure their strategies in view of the experiences described for Lovelace. At the heart of successful recruitment is laying a foundation of basics—a well-structured and informative process. Organizations should also contemplate means to tap the collegial and professional network of their physicians. Central in this effort is continual questioning of whether the existing medical staff members have contributed to the recruitment process by spreading the word in the professional and collegial grapevine. Furthermore, organizations should build on their distinctive qualities and assets in attracting candidates. Special attention can be focused on the collegial environment, quality of care, and emphasis on medical care delivery. With these ingredients in mind, the prognosis for successful recruiting improves.

REFERENCES

1. Grayson, M.A. "Physician Recruitment Takes Center Stage." *Hospitals* 63, no. 7 (1989): 30–34.
2. Korcok, M. "U.S. Doctors Flocking to Salaried Employment." *CMAJ* 136, no. 1 (1987): 73–75.
3. Crandall, L.A., Dwyer, J.W., and Duncan, R.P. "Recruitment and Retention of Rural Physicians: Issues for the 1990s." *Journal of Rural Health* 6, no. 1 (1990): 19–37.
4. Jacobs, M.O., and Mott, P.D. "Physician Characteristics and Training Emphasis Considered Desirable by Leaders of HMOs." *Journal of Medical Education* 62, no. 9(1987):725–31.
5. Thomas, M.C. "Groups Are Still Bidding Top Dollar for the Doctors They Want." *Medical Economist* 67, no. 4 (1990): 52–60.
6. Steinwachs, D.M., et al. "A Comparison of the Requirements for Primary Care Physicians in HMOs with Projections Made by the GMENAC." *New England Journal of Medicine* 314, no. 4 (1986): 217–22.
7. Powills, S. "Physicians Join HMOs Reluctantly." *Hospitals* 61, no. 19 (1987): 100.
8. Taylor, H., and Kagay, M. "The HMO Report Card: A Closer Look." *Health Affairs* 5, no. 1 (1986): 81–89.
9. Zoler, M.L. "Salaried Physicians: Decent Money, Great Call Schedule, But. . . ." *Medical World News* 29, no. 2 (1988): 34–36, 39.
10. Shouldice, R.G., "Characteristics of Physicians in HMOs." *Medical Group Management* 36, no. 4 (1989): 6, 9.
11. Koska, M.T. "Physician Recruiting 101: Avoid the Classic Mistakes." *Hospitals* 64 (1990): 46–49.
12. Martinsons, J.N. "What's the Top MD Recruitment Incentive?" *Hospitals* 62, no. 3 (1988): 69.
13. Muller, A., and Bledsoe, P. "Physicians' Ranking of Hospital Attributes: A Comparison by Use Group." *Health Care Management Review* 14, no. 3 (1989): 77–84.
14. Ripley, R.A., and Nichols, R. "Hiring Winners." *Medical Group Management* 34, no. 1 (1987): 45–47.
15. Taylor, M.W. "The Interviewing Process." *Medical Group Management* 34, no. 2 (1987): 40–44.
16. Fink, R. "HMOs and Physician Recruiting: A Survey of Problems and Methods Among Group Practice Plans." *Public Health Reports* 96, no. 6 (1981): 568–73.
17. Hay Group Consulting. *Survey of Physician Attitudes.* Chicago, Ill.: Hay Group Consulting, 1991.
18. Schulz, R., et al. "Physician Adaptation to Health Maintenance Organizations and Implications for Management." *Health Services Research* 25, no. 1 (1990): 43–64.
19. McKinlay, J.B., and Stoeckle, J.D. "Corporatization and the Social Transformation of Doctoring." *International Journal of Health Services* 18, no. 2 (1988): 191–205.

12

Physician Responses to a Managed Environment: A Perceptual Paradox

Gloria J. Deckard

Whether one views the future of health care to be "*managed* competition" or "managed *competition*," increased management of physicians is inevitable. Dictates established by insurers, government regulatory bodies, and organized practice settings are altering the practice of medicine. An escalation of administrative requirements and the concomitant erosion of professional autonomy have been coupled with growing physician frustration and dissatisfaction with the general practice of medicine.[1-4] A recent survey[5] found that most physicians were dissatisfied with their autonomy or loss of control over clinical decision making. Seventy-six percent of practicing internists agreed that restrictions imposed by regulations make it increasingly difficult to practice good medicine, and fewer than one half (43%) responded positively concerning the future of medicine.[6]

Perceived infringements on individual professional autonomy generally are intensified when physicians affiliate with an organized delivery system, particularly HMOs.[7-9] Hence, one might expect an amplification of dissatisfactions with the practice of medicine for physicians affiliated with an HMO. This supposition, however, does not necessarily hold true. While negative expectations of practice within managed care environments prevail, the experience of practice in organized settings can counter negative expectations. Results from various studies suggest that managed care affiliation does not have a uniformly negative effect on physician satisfaction.[10-12]

Physician satisfaction is important for both policy and administrative purposes. Physician satisfaction can impact outcomes and perceived quality of patient care as well as patient satisfaction.[13-15] The practice of medicine and management of practice in organized settings encompass numerous factors. While autonomy is perhaps the most critical influence, other aspects of medical practice also contribute to overall physician satisfaction.[16-18] Additional factors important in both general and organized practice settings include income, paperwork and administrative burdens, patient relationships, time with patients, hours worked, resources, professional relationships, control, participation, and quality.[19-23]

Managers need to understand and respond to physician perceptions of individual practice-related factors, as well as their overall satisfaction. Perceptions, however, do not always coincide with objective experience. Perceptions also should be examined in relation to more directed and/or objective data to determine consistency. If perceptual and objective data provide dissimilar information, managerial responses will need to target this disparity.

Methods

Subjects and procedure

The study sample included 1,000 physicians randomly selected from the 15,000 member Florida Medical Association (FMA). The sample received a cover letter from the FMA and a pencil-and-paper survey. A follow-up letter was sent to all physicians in the sample one month later to increase the overall response rate.

Measures

The survey was composed of three parts. The first part requested demographic and professional information, including age, sex, race/ethnicity, income, practice location, and specialty, average hours worked per week, and annual income.

The second part obtained physician evaluations regarding the general practice of medicine and specific aspects of practice, including current and future earnings, the amount of time spent with patients, average hours worked per week, amount of paperwork required,

Health Care Manage Rev 1995; 20(1): 40–46

systems for specialty referral, autonomy (the opportunity to practice medicine as one wants), overall quality of medical care one felt able to provide, and overall satisfaction with the medical practice. Physicians currently affiliated with an HMO were asked to complete the third portion of the study, which rated the same aspects of practice named above in relation to their experience with HMOs. In addition, these physicians were asked to evaluate specific HMO procedures and processes, including their input into management decisions, their control over the organization and delivery of services, the way payment level was determined, the utilization review (UR) process, the appeals process for utilization review decisions, and the overall management of the HMO. The evaluative ratings of all of the practice factors were based on a 5-point Likert-type rating scale (1 = poor, 2 = fair, 3 = good, 4 = very good, 5 = excellent). Other questions in this section obtained information on the functions performed for the HMO, perceived relationship between the UR process and quality of patient care, change in earnings, payment coverage and costs of service, perceived cost-effectiveness, and plans to continue affiliation.

Results

Demographic and professional characteristics

A total of 372 physicians responded to the survey, representing a response rate of 37.2%. Of these, 114 (30.6%) reported affiliation with an HMO and completed the third portion of the survey that addressed HMO practice experience.

Table 12–1 provides descriptive measures of the personal and professional characteristics for the total sample and the two subsamples (nonaffiliated and HMO-affiliated). The vast majority of the total respondents were male, white, medical specialists who practiced in an urban area and earned more than $100,000 a year. The average age of the respondents was 49.6 years, and the average hours worked per week was 57.

The two subsamples of physicians (nonaffiliated and HMO-affiliated) were compared across all demographic and professional factors. Only one factor, practice location, displayed a statistically significant difference. Physicians practicing in small towns and rural areas were less likely to report an HMO affiliation.

Group model HMOs were the most frequent type (62.5%) of affiliation. The predominant payment rela-

tionships were discounted fee-for-service (50.9%) and capitation (31.5%). The majority (66%) reported having contracts with more than one HMO, with the average number of affiliations being 2.29. The modal number of affiliations, however, was one (44% of affiliated respondents). For 80% of the HMO-affiliated respondents, the number of HMO patients translated into less than 20% of their patient base, the average percentage reported was 15.9% and the median and mode were both 10%.

Physician evaluative ratings of general and HMO-affiliated practice

Physician ratings of quality, practice autonomy, specialty referral and time with patients for general medical practice received average rating scores corresponding to good or very good (Table 12–2). While overall satisfaction with general practice was rated as good, the encroachment of managed care appears to be reflected in the "fair" ratings for paperwork, future earnings, and average hours worked. Both independent and paired t-test comparisons of general versus HMO-affiliated practice ratings displayed no significant differences in the areas of paperwork and average hours worked. All other aspects of practice, however, displayed statistically significantly lower ratings for HMO-affiliated practice (Table 12–3). Overall satisfaction, as well as the general aspects of practice associated with HMO-affiliation, received only fair ratings.

An examination of the percentage respondents for each scale rating finds 50% of the HMO-affiliated physicians rating overall satisfaction with their HMO practice experience as poor or fair. In contrast, only 26% of the overall satisfaction ratings for general medical practice were reported within these two categorizations. Similarly, nearly 60% of the respondents rated future earnings with HMO-affiliated practice poor or fair, while these values represented only 40% of the responses for general practice. With the exception of quality of care, all aspects of HMO-affiliated practice experience were viewed by nearly 40% to 60% of the respondents in the two lowest categorizations—poor or fair.

Ratings and targeted questions for HMO procedures and processes

HMO specific procedures and policies were rated either poor or fair by the majority of HMO-affiliated

Table 12–1

Demographic and professional characteristics of physician sample

	Total sample $n = 372$	Nonaffiliated subsample $n = 258$	HMO-affiliated subsample $n = 114$
Age			
< 39	21.5	23.0	18.0
40–49	29.2	25.8	36.9
50–59	29.5	30.2	27.9
> 60	19.8	21.0	17.1
Sex			
Male	92.7	91.9	94.7
Female	7.3	8.1	5.3
Ethnicity			
Asian-Pacific Island	7.1	8.7	3.6
Black	.5	.8	
Hispanic	5.5	4.3	8.2
White	86.8	86.2	88.2
Professional categorization			
Primary care	43.0	40.7	48.2
Specialist	57.0	59.3	51.8
Practice location			
Rural	.3	.4	
Small city or town	14.0	17.9	5.3
Suburb	9.2	7.4	13.2
Medium size city	41.5	40.5	43.9
Large city	35.0	33.9	37.7
Average hours worked			
< 40	17.8	18.5	16.4
41–50	20.3	21.7	17.3
51–60	34.3	29.7	44.5
61–70	13.9	14.9	11.8
> 70	13.6	15.3	10.0
Annual income			
< $50,000	3.4	4.5	1.0
$50,000 to $74,999	9.5	10.1	7.8
$75,000 to $99,999	14.3	12.6	18.6
$100,000 to $149,000	24.9	25.5	23.5
$150,000 to $199,000	16.9	15.4	20.6
$200,000 and over	30.9	32.0	28.4

respondents (Table 12–4). The average ratings fall into the fair categorization for all items, with the exception of control over the organization and delivery of services. This vital area of physician concern received an average rating of poor, with 68% of the respondents reporting only poor or fair ratings. Consistent with these ratings, few (11.4%) reported committee or management responsibilities as part of their HMO affiliation. Most physicians (88.4%) reported direct patient care as the sole function of their HMO affiliation.

Conflicts between professional and administrative authority were reported to occur seldom or never by 61% of the HMO-affiliated physicians. Another 26% reported only occasional conflicts. Similarly, 56% reported restrictions on professional autonomy to occur seldom or never, with an additional 19% reporting only occasional restrictions.

The HMO UR process, as well as the appeal process for utilization review decisions, were rated as fair. Though UR is generally considered a resource, as well

Table 12–2

Evaluative ratings of general practice*

Variable	Mean[†]	Percentage rating as[‡]				
		1	2	3	4	5
Current earnings	3.26 ± 1.07	4.4	19.3	36.8	24.5	15.0
Future earnings	2.83 ± 1.10	10.5	29.4	35.5	15.8	8.9
Average hours worked	2.67 ± .99	12.4	29.8	41.0	12.1	4.7
Time with patients	3.31 ± .94	2.2	15.7	41.4	29.6	11.0
Amount of paperwork	2.14 ± 1.01	30.8	36.0	21.9	10.1	1.2
Specialty referral	3.31 ± 1.12	6.7	15.7	33.1	28.6	16.0
Quality of care	4.22 ± .71	0	1.4	12.7	48.6	37.3
Practice autonomy	3.49 ± 1.06	3.2	15.1	29.2	34.1	18.4
Overall satisfaction	3.19 ± 1.08	6.2	20.1	34.1	27.9	11.7

*n = 372
[†]± = Standard deviation
[‡]Scaling: 1 = poor; 2 = fair; 3 = good; 4 = very good; 5 = excellent

as a quality control measure, the majority of the HMO-affiliated physicians (64.4%) perceived the UR process as having no impact on the quality of care. While 18.8% thought the UR process improved the quality of care provided within the HMO practice, a similar percentage (16.8%) indicated that the process reduced quality of care. The majority (56%) did not feel that HMOs are more cost-effective than other types of health delivery systems.

Physicians expressed only fair ratings for the way in which payment level for services was determined. Yet, 80.8% of the respondents reported that the payment covered the costs of serving the HMO patients. In addition, 34% of the HMO-affiliated physicians reported an increase in earnings as a result of their HMO affiliation. Earnings remained approximately the same for 50.9% of the respondents, while 15.9% indicated a decrease in earnings since joining the HMO.

Table 12–3

Evaluative ratings of HMO-affiliated practice*

Variable	Mean[†]	Percentage rating as[‡]				
		1	2	3	4	5
Current earnings	2.56 ± 1.04	18.8	27.1	36.5	15.6	2.1
Future earnings	2.26 ± 1.06	28.7	30.9	29.8	7.4	3.2
Average hours worked	2.60 ± .84	7.9	37.1	44.9	7.9	2.2
Time with patients	2.70 ± .97	10.8	28.9	44.6	10.8	4.8
Amount of paperwork	2.23 ± 1.12	33.7	27.6	23.5	13.3	2.0
Specialty referral	2.62 ± 1.03	19.4	20.4	43.0	15.1	2.2
Quality of care	3.42 ± .93	1.0	14.7	38.2	33.3	12.7
Practice autonomy	2.62 ± 1.14	20.2	25.5	30.9	19.1	4.3
Overall satisfaction	2.42 ± .97	20.2	29.8	39.4	8.7	1.9

*n = 114
[†]± = Standard deviation
[‡]Scaling: 1 = poor; 2 = fair; 3 = good; 4 = very good; 5 = excellent

Table 12–4

Evaluative ratings of HMO specific characteristics*

Variable	Mean[†]	Percentage rating as[‡]				
		1	2	3	4	5
Input	2.12 ± 1.14	39.5	25.0	23.7	7.9	3.9
Control over organization and delivery	1.93 ± 1.07	48.6	20.0	22.9	7.1	1.4
Payment level	2.13 ± .93	27.8	38.1	28.9	3.1	2.1
UR process	2.41 ± .88	14.3	40.0	37.1	7.1	1.4
UR appeal process	2.30 ± 1.00	25.9	29.6	35.2	7.4	1.9
HMO management	2.49 ± .90	11.7	41.6	33.8	11.7	1.3

*$n = 114$

[†]± = Standard deviation

[‡]Scaling: 1 = poor; 2 = fair; 3 = good; 4 = very good; 5 = excellent

Discussion

The changing health care environment places both managers and physicians in a continual process of adaptation. For physicians, affiliation with HMOs may be a reluctant choice deemed necessary to maintain a viable patient base in an increasingly dominant managed-care market.[24,25] The reluctance present in this decision is based, at least in part, on the negative perceptions of HMO practice documented in other studies[26–28] and largely corroborated here. Overall satisfaction with, as well as most aspects of medical practice associated with, HMO affiliation were rated significantly lower than general medical practice. Yet singular directed questions revealed a paradox.

The differences between perceptions, expectations, and experience provide an ambiguous picture. Physicians are concerned about autonomy, yet the majority report few conflicts between professional and administrative authority. Nor do many physicians report frequent restrictions on autonomy. Income concerns are countered by an increase in earnings by some, and maintenance of income by most. The vast majority reported payment covered the cost of providing care. These paradoxical views suggest the need for managers to provide objective information to physicians, which may alleviate concerns and improve perceptual attributions.

The onus is also upon management to demonstrate the effectiveness of UR procedures in both maintaining quality and controlling costs. Previous research found that satisfaction and support of HMOs were strongly linked with the belief that the HMO was cost-effective.[29]

Managers must be responsive to physician perceptions and strive to achieve physician satisfaction. Faced with a paradox between perception and experience, however, requires that managers first address the disparity. Educational efforts should be coupled with increased physician participation in policy and operational decision making. Organizational structures designed to encourage participation provide the opportunity to dispel negative perceptions, and lead to improved, cooperative relationships between physicians and management.

REFERENCES

1. Astrachan, J., and Astrachan, B. "Medical Practice in Organized Settings." *Archives of Internal Medicine* 149 (1988): 1509–13.
2. Relman, A. "The Changing Climate of Medical Practice: Introduction." *New England Journal of Medicine* 316, no. 6 (1987): 333–4.
3. Berrien, R. "What Future for Primary Care Private Practice?" *New England Journal of Medicine* 316, no. 6 (1987): 334–7.
4. Lindquist, J. "Letter-to-Editor." *New England Journal of Medicine* 317, no. 7 (1987): 456.
5. Lewis, C., et al. "How Satisfying is the Practice of Internal Medicine?" *Annals of Internal Medicine* 114 (1991): 1–5.
6. Hershey, C., McAlloon, M., and Bertram, D. "The New Medical Practice Environment: Internists' View of the Future." *Archives of Internal Medicine* 149 (1989): 1745–9.
7. Murray, J. "Physician Satisfaction with Capitation Patients in an Academic Family Medicine Clinic." *The Journal of Family Practice* 27, no. 1 (1988): 108–13.

8. Weisman, C., and Nathanson, C. "Professional Satisfaction and Client Outcomes: A Comparative Organizational Analysis." *Medical Care* 23, no. 10 (1985): 1179–92.

9. Mechanic, D. "The Organization of Medical Practice and Practice Orientations Among Physicians in Prepaid and Nonprepaid Primary Care Settings." *Medical Care* 13, no. 3 (1975): 189–204.

10. Topping, S., and Fottler, M. "Improved Stakeholder Management: The Key to Revitalizing the HMO Movement?" *Medical Care Review* 47, no. 3 (1990): 365–93.

11. Baker, L., and Cantor, J. "Physician Satisfaction Under Managed Care." *Health Affairs, Supplement* (1988): 258–70.

12. Schulz, R., Girard, C., and Scheckler, W. "Physician Satisfaction in a Managed Care Environment." Paper presented at the Annual Meeting of the Academy of Management, Miami, Fla., August, 1991.

13. Kravitz, R., Linn, L., and Shapiro, M. "Physician Satisfaction Under the Ontario Health Insurance Plan." *Medical Care* 28, no. 6 (1990): 502–12.

14. Bertram, D., et al. "A Measure of Physician Mental Work Load in Internal Medicine Ambulatory Care Clinics." *Medical Care* 28, no. 5 (1990): 458–67.

15. McCue, J. "The Effects of Stress on Physicians and Their Medical Practice." *New England Journal of Medicine* 306 (1982): 458–63.

16. Breslau, N., Novack, A., and Wolf, G. "Work Settings and Job Satisfaction: A Study of Primary Care Physicians and Paramedical Personnel." *Medical Care* 16, no. 10 (1978): 850–62.

17. Cashman, S., et al. "Physician Satisfaction in a Major Chain of Investor-Owned Walk-in Centers." *Health Care Management Review* 15, no. 3 (1990): 47–57.

18. Freeborn, D. "Physician Satisfaction in a Prepaid Group Practice HMO." *The Group Health Journal* (Spring, 1985): 3–12.

19. Barr, J., and Steinberg, M. "Professional Participation in Organizational Decision Making: Physicians in HMOs." *Journal of Community Health* 8, no. 3 (1983): 160–73.

20. Fisher, N., Smith, H., and Pasternak, D. "Critical Factors in Recruiting Health Maintenance Organization Physicians." *Health Care Management Review* 18, no. 1 (1993): 51–61.

21. Lewis, C., et al. "How Satisfying is the Practice of Internal Medicine?" *Annals of Internal Medicine* 114 (1991): 1–5.

22. Lichenstein, R. "Measuring the Job Satisfaction of Physicians in Organized Settings." *Medical Care* 22, no. 1 (1984): 56–68.

23. Mawardi, B.H. "Satisfaction and Dissatisfaction and Causes of Stress in Medical Practice." *Journal of the American Medical Association* 241, no. 14 (1979): 1483–6.

24. Powills, S. "Physicians Join HMOs Reluctantly." *Hospitals* (October 5, 1987): 100.

25. Topping, S., and Fottler, M. "Improved Stakeholder Management: The Key to Revitalizing the HMO Movement?" *Medical Care Review* 47, no. 3 (1990): 365–93.

26. Baker, L., and Cantor, J. "Physician Satisfaction Under Managed Care." *Health Affairs, Supplement* (1988): 258–70.

27. Schulz, R., Girard, C., and Scheckler, W. "Physician Satisfaction in a Managed Care Environment." Paper presented at the Annual Meeting of the Academy of Management, Miami, Fla., August, 1991.

28. Schulz, R., Girard, C., and Scheckler, W. "Physician Satisfaction in a Managed Care Environment." Paper presented at the Annual Meeting of the Academy of Management, Miami, Fla., August, 1991.

29. Schulz, R., et al. "Physician Adaptation to Health Maintenance Organizations and Implications for Management." *Health Services Research* 25, no. 1 (1990): 43–64.

13

Capitated Hospital Contracts: The Empty Beds versus Filled Beds Controversy

Steven A. Finkler

Recently, the importance of keeping hospital beds empty under capitated arrangements has been pointed out. Although everyone would agree that there is no reason to hospitalize an individual who does not need hospital care, we would not all necessarily agree on the implications of managed care contracts.

This article contends that the financial incentives of fundamental cost accounting dictate keeping beds filled, not empty, under capitated arrangements. It argues that hospitals that equate the philosophy of keeping patients healthy and out of the hospital with the philosophy of keeping beds empty are doomed to failure.

A Base Case Scenario

To understand the financial incentives that exist under capitation, we will start with a base case situation and then examine what happens under alternative hospital payment or reimbursement approaches. Assume the following information:

Fixed costs for a hospital	$1,000,000
Original number of patients per year	1,000
Original average length of stay	10
Hospital capacity inpatient days (i.e., hospital is full)	10,000
Variable cost per patient day	$200
Original per diem reimbursement rate	$280
Weighted average diagnostic-related group (DRG) rate	$2,800

These base data will be used throughout this article.

Health Care Manage Rev 1995; 20(3): 88–91
© 1995 Aspen Publishers, Inc.

Per Diem Environment

Historically, per diem reimbursement has been a common approach in some states. For example, until just a few years ago, care for most hospital inpatients in New York was paid for on a per diem basis. Using the base case scenario information, we can calculate the expected revenues, costs, and profits for a hospital under that form of reimbursement.

Revenue	
1,000 patients × 10-day stay × $280/day	$2,800,000
Expenses	
Fixed cost	$1,000,000
Variable cost $200/day × 1,000 patients × 10 days/patient	2,000,000
Total expenses	$3,000,000
Loss	$(200,000)

Under this simple per diem approach to reimbursement, the hospital in our base case scenario will lose $200,000.

What if the hospital attempts to become more efficient by lowering average length of stay by 10 percent? How will that alter its revenues and expenses?

Revenue	
1,000 patients × *9-day stay* × $280/day	$2,520,000
Expenses	
Fixed cost	$1,000,000
Variable cost $200/day × 1,000 patients × *9 days*/patient	1,800,000
Total expenses	$2,800,000
Loss	$(280,000)

What impact did improved efficiency have on the hospital? The loss got greater rather than smaller.

Why? Although revenue declined in direct proportion to reduced patient days, expenses did not. Variable costs declined, but fixed costs did not. This fundamental behavior of costs should indicate the desirability of increasing volume up to capacity. Revenues generally will rise faster than costs when volume increases and fall faster than costs when volume decreases. Under a per diem reimbursement approach, volume is measured in terms of patient days, and more patient days are desirable.

DRG Environment

Most hospitals currently have at least some of their inpatients paid on a DRG basis. What are the revenues and expenses for our base case scenario under a DRG payment system?

Revenue	
1,000 patients × $2,800/discharge	$2,800,000
Expenses	
Fixed cost	$1,000,000
Variable cost	
$200/day × 1,000 patients	
× 10 days/patient	2,000,000
Total expenses	$3,000,000
Loss	$(200,000)

Note that the loss is the same as the initial per diem result in the example.

Suppose that under a DRG payment system, the hospital lowers length of stay by 10 percent? In the per diem example, we found that such an approach would increase the loss.

Revenue	
1,000 patients × $2,800/day	$2,800,000
Expenses	
Fixed cost	$1,000,000
Variable cost	
$200/day × 1,000 patients	
× 9 days/patient	1,800,000
Total expenses	$2,800,000
Loss	$0

Now the loss has been completely eliminated.

There is clearly an incentive to shorten length of stay under a DRG payment system. Revenues did not change as length of stay declined, nor did fixed costs.

However, variable costs were reduced as the length of stay declined. With the reduced length of stay, the hospital is no longer full. It has some empty beds. Would one conclude that we want to reduce length of stay and keep beds empty under a DRG payment arrangement? That is unlikely, as the following example demonstrates.

Suppose the hospital fills some of the newly empty beds with more patients. What if it adds 100 patients?

Revenue	
1,100 patients × $2,800/discharge	$3,080,000
Expenses	
Fixed cost	$1,000,000
Variable cost	
$200/day × *1,100 patients*	
× 9 days	1,980,000
Total expenses	$2,980,000
Profit	$100,000

Now the hospital is earning a profit on those newly emptied beds. Under a DRG payment approach, there is clearly an incentive to keep the hospital full, albeit with patients that have a shorter length of stay. Note that because hospitals still want to be full, ultimately fewer hospitals will be needed. Therefore, a reduction in the number of short-term acute care hospitals is likely under a DRG payment system. In fact, during the past 10 years, there has been significant consolidation and a reduction in the number of hospitals.

Managed Care and Capitation

Are the same set of incentives likely to hold in a capitated environment? Suppose all patients come from HMOs and that the hospital is paid on a totally capitated basis. This is the scenario under which many have said that a hospital must learn to keep patients healthy and beds empty: The fewer inpatients the better, once all of the payments are capitated. The following examples will show the fallacy of that argument.

Suppose there are 1,100 inpatients with an average length of stay of 9 days. Suppose further:

Total population in area	1,000,000
Lives covered by arrangements with managed care providers	50,000
Per member per month (PMPM) rate	$4.50

The hospital will be paid $4.50 per covered life per month for inpatient services.

Revenue
50,000 members × $4.50 PMPM	
× 12 months	$2,700,000

Expenses
Fixed cost	$1,000,000
Variable cost	
$200/day × 1,100 discharges	
× 9 days	1,980,000
Total expenses	$2,980,000
Loss	$(280,000)

The hospital is operating relatively efficiently. It has reduced length of stay from 10 days to 9 days, and it is utilizing its facility (spreading its fixed cost) by treating 1,100 instead of 1,000 patients. However, the managed care company, perhaps an HMO, has negotiated a low price. Under the current arrangement, the hospital has a loss. This loss gives the hospital an incentive to try to achieve even greater efficiency. Suppose the average length of stay is reduced to eight days.

Revenue
50,000 members × $4.50 PMPM	
× 12 months	$2,700,000

Expenses
Fixed cost	$1,000,000
Variable cost	
$200/day × 1,100 discharges	
× *8 days*	1,760,000
Total expenses	$2,760,000
Loss	$(60,000)

The reduced length of stay has helped, but the hospital is still losing money.

The HMO works to find ways to keep the members healthier, reducing the number of people needing inpatient hospitalization to 1,050:

Revenue
50,000 members × $4.50 PMPM	
× 12 months	$2,700,000

Expenses
Fixed cost	$1,000,000
Variable cost	
$200/day × *1,050 patients*	
× 8 days	1,680,000
Total expenses	$2,680,000
Profit	$20,000

The hospital is now earning a profit. However, it has capacity for 10,000 patient days but is generating only 8,400 (1,050 x 8). It has 1,600 empty bed days. Does it want to keep those beds empty?

What if those beds are filled with patients who are currently part of the hospital's 50,000 covered lives? How much do costs go up per patient? For each extra patient, there will be $200 of variable cost per day for 8 days or an incremental cost of $1,600 per patient. How much does revenue go up per patient? Because payment is on a capitated basis, there is no revenue increase. This is the source of the idea that hospitals want to keep their beds empty under capitation.

However, what if the hospital *covers more lives*? Suppose it makes an additional arrangement with another HMO and covers an additional 9,000 lives. This is an 18 percent increase from the previous 50,000 lives covered. Assume that the 1,050 patients treated will increase by 18 percent to 1,239.

Revenue
59,000 members × $4.50 PMPM	
× 12 months	$3,186,000

Expenses
Fixed cost	$1,000,000
Variable cost	
$200/day × 1,239 patients	
× 8 days	1,982,400
Total expenses	$2,982,400
Profit	$203,600

Profits have increased substantially. Why did the profits increase? Didn't both revenue and cost rise by 18 percent? No! Revenue rose by 18 percent and variable costs rose by 18 percent, but fixed costs did not rise at all.

Revenue-generating volume increases will generally increase profits unless all costs are variable. Volume decreases that reduce revenues will generally result in reduced profits or increased losses unless all costs are variable.

Certainly, one can argue that inpatient hospitalization should be minimized for any fixed number of covered lives. Keeping members healthy and out of the hospital may well make sense. However, that does not translate into keeping a hospital empty under capitation. Full hospitals spread fixed costs over a broad number of patients, minimizing the cost of treating each one. If capitation reduces the number of admissions, this is not likely to result in many hospitals operating at low volumes. It is more likely to result in further reduction in the number of hospitals. Managers who fail to note this key point place their hospitals at risk of closure.

Extending the Case to Physicians

A similar caution should be extended to physicians. At one time the economics of medical care indicated that physician supply increases were accompanied by price increases. Studies had shown that as more surgeons moved into an area, both the quantity of and price for surgery increased. This, of course, is contrary to the normal functioning of supply and demand, which dictates that as supply increases, prices fall. Quite simply, supply and demand rules did not function normally in the marketplace for physician services.

Managed care is dramatically changing that. As HMOs control utilization, especially of specialist services, the wise physician response cannot be to increase price in response to the decrease in demand. The concept of pricing physician services to attain an expected "target income" no longer holds in the new environment. Managed care will assure that an excess of surgeons does not simply increase the number of surgeries. Nor will it allow for price increases.

In such an environment, physicians will need to keep a large number of patients to maintain an income. Just as hospitals will desire to cover more and more lives, and stay full, physicians will need to do the same. Just as some hospitals will inevitably close, some physicians will wind up leaving the profession. The last to realize this are the most at risk.

14

Economic Credentialing Moves from the Hospital to Managed Care

John D. Blum

In the early 1990s, a telling and controversial issue emerged in the world of hospital medical staff relations: economic credentialing. While credentialing has been the focal point of numerous hospital-physician disputes, the process was by and large controlled by the medical staff. The concept of evaluating physicians for appointment, reappointment, and privilege delineation with financial criteria shifts the focus of credentialing away from quality and, in turn, increases the involvement of hospital administration in the process. In many ways the controversy over economic credentialing was a harbinger of changes in physician evaluation that would be incorporated into managed care. This first article examines economic credentialing in the hospital context and then attempts to explore the implications of this process in the current medical practice environment.

Background

Definitions

The American Medical Association (AMA) has defined economic credentialing as "the use of economic criteria unrelated to quality of care or professional competency in determining an individual's qualifications for initial or continuing medical staff membership or privileges."[1]

The definition adopted by the AMA was originally developed by the California Medical Association (CMA). In 1990 CMA conducted a study of the use of economic criteria in hospital credentialing.[2] The California study distinguished among three types of physician evaluation criteria: those dealing with cost, quality, and a combination of the two factors. According to CMA, factors that were strictly linked to cost should not be part of physician evaluation in credentialing. On the

other hand, elements such as length of stay, improper use of hospital resources, and intensive care unit days were identified among a list of other factors that combined cost and quality, and could be viewed as relevant to credentialing. Also included in the orbit of economic credentialing is the practice of exclusive contracting, which has been characterized as a vehicle hospital administrations have used to circumvent medical staff decision making.[1]

While there are considerable bottom-line pressures on hospitals, it is not likely that credentialing will be based strictly on financial considerations, as envisioned by the AMA definition. Before a hospital would remove someone from a medical staff as a result of cost considerations, extensive educational interventions would likely be tried. Also, it seems difficult to identify factors that are pure cost measures, devoid from quality. In the current environment of medical practice, business issues have a direct bearing on institutional efficiency, and as such, can be seen as having quality implications. Certainly motivating factors for entering into exclusive contracts are business related, but departmental efficiency bears directly on the quality of patient care. In the future, institutions that base credentialing and physician contracting strictly on financial measures may miss the next wave of marketing, the ability to distinguish oneself on the basis of quality.

While becoming embroiled in definitional debates often gets into pointless exercises in semantics, organized medicine's definition of economic credentialing is not the only way to look at this concept. It can also be viewed as part of the broader trend in health services research that has shifted the focus of practice evaluation to a consideration of variability in performance and outcome. Economic credentialing is a way of assessing clinical practice variation from an economic vantage point. It is not a stand-alone process, but a part of an overall performance evaluation program. With current

J Health Care Financ 1995; 22(1): 60–71

information technology, physician practice can be isolated in ways that highlight clinical and financial measures, and this information, in turn, can be incorporated into practitioner profiles that can be used in credentialing, contracting, and marketing.

Practices in the field

Even at the height of the economic credentialing controversy, there was little evidence to demonstrate a widespread use of this practice in many hospitals. Only one small Maryland hospital system implemented a formal economic credentialing program, which is based on the use of evaluation screens and is supported by an extensive counseling program prior to actual removal from the medical staff.[3]

More typically, hospitals have developed evaluation methodologies, spurred by accreditation and business concerns, that could act as the foundation of an economic credentialing program. For example, many hospitals have adopted physician profiling systems that allow assessment of individual performance over a given period of time. In addition to clinical information, physician profiles can highlight economic performance measures, and profiles can be effective assessment tools for credentialing purposes.[4] Also, hospitals have incorporated economic assessments that occur in established areas, such as utilization review and quality assurance, into staffing and privileging determinations.

Studies have demonstrated that the majority of hospitals have entered into exclusive contract arrangements, particularly in the institutionally based specialty areas.[5] Exclusive contracting has a strong business motivation attached to it, as institutions make decisions to use only certain practitioners with the goal of making departmental operations more efficient. A secondary form of economic credentialing can be seen in medical staff development plans that base recruitment planning on the economic viability of certain practice areas, and as such affect appointments.

The Legal and Political Battle Over Economic Credentialing

Legal battles

The controversy surrounding economic credentialing was waged on two fronts, one legal and the other political. The legal dispute over economic credential-

ing occurred within the context of one of the most frequently litigated areas of hospital law: physician staffing. In addition, there is a large body of state legislation dealing with hospital medical staff credentialing, as well as the federal Health Care Quality Improvement Act and the Joint Commission on Accreditation of Health Care Organizations' (Joint Commission's) accreditation criteria.[6] Those opposing economic credentialing drew on this extensive body of law and constructed arguments that this new evaluation process violated the independence of the self-governing medical staff. Under state law, as well as Joint Commission accreditation, the medical staff has a delegated responsibility for credentialing. Opponents argued that if economic factors are used in credentialing, the medical staff must make such a decision, not a hospital board.

The same body of law referenced above can be read to support the conclusion that economic credentialing is a legitimate process that can be entered into by a hospital board. Review of hospital law leads to an irrefutable conclusion that the board has the final say in credentialing matters, even if the process is delegated to the medical staff. It is telling that when credentialing goes astray, the hospital corporation and its trustees bear the liability, not the medical staff. As the final arbiter of credentialing, state laws provide the board with adequate discretion to adopt reasonable criteria that would include economic measures. Beyond that, it can be argued that the board, as the institution's fiscal fiduciary, has an affirmative responsibility to take action against a physician, or group of physicians, whose practices are adversely affecting a hospital's bottom line.

To date there has been only one litigated case of economic credentialing, Rosenblum v. Tallahassee Memorial Regional Hospital.[7] In Rosenblum, the plaintiff challenged a Florida hospital board decision to deny him open-heart surgical privileges because of a perceived economic conflict of interest. The Tallahassee board was concerned that Rosenblum, who had a contract to run a competing hospital's open-heart program, would refer patients from Memorial Hospital to the competitor. In refuting Rosenblum's challenge, the court was influenced by the fact that the plaintiff did not have privileges at Memorial, and thus had no property interest adversely affected nor any contractual claim to a hearing. The judge felt that the

Florida law was broad enough to allow boards to consider reasonable factors in credentialing, and that economic issues fell under the trustees' discretion.

While Rosenblum has to be viewed narrowly because it is a single lower court opinion, it does seem that most courts, if they follow state hospital law, would reach a similar conclusion. Many more cases have been litigated concerning the validity of exclusive contracts, and by and large these agreements have been upheld. Problems can arise in the situation where the continuation of an exclusive physician deal and staff privileges are not linked.[5]

Other legal challenges that have been raised against economic credentialing involve antitrust and Medicare fraud and abuse violations. Clearly, scenarios can be constructed in which the improper use of economic criteria could become a restraint of trade, but in today's environment, operational efficiency concerns would provide a strong defense. As far as fraud and abuse is concerned, it is unlikely that a hospital would be reckless enough to develop a physician admission quota system linked to credentialing. It is more likely that a hospital would consider admission patterns as part of a broader practitioner staffing evaluation.

Politics

Due to the transitory nature of the hospital economic credentialing issue, the legal issues have never been played out fully. The battles over economic credentialing have been waged largely in the arena of medical politics rather than the courts. While the issue is partly rooted in law, ultimately economic credentialing raises a political question about who will control medical staff appointments, reappointments, and privilege delineation. Organized medicine opposes the introduction of economic measures into credentialing in large part because that movement was spurred by hospital management and trustees, not physicians. The issue is thus one that ultimately centers on control, and the fight is over who is to retain the dominant voice in physician evaluation.

As noted, the AMA took the lead in defining and opposing economic credentialing nationally. On the state level a number of medical societies adopted positions opposing economic credentialing and proposed legislation outlawing the practice. In California, a political dispute over economic credentialing between organized medicine and the hospital community resulted in the establishment of a medical staff arbitration program.[8] Only one state, Illinois, actually passed legislation that put some limits on economic credentialing.[9]

Sparked by an individual case, the Illinois State Medical Society embarked on a two-year process to legislatively restrict economic credentialing. The medical society argued that economic credentialing would adversely affect consumers in that physicians with high indigent or Medicaid patient loads would be excluded from medical staffs. With no evidence demonstrating the prevalence of economic credentialing, the Illinois Health Facilities Planning Commission, in a 1993 study of the matter, recommended that no specific legislation barring economic credentialing be enacted.[10]

Nevertheless, captured by the winds of medical politics, the Illinois doctors persisted, and in 1994 a bill was enacted after a compromise was reached with the state hospital association. The Illinois legislation does not ban the practice of economic credentialing, but merely cautions against the inappropriate use of economic criteria in the medical staffing area. The law creates new physician procedural safeguards for adverse credentialing decisions, as well as exclusive contract terminations. Also, the Illinois law requires that initial applicants who are rejected for staff membership be given reasons in writing, including specific economic factors.

The fight over the Illinois law certainly raised general awareness about economic credentialing around the state. But the actual law itself only modifies hospital credentialing procedures and does not present a major barrier to the use of economic criteria in hospital physician evaluations. In view of the ongoing changes in the environment of medical practice, it seems unlikely that other state medical societies will pursue legislative goals directed against hospital economic credentialing.

Economic Credentialing Crosses the Street

Framed within the four walls of the hospital, the issue of economic credentialing becomes murkier when it moves into the managed care arena. All of the variables—politics, law, evaluation methodologies, and business issues—affecting physician assessment and staffing take on a different cast when viewed in the new and evolving medical practice environment. In the world of managed care it seems that economic credentialing would be a natural focal point of physician evaluation and that the concerns over this practice would have little relevance to current realities. Clearly, the need to evaluate physicians from an economic perspective is more compelling than ever. The issues raised by economic evaluation of practice in managed care are complex due to the fluidity of practice models, the types of fiscal pressures affecting physicians in managed care organizations (MCOs), and the lingering controversy still associated with economic credentialing generally.

New guidelines

In the context of managed care, the issue of credentialing becomes a matter of contract policy. The relationships between plans and providers are fundamentally contractual ones, and the very term credentialing falls by the wayside to the notion of selective contracting. While each managed care plan offers unique features, all share the commonalities of attempting to construct and maintain the "right" mix of physicians.

Unlike in a hospital setting, credentialing in the managed care context has dimensions attached to it that go beyond the traditional quality mandate. While quality is still a fundamental concept in managed care contracting, plans are selecting and retaining physicians (or groups) based upon the need to provide services in a cost-effective manner. The providers offered by plans must be able to function in a capitated reimbursement environment, and those providers whose profiles do not hold the promise for such an ability become less attractive to the managed care entity.

In addition, MCOs construct physician panels for marketing purposes. While cost is not the sole factor that sways purchasers and enrollees to join and stay with a particular plan, it is clearly a core issue that affects the long-term viability of any managed care product.[11]

Credentialing also varies in managed care because the organizational structure, the operating political dynamics, and provider expectations are different from that of the hospital. In the traditional hospital medical staff setting, most physician staffs still engage in credentialing activities somewhat removed from the realities of medicine as a business. In managed care, however, those providers who join the established plan models realize that financial structures will affect practice styles. The very essence of the managed care gatekeeper model is one that requires judicious use of resources.

Within the rapidly emerging transitional MCO vehicles, such as the physician-hospital organization (PHO), the need to assess the medical practice from an economic vantage point is shared by both the administration and the practitioner. In fact, the most zealous advocates of using economic measures in PHO contracting are often physicians who have strong economic stakes in associating with other doctors whose practices will have a positive impact on the bottom line. Without the strictures of traditional medical staff processes, managed care staffs are free to endorse credentialing and recredentialing models that overtly consider economic practice questions.

Current criteria

Detailed information about what selection criteria managed care plans use for initial physician contracting and contract renewals is difficult to obtain. Generally, plans appear to be using criteria that take into account professional credentials, cost-effective practice patterns, and subscriber access.[12] Many managed care plans are following the broad dictates of accrediting bodies such as the National Committee on Quality Assurance (NCQA).[13]

The specific criteria that plans are using for assessing physicians can be gleaned from the multitude of plan report cards that are being compiled.[14] Physicians are being evaluated on the basis of time schedules, hospital reimbursement, referrals, consultations, medication costs, liability issues, patient satisfaction measures, and so on. What appears to be happening is that physician evaluation in managed care entails a process in which relevant cost and quality measures are impossible to unbundle.

As the managed care marketplace matures, the cost differential from one plan to another will be minimal, and physician evaluation and plan marketing will shift to a stronger emphasis on quality.[15] But even if quality factors eventually become dominant in MCO credentialing, it seems unlikely that economic evaluation criteria of some sort will be scrapped.

NCQA

Like a hospital credentialing process, managed care credentialing under the NCQA standards is broken up into the phases of initial appointment and reappointment.[13] Among the list of requirements is the need for an applicant to have clinical privileges in good standing at a hospital that is his or her primary admitting facility. Presumably, if the hospital in question is outside the managed care plan network, the applicant's privileges at that hospital may not be acceptable. Other criteria involving education, board certification, health status, liability exposure, and requisite background checks with the National Practitioner Data Bank, the peer review organization (PRO), and the state licensing authority are compatible with hospital requirements. What is unique is the requirement that there be an office visit by the MCO to evaluate the structure of the applicant's office and the record-keeping practices.

NCQA has also established a process for recredentialing that includes a series of validation checks, as well as a repeated office visit for primary care, obstetrics and gynecology, and high volume specialist physicians. Also, NCQA recredentialing requires a review of member complaints, satisfaction surveys, quality assurance, and utilization management data. Undoubtedly, the successful managed care plans will have state-of-the-art information systems that can generate profiles and report cards that will be valuable in recredentialing assessments. Finally, NCQA requires plans to have processes in place for contract suspension and termination. Plans are required to have formal appeal mechanisms available to physicians who are not renewed.

General legal issues

As might be expected, managed care credentialing raises a number of legal issues, but these issues are far less developed than those noted previously on the hospital side. Like acute care facilities, managed care plans have a corporate responsibility to select and retain competent physicians. But the nature and scope of this duty is undeveloped, for there are only a handful of reported cases articulating MCO credentialing responsibilities.[16] While managed care plans rely heavily on the hospital credentialing process, their own corporate duty in this area necessitates an independent evaluation.

Related to the common law credentialing duties, managed care plans are statutorily bound by the federal Health Care Quality Improvement Act reporting requirements. Under NCQA dictates, plans should check the National Practitioner Data Bank on a regular basis to determine if any of its members have been reported for malpractice or credentialing problems. Failure to access the databank could result in allegations of negligent selection.

Safeguarding providers

Providers have been particularly concerned about the lack of protections they have if suspended or subjected to nonrenewal by a managed care entity. The battery of legal arguments seen in hospital credentialing does not exist yet in managed care. Relationships between physician and MCO are a matter of contract law, and if procedural safeguards are not incorporated into specific contracts, practitioners have little to stand on in challenging nonrenewals. Some states have enacted "any willing provider" legislation that offers practitioners some assistance in being able to secure initial contracts with an MCO. With the exception of Texas and California, states have not enacted protections for individual providers who wish to challenge contract terminations. Suing managed care plans for inappropriate credentialing is complicated by the existence of the Employee Retirement Income Security Act (ERISA), which covers the majority of plans and raises complex state law preemption problems.[17]

To date, only one case has been successfully litigated in which a court required a plan to provide a fair hearing before making a final decision in a provider fee dispute. The case of Delta Dental Plan v. Banasky was decided by a California Appellate court on the basis of a unique feature of state law, the fairness doctrine.[18] Under the fairness doctrine, individuals whose economic interests are affected by a particular entity have the right to procedural safeguards, such as a formal hearing. In Banasky, two dentists who had contracts with the Delta plan requested arbitration to resolve a fee dispute. While arbitration was not granted, the court ruled that under the fairness doctrine the two dentists were entitled to an administrative hearing because the plan's action affected their economic interests.

It would not be a major extension of Banasky to argue that the same application of the fairness doctrine could be applied to cases involving managed care credentialing, particularly contract renewal situations. Procedural fairness arises from the law's protections against economic injury, and as such, the doctrine has strong application to individuals who have an established property interest. A physician who is refused an initial contract may be hurt financially, but under the fairness doctrine the physician whose contract is not renewed has a more compelling argument to ask for administrative redress. Although the fairness doctrine is unique to California, administrative review is required under NCQA standards and may also be promoted by legislatures elsewhere.[13]

The development of provider procedural rights in managed care credentialing should serve as a catalyst for plans to more carefully develop the criteria on which contracting decisions are based. The validity of specific contracting criteria will undoubtedly be challenged by aggrieved physicians, provided that such evaluation measures are made public or can be legally discovered. Recently, the Medical Society of the District of Columbia (MSDC) settled a challenge against the Blue Cross/Blue Shield Association of the National Capital Area (BCBSNCA) involving a dispute over the criteria used by the insurer to select physicians for its preferred provider network. The medical society had alleged that the Blues' plan made false and misleading statements about its provider selection processes. Also included among MSDC's multiple allegations was a challenge against the Blues' selection software. It was argued that the methodologies used to develop the software were flawed. The medical society also advocated that the criteria for software development be made public.

In the settlement, BCBSNCA agreed to establish quality improvement and creden-tialing advisory committees comprising physicians and insurance company representatives. A two-stage appeal process was developed that allows nonselected providers the right to challenge the insurer's decision and obtain information about the specific reasons for nonselection. Under the terms of the settlement, the quality improvement committee will be responsible for reviewing practice guidelines and monitoring aspects of care. The committee responsible for credentialing will make recommendations about spe-

cific credentialing decisions, and it will oversee selection and appeals generally. The settlement in the MSDC case should serve as a model to other managed care plans to mitigate nonselection disputes. A structure for nonselection decisions that involves physicians' input and an appeal process will make provider challenges in this area difficult to mount.[19]

Any willing provider provisions

A fundamental issue in MCO credentialing is the application of state laws referred to as "any willing provider" (AWP) provisions. Spurred by certain sectors of the health industry, particularly pharmaceutical companies and independent surgicenters, over 20 states have enacted provisions that open MCO membership to qualified providers.[20,21] Generally, AWP laws require MCOs to offer participation to those providers who accept a given plan's fee structure and practice standards. Such statutes appear to make selective contracting difficult and would also appear to constrict plan discretion in credentialing. Even the most comprehensive AWP laws, however, still allow plans to set membership ground rules and, by so doing, narrow the field of potential participants. As far as credentialing is concerned, the existence of an AWP law will require plans to be cautious in denying provider contracts, taking care to identify specific reasons for membership denials.

Some have argued that AWP laws are only transitional provisions and that once markets jell into comprehensive capitated networks, their usefulness will be outlived.[22] In the meantime, the bounds of AWP laws have not been subjected to many legal challenges. In the cases dealing with AWP provisions, the courts have demonstrated their propensity to interpret laws narrowly and have also accepted the argument that ERISA is a barrier to their enforcement.[22] It will be interesting to note how much discretion courts will give plans to reject applicants, based not on specific evaluation criteria, but on broad business plans and perceptions about staffing needs generally. It does not appear that any current AWP provision restricts plans from developing membership criteria that are based on economic assessment measures. It is conceivable that attempts will be made to pass legislation limiting the contract determinations to criteria based on quality of care, but in a managed care context, it is unlikely that even such a provision would rule out the application of all economic evaluation measures.

Other legal concerns

In addition to legal considerations dealing with process and statutory/accreditation mandates, MCO credentialing is also subject to antitrust law and the application of the Americans with Disabilities Act (ADA). Clearly, plan contracting decisions must not be motivated by a strategy to create a monopoly or restrain a given provider (or group of providers) from practicing in the MCO's market area. In practice, antitrust challenges are difficult to mount. The plan being challenged must have significant market power, and the aggrieved party must show the plan's action was detrimental, because other practice options do not exist.

As far as the ADA is concerned, MCOs must be conscious of the law's statutory requirements in that plans will be seen as employers under the ADA law, even if the relationship with a provider is strictly as an independent contractor. For example, questions asked about physical capabilities in the initial credentialing phase must be framed around inquiries about the ability to perform specific tasks, as opposed to general health questions.

Taking into account all the legal considerations discussed, the law as it now stands does not act as a barrier to an MCO's discretion in reviewing physicians for credentialing purposes. Unlike the hospital setting, there are no major legal constraints against a plan adopting economic measures to assess a particular physician or group of physicians. If an organization follows the NCQA credentialing standards literally, it may not necessarily focus on economic measures, but it is not restricted from doing so. Under NCQA, a plan can delegate credentialing to a hospital, and it is conceivable that economic credentialing will not be pursued there, but such inquiry can easily be added on by a particular plan.

Legislative initiatives to protect physicians

In order for economic credentialing to be restricted in managed care, a legal foundation similar to that seen in the hospital world must be developed. Such a movement is now underway, driven primarily by the efforts of organized medicine.[23] In 1993 the AMA, in conjunction with the Health Insurance Association of America, the National Blue Cross/Blue Shield Association, and the Cigna Corporation, developed "Guidelines for Conduct of Managed Care." Under the selective contracting section of the guidelines it was noted that cost efficiency related to quality medical care was an appropriate way in which physicians could be evaluated.

The voluntary guidelines set the stage for the AMA's ongoing initiative to pass a national Patient Protection Act.[24] In the most recent version of the AMA Patient Protection Act, several sections have a direct bearing on the managed care economic credentialing issue. Generally, the AMA is proposing that plans be required to establish formal mechanisms for participating physicians to have input into the credentialing process, and that procedural fairness standards be developed. The AMA argues that all MCOs should have a Physician Executive Committee that is responsible for conducting credentialing and making recommendations to the plan's governing body regarding initial and ongoing physician participation matters. Specific to credentialing, the AMA bill recommends that objective standards be developed and published and that plans not discriminate against physicians whose patient mix includes a high number of risky or vulnerable patients or populations.

In effect, the AMA is proposing the establishment of a type of medical staff arrangement for MCOs in which credentialing becomes a delegated medical function, akin to a hospital. If control for MCO credentialing is vested in its medical staff, presumably the application of economic criteria will be pursued more cautiously than if the process is totally managed by a governing board. It is unlikely that an MCO medical staff model will result in an entity with the independence of a hospital medical staff.

Passage of the 1995 Patient Protection Act may result in greater physician control over plans, but it is not likely to stem the tide against the adoption of economic evaluation measures that both the marketplace and, in turn, certain sectors of the medical community may demand. It is interesting to note that the AMA has not endorsed the AWP laws. The Patient Protection Act recommends that contracting decisions be made consistent with an MCO's business needs, capacity, and objectives. The awareness by the AMA of plan business realities could be pushed to the next logical step, supporting individual analysis of economic practice patterns for MCO contracting purposes, but politically such a leap still lies in the future.

●　　●　　●

As in many other areas of medical practice, the economic credentialing issue has been caught up in the changes affecting medicine generally as it moves into managed care. Unquestionably, economics plays a central role in the relationship between a physician and a managed care plan. But at this point, the extent and nature of MCO fiscal pressures over individual medical practice are not fully understood. It does seem clear that physician economic performance, however it is defined, will be essential to the successful managed care operation. And as such, the ongoing movement to measure the economic factors in medical practice will not subside in this new environment. The economic credentialing controversy played out in hospital settings lingers, but is more illusive in managed care. To dismiss economic credentialing as passé in MCOs would be to ignore the fact that what is at issue is the efficiency and control of medical practice, and while the nature of evaluation issues may change, the core debates will not.

REFERENCES

1. American Medical Association. *Report of the Hospital Medical Staff Section Governing Council Report Q, Economic Credentialing* (I-93). Chicago, Ill: AMA, 1993.
2. Rotenberg, J. "Report to the Council from the Taskforce on Exclusive Contracting and Economic Credentialing" July 1990 (on file with the California Medical Association).
3. Bader, B. "Economic Factors and Credentialing: Turning a Volatile Mix into a Quality Improvement Tool." *The Quality Letter for Healthcare Leaders*, 3 (1991): 2–6.
4. Montague, J. " Profiling in Practice; Comparing Physician Practice Profiles." *Journal of Hospitals and Health Care Networks,* 68, no.2 (1994): 50–52.
5. Koska, M. "Review of Exclusive Contracts in Light of Recent Challenges." *Hospitals* 66 (1992): 38–42.
6. Health Care Quality Improvement Act of 1986 sec. 402, 42 U.S.C. sec.11101-52 (1988).
7. *Nations v Wausau Insurance Companies*, No. 91-589 (Fla. Cir. Ct. App. Feb. 12, 1992). Unpublished decision referenced in Southern Reporter in a table captioned "Florida Decisions without Published Opinions" at 593 So.2d 1055.
8. Lang, H., and Dauner, C.D. *Statement on Economic Credentialing and Exclusive Contracting.* Feb. 13, 1992 on file with the California Association of Hospitals and Health Systems.
9. Hospital Licensing Act, 210 ILCS 85/2 (1994).
10. Illinois Health Facilities Planning Board. *Report to the General Assembly Pursuant to Senate Resolution 667.* Assembly no. 88, Jan. 1, 1994.
11. Kolb, D., and Horowitz, J. " Managing Transition to Capitation." *Journal of Healthcare Financial Management* 49, no.2 (1995): 64–74.
12. Bureau of National Affairs. "Blue Cross' Physician Criteria Software Discriminatory Medical Society Charges." *Health Law Reporter* 3, no. 27 (July 7,1994): 911.
13. National Committee on Quality Assurance. *Managed Care Accreditation Guidelines.* Washington, D.C.: NCQA, 1994.
14. Accountability News for Health Care Managers. *Health Care Report Cards.* Washington, D.C.: Atlantic Information Services, 1995.
15. Rosenstein, A. "Cost Effective Health Care: Tools for Improvement." *Health Care Management Review* 19, no. 2 (March 22, 1994): 53–61.
16. Younger, P., et al. "Basis for Liability Sec. 2-1 Selection of Providers." In *Managed Care Law Manual.* Gaithersburg, Md.: Aspen Publishers, 1994.
17. For example see, *Tolton v. American Biodyne, Inc.* 1995 U.S. App. Lexis 4083.
18. *Delta Dental Plan v Banasky* 27 Cal. App. 4th 1598 (1994).
19. *MSDC v Blue Cross Blue Shield*, No 1 CV01426 (Washington, D.C., June 28, 1994).
20. "More States Enact AWP Laws but Some Have Second Thoughts on Passage." *Managed Care Law Outlook* 7, no. 3 (March 1995): 5–6.
21. "Any Willing Provider Laws, Bills Proliferate at State Level, AMCRA Finds." *Health Care Policy Report* 2, no. 48 (Dec. 5, 1994): 2011.
22. Hudson, T. "State Laws: A Stumbling Block for Systems Integration ?" *Journal of Hospitals and Health Networks* 68, no. 8 (April 20, 1994): 40.
23. For example, see Medical Society of the State of New York. "Talking Points." *Important Health Issues Before the NYS Legislature.* I sec. 3(c). Medical Society of the State of New York, 1995.
24. American Medical Association. *1995 Patient Protection Act.* On file with the American Medical Association Office of the General Counsel. Chicago, Ill: AMA, 1995.

Part IV
Medical Management

15

Comparison of Inpatient Utilization to Optimal Standards

Robert J. Dymowski

Managed care delivery systems are an important element in the medical benefit programs of most employers, whether in the form of health maintenance organizations (HMOs), preferred provider organizations (PPOs), exclusive provider organizations (EPOs), or utilization review vendors working with indemnity benefit programs. Furthermore, their ability to deliver enhanced benefits for lower costs or to offer lower rates of increase in cost has made it likely that managed care organizations will play a major role in any future health care reform proposals. This was certainly the case with the Clinton administration's Health Security Act. While the direction of health care reform efforts in 1997 or after is uncertain, it is likely that managed care will be an important element.

How much difference can managed care make in program costs? Are all managed care delivery systems the same? How can an employer evaluate the effectiveness of a managed care delivery system? Against what standards should the performance of managed care organizations be measured? Two recent research efforts completed within Milliman & Robertson, Inc. (M&R), illustrate the potential value of effective management of medical care. One addressed the issues of unnecessary utilization of inpatient services, and the other compared the efficiency of HMOs versus non-HMOs in hospital admissions. Both of these research efforts produced results that should be considered by employers in evaluating their current benefit programs or in considering the choice of a managed care delivery system. The implications of the results of this research for managed care organizations are also significant, in view of the increasing acceptance of The Health Plan Employer Data and Information Set (HEDIS). This article describes the recent M&R re-

search and its results, and comments on the value of the utilization data included in HEDIS for comparison with similar benchmarks. Most of these comments are from the perspective of an employer's evaluation of the effectiveness of a managed care organization, but some will reflect the latter's point of view as well.

Medically Unnecessary Inpatient Services

The M&R report titled "Analysis of Medically Unnecessary Inpatient Services"[1] was based on chart reviews completed throughout the United States in a period of over a decade with a wide range of health care delivery systems, including managed care organizations. The purpose of these reviews was to determine the level of efficiency in the delivery of medical care services of these organizations. This is done by reviewing all services provided for a sample of patients, and by identifying medically unnecessary services, based on actual patient charts. A medically unnecessary inpatient day is defined as one in which neither the medical condition of, nor the level of treatment being provided to, a patient requires confinement as an inpatient in a hospital.

The experience noted by the authors of that report is that a high level of medical efficiency is generally not present in the case of ineffective utilization review programs. They also observed that aggregate outcomes of cases being managed by managed care organizations are likely to be favorable when a majority of the routine uncomplicated individual cases are cared for efficiently. Overutilization of inpatient care is seen not solely as a result of treating catastrophic illness, complex disease, or use of high technology. Rather, waste in the provision of routine care, even under supposed utilization management programs, causes the overutilization problem.

The authors relate their observations to guidelines[2] published by their firm, *Milliman & Robertson*

Managed Care Quarterly 1997; 5(1): 33–41

Healthcare Management Guidelines. Volume 1 of these guidelines focuses on inpatient care, and contains a level of performance identified as optimal management. This represents the level corresponding to current best observed practices: the pattern of delivery of care observed in the high-quality, safe, efficient treatment of routine uncomplicated cases. This provides an explicit clinical standard of "what should happen" in such cases. The level of inpatient utilization corresponding to this pattern of delivery represents the level being observed in well-managed HMOs, especially in California. The report presents a summary of estimated unnecessary utilization for the 40 largest markets in the United States.

The report defines optimal utilization levels of 58 admissions and 184 days per 1,000 population for the commercial population (under age 65), and corresponding values of 234 admissions and 1,565 days per 1,000 population for the Medicare population. Utilization levels for the unmanaged system for each region were estimated by using the area cost variation data contained in another proprietary Milliman & Robertson data source. The authors' analysis then considered the ratios of optimal to unmanaged admissions and total inpatient days per 1,000 of population. The authors estimated that the nationwide average was that 31 percent of admissions were medically unnecessary for the under-65 population, while 59 percent of days were considered medically unnecessary.

It should be noted in both these comparisons that the frame of reference was to *unmanaged* levels of care. In actual experience, the care being provided may represent some degree of management. In the case of a single employer, for example, the total experience of the employer's group might represent a combination of experience for employees and dependents enrolled in an HMO and the experience of employees and dependents covered under a fee-for-service program. The comparison between the optimal level of care and unmanaged care indicates the total potential that exists for savings if care could be delivered at the optimal level. Employers may already have achieved some portion of this savings, depending on the proportion of their care being provided on a managed care basis, and the medical efficiency of the managed care organizations providing their care.

By way of comparison, the estimated level of inpatient services for the under-65, non-Medicaid population on an unmanaged basis is approximately 450 days per 1,000 per year. A moderately managed system might experience days in the range of 300 to 350 per 1,000 per year. The results estimated for the Medicare population were that 23 percent of admissions and 49 percent of days were medically unnecessary.

It should be recognized that the optimal level represents an aggressive target, and assumes the availability of home care and other services as alternatives to inpatient confinement. The experience of specific employer groups may differ significantly from these levels due to demographic or other factors, however. For example, the utilization of hospital inpatient medical-surgical services for males aged 35 to 39 is about 72 percent of the overall per capita utilization, while that for females in the same age bracket (excluding maternity) is about 96 percent of the average. In the 55 to 59 age bracket, these levels increase to 236 percent and 225 percent for males and females, respectively.

Variations in the unmanaged inpatient utilization levels between geographic regions are also substantial. These ranged from an estimated low of 322 days per 1,000 in Portland, Oregon, to 600 days per 1,000 in New York for the under-65 population. The range for the Medicare population was from 2,255 days per 1,000 in Portland, Oregon, to a high of 4,199 days per 1,000 in New York. Tables 15–1 and 15–2 show the results of the study for the commercial under-65 and Medicare populations, respectively. Table 15–1 shows that the admissions in Minneapolis were closest to the optimal level, at 85 percent, closely followed by several other locations between 70 percent and 80 percent. Portland and Seattle had the highest ratios of optimal to unmanaged days per 1,000 at 57 percent. The largest ratio of projected unnecessary days was estimated to be in New York, at 69 percent. These patterns of delivery of care appear to carry over into the Medicare population as well, as shown in Table 15–2. In this case, however, two regions (Honolulu and Salt Lake City) are estimated as having admission rates lower than the optimal level, although by only minor amounts.

The results of this study indicate that the application of tight controls over the utilization of inpatient services can result in significant reductions of the level of utilization that would be observed if no managed care controls were applied. These reductions result from eliminating the excess days, or waste,

Table 15–1

Inpatient Utilization Statistics by Region: Under-65
Population (Non-Medicaid)

Region	Ratio of optimal to unmanaged (%)	
	Admissions	Days per 1,000
Atlanta	63	40
Baltimore	61	35
Birmingham	58	34
Boston	65	35
Chicago	64	37
Cincinnati	68	42
Cleveland	68	41
Dallas	69	42
Denver	66	42
Des Moines	68	37
Detroit	69	38
Hartford	69	37
Honolulu	83	47
Houston	68	37
Indianapolis	67	38
Kansas City	70	42
Las Vegas	77	47
Little Rock	67	38
Los Angeles	70	43
Louisville	64	37
Memphis	62	33
Miami	66	37
Milwaukee	62	43
Minneapolis–St. Paul	85	55
Newark	81	36
New Orleans	63	33
New York	75	31
Norfolk	72	42
Oklahoma City	75	43
Philadelphia	68	34
Phoenix	75	53
Pittsburgh	62	34
Portland	78	57
Salt Lake City	73	45
San Diego	75	51
San Francisco	67	43
Seattle	80	57
St. Louis	66	37
Tampa	70	43
Washington, D.C.	73	40
Nationwide average	69	41

Source: "Research Report: Analysis of Medically Unnecessary
Inpatient Services." David V. Axene and Richard L. Doyle. Seattle,
Wash.: Milliman & Robertson, Inc., © 1994. Reprinted with per-
mission.

from the current level of delivery of care. This identifies for an employer the value of introducing such
controls into a benefit program. It also provides a
target against which managed care organizations can
evaluate their performance.

Of course, reducing inpatient utilization as severely
as indicated will not occur without some degree of
corresponding increase in outpatient utilization. It
also may result in changes by providers in the pricing
of inpatient services. Thus, it is not easy to predict net
savings resulting from the imposition of managed care
controls. These will be affected by factors such as the
relative cost of inpatient versus outpatient charges,
the cost of the eliminated days versus the cost of an
average day, or other considerations. Nonetheless,
this study indicates that substantial reductions in
inpatient utilization can be achieved through aggressive management.

Florida Hospital Experience

If managed care can work, is it fair to expect that all
managed care organizations operate at the optimal
level of efficiency? The other report ("An Analysis of
the Efficiency of HMO Inpatient Lengths of Stay in
Florida")[3] comparing HMO and non-HMO utilization
in Florida hospitals provides some interesting insights into this question.

All hospitals in Florida are required to report certain data to the state in a data source known as the
Florida Hospital Discharge Patient Data. This information is compiled on a quarterly basis and is made
available as a public data tape providing detailed
information for each hospital admission. The research
team gathered the information reported for Florida
hospitals for 1992, and separated the data into HMO
versus non-HMO components for individuals under
age 65. The author then compared the average length
of stay (ALOS) of the HMO versus the non-HMO
admissions and established an LOS Efficiency Index
based on the optimal levels of management contained
in the same guidelines referenced above. In order to
avoid one source of possible distortion in the comparisons, the estimated admissions and lengths of
stay for the optimal management samples were adjusted to reflect the same distribution of cases within
broad groupings called Major Diagnostic Categories
(MDCs).

Table 15–2

Inpatient Utilization Statistics by Region: Medicare Population

	Ratio of optimal to unmanaged (%)	
Region	**Admissions**	**Days per 1,000**
Atlanta	72	54
Baltimore	64	45
Birmingham	61	45
Boston	68	42
Chicago	73	47
Cincinnati	72	47
Cleveland	72	46
Dallas	81	59
Denver	84	57
Des Moines	85	58
Detroit	79	46
Hartford	88	46
Honolulu	104	68
Houston	79	54
Indianapolis	73	47
Kansas City	80	50
Las Vegas	91	66
Little Rock	71	51
Los Angeles	80	55
Louisville	72	44
Memphis	75	44
Miami	76	50
Milwaukee	80	56
Minneapolis–St. Paul	88	63
Newark	77	41
New Orleans	67	47
New York	79	37
Norfolk	75	53
Oklahoma City	77	61
Philadelphia	70	42
Phoenix	80	62
Pittsburgh	63	41
Portland	84	69
Salt Lake City	101	75
San Diego	88	60
San Francisco	76	55
Seattle	88	69
St. Louis	75	47
Tampa	83	55
Washington, D.C.	78	42
Nationwide average	77	51

Source: "Research Report: Analysis of Medically Unnecessary Inpatient Services." David V. Axene and Richard L. Doyle. Seattle, Wash.: Milliman & Robertson, Inc., © 1994. Reprinted with permission.

The results of this study indicated that in 1992 the average LOS of Florida HMOs was 9 percent less than the LOS for other private payers (4.69 versus 5.15 days). After adjusting for case mix differences, however, the HMO LOS was less than 5 percent more efficient than other private payers. Moreover, under the adjusted case mix, the Florida HMO LOS is 46 percent greater than the adjusted well-managed LOS (the optimal level of management) at 4.69 versus 3.22 days. Furthermore, the Florida HMO LOS is more than 10 percent above the case mix adjusted estimated LOS shown in the *Guidelines* for a moderately managed HMO (4.48 vs. 4.06 days) and only 3 percent below the estimated level of an unmanaged HMO (4.48 vs. 4.63 days), also considered on a case mix adjusted basis.

A significant observation from this study is that the difference in efficiency between managed and unmanaged care is much less than the difference between the average managed care result and the optimal level. Since the average level of managed care is a result of HMOs operating better and worse than the average, this highlights the importance to employers of seeking the HMO that is able to demonstrate better than average results, or to HMOs, of being able to demonstrate superior performance.

This analysis implies that on average over one third of the non-Medicare hospital days in Florida could be eliminated through more efficient inpatient LOS management. This does not recognize additional potential savings for the elimination of unnecessary admissions. Conservatively, assuming the elimination of just room and board costs of $425 for each day saved would have reduced costs to consumers by nearly $2.3 billion in the state of Florida in 1992. Extrapolating such a figure nationally would have produced potential non-Medicare savings of over $45 billion in 1992.

This comparison indicated that there is considerable room for many HMOs, hospitals, and other managed care organizations in Florida to significantly improve the efficiency of their inpatient utilization management. As noted earlier, such improvement would require an adequate infrastructure of home health services, outpatient surgery suites, infusion therapy, and other support services to minimize the in-hospital usage. Table 15–3 indicates the LOS Efficiency Indices for the HMO and non-HMO categories for the MDCs considered in the study.

Table 15–3

Comparison of Florida HMO and Non-HMO Inpatient Lengths of Stay (LOS)

Major diagnostic category (MDC)	LOS efficiency index*	
	HMO	Non-HMO
Nervous system	1.40	1.49
Eye	1.40	1.50
Ear, nose, mouth, and throat	2.49	2.59
Respiratory system	1.67	1.79
Circulatory system	1.48	1.48
Digestive system	1.42	1.44
Hepatobiliary system and pancreas	1.47	1.66
Musculoskeletal system and connective tissue	1.54	1.65
Skin, subcutaneous tissue, and breast	1.29	1.23
Endocrine, nutritional, and metabolic	1.99	2.13
Kidney and urinary tract	1.59	1.63
Male reproductive system	1.45	1.49
Female reproductive system	1.26	1.28
Pregnancy, childbirth, and the puerperium	1.41	1.41
Newborns in the perinatal period	1.25	1.18
Blood, blood forming organs, and immune system	1.22	1.39
Poorly differentiated neoplasms	1.48	1.36
Infectious and parasitic diseases	1.63	1.76
Mental diseases and disorders	1.33	1.61
Substance use	0.86	1.10
Injury and poisoning	1.30	1.45
Burns	1.30	1.54
Factors influencing health status	2.26	2.38
Multiple significant trauma	1.23	1.35
Human immunodeficiency virus	1.11	1.29
Heart transplants	1.20	1.39
Kidney transplants	1.11	1.16
Liver transplants	2.24	1.81
Bone marrow transplants	1.16	1.19
Total	1.46	1.53

Source: "An Analysis of the Efficiency of HMO Inpatient Length of Stay in Florida." John P. Cookson. Radnor, Penn.: Milliman & Robertson, Inc., © 1994. Reprinted with permission.

*LOS Efficiency Index represents the ratio of (a) the length of stay for the MDC/admission source combination to (b) the length of stay for the category based on optimal management. Thus, an LOS Efficiency Index of 1.00 indicates an average LOS equal to the optimal.

The range of results observed for the HMO indices is from 0.86 for MDC 20 (substance use) to 2.49 for MDC 3 (ear, nose, mouth, and throat). These same MDCs represented the range of indices for the non-HMO admissions also (1.10 to 2.59). The author notes that the relatively low HMO index shown for MDC 20 may be influenced by the fact that psychiatric hospitals with a greater proportion of longer substance abuse rehabilitation programs were not included in the data used.

Implications for Managed Care Organizations

Analysis of such data, compared to an optimal level of performance, can be used as a powerful tool in managed care in the following ways:

- First, any HMO can evaluate its performance relative to both its peers and to the well-managed level of performance. This process can also identify the admissions (diagnoses) with inadequate performance and the greatest potential for improvement. The HEDIS utilization data are an example of comparative data that will be reviewed by prospective customers.

- Second, this method, after adjusting the data for severity, allows the development of a ranking system for each hospital's efficiency by diagnosis category. The ranking illustrated here represents a proprietary database of Milliman & Robertson, Inc., and is called the LOS Efficiency Index. It allows a hospital to compare the effectiveness of its performance relative to its competitors and to use this information to help improve its efficiency and compete for managed care contracts. Furthermore, this ranking provides HMOs and other managed care vendors an efficient method to evaluate the diagnosis-specific performance of contracting hospitals. This information can be used to improve an HMO's efficiency and competitiveness through selective contracting. These data can be supplemented by chart audits to determine whether admissions are appropriate or the LOS is biased by unnecessary admissions. Chart audits can also be used to pinpoint specific reasons for inefficiencies.

- Third, this method allows an HMO or hospital to measure its progress toward achieving greater efficiency. This can be accomplished by comparing the progression of its LOS Efficiency Index over time. As the index approaches 1.0, the average adjusted LOS is approaching the well-managed level in the guidelines referenced by the author.

- Fourth, this important advance in information technology can have a significant impact on competition between HMOs and other managed care vendors and also between hospitals, by improving the capability of selecting more efficient organizations as part of a network.

Hospital Ranking

As an example of the hospital ranking process, the results of eight hospitals in one geographic area for five different diagnosis-related groups (DRGs) and all DRGs combined are illustrated in Table 15–4. The hospitals are labeled A to H and are ranked relative to a well-managed model based upon the LOS Efficiency Index. The All DRGs and any subtotals reflect the actual mix of admissions by DRG in each hospital. The use of the well-managed HMO LOS reflects the case mix of each hospital so that the LOS Efficiency Index is based on the hospital's actual usage pattern for the services it provides. In an actual analysis, results would be shown before and after severity adjustment. The results by DRG sometimes show a wide statistical confidence range due to the small number of cases. However, the results can be summarized by MDC and by Medical versus Surgical to provide tighter confidence levels. Furthermore, for All DRGs by hospital the range is generally much tighter and provides a very good estimate of a hospital's overall efficiency. In these examples, except for one small hospital, the All DRG confidence levels were generally within 2 percent to 3 percent of the mean.

The LOS Efficiency Index in the table represents the ratio of the hospital relative LOS for each DRG to the corresponding case mix adjusted well-managed LOS. Thus, an index of 1.75 for DRG 14 in Hospital E means the hospital average LOS for this diagnosis is 75 percent longer than the well-managed LOS. Note that an index of less than 1 for some hospitals for DRG 198 (Total Cholecystectomy Without Complicating Conditions) may imply that a higher percentage of laparoscopic cholecystectomies with a lower LOS is being done on an inpatient basis than is anticipated in the well-managed model. This would anticipate a higher percentage of the laparoscopic cholecystectomies on an outpatient basis, which would increase the average LOS for the inpatient procedures. This could be evaluated by examining the percentages of laparoscopic versus open procedures in the database.

Implications for Employers

The first implication of the results of these studies is that significant differences in the levels of utilization can result from the application of managed care. This only occurs when there is a strong dedication on the part of the managed care organization to making this happen. Thus, all managed care organizations are not equal, and do not achieve the same degree of success in reducing utilization. The primary factors that might affect the ability of a managed care organization to achieve improved performance include the process by which it assembles its network of providers, and the nature of its utilization controls.

In addition to consideration of their qualifications, specialties, and geographic location, providers should be selected on the basis of their demonstrated medical effectiveness. This is determined by comparing their practice patterns to optimal levels. Similarly, such comparisons would form the basis of ongoing monitoring, or of the authorization of admissions. Only the adoption of optimal performance levels as targets will lead to results significantly lower than the marketplace norm.

These optimal levels of utilization reflect underlying physiological and biological considerations, and are thus independent of regional practice variations. The performance of medical groups in California or elsewhere has demonstrated that such levels are attainable, and that the continued application of quality improvement processes can result in further improvements.

Thus, employers should evaluate the experience of their programs against optimal levels of performance, not in comparison to their competitors or in terms of trends over the previous year's performance. This means selecting managed care organizations based on their demonstrated ability to deliver care effectively at levels approaching the optimal level. Such organizations should be able to demonstrate their effectiveness by citing their statistics for inpatient utilization and by describing the process by which they monitor

Table 15–4

Comparison of Hospital-Specific LOS Efficiency Index for Select DRGs

DRG	Hospital A LOS efficiency index	Rank	95 Percent confidence level Lower bound	Upper bound	Hospital B LOS efficiency index	Rank	95 Percent confidence level Lower bound	Upper bound	Hospital C LOS efficiency index	Rank	95 Percent confidence level Lower bound	Upper bound	Hospital D LOS efficiency index	Rank	95 Percent confidence level Lower bound	Upper bound
14	1.582	6	1.261	1.904	1.650	7	0.555	2.745	1.436	4	1.071	1.802	1.264	1	1.020	1.508
97	1.324	1	1.094	1.554	1.484	2	0.996	1.972	2.247	7	1.953	2.541	2.527	8	1.759	3.295
167	1.142	1	1.020	1.264	1.202	3	0.869	1.535	1.190	2	1.083	1.296	1.374	6	1.077	1.670
198	1.871	7	1.532	2.209	0.746	1	0.402	1.091	0.949	2	0.827	1.071	1.451	4	0.999	1.903
373	1.512	3	1.471	1.553	NA				1.488	1	1.454	1.521	NA			
Total	1.574	6	1.557	1.592	1.478	2	1.379	1.577	1.538	5	1.519	1.556	1.421	1	1.392	1.451

DRG	Hospital E LOS efficiency index	Rank	95 Percent confidence level Lower bound	Upper bound	Hospital F LOS efficiency index	Rank	95 Percent confidence level Lower bound	Upper bound	Hospital G LOS efficiency index	Rank	95 Percent confidence level Lower bound	Upper bound	Hospital H LOS efficiency index	Rank	95 Percent confidence level Lower bound	Upper bound
14	1.750	8	0.711	2.789	1.280	2	0.808	1.752	1.519	5	1.210	1.827	1.404	3	1.091	1.717
97	1.492	3	1.119	1.864	1.583	4	0.993	2.173	1.712	6	1.461	1.963	1.701	5	1.479	1.922
167	1.282	5	0.857	1.707	1.572	7	1.249	1.894	1.231	4	1.018	1.444	1.937	8	1.583	2.291
198	1.928	8	1.398	2.457	1.750	6	1.398	2.101	1.408	3	1.135	1.681	1.519	5	1.204	1.834
373	1.572	4	1.505	1.639	NA				1.504	2	1.466	1.542	1.731	5	1.635	1.827
Total	1.489	4	1.447	1.530	1.600	7	1.576	1.624	1.480	3	1.464	1.496	1.797	8	1.776	1.818

DRG	Description
14	Specific Cerebrovascular Disorders Except Transient Ischemic Attack
97	Bronchitis and Asthma Age Greater Than 17 with Complication or Comorbid Condition
167	Appendectomy Without Complicated Principal Diagnosis Without Complication or Comorbid Condition
198	Total Cholecystectomy Without Common Duct Exploration Without Complication or Comorbid Condition
373	Vaginal Delivery Without Complicating Diagnoses

Source: "An Analysis of the Efficiency of HMO Inpatient Length of Stay in Florida." John P. Cookson. Radnor, Penn.: Milliman & Robertson, Inc., © 1994. Reprinted with permission.

the patterns of care being provided through their network. Employers should accept only an ongoing commitment to reduce utilization levels to the optimal level.

Utilization Data Included in HEDIS

HEDIS 2.0 contains a Membership and Utilization component. An example of the capabilities provided by HEDIS for the comparison of performance among reporting plans was reported by the New England HEDIS Coalition in *1993 Baseline Performance Profile: October 14, 1993.*[4] The *Profile* reports data for 15 HMOs in New England for their 1993 experience. It is organized into five sections, which follow the HEDIS 2.0 format. The sections include quality of care, member access and satisfaction, membership and utilization, finance, and health plan management. The membership and utilization data are of most interest for purposes of this discussion.

The membership data allow a managed care plan or an employer to compare the membership distribution of the reporting organization to other plans, or to the employer's own mix of employees and dependents. As noted above, the utilization of medical care services increases with age; a comparison of the age distribution of an employer's group against that of the managed care organization will improve understanding of factors that might be affecting utilization by the group.

Data reported in the *Profile* concerning inpatient utilization include measures such as discharges per 1,000 members, days per 1,000 members, and ALOS. These are reported in total for a plan, as well as for broad categories such as medical/surgical and maternity. Outpatient utilization data, including outpatient visits, emergency department visits, and outpatient drug utilization, are also included. Additional utilization data include the rates of selected procedures per 1,000 members, and discharges per 1,000, average costs per discharge, and ALOS for selected DRGs. Compilation of these data for all of the reporting plans allows for comparisons across the plans. Plans can use these data to determine the extent to which their performance differs significantly from the norm of all of the reporting plans. Employers can similarly use them to evaluate plans. A comparison of the reported data to an optimal target such as the *M&R Healthcare*

Management Guidelines can be used to identify the levels of efficiency of the reporting plans.

For example, the median ALOS reported in the *Profile* for 11 plans for DRG 14 (Specific Cerebrovascular Disorders Except TIA) is 7.8 days. By comparison, the *Guidelines* identify an ALOS for a well-managed delivery system of 5.0 days. The reported 25th percentile ALOS for the 11 plans is 6.5 days, with the lowest reported ALOS being 3.4 days. The *Profile* results for the same 11 plans for DRG 15 (Transient Ischemic Attack and Precerebral Occlusions) are a median ALOS of 3.3 days, and a 25th percentile of 2.9 days. The *Guidelines* identify an ALOS of 2.17 days for the combined DRGs 15–17. Again, the lowest ALOS reported in the *Profile* for this DRG is 1.9 days. Similar results are observed for the other selected DRGs presented in the *Profile*. While this is a very small sample, it shows that the optimal levels of performance identified in the *Guidelines* are being achieved in practice. The gathering and publishing of plan-specific data on performance will be of considerable benefit to employers or other benefit plan sponsors in their selection of managed care organizations. It also seems inevitable that there will be continued pressure on plans to match the best reported levels of performance.

•   •   •

Efficiency in the delivery of care starts with the providers. While the application of practice guidelines and utilization management by a managed care organization can improve the efficiency of a provider network, selection of the most efficient providers for inclusion in the network creates the best foundation. Employers should explore with managed care organizations the ways in which they select providers for their networks in order to maximize their opportunity for realizing the benefits of the management process.

Quality and efficiency of medical care are closely related. Targeting utilization at optimal levels represents a rationalization of the delivery of care, not a rationing of care. Employers need to use the same techniques in selecting efficient medical care vendors as they use in other aspects of their business. The payoff comes in the form of lower costs and better quality care.

REFERENCES

1. Axene, D.V., and Doyle, R.L. *Analysis of Medically Unnecessary Inpatient Services.* Seattle, Wash.: Milliman & Robertson, Inc., 1994.

2. *Milliman & Robertson Healthcare Management Guidelines.*

3. Cookson, J.P. *An Analysis of the Efficiency of HMO Inpatient Lengths of Stay in Florida.*

4. New England HEDIS Coalition. *1993 Baseline Performance Profile: October 14, 1993.*

16

How HMOs Structure Primary Care Delivery

Suzanne Felt-Lisk

Managed care's increased influence on health care delivery highlights the need to better understand how people in managed care obtain primary care and referrals. A recent literature search found that previously published research on the topic is generally dated, derived from a limited subset of plans, inattentive to important structural differences between plans, and responsive to a narrow set of related issues.[1] Here, results are presented from a detailed study of primary care staffing in 23 health maintenance organizations (HMOs). Differences among HMOs are explored: who they use as "gatekeepers," how they use nurse practitioners (NPs) and physician assistants (PAs), and their policies on how people obtain referrals to specialists. The study also explored plans' initiatives to expand or better define a scope of practice for primary care physicians. To conclude, the implications of the findings are discussed.

Study Design

The study design consists of on-site interviews with senior health plan officials in 23 HMOs nationwide in winter and spring of 1994. The study was conducted by Mathematica Policy Research, Inc. for the federal Health Resources and Services Administration.[2] This sample of HMOs was constructed using a two-stage process, in which markets of varying HMO penetration and provider supply level were selected, and then a variety of plans were selected within these markets. The final sample consists of nine group or staff model plans in eight large urban areas and one rural area, nine network or IPA model plans in the same eight large urban areas and in one small urban area, and five plans selected because they have relatively high Medicaid enrollment (25 percent or more of their total enrollment). Mixed-

model plans were accommodated by selecting plans based on predominant model type and studying the staffing of each model type component.

The eight selected urban markets cover the range of the 54 largest metropolitan statistical areas in terms of their population, physician-to-population ratio, and HMO penetration rate. A greater proportion of large plans than exist nationwide was selected so as to include greater numbers of physicians and enrollees. Thus, the sample is more representative of HMOs that have enrollments greater than 50,000. It is also more representative of the distribution of enrollees in HMOs nationally.

At each HMO, the site visitors used semistructured interview protocols to interview the key personnel who make staffing decisions, usually the medical director, provider relations or network development director, and marketing representative, and often also the chief executive officer, a government programs staff person, and a regional representative if the plan was large and somewhat decentralized. Generally, one or two site visitors spent about a day on site.

The sample of HMOs was designed to represent the full range of HMOs in the nation and to facilitate an

The analysis presented in this article was developed under a contract awarded to Mathematica Policy Research, Inc. by the Health Resources and Services Administration (task order no. 240-93-0403 under contract no. 240-91-0007).

The 23 health plans that volunteered senior management time to participate in the site visit interviews on a confidential basis are gratefully acknowledged. Marsha Gold, a Senior Fellow at Mathematica Policy Research, Inc., acted as a senior advisor to the study and provided useful comments on an earlier draft of the manuscript. Jessica Townsend, at the Office of Planning, Evaluation, and Legislation within the Health Resources and Services Administration, saw the need for this study, served as the project officer for the study, and also provided useful comments on a draft of this manuscript. Hilary Frazer, Karyen Chu, and Timothy Lake were other project team members who contributed to collecting the information for this analysis.

Managed Care Quarterly 1996; 4(4): 96–105
© 1996 Aspen Publishers, Inc.

understanding of how differences in model type, high Medicaid enrollment, and market factors affect primary care staffing. However, about half the HMOs originally selected declined to participate, requiring substitution of another HMO with similar characteristics, and the sites were selected primarily through a judgmental rather than random process; thus, both the study design and the relatively small number of plans mean that the results are more useful for providing insight about staffing processes than specific point estimates of prevalence.

Selection of a "Gatekeeper"

Basic to managed care is the idea that a patient accesses care through primary care providers chosen from a health plan's associated network of providers. However, the study found wide variation in the extent to which enrollees were required, versus encouraged, to select a single primary care provider to act as a gatekeeper.

New health plan enrollees generally are asked to choose a specific medical group/IPA or health center in the plan's provider network; they are then encouraged or required to select one primary care provider. As Table 16–1 shows, just over half of the group/staff model plans and a quarter of the network/IPA model plans required enrollees to select a specific primary

care provider (6 of 11 plans and 3 of 12 plans, respectively). Half of the network/IPA model plans delegate the selection rules to the contracted group or IPA—typically because of the plan's payment policy, which capitates the group or IPA only, not individual providers.

The plan's decision to require rather than encourage selection of a primary care provider may be related to its proportion of Medicaid enrollees, since plans with high Medicaid enrollment appear less likely to have this requirement. The reason for this is unknown, although the pattern is consistent with what plans cite as the challenges of treating Medicaid patients. For example, the basic challenge of promoting appropriate use of primary care providers rather than emergency departments might be more easily met than expectations for compliance with more strict requirements for contacting a particular provider.

Regardless of whether a plan requires enrollees to select a provider, the plan typically allows providers other than the one selected to also provide primary care to the patient. For example, group/staff model plans accommodate enrollee "crossover"; that is, enrollees sometimes seek care at two or more different health centers in the plan, and the plan accommodates this. Network/IPA plans that contract with large medical groups mentioned that some of the primary

Table 16–1

Types of Plans Requiring Selection of One Primary Care Provider

	Rules for selecting a primary care provider (n = 23) Percentage of HMOs			
	Encouraged but not required to select an individual	Required to select an individual	Neither encouraged nor required to select an individual	Plan has no preference/ groups or IPAs determine rules
All plans (n = 23)	30	39	13	17
Predominant model type				
Group/staff (n = 11)	36	55	9	0
Network/IPA (n = 12)	25	25	17	33
Medicaid enrollment				
None (n = 12)	25	42	8	25
1–24 percent of total enrollment (n = 3)	0	100	0	0
25+ percent of total enrollment (n = 8)	50	13	25	13

care providers in these groups see one anothers' patients freely (without restriction) within the same site.

Types of Providers Used as Gatekeepers

HMOs typically use a combination of family practitioners (FPs), general practitioners (GPs), pediatricians, and internists as gatekeepers. Obstetrician/gynecologists (OB/GYNs) and subspecialist physicians may deliver primary care but are not often used as gatekeepers. Similarly, plans generally do not offer NPs and PAs as gatekeepers.

Primary care gatekeepers for adults

Generally, adult enrollees select a primary care provider from a list of FPs, GPs, and internists who focus most of their practice on primary care. (Plans told us some of these internists have specialist designations, but they have chosen to largely practice primary care and so the plan lists them with general internists as primary care providers.) Though these providers form the core of plans' primary care provider lists and are most often selected by enrollees for this role, most plans also allow some other providers to be selected. In a third of the network/IPA type plans, the contracted groups or IPAs have the flexibility to set their own rules on provider selection, with the result that some allow OB/GYNs and/or subspecialists to be selected as primary care physicians. In fact, a significant minority of plans (10 of 23) allow selection of OB/GYNs as gatekeepers, though the extent to which OB/GYNs actually play this role is reported to be minimal. Although not often selected as a primary care provider through which care is channeled, OB/GYNs appear to provide a substantial amount of primary care. Most plans reported that OB/GYNs provide well-woman and obstetric and gynecological care upon patient self-referral to complement care delivered by the regular primary care provider; about three fourths of plans allow at least some self-referral for OB/GYN care.

Other common policies on who acts as a gatekeeper are allowing specialists to serve as primary care providers on a case-by-case, approved basis, and allowing NPs and PAs to be selected if specifically requested by the patient although these providers are not on the publicized list of primary care providers. A few plans had a unique approach reflecting their particular philosophy or circumstances; for example, in remote rural areas served by one plan, PAs or OB/GYNs may be selected due to a lack of the types of providers the plan uses in other parts of its service area.

Plans do not frequently use subspecialists as primary care providers, though more than three fourths of the plans allow them to play this role on a rare or exceptions basis, and about a third freely allow enrollees to select these providers as gatekeepers. Many plans view subspecialists without additional primary care training as poor providers of primary care, reporting that they tend to do more specialty care than other primary care providers, to be unhappy and want to return to their specialty, and refer to others too much for conditions they, as primary care providers, should handle. The eight plans that allow subspecialists to be selected as a primary care provider on more than an exceptions basis generally reported they do so because (1) they believe this practice is cost-effective (e.g., the plan otherwise had excess specialist capacity), (2) there is a large number of subspecialists in the market area who would not be able to stay based only on the basis of demand for specialty care, or (3) they want to provide consumers with as much choice of providers as possible within their network. These plans generally reported that while subspecialists are permitted to act as primary care providers with few restrictions, they generally do not play this role often, either because they are not selected by patients or because they do not choose to act in this role.

Plans vary in the extent to which they rely on internists compared with FPs for primary care. (Plans almost never distinguished between FPs and GPs in their policies or statistics, so following their lead both groups are labeled FPs for simplicity.) In over 60 percent of the plans (14 of 23), internists greatly outnumber FPs, or vice versa—that is, the plan clearly prefers and has experience with one type of primary care provider or the other. The remaining nine plans (39 percent) have a relatively even mixture of internists and FPs. Table 16–2 shows plan differences in this mix by model type. The reasons for the fact that internists greatly outnumber FPs in some plans did not always surface in discussion, but seem likely to be related to the plan's origin, when it was closely associated with a multispecialty group, to restrictions in some areas on admitting privileges for FPs by the hospitals with which the plan contracts, and to plan-imposed restrictions on FP practice, such as not al-

Table 16–2

Differences in Mix of Internists and Family Practitioners by Model Type

	Percentage of HMOs		
Primary care physician mix*	**Group/staff** **($n = 11$)**	**Network/IPA** **($n = 12$)**	**All types** **($n = 23$)**
Internists greatly outnumber family practitioners	46	17	30
Near even mix of internists and family practitioners	27	50	39
Family practitioners greatly outnumber internists	27	33	30

*Internists were considered to greatly outnumber FPs if the number of internists providing primary care was at least 50 percent greater than the number of FPs, or the plan described itself as heavily reliant on internists relative to other primary care providers. (The two pieces of information never conflicted but we did not have both pieces for every plan.) The reverse was true for categorizing plans where FPs greatly outnumbered internists.

lowing FPs to see children under a certain age or not allowing them to deliver infants, which would make plans with these restrictions less desirable to FPs seeking a full range of patient types. Differences in the competitive environment of HMOs may be another reason for different use of internists versus FPs, among network/IPA model plans. None of the network/IPA model plans in areas with high HMO penetration heavily used internists relative to FPs, although internists heavily outnumbered FPs in two of four plans in low penetration areas. If this pattern is real rather than coincidental, it could reflect greater pressure to reduce costs in areas with high levels of HMO competition.

Several plans now using some FPs expressed their intent to use more of them. For example, one found it more cost-effective when moving into a new area to hire one FP rather than both an internist and pediatrician. Several plans see them as more flexible than internists given the larger range of ages they treat. However, other plans are more ambivalent about FPs and thus are not planning to use them more relative to other primary care providers. One plan found that FPs are more acceptable in the lower income areas than in other areas in its market. Another noted that while adults in its market are indifferent to seeing an internist or FP, they prefer that their children see a pediatrician.

Primary care gatekeepers for children

Children in the study plans have a pediatrician or an FP as their primary care physician gatekeeper. Plans in which internists heavily outnumber FPs tend to use more pediatricians for their enrolled children, since internists do not treat children. Few plans (only

three) require children to see pediatricians rather than the FPs who are available. There were not many rules or specific policies on primary care for children. The exceptions were one plan that had a specific policy requiring contracted providers to arrange with other providers to ensure 24-hour coverage for their practice, and that those who agree to provide coverage must treat patients of the same ages as those treated by the provider being covered (many pediatricians restrict their practice to children under a certain age, e.g., 15 or 18; and many internists see patients only over a certain age, e.g., 15 or 18, but the age limits vary by practice). A second plan had specific guidelines for when children must be seen by a pediatrician rather than another type of provider (e.g., sick children under age 1). Plans generally do not specify an age at which a patient must switch from a pediatrician to an internist but allow this to vary by pediatrician and internist practice.

Using Nurse Practitioners and Physician Assistants

Only two plans (of the 23) allow routine selection of NPs or PAs as gatekeepers; two others allow enrollees to select an NP or PA as a primary care provider if they specifically ask to or if medical group/IPA rules allow. Importantly, however, NPs and PAs provide primary care as part of a patient care team in most of the HMOs we visited. NPs, in particular, make up a large part of group/staff model plans' primary care staff, as shown in Table 16–3. Nearly two thirds of group/staff model plans use NPs extensively, and one third use PAs to

Table 16–3

Use of Nurse Practitioners by Model Type

	Group/staff model plans (Percentage of HMOs)	Network/IPA model plans (Percentage of HMOs)
Heavy use	64	0
Some use	9	33
Rare use	18	59
No use	9	8

some extent (more than "rarely"). (Plans were classified by frequency of use of NPs and PAs to show the major patterns of use, but the classifications are rough rather than precise. For example, plans were considered "heavy" users of NPs or PAs if they had at least one NP or PA for every five primary care physicians, or, if this figure was not available, if they considered themselves or their physicians to be heavy users of these providers. In the case of a plan that used some NPs or PAs, did not qualify as a "heavy" user, and did not specifically describe use as "rare," we classified the plan as having "some use.") Only one group/staff model plan does not use NPs, all use PAs to some extent, and much but not all of this use was for primary care. The general pattern of use for NPs and PAs was similar, though PAs were used somewhat less than NPs.

Group/staff model plans in the sample in areas with high levels of HMO penetration use NPs more heavily than other plans; all four of the group/staff model plans in areas with high HMO penetration (25 percent or more of the insured population) heavily used NPs, versus only two of the four in lower penetration areas. If the difference is real and not only a result of the markets we selected or other contributing causes related to these markets (e.g., the location of markets with high penetration), potential reasons for it could include better consumer and physician acceptance of NPs in areas with a long history of managed care, or increased pressure on plans to reduce service delivery costs in areas with heavy competition from other HMOs.

Plans reported that NPs and PAs most commonly work six areas:

1. general primary care (13 plans)
2. urgent care (7 plans)
3. specialized positions (6 plans)
4. pediatric care (6 plans)
5. OB/GYN care (5 plans)
6. telephone triage (3 plans)

Four plans expressed a desire to increase use of NPs or PAs, but were finding recruiting very difficult. For example, one plan reported having to raise NP and PA salaries twice by mid-1994 to keep up with the competition and retain its own providers. It has also begun to use market surveys on a continuing basis to gauge this trend and keep its salaries in line.

A large minority of plans (8 of 23) are very supportive of NPs and PAs, and the rest are less supportive, neutral, or negative. (The classification of plans into "very supportive" or "less supportive, neutral, or negative" was considered both in terms of their use of NPs and PAs, and in terms of any special actions or plans to enhance their role or increase their number.) Only one or two plans could be categorized as being generally negative toward these providers. As Table 16–4 shows, very supportive plans tend to be group/staff model plans and plans without Medicaid contracts. It is not surprising that group/staff model plans were found to be more supportive, given that their general structure (organized multispecialty group or medical center settings rather than individual offices) is more conducive to providing ample work for NPs or PAs. It is not clear how to interpret the finding that

Table 16–4

Types of Plans More and Less Supportive of Nurse Practitioners and Physician Assistants

	Very supportive	Less supportive, neutral, or negative*
All plans	35	65
Predominant model type		
Group/staff (n = 11)	64	36
Network/IPA (n = 12)	8	92
Medicaid enrollment		
None (n = 12)	50	50
1–24 percent of total enrollment (n = 3)	33	67
25+ percent of total enrollment (n = 8)	13	88

*Only one or two plans could be categorized as generally negative toward these providers.

Exhibit 16–1 Nature of Support for NPs and PAs

Supportive Actions
- Two plans already heavily using NPs and PAs are considering expanding their use—one created a task force to review the advantages and disadvantages of more extensive use.
- One group/staff model plan was raising the status of NPs and removing their nursing duties in hopes of better retaining them.
- One plan had recognized some group physicians using NPs as nurses and influenced them to more appropriately use these providers.
- Heavy use of NPs by 7 plans and PAs by 2 plans.

Supportive Comments
- NPs and PAs are cost-effective providers.
- Consumers in the plan feel more comfortable talking to them than to physicians.
- Consumers like them (generally).
- NPs have a feel for preventive care and teaching due to their training.
- Physicians like them because it enables their practice to be more productive, thus benefiting them financially.

Other Comments
- Most network/IPA plans were neutral or offered verbal support only, because they viewed

decisions on NPs and PAs as an IPA or medical group decision.
- Many of the network/IPA plans did not track NP or PA use by their contracted providers.
- Several plans reported physicians were mixed in their views on these providers:
  — Some physicians favored using them.
  — Others viewed them as not cost-effective, too inclined to refer patients back to them, too inclined to spend excessive time with patients, or requiring too much supervision.
- Some plans reported mixed views by consumers. One plan's consumer-based strategy was in part distinguishing itself from its competitor by not using NPs or PAs.
- One reported being cautious about contracting with groups that use PAs due to the medical director's past experience with finding they were used without appropriate supervision.
- One heavy-Medicaid plan reported that it does not view NPs and PAs as very useful for its enrollees because the Medicaid clients tend to be sicker than other populations.
- One plan cited lack of availability of hospital privileges as a factor for NPs and PAs.

plans with Medicaid contracts tend to be less supportive of NPs and PAs. Exhibit 16–1 provides examples of how and why plans are more or less supportive of NPs and PAs. The most common reason for lower levels of support is that the plan views decisions on NPs and PAs as being within the discretion of the medical group or physician.

Both plans that are generally supportive of NPs and PAs and those less supportive reported that a substantial proportion of their physicians have negative views on the usefulness or cost-effectiveness of these providers. Such views appear to be a major barrier to increasing the use of NPs and PAs.

Structuring Access to Referrals

The primary care provider selected by enrollees generally functions as a gatekeeper, authorizing refer-

rals for all or most specialty care according to plan rules. In less restrictive plans, any primary care provider the patient sees may perform this function, or, rarely, patients are free to make their own referral choices. Even when gatekeeping policies are generally restrictive, plans normally specify certain services that patients may access without a referral. The most common clinical areas for which plans allow self-referrals are shown in Table 16–5.

Plan policies for gatekeeping and referral vary widely, and although there are not strong patterns by model type, there is some tendency for network/IPA plans to delegate gatekeeping policies to their contracted groups/IPAs. Thirty percent (7) of the 23 plans use a strict or fairly strict gatekeeper model. That is, these plans require enrollees to select a primary care provider, then limit self-referrals requiring most care to be referred by the primary care provider. Even among these plans,

Table 16–5

Common Clinical Areas Where HMOs Allowed
Enrollees to Self-Refer

Clinical area	Number of HMOs ($n = 23$)
Limited OB/GYN	15
Mental health	7
Optometry	7
Substance abuse	5
Dermatology	2
All or nearly all care	3
No self-referrals	1

however, most permit self-referral for limited OB/GYN care (6 of 7 plans). At the other extreme, 30 percent have very open policies or practices. Enrollees in these plans are able to access a wide range of primary care and specialty providers without getting a referral from their gatekeeper (if they chose one). Two plans in this group allow any physician within a patient's chosen health center to treat the patient without a referral, although referrals are required for any other care. Seventeen percent (4 plans) lie between these extremes. For example, they require a primary care provider to be chosen but allow nearly unrestricted access to other providers. Or they encourage but do not require selection of a primary care provider. The requirements for referrals to specialists are more strict than those of the plans described in the preceding item.

The remaining 22 percent of plans (5), all of which are network/IPA plans, either allow their contracted groups or IPAs to make these policies (4 of the 5 plans), or the rules differ depending on whether the contracted entity is a group or an IPA. If the entity is an IPA, a primary care provider must be chosen on the theory that more loosely structured entities need this rule to manage care by their providers.

The higher level of competition that plans face in areas with high HMO penetration may tend to influence them toward more open gatekeeping policies, (e.g., because of consumer preferences for more open access) although the small numbers prevent conclusions on this point. Only 1 of 7 plans (14 percent) in areas with high HMO penetration maintained strict gatekeeping policies versus 4 of 8 plans in areas with low to moderate HMO penetration.

Referrals must usually be in writing, although some plans allow referrals by phone or are equipped for electronic referrals. Face-to-face contact between a patient and a physician is not always required for a referral, for example, if the physician knows the patient and has discussed his or her problem by phone. Most plans allow patients to self-refer to specialists for at least one or two types of care, most often for a limited amount of OB/GYN care (Table 16–5).

In general, plans appear to be moving toward tighter gatekeeping arrangements and self-referral policies. Even two of the three most open plans support tighter gatekeeping arrangements in theory; their policies are open only because of major transitions. The main reasons plans gave for tighter arrangements is the perception that they enhance access to and continuity of care, and permit the plan to hold a provider accountable for a patient's care. Concerns about access and accountability are perhaps best explained by one plan as follows. Before the plan required patients to select a primary care provider, they would sometimes diagnose themselves as needing a specialist and call the specialist's office for an appointment. The administrative assistant who received the patient's request would often have to inform the patient that the physician had no appointments for many weeks, and the patient would try another specialist, perhaps in a related field, to gain access to care, perhaps with a similar lack of success. The frustrated patient would complain to the plan, but the plan had no one to hold accountable for the care of the patient. In the current system, the primary care provider can (1) ensure the patient is referred to the correct specialist, (2) facilitate access to this provider, and (3) be held accountable by the plan if he or she does not perform the first two functions.

Plans that have recently tightened their gatekeeping arrangements or are considering doing so indicated that the process takes considerable time and effort. One plan just completed an 18-month process; another reported it would probably tighten its system in the near future, but the medical director knows from experience about the difficult and controversial nature of the process.

Plans are not uniformly moving toward tighter gatekeeping. Five plans reported having recently and selectively eliminated referral requirements, for example, for optometry, after finding that primary care providers do not do any related screening or care, and thus contact with the primary care provider seemed unnecessary. Further, several plans are content with an open policy of care at the chosen health center and require referrals for care from physicians outside the center. Two predominantly group/staff model plans feel this way, and one network/IPA model plan noted that it often finds the groups that are more experienced with managed care are open about on-site referrals (these tend to be large, organized multispecialty group or health center settings). Only one plan directly challenged the concept of gatekeeping as a useful tool for managing care or containing costs. This plan believes that patients can effectively refer themselves for many conditions, and that capitating specialists should be the main mechanism for encouraging appropriate allocation of both resources and care between primary and specialty care providers.

Scope of Practice

Overall, plans perceive that the scope of practice of primary care physicians has not changed much in recent years. Beyond this generalization, all agree that there is not one agreed-upon set of conditions or treatments that constitute the scope of practice of primary care. Thus, the level of care received from a primary care provider may vary depending on the provider's comfort level and experience with certain procedures or conditions more than on any consensus about the scope of practice for primary care providers.

Specific primary care responsibilities may be defined under primary care capitation arrangements; that is, to the extent that physicians are capitated for primary care, they will have responsibility for a defined set of services associated with the capitation amount. (Since examining individual physician payment arrangements was beyond the scope of the study, the evidence is suggestive rather than conclusive in terms of the link between the definition of primary care and payment strategy.) However, not all primary care providers are paid on a capitated basis; in some and perhaps many cases, the medical group or IPA is capitated but chooses to pay its physicians on a discounted fee-for-service basis.

While the content of care practiced by primary care physicians does not appear to have changed substantially, or while such changes are at most limited to a few areas, there is some evidence that changes may soon occur. The study identified three main factors affecting what services are provided by primary care providers rather than specialists: (1) plan financial or other incentives to increase the range of primary care practice (six plans); (2) malpractice liability risk, which has reduced the range of primary care practice in certain areas (two plans); and (3) plan efforts to standardize what is considered primary care; in theory the efforts could either increase or decrease the range of primary care practice (three plans). In practice, it seems likely that plans are interested in standardizing the definition in order to encourage a wider range of practice for those primary care providers who tend to do less than others in their plan.

The financial or other means to increase the range of primary care practice include expanding lists of procedures considered to be primary care. For example, one plan reported adding ECG, minor acne, and allergy injections to its list; another added immunizations, ECGs, pregnancy and other routine tests, colonoscopies, and endoscopies. One plan pays a higher capitation amount to the primary care provider if the patient sees him or her rather than an OB/GYN for a routine gynecological exam. Another provides a financial incentive to primary care providers for performing instead of referring flexible sigmoidoscopies. Other plans simply noted that their compensation models (e.g., capitation to a group that includes specialty services) encourage a broadening of primary care practice.

In addition to expanding the list of procedures, another effort to increase the range of primary care involves redirecting patients with defined borderline conditions back to primary care providers. The plan making this attempt has identified low back pain, minor lacerations, and mild inflammatory bowel disease, for example, as conditions that primary care providers, rather than surgeons, should be treating. The plan is assessing referral patterns for these conditions to develop practice guidelines.

On the other hand, plans in two markets reported that malpractice liability risk has reduced the scope of practice for primary care providers. Some of those who once provided obstetrical care or care for newborns have now reportedly discontinued these services because of the real or perceived high risk of malpractice suits.

The study found three examples of plan efforts to standardize the definition of primary care. The first plan is more specifically defining what primary care providers should do by using lists of procedures because of the current need for computer software packages that could identify payable bills versus procedures included in a primary care capitation amount. The second plan is circulating among providers medical management guidelines that define what primary care providers should be doing. Providers were to comment on the guidelines. The medical director's intent is to encourage physicians to buy into the list of guidelines. The effort stemmed from his observation of wide differences among individual primary care providers in the types of patients they feel comfortable treating. The third plan is analyzing the types of conditions that are being referred from primary care providers, then convening groups of specialists and primary care providers to attempt to reach a consensus on what can be done by primary care physicians. This plan reported that additional training for some primary care providers is the natural follow-up to such an effort, and that it is organizing and will support this training. The plan reported a positive outcome from the process it used to develop this list. It perceived that the primary care and specialist physicians left the meetings with stronger working relationships and a better understanding of each other's capabilities and responsibilities.

The second and third efforts were in progress at the time of the site visit, and therefore the nature of primary care has not yet substantially changed in these plans.

Implications

While HMOs generally pursue a more organized primary care delivery strategy than the fee-for-service sector, their strategies vary substantially across plans. Even the plans with tight gatekeeping systems allow patients access to some services without referral (OB/GYN self-referrals were allowed on a limited basis in 15 of the 23 plans) though beyond OB/GYN plans do not agree on which services patients should directly access. Also, not all plans required selection

of a single primary care gatekeeper, though all at least encouraged it. Plans truly ranged from virtually unrestricted access to the plan's full network of providers at one extreme, to plans that strictly required nearly all care decisions be channeled through the chosen primary care provider.

Contracting provider groups have a large role in structuring primary care delivery in network/IPA model plans. This is an increasingly important observation since much of the growth of managed care is occurring in this type of plan.[3,4] Contrary to the popular notion that health plans determine most aspects of delivery, many of the network/IPA type plans we visited paid medical groups or IPAs on a capitated basis, then took a hands-off attitude toward delivery. It was often the medical group or IPA that was responsible for rules regarding choice of primary care provider, and use of NPs or PAs, for example.

Also, the care a patient receives from a primary care physician appears to vary depending on the provider's level of comfort and experience with certain procedures or conditions more than on any consensus about the scope of practice for primary care physicians. There are signs that the scope of practice of primary care physicians may expand for those physicians who now practice primary care within a narrower scope than their peers. For example, 6 of the 23 HMOs reported having financial incentives or educational initiatives to expand the content of primary care. However, they described these as small steps that were not likely to result in large changes in primary care practice in the near future.

Finally, plans' views on the use of subspecialists and OB/GYNs as gatekeepers raise a cautionary note. As policy makers and providers seek opportunities to balance the number of specialists relative to primary care providers, use of specialists in primary care roles may become more common. Yet the findings suggest that plans often view the primary care skills of such providers negatively. At a minimum, initiatives to retrain specialists to practice primary care will be critical to address the perceived problems of over-referral and specialty orientation. Further, some plans were skeptical that primary care was a fitting role for many subspecialists, since the skills used in primary care differ greatly from those attracting physicians to certain specialties (e.g., radiology).

In sum, the diversity among health plans in their primary care strategies is evident from the study. However, the relative desirability of the various strategies has to do with both value judgments (e.g., about what organization or person should be held accountable for an enrollee's care) and unanswered research questions about how different strategies and incentives toward expanded primary care practice affect health care costs, outcomes, and satisfaction with care.

REFERENCES

1. Gold, M., et al. "Behind the Curve: A Critical Assessment of How Little Is Known About Arrangements Between Managed Care Plans and Physicians." *Medical Care Research and Review* 52(3) (September 1995): 307–341.
2. Felt, S., Frazer, H., and Gold, M. "HMO Primary Care Staffing Patterns and Processes: A Cross-Site Analysis of 23 HMOs." Washington, D.C.: Mathematica Policy Research, Inc., December 23, 1994R.
3. Group Health Association of America. *1995 National Directory of HMOs*. Washington, D.C., GHAA: June 1995.
4. Group Health Association of America. *1993 National Directory of HMOs*. Washington, D.C., GHAA: June 1993.

17

Managing Care for Mental Illness: Paradox and Pitfalls

Leslie J. Scallet

The potential for applying "managed care" techniques in caring for people with mental illnesses and disorders seems at once the most natural development possible and the most dangerous. Managed care fits beautifully with the direction of the field toward comprehensive systems of care (community mental health centers, community support systems, case management). However, its threat to the existing service structures and programs creates a very real possibility that in making the shift, vital elements will be lost and the most vulnerable populations once again will be ill-served.

This seeming paradox is deeply rooted in some basic realities of the mental health care system, how it has differed from the rest of health care, and why those differences present somewhat distinct challenges and opportunities. Today's choices—public versus private responsibilities, scope and design of benefits, integrated or carve-out models—grow directly from the particular history and structure of mental health care. In turn, that history gave mental health care an early introduction and long experience with many of the key elements of managed care now sweeping the entire health care field.

Massachusetts has played a pioneering role in the ongoing drama of mental health care, so it is no accident that the two articles presented here focus on how managed care programs are evolving in that state. These two examples in fact represent the two current leading choices in managed care systems for people experiencing mental disorders: the integrated model (Stelovich) and the carve-out model (Counihan et al.). Their history is extensive enough to provide a basis for some observations.

Two Dual Systems

Historically, mental health care has been regarded as separate from physical health care. Following World War II, this traditional pattern began to break down. However, the history of segregation remains a powerful current in health care and health policy today.

While the medical model dominated in mental health, the disorders and their treatment as well as their funding and reimbursement mechanisms remained largely separate from medical care in the minds of practitioners, patients, and the public. For example, mental health care had strong public sector support for well over a century before the advent of significant public responsibility for physical health conditions. Separate treatment facilities were the rule. In addition to psychiatry, a whole coterie of separate specialty professionals developed.

Within the mental health sector a second duality historically obtained: between a public system, largely hospital-based and often involuntary, and a private-practice system, largely office-based and voluntary. However, both remained over many years essentially distinct from the physical health care domain.[1–3]

After World War II the growing popularity of psychoanalysis and psychotherapy, the appearance of the first effective medications for the symptomatic relief of severe mental disorders, and, somewhat later, a growing recognition of the civil rights and dignity of individuals suffering from mental disorders combined to begin bringing mental health care into the mainstream. However, this development was shaped in significant ways by two underlying dualities: mental/physical and public/private.

In the private sphere, acknowledgment grew that mental disorders affected large numbers of people, that there was a wide spectrum of disorder ranging from transient and minor problems to very severe and dysfunctional conditions, and that effective treat-

Managed Care Quarterly 1996; 4(3): 93–99
© 1996 Aspen Publishers, Inc.

ments could help people to recover. The spread of private health insurance, along with employer recognition that mental problems affected productivity and absenteeism fueled an expansion of mental health coverage as an element of health insurance. However, these benefits typically were circumscribed through differential limitations.

Throughout the private health insurance market, an assumption prevailed that policies could be limited safely for mental health, because anyone needing additional care could (and should) turn to the public sector safety net. Early models of managed care, such as health maintenance organizations (HMOs), incorporated this view.[4,5]

The public mental health system, however, had a life of its own, and increasingly diverged from that assumption. From the 1950s on, the projected costs of state mental hospitals spurred an exploration of less expensive alternatives and an imperative to define priorities for limited public dollars. These changes retained the separate public role but significantly reduced its capacity to provide the safety net assumed by the health system in general and private insurance in particular.

Two developments of the 1960s—the creation of Medicaid and the Community Mental Health Center (CMHC) movement—illustrate the converging mental health and health systems tempered by the ongoing influence of historical dualities. Today's managed care models, including the two in Massachusetts, grow directly from these forces.

Community Mental Health Centers, Medicaid, and Managed Care

The Community Mental Health Center movement was in many respects a forerunner of managed care.[6] Its avowed purpose was to contain or reduce costs while providing more appropriate and less intensive care. It postulated a defined population, limited dollars, flexible coverage of care for a spectrum of disorders, a focus on prevention and early intervention, and a team of multidisciplinary providers implementing an organized plan of care for an individual.

The CMHC also was designed as a bridge between public and private mental health care. It created an alternative system to serve people with severe and chronic illness who might otherwise spend years in the state institutional system, as well as a broad range of people in the community who might have limited or no access to insurance or who might need something other than the traditional model of private office-based therapy. The network of local centers was to be established with federal seed funds, declining over time, and eventually replaced by a mix of state and private insurance dollars.

CMHCs (along with civil rights lawyers) have sustained often bitter criticism for the "failure of deinstitutionalization" and the suffering of many people with severe and chronic mental illnesses who never received the care and services in the community that were supposed to replace the comforts of the state hospital. That subject deserves more attention than this brief treatment can offer. Suffice it to say here that the failure to establish even half the planned number of centers, and the gross underfunding of an ever-increasing array of required services, represented a failure of political will that doomed the centers' attempt to fulfill their mandate.[7]

States discharged many patients to communities but also resisted funding upstart "independent" centers at the expense of state-run institutions with politically powerful constituencies. Survival instincts drove many centers to focus on insured or paying populations, and later toward provision of contract services such as employee assistance programs (and now, managed care).

In sum, while one of the most effective arguments for creating a community-based system was the goal of replacing expensive and often horrific state hospitals, the ultimate result was that the population previously served in the hospitals too often were ill-served by the new community-based system. However, by the late 1970s this problem was well understood, and steps were taken by both the federal and state governments to address it.

The resulting Community Support System (CSS) concept drew on the CMHC model: defining a target population, designing services needed by that group, and providing a flexible, individualized plan of service. Instead of bypassing the states or decreeing a one-size-fits-all approach, starting in 1977 it engaged them in a participatory process that identified essential common elements but accommodated differences among state environments. Direct federal funding to CMHCs was replaced over time by block grants to the states focused exclusively on the target population but "grandfathering" the CMHCs as service providers, drawing the community mental health centers and the states into alliance around a target population of individuals with severe and persistent mental illnesses.[8–10]

This 10-year effort (1977–1987)[11] provides one of the best examples of a true federal-state partnership. A related effort focused on children with severe emotional disturbances. The Child and Adolescent Service System Program (CASSP) conceptualized a "system of care" for children living in communities and utilizing multiple service systems, e.g., education, juvenile justice, child welfare as well as mental health and health. The Federal CSP program has continued to the present time. However, beginning in 1988, it shifted toward a research demonstration model rather than the catalyst/learning community model.

A key element of both the CSS and CASSP strategies was to maximize Medicaid as a source of payment for community-based mental health and support services. When Medicaid was created in the mid-1960s the drafters, like their contemporaries designing expanded private health insurance policies, recognized that the general run of beneficiaries might need mental health care and included a measure of general coverage as part of the mandatory package. Also like their counterparts, they had no desire to assume the safety net responsibility traditionally belonging to the states. Therefore they limited most mental health services to the optional category, and carefully excluded coverage for people over 22 or under 65 residing in "institutions for mental disease" (IMDs), that is the population thought to be resident in state mental hospitals. States continued to reflect the separate sense of public responsibility for mental health, retaining separate departments of mental health even as they established large health bureaucracies to administer the new Medicaid program.

However, by the late 1970s much of the population formerly residing in state hospitals for years actually now lived much or all of the time in the community. Also the growth of health insurance, including mental health benefits (despite limitations) had encouraged the expansion of private hospitals specializing in mental health care but not eligible (since they were IMDs) for Medicaid reimbursement for nonelderly adults. The interests of public and private sector mental health interests found common ground in advocating effectively for the expansion of Medicaid plans to cover inpatient reimbursement for eligible populations (children/adolescents and the elderly) and community-based services under the clinic option and later the rehabilitation option.[12–14]

At the same time, private insurance coverage for the employed population was also expanding in response to greater acknowledgment of the needs and benefits of such care for both employees and employers. For a brief time in the mid-1980s, it appeared that public and private roles in both health and mental health were stabilizing and converging and that mental health had established its place within both public and private health care financing systems. However, accelerating cost pressures in both public and private sectors derailed that progress and threatened to turn back the clock.

Managing Mental Health Care

The timing of mental health's advances could not have been worse. During the 1980s health costs assumed crisis proportions in the minds of private sector payers. The recent expansion of mental health benefits had produced disproportionately large percentage increases in costs, since they started from such a small base, creating a perception that those costs were out of control and perhaps one of the chief causes of the overall problem. Well-publicized abuses of insurance, particularly for long-term hospitalization for adolescents covered under their parents' policies and for substance abuse treatment, added fuel to the fire.

Mental health benefits became one of the first targets of "managed care" in the private sector, with the avowed goal of containing and reducing costs. Strategies included higher deductibles and copayments, lower limits on annual and lifetime benefits, and more limits on inpatient and outpatient visits for mental health than for physical health care.

Soon specialty firms began to appear, offering to "manage" mental health benefits to save even more. Some focused on utilization review, primarily for hospital admissions and length of stay and for long-term psychotherapy. Others developed a more flexible approach, willing to waive specific benefit limits and cover additional or newer forms of service that offered the promise of containing total costs. However, the primary focus was clearly on cost management rather than care management.[15]

In the public sector, state and local mental health services had come to rely increasingly on Medicaid dollars in order to obtain shared federal financing.[16] As costs rose, and political pressures protected hospital budgets, state mental health agencies managed costs by increasingly limiting their priorities (and most access to public services) to individuals who could qualify for Medicaid and those few others who could gain a claim on the state through the justice system or as a "state [hospital] patient."

As hospitalization was discouraged and lengths of stay decreased, fewer and fewer patients could meet admission criteria, which usually now required an extreme form of illness or demonstration of dangerousness even for voluntary admission. Public hospital emergency rooms began to face barriers in sending people to state hospitals. Individuals who exhausted their private insurance benefits simply could not access public services unless they became indigent and enrolled in Medicaid or demonstrated extreme or dangerous behavior. By the mid-1980s the old, comfortable assumption that a state mental health system was available to back up private health insurance, HMOs, and public hospitals had become obsolete. Instead, both the public and the private systems were managing the costs of mental health care by limiting services and access.

However, both sectors also provided models of "care management." It is no accident that many of the early developers of "managed behavioral health care" came out of the community mental health center movement, or that private sector–managed behavioral health care companies today are competing vigorously for talented staff from state mental health agencies and national nonprofit organizations. Aside from representing the one area of growth in the field today, managed care offers what many see as a new and in some ways better way to pursue their professional goal of rationalizing and improving care.

The Community Support System (CSS) and Child and Adolescent Service System Program (CASSP)—public sector models for adults and children, respectively, with severe mental disorders—demonstrated effective strategies to both assemble resources and provide a flexible array of services geared to the changing needs of a long-term and often very expensive population. Some progressive private employers pioneered a flexible, managed mental health benefit that allowed reimbursement for essentially any mental health service that was cost-effective in the long run.[17] Some progressive HMOs (as illustrated in the Stelovich article) began to experiment with including a broader range of mental health services than the original, intentionally limited design, including services for people with severe mental illnesses.

In the late 1980s and 1990s, managed care advanced rapidly in all areas of health, receiving a boost from the national health care reform debate of 1993–1994. Private insurance increasingly incorporated managed care for all benefits, and HMOs and insurers competed on ways to handle the mental health benefit. Some HMOs and newer forms of managed care chose an integrated strategy; others a specialized "carve-out" for all mental health care or for long-term mental health care. Managed behavioral health care firms grew rapidly in response to these opportunities, shaping their approaches to meet the needs of their customers—primarily large corporations. In 1993 these firms were responsible for over 86 million covered lives. By 1995 the total was almost 111 million covered lives.[18,19]

States began to believe that managed care could be the answer to their escalating Medicaid budgets, and developed such lucrative contracts that managed behavioral health care firms jumped into this new market, immediately challenging the expertise and livelihood of longstanding public "care management" providers, such as CMHCs and psychosocial rehabilitation centers.

Dilemmas and Doubts

Read in this context, the two articles here present acute dilemmas for the future development of managed care for individuals with mental illnesses. Managed care, as traditionally understood, would seem to offer the potential to further goals long promoted by reformers in the mental health system: reducing service fragmentation, increasing access to individualized care, establishing accountability, reducing costs, and shifting from unnecessary institutional care to more appropriate and less restrictive community services. However, experience to date in both the mental health and health arenas underscores significant risks.[20]

Underfunding

Mental health traditionally has been underfunded in relation to its impact on the population, in public systems, insurance, and HMOs.[21–23] Cost estimates today are suspect, since they are highly skewed by the current dualities and their opportunities for cost shifting (e.g., "dumping" of expensive patients onto the public mental health system, or out of all mental health care and into the criminal justice system or the street). The usual assumption of cost savings engendered by a move to managed care simply may be unrealistic, and attempts to wring savings from the system may produce dangerous cuts in services.

No Net

A casualty of the move toward increased reliance on private, for-profit managed care may be the public sector safety net. In the early years of managed mental health care, big profits nurtured the development of the managed behavioral health care industry. They now are rapidly taking over many of the functions formerly provided by public agencies and a large network of not-for-profit providers. In some cases they are in fact "buying up" key staff and incorporating service providers into the for-profit networks. But as both private sector and then public sector learn better how to estimate costs, and the profit margin falls, companies may simply withdraw from a market and move on to greener pastures. What service structures will be left to serve the people who need care the most?

Going Backwards

The field has made significant advances in the past 15 or 20 years.[24] A lot is known about the constellation of services and supports needed to serve individuals with severe mental illnesses and children with severe emotional disturbances outside hospitals and institutions. However, the applications of this knowledge have occurred within publicly dominated service and financing structures. Now the rush is on to replace these structures with contracts to managed care companies whose experience was shaped by serving a private sector, employed population base—an experience largely devoid of focus on the populations with the most complex needs. The rapidity of change risks failure to translate the substantive learning about how best to serve seriously disabled populations into this new environment.

For example, it took long years of effort in the public sector to gain understanding and acceptance of the vital role of "ancillary" support services for the success of medical services provided by Medicaid. In an era of Medicaid cutbacks, and loss of visibility for mental health constituencies within an integrated public financing system, how long will it be before Medicaid managed care contracts include adequate community support requirements in their definitions of "medical necessity?"

Loss of Focus and Memory

The prospect of integration of mental health with health care strikes chords of ambivalence in the field. On the one hand, mental health has struggled mightily for recognition as a serious, medical concern. The long and ultimately successful battle to return the National Institute of Mental Health to the National Institutes of Health vividly illustrates the determination to be a part of the larger health structure. On the other hand, many fear that integration would mean a loss of visibility and focus on mental health problems. They note the low priority and prestige of mental health in many academic, clinical, and policy settings concerned with health broadly. They believe in integration, but not yet.

Part of this struggle involves habit and established ways of thinking and relating with each other and with the relevant environment. Part is also a pragmatic fear of losing resources that they have now.[25] The risk involved in integration is that mental health must put its hard-won categorical funding (state, federal, local, as well as private insurance) on the table, with no assurance and often little confidence that they will break even in the political and popularity contest. If national and state mental heath agencies disappear or become low-level bureaus within giant health financing and contracting structures, what kind of priority will go to the needs of people with severe and persistent mental illnesses? Will we have to learn the lessons of deinstitutionalization again?

Institutional memory is a fragile commodity, now at great risk. Faced with the assault of managed care, the federal agencies and organized constituency groups are so busy trying to cope and protect their current program budgets that precious little attention is devoted to thoughtful consideration of long-term trends or opportunities. Few private foundations focus on mental health, or recognize the interrelationship of mental health over time with their priority concerns in physical health or social problems.

Managed Care Is Not a Panacea But an Opportunity

As daunting as these dilemmas may seem, they yet do not obviate the potential benefits of the managed care revolution. First, a primary institutional memory about mental health services is that the old system has never been very good for individuals with the most serious and chronic conditions. Yes, over the past couple of decades we have done better, and now have a good deal of confidence that we know what both adults and children need. But in practice, model systems have been few. We simply have never found a way to bring the benefits of our knowledge to most people in need.

Managed care, at least, offers an opportunity to rethink and restructure, to test a different approach. This experimentation entails real risks. The unfamiliar hazards of managed care seem even greater than those posed by the current system; many in the field would prefer "the devil they know."

One prime example of the new equation of risk and opportunity will be the role of consumer responsibility and choice. For the past 20 years, mental health consumers and families have demanded, and finally attained, a significant measure of participation in decisions affecting their care and their lives: the development of patients' rights charters in states and facilities; the spread of protection and advocacy programs to assist consumers; the establishment of consumer affairs offices in state mental health departments; and the vocal representation of consumer and family groups on planning, advisory, and governing councils.

Managed care posits an active and responsible consumer role for patients, entailing active participation in their own treatment as well as monitoring the system's performance through complaints and griev-

ances. How will the consumer activism of the mental health field translate into the context of managed care? On the one hand, the acceptance and reliance on consumers to participate will strengthen and extend a role that was won only with great effort and political pressure in the old system. On the other hand, what will private sector managed care do to assure that people receiving mental health care have access to the decision processes, information, and advocacy assistance they may need to play their designated role as responsible consumers? This challenge will help to define the success of managed care for mental health.

REFERENCES

1. Grob, G. N. *Mad Among Us: A History of the Care of America's Mentally Ill.* New York, NY: Free Press, 1994.
2. Rochefort, D. A., ed. *Handbook on Mental Health Policy in the United States.* Westport, CT: Greenwood Press, 1989.
3. Goldman, H.H., and Morrissey, J.P. "Alchemy of Mental Health Policy: Homelessness and the Fourth Cycle of Reform." *American Journal of Public Health* 75(7) (1978):727–731.
4. P.L. 93-322, Health Maintenance Organization Act of 1973.
5. Stelovich, S. "Evolution of Services for the Chronically Mentally Ill in a Managed Care Setting: A Case Study." *Managed Care Quarterly* 4(3) (1996):78–84.
6. Feldman, S. "Managed Mental Health—Community Mental Health Revisited?" *Managed Care Quarterly* 2(2) (1994):13–18.
7. Scallet, L.J. "Mental Health and Homelessness: Evidence of Failed Policy?" *Health Affairs* 8(4) (1989):185–188. Review of Torrey, E.F. *Nowhere to Go: The Tragic Odyssey of the Homeless Mentally Ill.* New York, NY: Harper and Row, 1988.
8. Mulkern, V. *Community Support Program: A Model for Federal-State Partnership.* Washington, D.C.: Mental Health Policy Resource Center, 1995.
9. Carling, P.J. *The National Institute of Mental Health Community Support Program: History and Evaluation.* Burlington, VT: University of Vermont, 1984.
10. Turner, J.C., and TenHoor, W.J. "The NIMH Community Support Program: Pilot Approach to a Needed Social Reform." *Schizophrenia Bulletin* 4(3) (1978):319–348.
11. Mulkern, *Community Support Program.*
12. Toff-Bergman, G. *Medicaid Plans and Mental Health: 1992 Profiles of State Options and Limitations.* Washington, D.C.: Mental Health Policy Resource Center, 1993.
13. Folcarelli, C., and Law, C. *Medicaid Plans and Mental Health: 1994 Updated Profiles of State Options and Limitations.* Fairfax, VA: Lewin/VHI, 1994.
14. Koyanagi, C., and Goldman, H.H. "Quiet Success of the National Plan for the Chronically Mentally Ill." *Hospital and Community Psychiatry* 42(9) (1991):899–905.
15. Trabin, T., and Freeman, M. A. *Managed Behavioral Healthcare: History, Models, Strategic Challenges and Future Course.* Tiburon, CA: CentraLink Publishers, 1995.

16. Counihan, C.W., et al. "A Medicaid Mental Health Carve-Out Program: The Massachusetts Experience." *Managed Care Quarterly* 4(3) (1996):85–92.

17. England, M.J., and Vaccaro, V.A. "New Systems to Manage Mental Health Care." *Health Affairs* 10(4) (1991):129–137.

18. Oss, M.E., ed. *Managed Behavioral Health Market Share in the United States, 1993.* Gettysburg, PA: Behavioral Health Industry News, Inc., 1993.

19. Oss, M.E., et al. *Managed Behavioral Health Market Share in the United States, 1995/1996.* Gettysburg, PA: Behavioral Health Industry News, Inc., 1995.

20. Iglehart, J.K. "Health Policy Report: Managed Care and Mental Health." *New England Journal of Medicine* 334(2) (1996):131–135.

21. Frank, R.G., and McGuire, T.G. "Estimating Costs of Mental Health and Substance Abuse Coverage." *Health Affairs* 14(3) (1995):102–115.

22. Stelovich, "Evolution of Services."

23. Counihan, "Mental Health Carve-Out."

24. Mechanic, D., Schlesinger, M., and McAlpine, D.D. "Management of Mental Health and Substance Abuse Services: State of the Art and Early Results." *Milbank Quarterly* 73(1) (1995): 19–55.

25. Stelovich, "Evolution of Services."

18

The End of Autonomy? Reflections on the Postprofessional Physician

Stephen J. O'Connor and Joyce A. Lanning

"Now hold on, hold on. You know just as well as I do that a high-priced man has to do exactly as he's told from the morning till night. You have seen this man (the taskmaster) before, haven't you?"

"No, I never saw him."

"Well, if you are a high-priced man, you will do exactly as this man tells you to-morrow, from morning till night. When he tells you to pick up a pig and walk, you pick it up and you walk, and when he tells you to sit down and rest, you sit down. You do that right straight through the day. And what's more, no back talk. Now a high-priced man does just what he's told to do, and no back talk. Do you understand that? When this man tells you to walk, you walk; when he tells you to sit down, you sit down, and you don't talk back at him. Now you come on to work here to-morrow morning and I'll know before night whether you are really a high-priced man or not."

—Frederick W. Taylor,
to his pig-iron handler, "Schmidt."[1(pp.45,46)]

Students of health care administration learn early on that the role of physician professionals in health care delivery distinguishes health administration from its more generic business administration counterpart. These students also recognize that the physician presence has major implications for the way in which health care organizations are designed and managed.

In dealing with physician professionals, nonphysician health care managers have faced constraints and limitations to their own organizational power and authority: Justification for this arrangement has typically been based on the premise that management and health care organizations must not interfere with the practice of medicine. Physicians alone may practice medicine; administrators manage the nonmedical bureaucratic structure that supports the physicians' work.

In many health care organizations, especially community hospitals, these distinct domains have resulted in the oft-cited dual line of authority: one medical, the other administrative.[2] The two domains, like oil and water, do not mix well. Physician professional and bureaucratic management discord is not a new phenomenon, but has occurred in the United States since the time of the Revolutionary War. General George Washington (ostensibly a bureaucratic manager with substantial power and authority), after his first inspection of the Continental Army, lamented in a letter to the early Congress:

> I have made inquiry into the establishment of the hospital, and find it in a very unsettled condition. There is no . . . subordination among the surgeons; of consequence, disputes have arisen, and must continue until it is reduced to some system. I could wish it was immediately taken into consideration, as the lives and health of both officers and men so much depend on due regulation of this department.[3(p.33)]

Although military surgeons during the Revolutionary War did not have the freedom or professional autonomy later accorded to their 20th century paral-

An earlier version of this paper was presented at the 1990 Annual Meeting of the Academy of Management. The authors gratefully acknowledge the helpful comments of Marlene Beggelman, M.D., President, Medical Intelligence (Brookline, MA); B. Kay Snavely, Ph.D., Miami University; and three anonymous reviewers.

Health Care Manage Rev 1992; 17(1): 63–72
© 1992 Aspen Publishers, Inc.

145

lels, they nonetheless made it difficult to manage even a highly disciplined bureaucratic military unit. The duality in the structure of authority observed in many modern health care organizations has been a frequent source of frustration, conflict, disagreement, and uncooperativeness for both professional physicians and bureaucratic managers alike. New economic pressures have extended the arena of conflict. As Shortell points out, "No longer is the issue who will control the hospital, but rather who will control the delivery system from the patient's home to the physician's office, to the hospital, to the postacute facility, and back again to the patient's home."[4(pp.11–12)]

This article examines the medical profession, first by analyzing the important role autonomy plays in defining a profession and how it has supported physician professional dominance in both health care organizations and society. The second section discusses the array of macro and micro influences in the health care environment that have contributed to reduced autonomy. The third section explores the consequences of diminished autonomy, and its effect on the medical profession, patients, payors, and on health care organization and management. This article should be of interest to anyone wishing to better understand current directions in the medical profession and how health care organizations are adapting to these altered circumstances.

What is a professional? Autonomy is the key!

A profession is often defined primarily in terms of the amount of autonomy and self-direction it maintains.[5–7] One way of establishing and maintaining professional dominance is to obtain autonomy over work.[6,8] Reed and Evans specify 10 major characteristics that bestow professional status on an occupation:

1. The profession is in possession of a circumscribed and socially valuable body of knowledge.
2. The members of the profession determine the profession's standards of knowledge and expertise.
3. The profession attracts high-quality students who undergo an extensive socialization process as they are absorbed into the profession.

4. The profession is given authority to license practitioners by the state, with licensing and admission boards made up largely of members of the profession.
5. There is an ostensible sense of community and mutuality of interest among members of a profession.
6. Social policy and legislation that relate to the profession are heavily influenced by members of the profession through such mechanisms as lobbying and expert testimony.
7. The profession has a code of ethics that governs practice, the tenets of which are more stringent than legal controls.
8. A service orientation supersedes the proprietary interests of the professionals.
9. Professions are terminal occupations (i.e., they are the practitioners' singular and lifelong occupational choice).
10. A profession is largely free of lay control, with its practitioners exercising a high degree of occupational autonomy.[9(p.3279)]

Figure 18–1 regroups these 10 characteristics in terms of the "who," "what," "why," and "how" of a profession. First is the selection, training, licensure, and cohesiveness of the profession, or who they are; second, their knowledge base and standards, or what they know; third, their service orientation and code of ethics, or why they act as they do; and fourth, their occupational autonomy and impact on social policy, or how they direct their activities. Autonomy is a necessary underpinning for all the other features. To the extent that the public questions physician adherence to the who, what, and why characteristics of professionalism or questions the benefits that society may derive, there is less willingness to allow autonomy—the central component of any profession.

Regardless of their theoretical base, all observers agree that legitimate, organized autonomy is the key feature of a profession. An occupation that is lacking this authentic autonomy may alternatively be given such designations as quasiprofession, paraprofession, semiprofession, subprofession, or a trade. A trade has been defined as a craft in which only skilled workers are employed.[10] Freidson, one of the most prolific writers on the topic of professionalism, places the medical profession squarely at the top of the para-

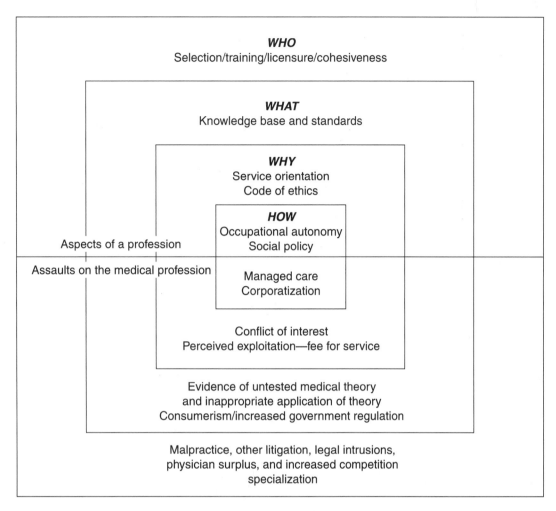

Figure 18–1. The medical profession: Aspects and assaults.

medical hierarchy, primarily as a result of its extraordinary autonomy—"the right to control its own work."[8(p.71)] Others have defined professional autonomy as controlling the content of professional work and the organization of medical practice,[11] or as "freedom from control either by peers or by organizational constraints,"[5(p.53)] or as "the authority and freedom to regulate themselves and act within their spheres of competence."[12(p.146)] In part, this autonomy has been protected in the past by professional physicians' ability to influence legislation and regulation of the profession.

Since 1910, when occupational autonomy was bestowed upon American physicians,[7,13] medicine has been viewed as the quintessence of professionalism. Now, however, assaults on this remarkable autonomy threaten the profession.

Assaults on Physician Autonomy

The challenges to physician self-determination are both direct and indirect. In search of value for their health care dollar, third-party payors seek to constrain payments directly for what physicians do and how they do it. Indirect erosion of autonomy is also occurring as the essential components of professionalism (as listed previously) are weakened. The following sections discuss the lower half of Figure 18–1, which indicates some of the forces that are undermining each of the profession's important components.

WHO: Selecting, training, and licensing a cohesive group

A profession must attract an ample supply of high-quality students who participate in a professionalization process as they are preparing for licensure. Until very recently, trends showed fewer applicants to medical school, and there were concerns that some state-based schools might have to lower admission standards.[14] Fall 1988 was the seventh consecutive year that 127 United States medical schools admitted fewer students than the previous year, and applicants have been decreasing in number since a peak in 1974. With 1.7 applicants in 1987 for each of the approximately 15,850 places, competition has declined substantially.[15]

Some credit the decline in applicants, at least partially, to the report of the Graduate Medical Education National Advisory Committee (GMENAC) in 1980,[16] which predicted a large oversupply of physicians by 1990. Other explanations include the fact that there are fewer people in the age group usually applying, increased tuition, and discouragement from practicing physicians.[15,17] The declining appeal of a medical career may also reflect the loss of social prestige accorded the profession.

The professionalization process for physicians is also under attack. The sharp demarcation between the 4-year undergraduate and 3- to 7-year graduate experience has been called into question, with a suggestion that clinical experience in the last 2 years of graduate medical education should be enough for the general internist, general pediatrician, and family physician.[14] The same authors also question the blurring of roles between teaching, research, and patient care for faculty members in the nation's academic medical centers, suggesting that good teaching be recognized and rewarded as a primary activity.[14] The extended hours and lack of supervision for interns and junior hospital residents have been questioned by the courts in the Libby Zion case, prompting the concern that "the threat of externally imposed controls over how physicians are trained remains very real."[18(p.213)] Libby Zion was a young college student who was admitted to a New York City hospital complaining of headache and fever. Eight hours later she died of coronary arrest. A grand jury investigating the case concluded that overworked residents contributed to Zion's death. Cur-

rently, New York is the only state constraining how many hours per week a resident physician may work. However, several other states are contemplating similar measures.[19]

Nor is the licensure process immune from interference. Congress enacted the Health Care Quality Improvement Act of 1986 because of physicians' inability to keep their incompetent members from moving across state lines where their history of incompetence would be unknown. Under the new system, the Department of Health and Human Services assists the licensing and credentialing bodies in each state by operating an independent information clearinghouse on license revocation or suspension, reprimands, and censures or probations for any licensed health professional. The Medicare and Medicaid Patient and Program Protection Act of 1987 expanded the list of information to be collected, as well as the proactive role of the clearinghouse, which presumably will make the information available to a wide variety of organizations and officials rather than merely respond to requests.[20]

Finally, the profession is no longer cohesive. Factors contributing to this condition include increased competition from an oversupply of physicians;[21] increased competition from provider brokers, such as hospitals;[22] fragmentation through specialization and growth of the specialty societies;[7,23,24] extreme disparity in rewards that the different physicians receive;[23] increased malpractice litigation;[25] the burgeoning business of peer review and managed care;[26] or any of a number of other causes. Whether the profession's current status can be attributed to these factors or not, there *is* a lessened sense of collegiality and cohesiveness.

WHAT: Maintaining the knowledge base and upholding standards

As professionals, physicians have a unique responsibility for developing and maintaining a specialized body of knowledge that they hold in trust for the public good. The current fervor over quality of care and outcomes research, however, is a result of the growing realization that physicians often don't know what works and what doesn't, and that they vary widely in the way they apply what they do know.[27] This evidence from the research on small area variations in practice patterns, coupled with a growing consumerism, threatens to undermine the patient's trust and dependency on the physician and further threatens professional autonomy.

With research backing his contention that physicians are guided as much by subjective factors as by science, Wennberg has made a compelling case for the need to evaluate medical practice.[28] Ellwood is among the voices calling for a renewed commitment to outcomes management based on a common national technology to measure the effect of medical care on patient outcomes.[29] The Agency for Health Care Policy and Research (AHCPR), formerly the National Center for Health Services Research, has a major research focus called the Medical Treatment Effectiveness Program. This program is based on the premise that some practice "variations are often the result of inadequate information about treatment effectiveness or differences in the 'practice styles' or preferences of physicians and other providers."[30(p.1)] The American Medical Association (AMA), in partnership with national specialty societies, has been increasingly active in the "development, evaluation and implementation of practice parameters."[31(p.2)]

This lack of certainty among medical professions is not lost on consumers, as the popular press has taken the message to the masses.[32–34] Calling the lack of knowledge about the appropriate test or procedure for a given condition an "intellectual crisis" helps undermine trust. Without this trust, a society will not be willing to accord physicians the professional autonomy they have had in the past.[35] Employers encourage their employees to question the physician about the proposed treatment and its costs, heightening a growing consumerism.[36]

WHY: A service orientation and code of ethics

The concern over the profession's capability to determine the efficacy of medical ministrations is coupled with a growing suspicion that some physician choices are driven by proprietary interests rather than a dedication to service. In some cases, parts of the code of ethics (e.g., the ban on advertising) have been interpreted by the courts to act against the interests of society. As a consequence, self-governance in this area has been replaced by a regulatory decision that overrules the profession's previous prohibition.[37,38]

Several recent *Wall Street Journal* articles reflect what one pundit has called the blood sport of doctor bashing: "Hospitals That Need Patients Pay Bounties for Doctors' Referrals,"[39] "Doctor-Owned Labs Earn Lavish Profits in a Captive Market,"[40] and "How Doctors Boost Bills by Misrepresenting the Work They Do."[41] All reflect a proprietary motivation for physicians rather than the service orientation expected of the profession.

The debate over the entrepreneurial role for physicians has raged in the professional literature. There is disagreement within the profession over the need to limit conflicts of interest by restricting physician financial interest. Some feel that entrepreneurship is essential to stimulating innovation, whereas others feel that the substantial decline in confidence in the medical profession warrants action.[42]

Based on the belief that current law and medical ethics fail to protect consumers from physician greed, Representative Stark introduced a bill that created the Ethics in Patient Referrals Act of 1989.[43] Such legislation, which Congress folded into the Omnibus Budget Reconciliation Act of 1989,[44] is designed to address perceived inadequacies in the profession's own service orientation and ethical standards, further eroding the autonomy of the profession.

HOW: Managed care and corporatization as direct threats to autonomy

Many physicians are beginning to feel their autonomy threatened as they react to individuals and events outside of their profession. This perception is reflected in a letter to the editor of the *New England Journal of Medicine*:

> Slowly but surely the medical profession is allowing itself to be controlled by nonphysicians, who are fast becoming the final authority on medical matters in this country. Lest anyone doubt that this is taking place, the evidence is all around us. Today's physician, instead of being governed by his or her peers, is now subservient to insurance companies or third-party payors and to the business tycoons who run worldwide hospital chains. It is of grave concern that nonphysicians with a smattering of medical knowledge, have deluded themselves into thinking that they can assume most of the functions of physicians.
>
> But the final degradation, the ultimate indicator of just how much we have relinquished

our power to nonphysicians and to the marketplace, is to have one's medically correct diagnosis changed to a more lucrative but less accurate one by a clerk recording DRGs. But then DRGs also originated with nonphysicians and were foisted on us by them. Why a once proud and independent profession has permitted this tragic takeover to occur is indeed incomprehensible.[45(p.390)]

However, if the physician is not trusted to know what is best, nor to always choose ethically even if he or she does know, then the social and economic system will step in with alternatives that constrain the physician's ability to define quality of care. The past resistance to such constraints as "cookbook medicine" have been replaced in some quarters with eloquent appeals to fellow physicians to help create practice guidelines as a means of preserving the autonomy of the profession, if not of the individual professional.[27,46] A major guideline developer states, "If the guidelines are developed with the aid of the best methods and if they are applied constructively, then the twin goals of increased health of the American public and physician satisfaction can be achieved."[47(p.3027)]

As more physicians assume full-time salaried positions in health care organizations, and as outside threats to their autonomy become intensified, there will be greater incentives for physicians to unionize. Describing the intrinsic objective of physician unions, Sobal and Hepner note that

> [t]he changes currently affecting the health industry represent a threat to the role that physicians have traditionally held in the industry and society in general. Therefore, the physician union often expends significant energy defending the professional integrity of physicians and their status in the medical profession, as opposed to the more traditional union negotiations.[48(pp.334,35)]

In addition, the changing structure and financial arrangements of the health care delivery system have led to the proliferation of payor watchdogs to oversee physician choices.[26] Originally, there were no third parties between the physician and the patient, a situation that the medical profession fought hard to preserve.[13] The advent of traditional insurance did little to change the relationship because the payor simply acted as a pass-through. With increasing concerns over cost, professional autonomy has been directly invaded by payment or service decisions that require preadmission certification, continued-stay review, in-office ambulatory care audits, protocol adherence, and other third-party interventions.

Clearly, changing structural and environmental forces are exerting increasing control over physicians. Deprofessionalization theory suggests that these changes have the effect of moving the profession toward greater rationalization[49] and reduced expectations of work autonomy.[6]

There is little hope of a return to the full autonomy and unhampered patient relationships physicians experienced at the height of their dominance. Brokers or agents will continue to work on behalf of purchasers and providers to buy or sell health care in the most effective and efficient way. The question for the profession and for those who work to administer the facilities in which they practice their art is how will these brokering organizations be structured and who will manage them?

Reduced professional autonomy: changing models of control

As the professional autonomy of physicians weakens, the health care organizations in which they work will begin to acquire commensurately greater control over them. This control will vary in its extent and intensity depending on the nature of the emerging structural models for the delivery of care.

In an attempt to understand and conceptualize these alternative models, several authors have independently enumerated three related structural categories.[50–52]

Madison and Konrad's alternatives of individual autonomy, administered autonomy, and heteronomous organizations serve as an example of these distinct organizational categories.[50] Individual autonomous and heteronomous structures are at opposite extremes on a continuum of physician self-direction. Heteronomy can be considered the opposite of autonomy.

As the name implies, under an individual autonomous structure, the autonomy of physicians is maintained at both the level of the individual and the physician organization, group, or collegium. At the other extreme, in the heteronomous structure, the individual physician is subordinate to the physician collegium which, in turn, is subordinate to the organization. In between is the administered autonomous organization. In this structural alternative, the physician is subordinate to the collegium or physician governing group; however, the collegium still enjoys professional autonomy at the group level.

Each of these structural categories, characterized by the type of control exerted over physicians—how they do their work—has implications for physician relationships with patients, payors, other physicians, and the organization. In addition, each organizational alternative may also influence who is attracted to a medical career, what they know, and why they act as they do—the other characteristics of a profession. Table 18–1 provides examples of each of these kinds of organizations and their implications for physician relationships and the profession.

Individual autonomy

In the individual autonomous structure, professional autonomy thrives along with the traditional aspects of the medical profession. As the name implies, autonomy is maintained at both the level of the individual professional and the physician collegium.

Physicians in these organizations control the patient care process without the intrusion of intervening parties. They are also unconstrained in their ability to freely access consults and seek referrals. Decision making is by physician consensus and typically results in a structure that is more reactive than proactive when it comes to the organization's future or external environment. For many professionals, the organizational inertia that often results from extreme individual autonomy is not viewed as a serious problem.[50]

Examples of these structures are the traditional solo practice or groups of fewer than 25 physicians. The growth of managed care arrangements coupled with the general reduction in traditional fee-for-service reimbursement, has meant a decline in the number of these arrangements for practicing medicine.

The self-directed individual attracted by this role has very little external guidance, and standards of practice vary widely. When fee-for-service funding systems were commonplace, there were incentives to innovate with new procedures and costly technology. The major threat to physicians still practicing this

way is the redistribution of income that is projected to result from Medicare's application of the resource-based relative value scale in 1992. The continued public debate over the appropriateness of physicians as entrepreneurs (e.g., owners of diagnostic and therapeutic facilities) applies in the other alternative structures as well as the traditional one.

Administered autonomous

Individual physicians practicing in an administered autonomous structure lose autonomy by subordinating themselves to a centralized negotiated policy; however, the physician group still maintains autonomy because it is the primary agent directing and controlling the exchanges of health care between patients and member physicians. Reed and Evans term this alternative the physician-driven organization (PDO).[9] Most PDOs are not-for-profit organizations that have a strong legacy of providing high-quality care. Well-known archetypes of PDOs include the Mayo, Ochsner, and Menninger clinics.[9] Numerous less well-known PDOs, primarily smaller group practices, currently exist with new ones regularly forming. The Permanente Medical Group in the Kaiser-Permanente Health Plan is an older example of this structural form.

The administered autonomous structure influences the relationship between individual physicians and patients primarily by requiring adherence to patient care protocols developed jointly by member physicians. The individual physicians' relationship to other physicians is still generally characterized by free access. The major difference in this structure is that consults, referrals, and treatment patterns are reviewed and overseen by peer physician managers. Shortell sees some hospital–physician relationships changing in this direction with the development of parallel structures, such as independent practice arrangements, or eventually the union of separate hospital and physician organizations through contractual arrangements.[4(p.26)] Physicians in such arrangements may be owner–operators or employees; in either case, there is a professional hierarchy for negotiations and oversight. This structure calls for a collaborative approach and requires managerial and research skills for the physician managers. Current communication problems, in the hospital, between the elected or appointed physician leadership and physicians with hospital privileges could also be a threat to this type of organization.

Table 18–1

Implications of medical group practice structural alternatives

	Individual autonomy	Administered autonomy (external control)	Heteronomous
Administrative style and accountability	Autonomy of individual physician protected as is autonomy of the group. Consensus by owner-operator physicians.	The physician organization is sovereign, but individual physician subordinate to centralized negotiated policy.	The physician organization is subsidiary to some other entity; physicians are subordinate to the organization. Executive command.
Examples	Traditional private practice or group with fewer than 25 physicians and few managed care payments.	Physician-driven organizations: Mayo, Ochsner, and Menninger Clinics.	Staff model HMO*; military hospital.
Physician relationship to:			
Patient	Direct; no intervening parties except payment constraints like precertification.	Medicated/collegial. Adhere to jointly negotiated protocols.	Mediated by organization that sets standards and protocols.
Client agents	Payors deal directly with each individual physician for constraints on payment.	Payors deal with organization that may negotiate discounts.	Must consider global resources. Organization negotiates with payors; guarantees adherence.
Other physicians	Free access to consults. Referrals unconstrained.	Consults, referrals, and treatment patterns reviewed by peer physician managers.	Consults and referrals out of group discouraged by organization.
Physician organization	Owner-operated with rule by consensus.	Owner-operated or employees; professional staff hierarchy for negotiation and oversight.	Employee subordinate to organizational hierarchy.
Aspects of the profession:			
Who			
Selection	Attracts self-directed entrepreneur; many applicants.	Collaborators, willing to take financial risks.	Fewer risk-takers, less income-oriented, more women, caretakers.
Training	Research-valued; individual decision making stressed.	Managerial, research skills; protocol development.	More emphasis on computer expert systems, decision support.
Licensure	Physician-directed; control most allied health professions, too.	Pressure to allow other health professionals own licensure.	May be some pressure to license alternative systems or providers.
Cohesiveness	Few threats, except RBRVS† fee schedule and income differentials.	Distance between manager and managed, specialty income gaps may decrease cohesiveness.	May increase with development of union-type professional organizations.
What			
Knowledge	Incentives to innovate and use new technology.	Pressure to evaluate medical theory before wide use.	Innovation only if cost-savings required for competitiveness.
Standards	Widely varied in practice, development, and use.	Greater use of guidelines; possibly selling protocols to others.	Strict adherence to cost/quality procedures.
Why			
Service	Continuing disputes over fees and proprietary facility ownership raise questions.	Ties to research and care of underserved could improve service image.	Lack of autonomy may obscure any service orientation of the employed physician.
Ethics	Entrepreneurship seen as conflicting with professional ethics.	Arms-length transactions with patient may limit conflict of interest.	Any capitated arrangement will be required to guard against underservice.
Social policy	"Fewer friends" in D.C.	Greater impact if service role seen to outweigh proprietary.	Ability to influence social policy altered by "union" status.

*HMO, health maintenance organization.
†RBRVS, Resource-Based Relative Value Scale.

Heteronomous configuration

Another alternative that has distinct ramifications for reduced professional autonomy has been called the heteronomous configuration. *Webster's Third New International Dictionary* defines heteronomy as "subjection to something else: a lack of moral freedom or self-determination."[10(p.1,063)] This structure is characterized by physician subordination to external control by some other entity. For the most part, these controls are developed apart from individual physicians and the physician group; nonetheless, subordination to this control is expected. Although few examples of the pure heteronomous structure exist, staff model health maintenance organizations and military hospitals are health care organizations that come close.

In the heteronomous structure, physician relationships with patients, payors, and other physicians are characterized by substantial intervention on the part of the organization. The organization sets the standards and protocols of patient treatment, conducts negotiations with external third-party payors, and strongly discourages or patently disallows referrals and consultations outside the organization. Finally, the physician's relationship to the organization is one of an employee, subordinate to the hierarchy of the organization.

Physicians in these organizations would be likely to be more risk-averse and less income-oriented. This structure could be more hospitable to the female physician in her child-raising years. More emphasis would be placed on computerized decision support systems and adherence to cost/quality procedures, with emphasis on cost-saving rather than cost-increasing technologies.

A movement away from the traditional individual autonomous organization toward newer forms is underway. It is not yet clear which, if any, of these forms will predominate in the future.

The end of autonomy?

We are witnessing the end to the remarkable absolute autonomy that has traditionally been the cornerstone of the American medical profession. The structure of the health care organization, with its separate dual lines of authority and its emphasis on individual and collective autonomy for the medical profession, is giving way to newer structural alternatives. Will the emerging structures that are eroding physician autonomy ultimately reduce the profession of medicine to a trade? This will not happen unless physicians abdicate responsibility for the major task of rationalizing the practice of their art.

Health care managers are exhorted to gain control of the most important component of the organization's mission—the management of the patient care process—[53] while physicians decry the intrusion of lay persons into their realm. The relationship between physicians and health care managers, however, will never resemble that of Frederick Taylor and his pig-iron handlers. Physicians will not become organizational automatons, especially if they actively develop and negotiate acceptable practice criteria and guidelines. As Eddy points out, "The solution is not to remove the decision-making power of physicians, but to improve the capacity of physicians to make better decisions."[27(p.290)] Increasingly, those decisions will acknowledge patient preferences. The challenge incumbent upon managers and physician professionals is to develop a set of mutually responsive solutions to the problems of who physicians are and how they are trained, what they know and how they apply this knowledge, and the service orientation and ethical base for their decisions.

•   •   •

It is apparent that society will no longer tolerate the inefficiencies and inequities in the current system. The newer management structures that preserve the autonomy of the physician group, while constraining the individual within that group, hold some promise for both sustaining the profession and meeting society's needs. The role of the American Medical Association and the specialty societies in meeting the call for better outcome research and criteria standards for quality patient care may be the salvation of the profession rather than its end. Managers must facilitate the application of these criteria by focusing physician skills on the "gray areas," where they will always be supremely important, rather than assuming that the process of patient care will ever be fully rationalized and routinized.

REFERENCES

1. Taylor, F.W. *The Principles of Scientific Management.* New York, N.Y.: Harper and Brothers Publishers, 1911.
2. Smith, H.L. "Two Lines of Authority Are One Too Many." *Hospitals* 84, (1955): 59–64.
3. Wylie, W.G. *Hospitals: Their History, Organization, and Construction.* New York, N.Y.: D. Appleton & Co., 1877.
4. Shortell, S.M. *Effective Hospital–Physician Relationships.* Ann Arbor, Mich.: Health Administration Press Perspectives, 1991.
5. Haug, M.E. "A Re-examination of the Hypothesis of Physician Deprofessionalization." *The Milbank Quarterly* 66, Supplement 2 (1988): 48–56.
6. Light, D., and Levine, S. "The Changing Character of the Medical Profession: A Theoretical Overview." *The Milbank Quarterly* 66, Supplement 2 (1988): 10–32.
7. Wolinsky, F.D. "The Professional Dominance Perspective Revisited." *The Milbank Quarterly* 66, Supplement 2 (1988): 33–47.
8. Freidson, E. *Profession of Medicine: A Study of the Sociology of Applied Knowledge.* New York, N.Y.: Harper & Row, 1970.
9. Reed, R.R., and Evans, D. "The Deprofessionalization of Medicine: Causes, Effects, and Responses." *Journal of the American Medical Association* 258, no. 22 (1987): 3279–82.
10. Gove, P.B. (ed). *Webster's Third New International Dictionary of the English Language, Unabridged.* Springfield, Mass.: Merriam-Webster, Inc., 1986.
11. Pinealt, R., Contandriopoulos, A.P., and Fournier, M.A. "Physicians' Acceptance of an Alternative to Fee-for-Service Payment: A Possible Source of Change in Quebec Medicine." *International Journal of Health Services* 15, no. 3 (1985): 419–30.
12. Wilensky, H.L. "The Professionalization of Everyone?" *The American Journal of Sociology* 70, no. 2 (1964): 137–58.
13. Starr, P. *The Social Transformation of American Medicine: The Rise of a Sovereign Profession and the Making of a Vast Industry.* New York, N.Y.: Basic Books, 1982.
14. Ebert, R.H., and Ginzberg, E. "The Reform of Medical Education." *Health Affairs* 7, no. 2 (1988): 5–48.
15. Jolly, P. "Datawatch: Medical Education in the United States, 1960–1987." *Health Affairs* 7, no. 2 (1988): 144–57.
16. Graduate Medical Education National Advisory Committee. *Report of the Graduate Medical Education National Advisory Committee to the Secretary.* Washington, D.C.: U.S. Department of Health and Human Services, September 3, 1980.
17. Stimmel, B. "The Study and Practice of Medicine in the Twenty-First Century: Ask Not for Whom the Bell Tolls." *The Mount Sinai Journal of Medicine* 57, no. 1 (1990): 11–24.
18. Hafferty, F.W. "Theories at the Crossroads: A Discussion of Evolving Views on Medicine as a Profession." *The Milbank Quarterly* 66, Supplement 2 (1988): 202–25.
19. Jasperse, P. "It's Training. It's Helping. It's Work. It's the Grind." *Wisconsin — The Milwaukee Journal Magazine* (September 16, 1990): 6–10, 15–16, 19, 30.
20. Kadzieski, M.A. From the *Health Care Law Newsletter,* in *Medical Benefits* (January 15, 1988): 8, 9.
21. McKinlay, J.B., and Stoeckle, J.D. "Corporatization and the Social Transformation of Doctoring." *International Journal of Health Services* 18, no. 2 (1988): 191–206.
22. American Medical Association, Council on Long-Range Planning and Development. "Health Care in Transition: Consequences for Your Physicians." *Journal of the American Medical Association* 256, no. 24 (1986): 3384–90.

23. Benjamin, W.W. "Will Centrifugal Forces Destroy the Medical Profession?" *New England Journal of Medicine* 321, no. 17 (1989): 1191–92.
24. Stoeckle, J.D. "Reflections on Modern Doctoring." *The Milbank Quarterly* 66, Supplement 2 (1988): 76–91.
25. Stuart, S.E., and Maldonado, W.E. "How PPS is Changing Hospital–Physician Relations." *Trustee* (April, 1986): 14–15.
26. Gray, B.H., and Field, M.J. (eds). *Controlling Costs and Changing Patient Care? Role of Utilization Management.* Washington, D.C.: National Academy Press, 1989.
27. Eddy, D.M. "The Challenge." *Journal of the American Medical Association* 263, no. 2 (1990): 287–90.
28. Wennberg, J.E. "Dealing with Medical Practice Variations: A Proposal for Action." *Health Affairs* 3, no. 2 (1984): 6–32.
29. Ellwood, P.M. "Shattuck Lecture—Outcomes Management: A Technology of Patient Experience." *New England Journal of Medicine* 318, no. 23 (1988): 1549–56.
30. Agency for Health Care Policy and Research. *AHCPR Program Note.* Rockville, Md.: Agency for Health Care Policy and Research, U.S. Department of Health and Human Services (March, 1990).
31. Kelly, J.T. "Editor's Report: Practice Parameters Called Key to Effective QA Programs." *QA Review* 2, no. 3 (1990): 1–3.
32. Gibbs, N. "Sick and Tired." *Time* (July 31, 1989): 48–53.
33. Ludtke, M. "Physician Inform Thyself." *Time* (June 26, 1989): 71.
34. Miller, A., Bradburn, E., and Hager, M. "Second-guessing Doctor's Orders." *Newsweek* (May 23, 1988): 44, 45.
35. Winston, R. "Patient Data May Reshape Health Care." *Wall Street Journal* (April 17, 1989): B1.
36. Ricks, T.E. "New Corporate Program Lets Employees Compare Local Doctors' Fees and Training." *Wall Street Journal* (August 4, 1987): 37.
37. Barney, D.R. "Regulation of Health Services Advertising." *Hospital & Health Services Administration* 28, no. 3 (1983): 85–110.
38. Havighurst, C.C. "Antitrust Enforcement in the Medical Services Industry: What Does It All Mean?" *Milbank Memorial Fund Quarterly* 58, no. 1 (1980): 89–124.
39. Waldholz, M., and Bogdonich, W. "Hospital that Need Patients Pay Bounties for Doctors' Referrals." *Wall Street Journal* (March 1, 1989): A1, A6.
40. Bogdonich, W., and Waldholz, M. "Doctor-Owned Labs Earn Lavish Profits in a Captive Market." *Wall Street Journal* (February 27, 1989): A1, A4.
41. Rundle, R.L. "How Doctors Boost Bills by Misrepresenting the Work They Do." *Wall Street Journal* (December 6, 1989): A1, A8.
42. Hyman, D.A., and Williamson, J.V. "Fraud and Abuse: Setting the Limits on Physicians' Entrepreneurship." *New England Journal of Medicine* 320, no. 19 (1989): 1275–78.
43. Iglehart, J.K. "The Debate Over Physician Ownership of Health Care Facilities." *New England Journal of Medicine* 321, no. 3 (1989): 198–204.
44. House of Representatives. *Omnibus Budget Reconciliation Act of 1989. Conference Report to Accompany H.R. 3299.* Washington D.C.: U.S. Government Printing Office (November, 1989).
45. Norstrand, I.F. "Takeover of the Medical Profession by Nonphysicians." *New England Journal of Medicine* 314, no. 6 (1986): 390.
46. Leitner, W.A. "The Third Revolution." *Alabama Medicine* (November, 1988): 7, 8, 11, 12.

47. Brook, R.H. "Practice Guidelines and Practicing Medicine: Are They Compatible?" *Journal of the American Medical Association* 262, no. 21 (1989): 3027–30.

48. Sobal, L.V., and Hepner, J.O. "Physicians Unions: Any Doctor Can Join, But Who Can Bargain Effectively?" *Hospital & Health Services Administration* 35, no. 3 (1990): 327–40.

49. Ritzer, G. and Walczak, D. "Rationalization and Deprofessionalization of Physicians." *Social Forces* 67, no. 1 (1988): 1–22.

50. Madison, D.L., and Konrad, T.S. "Large Medical Group-Practice Organizations and Employed Physicians: A Relationship in Transition." *The Milbank Quarterly* 66, no. 2 (1988): 240–81.

51. Scott, W.R. "Managing Professional Work: Three Models of Control for Health Organizations." *Health Services Research* 17, no. 3 (1982): 213–40.

52. Mintzberg, H. *Structure in Fives: Designing Effective Organizations*. Englewood Cliffs, N.J.: Prentice-Hall, 1983.

53. Roher, J.E. "The Secret of Medical Management." *Health Care Management Review* 14, no. 3 (1989): 7–13.

19

Using Claims Data to Select Primary Care Physicians for a Managed Care Network

Philip Nathanson, Monica Noether, Ronald J. Ozminkowski,
Kevin M. Smith, Brendan E. Raney, Dale Mickey, and Philip M. Hawley, Jr.

H ow do you know your doctors are any good?" Anyone who has tried to explain managed care to a potential purchaser, or who has tried to convince someone to choose one managed care plan over another, has heard this question in one form or another. Today, many managed care organizations (MCOs) are attempting to develop what they hope are persuasive answers to this question, especially when it comes to physicians already participating in the plan or network. For example, at Aetna Health Plans (AHP), network primary care physician performance is now being measured in terms of clinical results, member satisfaction, cost effectiveness, and conformance to professional/clinical standards.

When it comes to selecting new physicians for network affiliation, or to developing a managed care network from scratch, the state of the art is less well developed and the answers to customer questions may be less persuasive. Historically, networks have used a variety of criteria for selecting new participating physicians, including office location, office procedures and ambiance, community reputation, and credentials. The latter typically include education, training, board certification, hospital affiliations, and employment and malpractice claims history. As evidence accumulates of the wide variation in costs and outcomes of health care, however, there is growing customer demand for ways to factor information about resource use and treatment outcomes into the managed care physician selection process.

For many MCOs, the best available source of information about prospective participating physicians is insurance claims data, whether from clients, from the MCO's own lines of business, or from public sources. This article outlines a way to use claims data to help select primary care physicians (PCPs) on the basis of their resource use, specifically on the basis of the differences between their observed and expected use of outpatient services. The article describes the limitations and challenges of using claims data for choosing "good" physicians, explains the technical and the philosophical choices the authors made in constructing the profiling methodology, and suggests avenues for possible further use and refinement of the methodology.

Background

A large self-insured employer engaged Pace Healthcare Management to design and implement a managed care program, including the selection methodology for providers. AHP was selected to administer the program and assist with data analysis and selection criteria application. Abt Associates was retained to provide statistical expertise during the physician selection process. The employer specified that the physician selection methodology should make the maximum possible use of insurance claims data as well as other less quantitative factors such as credentials, location, and community reputation. The claims data to be used would include two calendar years of data from two sources: AHP and

A technical discussion of the methodology and results used in this research is beyond the scope of this article. For more detailed information and analysis, contact Dr. Ozminkowski at Abt Associates, Inc., 4800 Montgomery Lane, Suite 600, Bethesda, MD 20814, phone (301) 913-0560.

Managed Care Quarterly 1994; 2(4): 50–59

the employer's self-insurance program. The universe of participating PCPs was to be selected from the medical staff rosters of 71 hospitals already selected for participation in the network. For the purposes of the research, PCPs were defined as internists, family practitioners, and pediatricians.

Data

The first task was to integrate the claims data from AHP and the employer. As is typical, the two source datasets used different systems for recording claims transactions and had different levels of detail and accuracy. For example, the AHP system reported procedures using the Current Procedural Terminology, fourth edition (CPT-4) codes, while the client's system used California Relative Value Scale (CRVS) codes. The AHP database used one place-of-service code to indicate outpatient care, while the employer's database had 10 codes including independent laboratory care, outpatient hospital care, and pharmacy. To create a common format, physician specialty, place-of-service, and type-of-service codes were mapped to a common definition table, and CRVS codes were converted to CPT-4 codes using an available crosswalk. The result was a database of over three million claims records, less than 10 percent of which were from the employer.

The next step was to match the names of PCPs on the participating hospital rosters with physician names in the AHP/employer dataset to develop a listing of PCPs who were affiliated at the appropriate hospitals and had claims activity reflected in either the AHP or employer dataset. The result was a single master file that included physician names and all applicable provider identification (ID) numbers for some 755 family practitioners, 1,045 internists, and 403 pediatricians.

The matching process itself was difficult. In many instances, physicians' names were not identical or in the same format among the claims datasets and hospital rosters. Common misspellings were handled with a phonetic matching system, the modified New York State Identification and Intelligence name coding procedure used by the National Center for Health Statistics to merge data from outside sources to its National Death Index.[1] Physician specialty codes were assigned using AHP's physician credentialing file, in which physician specialties had been verified and matched

with education and training. For those physicians not included in the credentialing file, hospital rosters or provider specialty information submitted on claims were used.

The claims data lacked some information about individual physicians in group practices who used the group practice tax ID number as well as their individual tax ID numbers for billing purposes. Because the master physician file was developed using hospital rosters, the names of these physicians were captured in the master file, and some of their claims data were studied. However, no information was available about the services these physicians provided and billed using the group tax ID number.

For physician profiling purposes, a key limitation in the data was the extremely low frequency with which individual physicians provided inpatient care. For example, the average PCP had fewer than four inpatient admissions to the 71 included hospitals. Lack of inpatient data has been noted by others who have worked with large insurance claims databases[2] and is not surprising given that the populations typically being studied consist mainly of active, relatively young employees and their dependents. In this database in particular, low frequency of inpatient admissions is a consequence of the fact that obstetricians were not being studied (childbirth is by far the biggest reason for inpatient admissions under age 65) and the fact that although all the PCPs admitted at least one patient to the 71 hospitals, it is likely that most of them admitted patients to other hospitals as well.

The implications of lack of inpatient data were significant for the research described here, and, potentially, for claims-databased physician selection in general. Many of the outcomes of inpatient care often used as clinical quality indicators—mortality, readmission, and complication rates—were simply not available. Thus, it was necessary to devise a physician performance measurement methodology that relied solely on outpatient care activity.

Another key limitation was that the claims data could not be used to measure the provision of pediatric immunizations, mammograms, Pap smears, and other preventive and well-care services. By definition, health maintenance is an important goal of managed care, and a "good" PCP should ensure that the assigned managed care plan members receive preventive care and periodic examinations appropriately. To measure this, however, data must be available for the physician for a panel, or stable population of members, over time. Since this database was being used to *select* PCPs, the claims information available did not relate to a panel of members; it included patients enrolled in a variety of insurance plans, including indemnity plans that did not have enrolled members and preferred provider organizations (PPOs) that did not cover preventive services.

Methods

Mathematical modeling was used to develop "expected" patterns of outpatient resource use for each PCP. Separate models for internists, family practitioners, and pediatricians were used because the statistically meaningful information available to evaluate each of these specialties varied somewhat. Expected patterns of resource use were those that reflected the practices of peers within the community, after taking into account differences in age, sex, and case mix among the patients treated by each physician. PCPs were then ranked according to deviations between their actual and their expected practice patterns. The closer a PCP's actual pattern of resource use approached the expected pattern, the higher the ranking.

Underlying this methodology was a critical assumption. Lacking up-front information on inpatient-linked quality outcomes, preventive care rates, customer satisfaction, and other dimensions of managed care performance, it seemed inappropriate to choose either relatively high or relatively low resource utilizers as PCPs. Relatively high utilizers are very rarely desirable in managed care networks. Relatively low utilizers may be efficient, highly desirable PCPs, or they may be withholding access to necessary services and referrals. Outpatient claims data—at least, the database available to this research—cannot distinguish between the two. Thus, the methods used here select primary care physicians whose resource use is similar to expectation, taking into account differences in demographics and case mix.

Measures of resource use

A large number of potential process and outcome measures obtainable from claims data were developed based on expert physician input, the literature, and previous analyses conducted by the consultants. The potential measures were analyzed against the database,

applying statistical tests to ensure that enough data existed to use the indicator to make fair comparisons among PCPs. Seven measures survived the elimination process for internists, six of which were used for family practitioners and five for pediatricians. The measures used to compare internists were:

1. Relative total outpatient charges,
2. Relative need for follow-up visits within 90 days of the first outpatient visit,
3. Relative use of consultations during the treatment process,
4. Relative use of laboratory services,
5. Relative use of radiology services,
6. Relative number of visits per patient per year, and
7. Relative level of intensity of care provided in the office visit, based on CPT-4 code.

The consultation rate was not used to compare family practitioners or pediatricians, nor was the revisit rate used to compare pediatricians, because rates among these physicians were extremely low (less than one percent), too low to permit meaningful analyses. The word "relative" appears in each measure to stress that each physician's performance was measured as a deviation from expectation.

Risk adjustment

Because primary care physicians treat patients presenting with a broad variety of symptoms and diagnoses, it was important to control, as much as possible, for systematic variation in age, sex, and case mix across physicians. For case mix, ambulatory patient groups (APGs) were used to develop clinically homogeneous categories of patients. APGs are the outpatient analog to the diagnosis-related groups (DRGs) used to group inpatient admissions into meaningful cohorts for resource-use analysis. There are 297 APGs, each of which defines a surgical procedure, a medical condition, an ancillary test or procedure, or a well-care or administrative activity.[3]

In addition to using APGs to adjust for case mix, APG weights were used as a crude proxy for severity. (Each APG is assigned a case weight to reflect its expected relative resource intensity, just as DRG case weights reflect relative resource intensity for inpatient admissions. APG weights are not a precise measure of severity of illness, because they include both severity and physician practices that may or may not be driven by severity.) Population-based severity adjustment methods such as ambulatory care groups (ACGs)[4] could not be used, because the database related to insurance claims and not to member populations.

Because insufficient patients existed in the database for each studied physician within a single APG, groups of APGs called APGSETs were created. APGSETs were defined by combining different APGs within a given body system (e.g., cardiopulmonary) or disease type (e.g., infectious diseases) or other major classification (e.g., administration and well care) until the number of claims per physician reached meaningful levels. As with the practice pattern measures, the APGSETs used for each specialty differed, as noted in Table 19–1.

Generating expected patterns of care

For each measure, a prediction about how much relative resources a physician should use was developed through a statistical technique (ordinary least squares or logistic regression analysis) that adjusted for differences in risk as described above. For example, in predicting how much laboratory services an internist should be expected to use compared to peers, the analysis took into account the age and sex of the physician's patients, the frequency with which various APGSET categories occurred in the claims data, and the APG case weight. It was then possible to compare each physician's actual use of laboratory services to predicted use. Figure 19–1 shows the laboratory use comparison for 10 internists, described as A through J to preserve confidentiality. The values in the figure represent the percentage of office visits for each physician that actually involved laboratory use versus the predicted percentage of visits involving laboratory use for that physician.

Once this analysis had been performed for each of the measures of resource use, a pattern of care for each physician was created by performing the actual-versus-predicted comparison for each measure. The result was a profile of differences that could be used to compare physicians. Figure 19–2 graphs the differences among Internists A, I, and J for all of the resource measures used to compare internists. Note that the measures are scaled differently in the graph for convenience of display, so that the variation in the amount of a physician's differences from expected use across the measures is visually overstated (laboratory, radiology, visit intensity, revisit rate, visits per year, consultations) or understated (total outpatient charges). However, the range of interphysician variation within each measure is accurately depicted.

Generating an overall measure of performance

Three options were available for transforming the individual scores in the pattern of care into an overall score that would permit the ranking of physicians. First, the scores could be combined to create an average or composite score in a way that weighted each measure of resource use equally. Second, arbitrary weights could be developed corresponding to subjective judgments about which measures are more significant than others. For example, the relative consultation rate could be weighted to count for twice as much as the relative laboratory visit rate, on the theory that propensity to use consultants is much more important in arriving at an overall judgment about a PCP than propensity to use the lab. Third, objective (i.e., data-driven) weights could be calculated for each measure before the overall scores were calculated.

The third option was chosen, using a method called principal components (PC) analysis. This process determined how much of the total variation among physician scores was caused by various combinations of the scores on individual resource use measures. The resulting values allow a weighting of each measure in proportion to its importance in driving the total scores. The PC analysis-derived weights for each measure are provided in Table 19–2.

Final scores

When the individual scores obtained on each measure were summed up, the physicians were ranked based on absolute scores (i.e., how far physicians deviated from expectation, regardless of whether the deviation was positive or negative). In other words, it counted against a physician to have relatively few revisits, as does Internist I in Figure 19–2, just as it counted against Internist J in Figure 19–2 to have a relatively high revisit intensity. Table 19–3 gives the final rankings of Internists A through J.

Results

A number of statistical tests and analyses were performed to determine the usefulness of the dataset and the predictive model. There were four principal findings.

Table 19–1

Grouping Outpatient Visits into APGSETs by Specialty

Specialty	Label	APG range
Internal medicine		
APGSET 1	Nervous	736–738
APGSET 2	Infectious diseases	721–724
APGSET 3	Ear, Nose, and Throat (ENT), and mouth; conjunctivitis and external eye	751–754, 766–772
APGSET 4	Cardiopulmonary	781–784, 796, 797, 800
APGSET 5	Digestive	811–817
APGSET 6	Skin/musculoskeletal/trauma	631–634, 841, 842, 856–860
APGSET 7	Endocrine/malignancy	601–605, 871–873, 933
APGSET 8	Urinary	886–916
APGSET 9	Well care and administrative	946–951
APGSET 10	All procedures	001–319
Family practice		
APGSET 1	Nervous/mental	654–659, 736–738
APGSET 2	Infectious diseases	721–724
APGSET 3	ENT and mouth; conjunctivitis and external eye	751–754, 766–772
APGSET 4	Cardiopulmonary	781–784, 796, 797, 800
APGSET 5	Digestive	811–817
APGSET 6	Skin/musculoskeletal/trauma	631–634, 841, 842, 856–860
APGSET 7	Endocrine/malignancy	601–605, 871–873, 933
APGSET 8	Urinary	886–916
APGSET 9	Well care and administrative	946–951
APGSET 10	Maternal peripartum	691–694
APGSET 11	All procedures	001–319
Pediatrics		
APGSET 1	Poisoning	616
APGSET 2	Skin/musculoskeletal/trauma	631–634, 841, 842, 856–860
APGSET 3	Neonate	676
APGSET 4	ENT and mouth; conjunctivitis and external eye	751–754, 766–772
APGSET 5	Cardiopulmonary	781–784, 796, 797, 800
APGSET 6	Digestive	811–817
APGSET 7	Skin	856–859
APGSET 8	Endocrine	871–873, 933
APGSET 9	Urinary	886–916
APGSET 10	Well care and administrative	946–951
APGSET 11	Infectious diseases	721–724
APGSET 12	Nervous	736–738
APGSET 13	All procedures	001–319

1. The adjustments made in this research for age, sex, and case mix explain a relatively small amount of the variation in physicians' use of outpatient resources. The regression analyses that predicted expected practice patterns took into account factors that are widely believed to affect resource use and that could be studied using insurance claims data. Most of these factors did have a statistically significant impact on each of the measures of resource use, meaning that they are likely to be important determinants of the

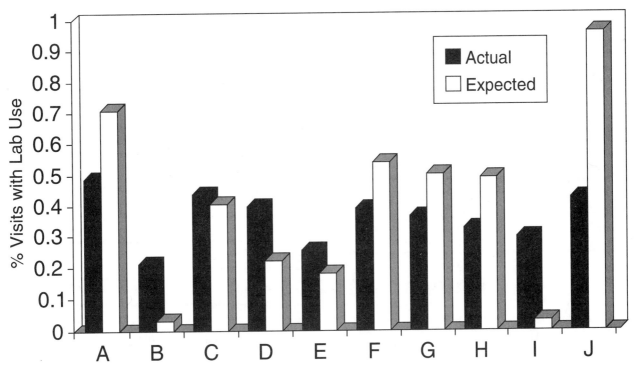

Figure 19–1. Relative outpatient laboratory use by internists after age, sex, and case mix adjustments

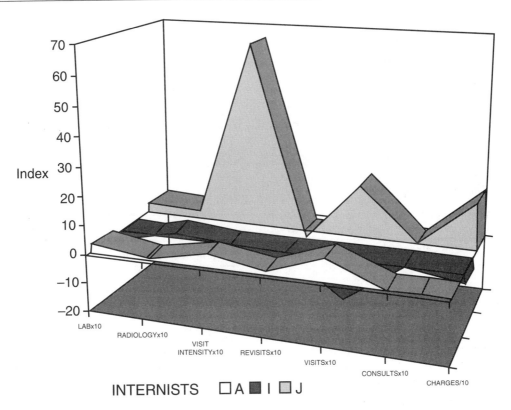

Figure 19–2. Actual/expected differences in relative resource use: Three internists

Table 19–2

Resource-measure-specific Weights for Family Practice, Internal Medicine, and Pediatrics

	Weights		
Criterion	Family practice	Internal medicine	Pediatrics
Outpatient charge	0.02	0.23	0.24
Visit weight	0.20	0.04	0.14
Visits per patient per year	0.25	0.11	0.18
Lab charge rate	0.15	0.19	0.31
Radiology charge rate	−0.09	0.20	−0.01
Revisit rate	0.19	−0.06	—
Consultation rate	—	0.09	—

Table 19–3

Final Scores and Rankings of Selected Internists

Physician	Score (absolute value)	Rank
A	.15941	332
B	.11123	226
C	.14169	301
D	.36254	717
E	.06491	127
F	.09164	185
G	.06326	123
H	.17510	366
I	.01156	20
J	1.35964	1040

way doctors practice. However, these factors explain less than three percent of the variability in resource use. Most probably, factors other than those that can be measured with claims data are major drivers of physician practice patterns. These factors could include differing levels of severity among patients that are not related to the APG case weight; different coverage levels, utilization review intensity, and reimbursement rules for the insurance "products" in which patients were enrolled; and real differences in physician opinion about what to do for patients presenting with the same symptoms.

2. Physicians differ significantly across the measures in their use of resources. It might be expected that physicians would be consistently heavy or consistently

light users of outpatient resources, regardless of the type of resources. However, the results do not support that hypothesis. Table 19–4 shows a correlation matrix for the seven internal medicine resource use measures. The higher the value shown in the cell in which two measures intersect, the more the variation in one of the measures relates to the variation in the other. As the table illustrates, these correlations often are low; for example, the correlation between relative radiology use and relative laboratory use is .35, and some of the correlations between other measures are negative. These results, while perhaps counter-intuitive, are consistent with others reported in the literature.[5]

3. Physicians' total scores did not vary greatly. Table 19–5 provides a number of measures of the size

Table 19–4

Descriptive Statistics for Overall Scores and their Absolute Value, by Specialty

	Overall scores				
Specialty	Number of physicians	Mean	Standard deviation	Range	CV*
Family practice	755	0.00	0.41	−1.35–1.79	Undefined
Internal medicine	1045	0.00	0.38	−0.93–2.95	Undefined
Pediatrics	403	0.00	0.46	−1.77–1.78	Undefined
	Absolute value of overall scores				
Family practice	775	0.31	0.27	0.00–1.79	0.87
Internal medicine	1045	0.30	0.24	0.00–2.95	0.80
Pediatrics	403	0.33	0.31	0.00–1.78	0.94

*Coefficient of variation

Table 19–5

Correlation Matrix for Internal Medicine Criteria

Criterion	Correlations						
	CHARGE	INTENS	VISITS	LAB	RAD	REVIS	CONS
Relative hospital charge **(CHARGE)**	1.00						
Relative visit intensity **(INTENS)**	0.18	1.00					
Relative number of visits **(VISITS)** per patient per year	0.25	0.01	1.00				
Relative lab use rate **(LAB)**	0.37	0.26	0.29	1.00			
Relative radiology use rate **(RAD)**	0.24	0.14	0.03	0.35	1.00		
Relative revisit rate **(REVIS)**	0.04	0.06	0.55	−0.12	−0.15	1.00	
Relative consultation rate **(CONS)**	0.13	−0.39	−0.02	−0.12	−0.04	−0.28	1.00

of variation—the mean, standard deviation, range, and coefficient of variation—of the profile scores. These statistics are provided both for the overall scores and their absolute values (i.e., the scores without pluses or minuses). Note that the mean of the overall scores is zero. This is the case by definition, because the technique used to generate the expectations (regression analysis) posits that the average physician does not deviate from expectation. A more important result is that the standard deviations and the ranges of scores are rather small, showing that physicians did not vary much in terms of overall performance. This also is illustrated by the coefficient of variation (CV), which equals the standard deviation divided by the mean. (The CV is calculated only for the absolute value of the overall score, because the calculation cannot be done if the mean is zero.) CV values of less than 1.0 are generally considered to reflect little variability in the data; Table 19–5 shows that all CV values were less than 1.0.

The limited variability of the scores and their absolute values makes it difficult to determine whether differences in scores would be meaningful for physicians who are close to one another in the overall ranking, such as Internists E and G in Table 19–3. Claims-data-driven profiles may be most useful for identifying physicians such as I and J in Table 19–3, who differed greatly from each other and from most of their peers.

4. The model appears to measure real differences among physicians. Reliability is an indication of the extent to which measured differences represent ac-

tual differences rather than chance variation, artifacts of the methodology, etc. Chronbach's alpha[6] was used as the measure of reliability. When this measure is close to 1.0, reliability is high. A complete lack of correlation between the items used to create the scores would result in a reliability coefficient of zero. The reliability coefficient for family practice was 0.61. Reliability coefficients for internal medicine and pediatrics were 0.39 and 0.47, respectively. This is lower than expected but does not mean that the measured differences among physicians are not meaningful. Chronbach's alpha is a "lower-bound" estimate; that means it slightly understates reliability. Also, Chronbach's alpha is directly affected by the correlations between the profiling measures, which in this case are low.

Obviously, reliability of the model would be enhanced by adding more performance measures, preferably valid ones that are correlated with one another but measure slightly different aspects of resource use or outcomes. Finding these measures in claims data is a challenging and potentially rewarding area for future research.

Discussion

This research suggests that there are both dangers and opportunities in attempting to use insurance claims data to help select "good" PCPs. First, like other efforts to learn from claims data, this work was based on several assumptions: that the information in the case datasets was reliable and valid, that physicians could be mapped accurately to patients and specialty, and that prevailing practice patterns can be useful for generating expected treatment and outcome measures in the absence of more detailed and scientifically established clinical algorithms or practice guidelines. Obviously, the extent to which all these are true affects the usefulness of the product.

Also, there are several caveats specific to this database and model. The difficulty of merging AHP and customer databases required the use of mapping techniques that might have resulted in more than the usual amount of data integrity issues. The mathematical model's performance against standard measures of "goodness" was less than excellent, a nearly universal problem when data is used for purposes for which it was not originally generated. And the methodology used to rank physicians was controversial, not only with the employer who commissioned the research but also among the researchers themselves. The notion of rewarding physicians for being "average" (after adjusting for case mix and demographic factors) seemed inappropriate to some—especially, perhaps, to physicians—even though average in this context meant as expected rather than mediocre. A more substantive objection was that those PCPs who achieved good results with low resource use were ranked low along with those who simply underutilized; thus, the method excluded some physicians who should be most sought for an MCO.

These concerns notwithstanding, there are reasons to consider the use of claims-driven profiles in selecting managed care PCPs. First, the current process of managed care network physician credentialing typically verifies training, education, and work experience, then simply checks for the absence of negative occurrences (e.g., malpractice claims, disciplinary actions by regulatory bodies, loss of hospital privileges). It would be difficult to argue that this process could not benefit from an infusion of performance-related data, even imperfect data. (Obviously, the data would be used as a supplement to, not a replacement for, current methods of physician selection.)

Second, depending on the specifics of the insurance claims databases available for use, several strategies could be employed to increase the usefulness of the kinds of profiles generated in this research, including incorporation of pharmacy data, which was unavailable to the current researchers; incorporation

of norms or data from a national physician claims database to "benchmark" and avoid local biases; and the addition of commercially available software that can generate a "compliance" profile based on the extent to which physicians' patterns of CPT-4 codes follow proprietary guidelines for appropriateness to the diagnosis.

Third, many alternatives exist to the scoring and ranking methodology used here. One approach would be to proceed as described above, but retain the plus and minus signs in computing the overall rankings for a first round of scoring. That would have the effect of identifying high outpatient resource users, who could then be eliminated. In a subsequent round (or iterative rounds), the entire modeling process would be replicated for the remaining physicians, but this time absolute values would be used in the scoring (pluses and minuses would be dropped). This approach would establish a "community standard" built around low-to-moderate resource users rather than around low, moderate, and high users.

Another option might be to eliminate the numerical rankings for each physician altogether. The individual scores on each resource use measure could be aggregated into a profile, possibly in control chart or other graphic format that highlighted outliers. (Figures 1 and 2 do this in different ways.) These profiles would be treated as useful information in the credentialing decision about each PCP, with particular attention being paid to any resource use measures for which the physician was a significant outlier.

•　　•　　•

Finally, it should be stressed again that the methodology in the current research was specifically intended to help in the initial selection of PCPs rather than in evaluating the practice patterns of PCPs who are already participating in managed care networks. For the latter purpose, much more sophisticated profiling approaches are possible, including comparisons of PCPs' relative provision of diagnostic and preventive care. In addition, expected resource use calculations for a managed care population assigned to a PCP can be adjusted specifically for severity of illness as well as for case mix.[4] Also, MCOs such as AHP are beginning to use such measures as member satisfaction and compliance with administrative rules and clinical guidelines, along with resource use information, to make multidimensional evaluations of PCPs who care for a significant number of managed care plan members.

REFERENCES

1. U.S. Department of Health and Human Services, Public Health Service. *National Death Index User's Manual.* DHHS Pub. No. (PHS) 90-1148. Hyattsville, Md.: 1990.
2. Lasker, R.D., Shapiro, D.W., and Tucker, A.M. "Realizing the Potential of Practice Pattern Profiling." *Inquiry* 29 (1992): 287–97.
3. Averill, R.F. et al. *Design and Evaluation of a Prospective Payment System for Ambulatory Care.* Final report to the Health Care Financing Administration, Office of Research and Demonstrations, 1991.
4. Weiner, J.P. et al. "Applying Insurance Claims Data to Assess Quality of Care: A Compilation of Potential Indicators." *Quality Review Bulletin* 16 (1990): 424–28.
5. Sanazaro, P.J. and Worth, R.M. "Measuring Clinical Performance of Individual Internists in Office and Hospital Practice." *Medical Care* 23 (1985): 1097–114.
6. Nunnally, J. *Psychometric Theory.* St. Louis, Mo.: McGraw-Hill, 1967.

20

Patient-Based Quality Measurement Systems

Eugene C. Nelson and Paul B. Batalden

Quality should be aimed at the needs of the consumer, present and future.

—W. Edwards Deming
Out of the Crisis

How do patients judge the quality of their health care? What do they expect? What do they need? How well do doctors, hospitals, and health plans meet patient needs and expectations? Where is the best place to purchase high-quality care at a fair price? Is the quality of care improving or deteriorating as changes are made to contain costs? How can health services be designed to delight patients and at the same time save money?

Questions like these are being asked by different players in the health care scene: consumers, purchasers, physicians, nurses, planners, and policy makers. The answers to these different questions are important for different users (of information) and have different uses (by those asking the questions). All of these questions require knowledge of the patient—the central customer of health care—and many of them require measurement that is patient based.

The aim of this article is to offer principles and processes that can be used to design patient-based quality measurement systems that will meet future needs. We begin by defining patient-based systems, reviewing the systems of today, and projecting the characteristics of future systems. After laying this groundwork, general design principles will be offered, followed by the description of a specific, yet flexible design process. Finally, to illustrate some of these ideas, features of tomorrow's patient-based systems are highlighted based on real-life examples.

Patient-Based Quality Measurement Systems Defined

What are patient-based quality measurement systems? A definition can be crafted by defining each of the terms and then combining them into a conceptual definition. First, *patient-based* refers to information that is provided by individuals who receive health care. Second, *quality* of health care can be thought of as the goodness of the match between patient total need (i.e., the need for health and health care that is effective, accessible, affordable, and acceptable) and the set of services delivered (i.e., tests, diagnoses, and treatments, that are based on current biomedical knowledge concerning efficacy and cost-effectiveness).[1] Third, a *system* of measurement integrates discrete processes (e.g., sampling, data collection, data analysis, feedback report production, distribution of report to users, and education of users on how to make best use of the information) to achieve the common aim of measuring the goodness of health care based on patients' evaluations for use by those professionals seeking to test whether improvement has occurred.[2]

Consequently, a patient-based quality measurement system is a planned method for gathering information on the goodness of health care from the perspective of the patient and for providing quantified feedback to educated user groups. The overall quality or "goodness" of health care, from the patient's perspective, is determined by the entire package of characteristics alluded to above, including the perceived health outcomes resulting from care and the patient's evaluation of the entire experience of seeking and receiving care (e.g., the accessibility, timeliness, and efficiency of services; the way providers interact and communicate with the patient; and the direct and indirect costs of illness and care). The users, the beneficiaries of the products of the measurement system, can take the knowledge gained from the system and utilize it for

Quality Management in Health Care 1993; 2(1): 18–30

different purposes based on their roles and attendant needs (e.g., purchasing health care; monitoring quality trends; identifying areas of strength and improvement opportunities; and innovating, designing, or redesigning care delivery processes).

Patient-Based Systems: Yesterday, Today, and Tomorrow

This section provides a very brief review of patient-based systems past, present, and future. Other reviews of the literature can be found to provide further background information.[3–5]

Broad interest in the measurement of quality is a fairly recent phenomenon. In the past, most efforts to measure quality have been led by health service researchers and quality assurance professionals. While quality assurance professionals, for the most part, have eschewed use of patient-based measures, health service researchers have used them from time to time to assess "satisfaction" with physicians, hospitals, health maintenance organizations (HMOs), and other providers.[6] On rare occasions, health service researchers have used both measures of outcomes and satisfaction. For example, the Health Insurance Experiment and the Medical Outcomes Study, both landmark projects, made extensive use of patient-based measures of quality, including patient-reported health outcomes and evaluations of care.[7,8]

Only within the past decade has the routine use of patient evaluations of quality started moving out of the lofty world of health services research into the daily world of health care delivery. Patient evaluations of care—commonly referred to as satisfaction studies—have become commonplace in hospitals, large group practices, and HMOs; they are, however, still relatively rare in other settings such as small medical practices and nursing homes.[9] During the past several years, health services researchers have made great advances in the development of patient-based measurement instruments. Many different investigators have developed assorted questionnaires. Some noteworthy and widely used patient evaluation surveys have been developed to assess health plans (e.g., Group Health Association of America)[10] and hospitals (Hospital Quality Trends: Patient Judgment System and Picker/Commonwealth Patient-Centered Care).[11–13] Other excellent patient-based measures of health outcomes have been developed and validated and are being used ever more widely. Some of the better known of these are the Sickness Impact Profile (SIP),[14] the Quality of Well Being (QWB) scale,[15] the Medical Outcomes Study Short-Form (MOS SF-36),[16] and the Dartmouth COOP Functional Health Status Charts (COOP Charts).[17]

Table 20–1 lists selected features that characterize many of the patient-based quality measurement systems in use today and contrasts them with the features projected for the future. The patient-based systems currently in use in most hospitals and large group practices tend to focus only on satisfaction with services; are done once or twice per year (or are casually made available to all patients all the time for comments); and generally suffer from low response rates,

Table 20–1

Features of patient-based quality measurement systems

Feature	Current	Future
Content	Satisfaction	Care evaluations, health outcomes
Validation	Rare	Common
Frequency	Annually or all patients	Continually on representative samples
Sampling	Not rigorous	Careful specification of sampling frame
Response Rates	Low (under 40%)	High (greater than 60%)
Comparative Data	Rare	Common
Users and Uses	Few and limited	Many and diverse and educated
Direct Link to Action	Limited, problem identification	Common
Feedback	Cross-sectional, tabular	Trends, graphic, layered measures

use of unvalidated instruments, and absence of longi-tudinal comparative information. Tomorrow's sys-tems, by contrast, will measure areas beyond satisfac-tion with services; will produce trend data based on continual, representative samples of patients; will have higher response rates; and will make greater use of validated measures for which comparative data will be available. Today's users of the measures often receive outdated, cross-sectional feedback summa-rized in tables; receive little education on how to use the information; and generally do not act on the results, except to identify problems. In the future, more diverse groups of people inside and outside of provider organizations will receive up-to-date graphi-cal feedback reports and will make extensive use of the information based on relevant education on how to interpret and apply it for multiple purposes. Be-sides tracking some critical, standard measures of quality and costs, flexible measures will be used to probe more deeply into areas of high interest.[18-20]

Design Principles

In the future, we predict that health care providers will need to compete on the basis of valid measures of value (i.e., the quality of care in relation to the total cost of care) and that health plan members (not patients) and purchasers of care (not third party payors) will be viewed as the main customers of the health care system. We also predict that health care providers who are best able to deliver high-value care to members or patients and to purchasers or payors will be the most successful providers over the long run. For these reasons and more, the following nine principles may be used to design patient-based quality measurement systems that will have high utility. Each of these principles is stated briefly; some are illustrated with a figure and discussed in the subsequent section.

Think like corn. Barbara McClintock, the Nobel laureate who did ground breaking genetic research based on the study of corn, alleged that before she could do good research on corn she needed to learn how to think like corn.[21] This principle is the most important one. For the most part, fundamental im-provements in patient care will come from learning to think (and feel) like patients.

Clarify the aims of the measures. Be clear about the aim of the measures, the users of the system, the uses of the information, and the nature of the system itself.

Basically, this principle addresses the need for the measures. For example, the aim of the measurement might be "to measure accurately overall trends in quality for use by senior leaders to confirm that the care is improving." Or it might be "to determine the major drivers of cardiac patient satisfaction for an interdisciplinary team engaged in the total redesign of the delivery process." Depending on the aim, differ-ent measurement and analysis methods are required.

Offer specific answers. Do not provide data. Give answers. Answers to the users' questions.[20] Clarify the data requirements by framing a specific question (or specific questions) that users must have answered (e.g., "What proportion of patients believe care is so good here that they would return again if they need care?"). This requires detailed knowledge of the in-tended application or use of the measurement.

Display measures on an "instrument panel." Do not rely solely on tables to show results; use graphical methods instead. Create an instrument panel to pro-vide "snapshots" as well as "moving pictures" that answer the basic questions. For example, control charts are akin to moving pictures and can reveal trends and instances of special causes. Flowcharts or patient care "maps" that have measures (gauges) at-tached to them can provide a numeric, cross-sectional snapshot of performance and variation in the delivery system.

Measure outcomes and care processes. Measure health status—biological, physical, mental, and so-cial function—over time as an indicator of health outcome. Measure patients' evaluations of the good-ness of care processes at meeting their needs—based on ratings and reports linked to steps in the care delivery process—as an indicator of care or service quality. Patient ratings and reports of processes and results can provide an important complement to more technical measures of care provision.

Link measures using "measurement trees." Provide a logical linkage between measures. One way to do this is to build a measurement tree. Based on a clear understanding of the aim of the measures and the answers needed by users, conceptualize the measures in the shape of a tree—complete with a trunk, main branches, and individual limbs. Measurement tree thinking helps to visually portray the logic in the linkage of the measures. For example, suppose lead-ers at different levels in the organization must know the answers to the following questions:

- Is patient satisfaction improving?
- What are the main drivers of patient satisfaction?
- What specific things should we do or not do to improve satisfaction?

The trunk measure might capture overall satisfaction, the branch measures might reflect the major drivers of satisfaction, and the limb measures might reflect highly specific features and actions related to the major drivers of satisfaction.

Use patient ratings and reports. Different types of questions are used for different levels of measurement. For example, patient ratings (e.g., excellent, very good, good, fair, poor) tend to be most useful for trunk measures, while specific reports tend to be most useful for limb measures (e.g., yes or no reports on things done or not done or features of care that are present or absent). Both ratings and reports can be useful for the middle level branch measures. Ratings can be constructed to cover a large span of connected processes of work (conceptual territory) and generate relevant overall judgments with only a few items—a shotgun strategy. Reports can be created to take aim at specific desired or undesired features and actions—a rifle shot strategy. Both strategies have value depending on the circumstances.

Seek the truth. Users want to know the truth. Measures are never perfectly truthful. They can only approximate and partly reflect part of the truth. However, by following the science of measurement, it is possible to construct measures that are more accurate.[22] To do so requires that the measures be

- valid (measure what they are supposed to measure),
- reliable (measures do not change if features, actions, or beliefs do not change), and
- representative (based on a representative sample of the relevant patient universe).

Whenever it is possible to adopt or adapt previously validated measures and methods, this should be done, because it can yield sound, professionally developed measures and methods at low start-up cost. Inventing new measures and methods of sampling, data collection, and analysis can be expensive. If the processes of sampling, gathering data and analyzing the results are not done with rigor, then truth (e.g., validity, reliability, and representativeness) is jeopardized.

Establish and continually improve utility. Ultimately, the value of patient-based measures depends on their utility. Utility is enhanced when the measures are readily accessible to users, when feedback is timely and made actionable through linkage to specific aspects of the process (i.e., inputs → actions → outputs → goodness of outcomes in the eyes of the customers), when the users have knowledge about how to interpret and use the feedback, and when there is a mix of standard and flexible indicators. Standard measures can be used to detect trends and afford apple-to-apple comparisons. Flexible measures can be used to explore all of the branches and limbs on an as-needed basis and to evaluate the success or failure of improvement trials and innovations.

Design and testing process

The best plan for designing and testing a patient-based quality measurement system is to adopt or adapt someone else's—if it is relevant, validated, and accessible. Many outstanding systems have already been developed and validated and are widely used. These should be considered before starting down the tortuous, expensive, and time-consuming process described below.

Unfortunately, circumstances often require new measure development work (e.g., an improvement team may be starting a long-term process to re-engineer diabetes care and may need highly specific, patient-based information) or the phenomenon of NIH (not invented here) may preclude local adoption of others' work.

The design process outlined in Figure 20–1 provides one way to design and pilot-test a patient-based measurement system. It is based on a quality-by-design strategy and is adapted from the model proposed by Moen and Nolan.[23] The design process begins with learning—learning about both the users and the patients.

First, query the user (or the multiple users) of the information: What key questions must be answered? How will they use the information? Then travel into the world of the patient to identify key subgroups and to gain full and complete knowledge of patients: What are their needs and expectations? What features and actions prompt their judgments about goodness and benefits? Then return to the users to learn how they would define a high-quality, high-value feedback report—something that might be tailored to meet their needs. Often, qualitative research methods (such as direct observation and the use of personal interviews and focus groups) are best suited for this initial spadework with patients and users.[24] It remains the responsibility of the provider to discern patient "need," though patients can often help provide clues to their needs. Assuming that the intended beneficiary of a service or product can define exactly what the provider should offer tends to limit ideas to those within the experience base of the beneficiary.[25]

Next, having defined quality of care based on knowledge of the patients' views and with feedback from the users' perspective, it is possible to begin work on the construction of potential, face-valid, patient-grounded measures and prototype feedback reports. The measures could be layered as discussed above to provide trunk, branch, and limb indicators based on user need. The feedback reports could be constructed treelike to afford users a clear view of the trunk, main branches, and individual limbs—again depending on user need.

It is especially important to construct alternate prototype feedback reports—each of which is designed to answer the users' questions—and then to obtain users' reactions to these "simulated" feedback reports before actually going to the trouble and expense of producing the report. The feedback report for pilot-testing can then benefit from the wisdom gained from the simulated prototype reports by building in useful features and designing out confusion, flaws, and useless features.

The next step is to move from high-level planning to preparing to run a small-scale pilot test that incorporates the best set of measurement and feedback report concepts in an overall initial trial. The pilot test may use the plan-do-study-act (PDSA) cycle for continual improvement (Figure 20–1).

Planning involves determining what sample of users will receive what type of prototype feedback reports from what set of patients using which methods of data collection on what measures of health care and health outcomes. The plan should include steps to ensure representativeness of the sample and respondents, safeguards to ensure data integrity in coding and analysis, user education and consultation before and after receipt of the report, and fast-as-possible feedback to users. This planning phase requires knowing the who, what, where, when, and how of the pilot.

Doing includes implementing the plan and carefully observing the processes of sampling, data collection, and report production and the use of the feedback by users. It is critical at this point to be close enough to the action to identify unanticipated problems and to uncover serendipitous events resulting from the work.

Studying the results can start by debriefing the users to explore utility—find out what they liked and did not like about the information and education they received, find out how they used or failed to use the feedback, and request suggestions for improvements. It also includes debriefing patients to determine if the measures that were pilot-tested made sense to them and adequately reflected their perceptions on the goodness of care as well as analyzing the patient-based measures: reliability, validity, variability, and representativeness. The analysis of measures may require expertise in fields such as psychometrics and statistics.

Acting on the results of the total experience involves learning all relevant lessons from the initial pilot test and using these to design a better way of gathering, analyzing, and using the patient-based measures. At this point, consideration should be given to dropping or adding measures, designing in flexibility to meet disparate user needs, streamlining and speeding up data management, and expanding the number of users.

A glimpse of tomorrow's systems

Previous sections of this article have laid out broad issues, design principles, and a specific design process. The aim of this section is to use real-world examples, taken from recent work, to provide a glimpse of tomorrow's patient-based quality measurement systems. The idea is to move from the abstract to the concrete. The work that is highlighted next is in constant evolution; consequently, these examples are offered to show elements of future systems, recognizing that the "perfect" system is, to the best of our knowledge, not up and running anywhere in the country.

Instrument panels: Processes and outcomes of care

Most people know what the cockpit of a jet airplane looks like. There are many dials and gauges that form an instrument panel to enable the pilots to fly safely from here to there. There are dozens of instruments to measure altitude, fuel consumption, air speed, engine performance, electrical systems, temperatures, and,

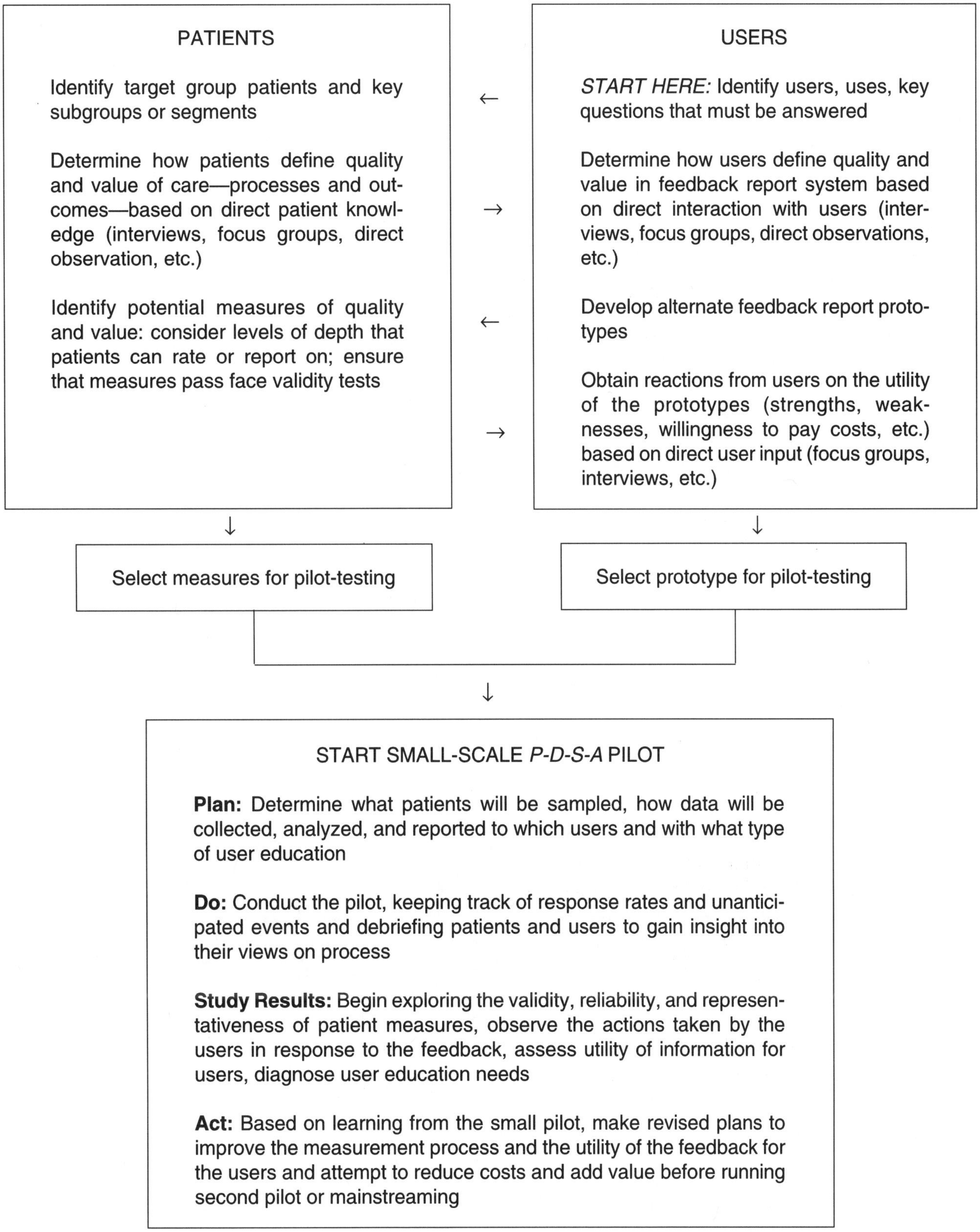

PATIENTS

Identify target group patients and key subgroups or segments

←

Determine how patients define quality and value of care—processes and outcomes—based on direct patient knowledge (interviews, focus groups, direct observation, etc.)

→

Identify potential measures of quality and value: consider levels of depth that patients can rate or report on; ensure that measures pass face validity tests

←

USERS

START HERE: Identify users, uses, key questions that must be answered

Determine how users define quality and value in feedback report system based on direct interaction with users (interviews, focus groups, direct observations, etc.)

Develop alternate feedback report prototypes

Obtain reactions from users on the utility of the prototypes (strengths, weaknesses, willingness to pay costs, etc.) based on direct user input (focus groups, interviews, etc.)

→

↓

Select measures for pilot-testing

↓

Select prototype for pilot-testing

↓

START SMALL-SCALE *P-D-S-A* PILOT

Plan: Determine what patients will be sampled, how data will be collected, analyzed, and reported to which users and with what type of user education

Do: Conduct the pilot, keeping track of response rates and unanticipated events and debriefing patients and users to gain insight into their views on process

Study Results: Begin exploring the validity, reliability, and representativeness of patient measures, observe the actions taken by the users in response to the feedback, assess utility of information for users, diagnose user education needs

Act: Based on learning from the small pilot, make revised plans to improve the measurement process and the utility of the feedback for the users and attempt to reduce costs and add value before running second pilot or mainstreaming

Figure 20–1. Method for designing and testing a patient-based measurement system.

most importantly, avionics to get the plane to the right destination safely.

Hospitals, clinics, and HMOs are, like jet aircraft, sophisticated systems. Leaders in these organizations need "instrument panels" much as an airplane pilot does. The instrument panels for health care leaders could put together—in one visual display—what we do with what we get (i.e., processes and outcomes). Others have noted the desirability of "balanced scorecards."[26]

Figure 20–2 shows an instrument panel for medical-surgical inpatients. This instrument panel was used by corporate executives of a health care system that operates a large number of medical-surgical hospitals. It is based on a random sample of 15,019 inpatients discharged from 69 hospitals. These particular patient-based measures were produced by the Hospital Quality Trend: Patient Judgments System (HQT: PJJ), a validated system that has been described fully in the literature.[11,12] Figure 20–2 lists elements of the patient care process (e.g., admitting, daily care, information, doctoring, nursing, ancillary, discharging, etc.) and provides measures of process performance and outcomes (e.g., perceived health outcome and overall satisfaction) based on patients' ratings.

For example, with regard to a rating of excellent, the median value for all 69 hospitals for the admitting process was 35 percent. The highest percentage for this rating among the hospitals was 47 percent and the lowest was 22 percent. That is, 47 percent of a randomly selected group of patients from one hospital rated admitting as excellent (the best hospital score on admitting), whereas only 22 percent of another hospital's patients rated admitting as excellent (the lowest hospital score on admitting). The comparable figures for nursing were 39 percent for the median hospital, 56 percent for the highest rated hospital, and

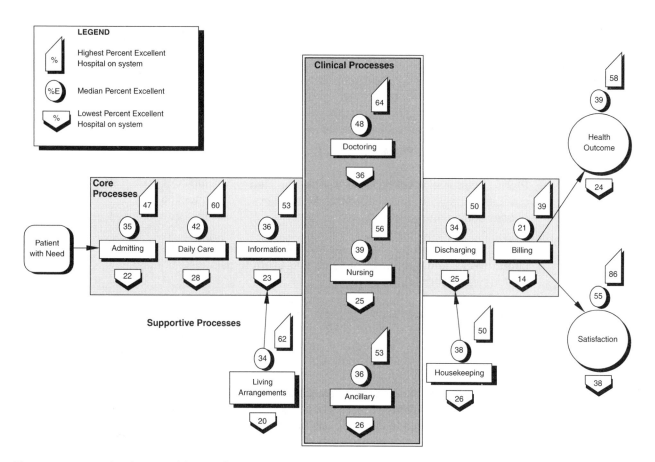

Figure 20–2. Medical-surgical hospital instrument panel: Excellence as rated by a random sample of patients (N = 15,019 patients discharged from 69 hospitals).

25 percent for the lowest rated hospital. In the case of health outcomes and satisfaction, median ratings were 39 and 55 percent, the best ratings were 58 and 86 percent, and the worst ratings were 24 and 38 percent respectively, with both health outcomes and satisfaction varying more than 100 percent across hospitals.

Figure 20–3 presents a more sophisticated instrument panel for acute myocardial infarction (AMI) patients. This instrument panel was used by a multi-disciplinary cardiac care improvement team. It combines 258 consecutive AMI patients' ratings of basic patient care processes (e.g., information and education, clinical information, nursing care, etc.), health status, and satisfaction with chart-abstracted data on clinical severity, diagnostic exploration, therapeutic recommendations and actions, and clinical outcomes. By scanning the instrument panel, it can be seen that 19 percent of patients died within eight weeks and 8 percent were readmitted. Among survivors, general health status improved dramatically, going from an average of 46 (on a 0–100 scale) two weeks prior to AMI to a score of 73 at eight weeks' postdischarge. It took 3.88 weeks on the average for the patients to return to work or normal routine; 29 percent rated their current health as excellent and 14 percent suffered from substantial angina. Almost one out of five patients (18 percent) rated information on medication side effects as inadequate.

Instrument panels like those shown in Figures 20–2 and 20–3 help users to visualize the process/outcome connection, easily identify improvement opportunities, know approximately where in the process to target improvements, and monitor the success of improvement work.[27]

Trunks, branches, and limbs: Overall satisfaction, ratings, and reports

Different users require different levels of information. Therefore, different levels of questions can be crafted to provide patient-based measures of different levels of performance. Figure 20–4 illustrates three different levels of questions related to AMI patient care that were used in a clinical improvement project.

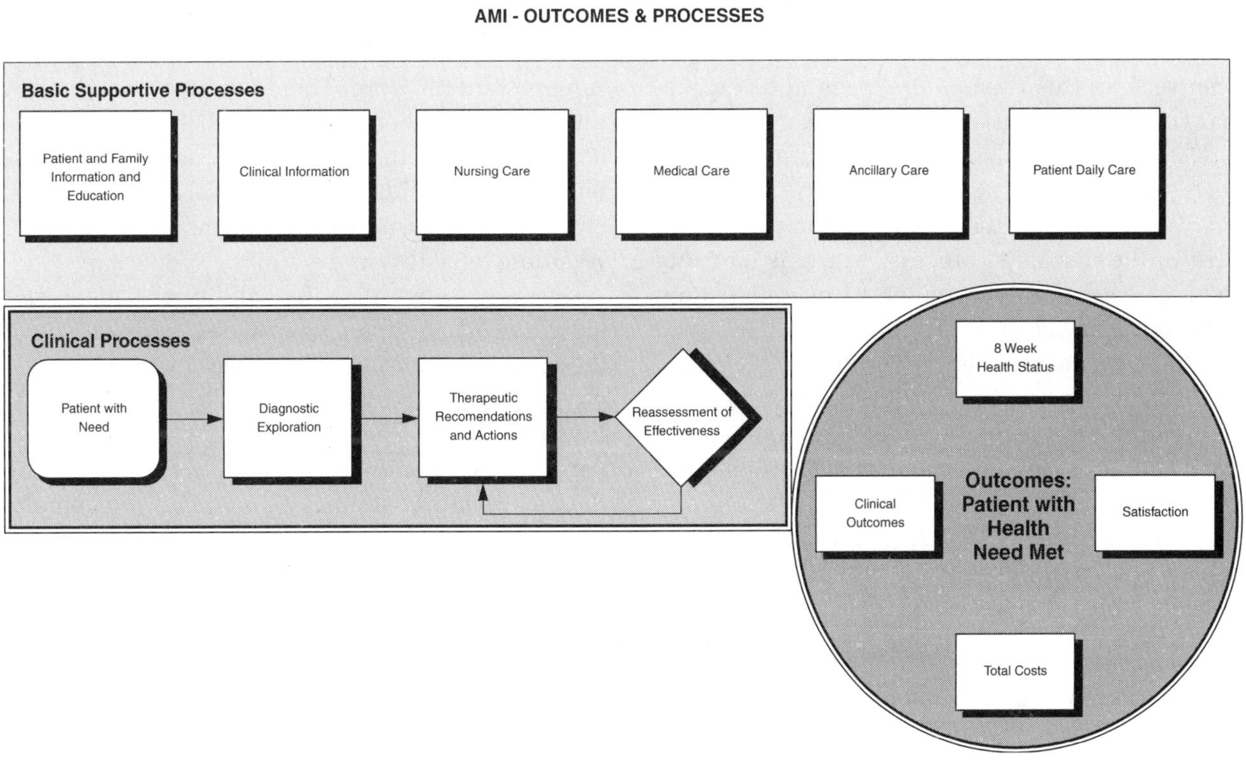

Figure 20-3. Acute myocardial infarction (AMI) process and outcomes draft instrument panel.

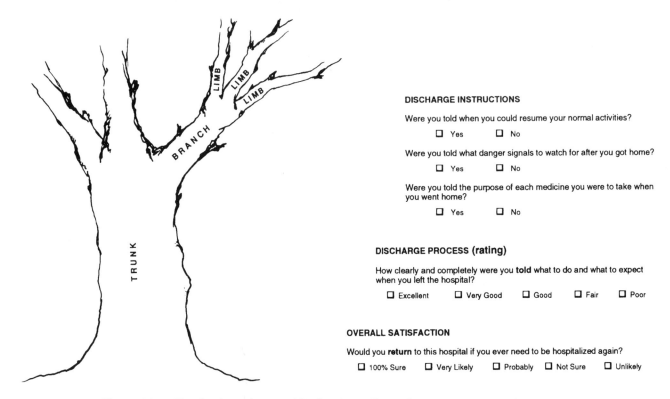

Figure 20–4. Trunks, branches, and limbs: Overall satisfaction, ratings, and reports.

The trunk in this example happens to be evaluations of care; it could just as well have been functional health status or clinical outcome. The trunk question reflects an overall rating of satisfaction (i.e., likelihood of return to hospital). The main branch shown relates to the discharge process, which is one subsystem of care that contributes to overall patient satisfaction. The question reflects how well informed the patient was at discharge. The limbs associated with discharge are concerned with specific reports on whether or not the patient was told when to resume normal activities, about danger signals, and the purpose of each prescribed medicine.

By thinking trunk ↔ branch ↔ limb, it is possible to have a relational information system that can provide users with different levels of detail to match their varied needs.

Truth by triangulation: Cross-customer quality measures

Users want information that is credible. Psychometricians want to construct measures that are valid. Con-

sumers want the truth. There is no way to ever prove unequivocally that a measure is reliable and valid, yet it is possible to gather evidence to establish the level of reliability and validity and to uncover systematic bias.[22] Outstanding measures have documented information regarding reliability and validity.

One way to establish the validity of patient-based measures is to compare the patients' perspective with the perspectives of other knowledgeable groups such as physicians and health care employees. Figure 20–5 illustrates a method to "triangulate" on the accuracy of patient-based measures by comparing and contrasting them with ratings of physicians and hospital employees. In this example, random samples of inpatient ratings of one aspect of nursing care (i.e., the degree of caring and concern shown by nurses) were compared directly with comparable ratings made by physicians and employees respectively. The results, shown thermometer style on the left panel of Figure 20–5, indicate that the overall level of association was quite strong (correlation coefficients of 0.68 for patients and physicians and 0.50 for patients and hospital employees).

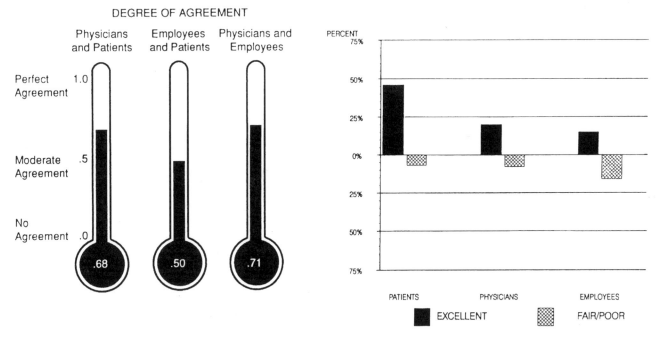

Figure 20–5. Patient, physician, and hospital employee ratings of the concern and caring of nurses (*N* = 15,019 patients, 2,532 physicians, and 14,724 employees associated with 69 hospitals).

However, the results displayed in the bar chart on the right side of Figure 5 reveal that, although the ratings of patients correlate highly with the ratings of physicians and employees, the absolute levels of ratings were substantially different. For example, almost 50 percent of patients rated nursing care and concern excellent whereas the figures were approximately 15 and 20 percent for physicians and employees respectively, and almost twice as many employees rated care and concern either fair or poor as patients or physicians.

Methods like this—asking different customer groups to evaluate the same thing from their own vantage point—can help provide evidence regarding the validity of measures and, at the same time, can provide a better context to understand how quality varies in the eyes of different beholders.

Automated, anytime, anyplace, anywhere measurement: The RT 2000

For patient-based measures to be integrated into the daily work of health care leaders and front-line workers, it will be necessary to explore new technologies for gathering, analyzing, and distributing information in a manner that is flexible, fast, and cheap. The RT 2000 is one promising technique that is already in use today.

Beyond devising instrument panels that comprise information trees filled with accurate patient-based measures, the RT 2000 permits both standardization and flexibility. In addition, it can provide scores for monitoring and improving care, measures to assess health outcomes and process variations, timely and cost-effective feedback, and utility for use by senior managers and front-line workers. A group from the Hospital Corporation of America, the New England Medical Center, and Response Technologies, among other organizations, designed the RT 2000 system in an attempt to accomplish all of these seemingly conflicting tasks.

Figure 20–6 summarizes and illustrates the RT 2000 system for gathering, entering, analyzing, and feeding back patient-based measures and for analyzing quality improvement data. This system combines a piece of hardware (the RT 2000 terminal, which is a computer plus a card reader plus a printer) with questionnaires and data collection forms (to measure patient satisfaction, health risk status, general and disease-specific health status, and quality improvement data) and with software to produce instant analyses (e.g., individualized feedback to a patient or aggregate feedback to a nonpatient in the form of run charts, control charts, histograms, or tabular data). The system can be thought of as providing *automated, anytime, anyplace, anywhere* instant feedback. It is being used in many different health care settings for the functions shown.[28]

•   •   •

It is probably fair to assert that most of today's health care executives, purchasers of care, and frontline health care professionals have only a casual interest in patient-based measures. Tomorrow, however, it is possible—and we believe likely and desirable—that senior leaders, purchasers of care, and front-line clinicians will all view patient-based measures as key indicators of system performance.[29] The patient-based measures will contribute to an instrument panel that will give these different user groups a clear and direct view of successes and failures, strengths and weaknesses, and improvements and declines in the organization's capacity to produce accessible and highly acceptable health care and desired health outcomes at a cost that represents value.[30]

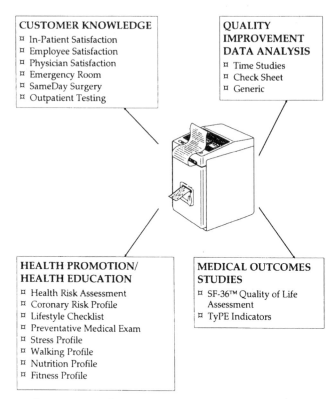

Figure 20–6. The RT 2000: Measurement in a box.

REFERENCES

1. U.S. Congress, Office of Technology Assessment. *The Quality of Medical Care: Information for Consumers.* Washington, D.C.: U.S. Government Printing Office, 1988.
2. Batalden, P.B., and Nelson, E.C. "Hospital Quality: Patient, Physician and Employee Judgments." *International Journal of Health Care Quality Assurance* 3, no. 4 (1990): 7–17.
3. Spilker, B., et al. "Quality of Life Bibliography and Indexes." *Medical Care* 28, suppl. (1990): DS3.
4. Davies, A.R., and Ware, J.E., Jr. "Involving Consumers in Quality of Care Assessment: Do They Provide Valid Information?" *Health Affairs* 7, no. 1 (Spring 1988): 33–48.
5. Ware, J.E., Jr., Davies-Avery, A., and Stewart, A.L. "The Measurement and Meaning of Patient Satisfaction." *Health and Medical Care Services Review* 1, no. 1 (1978): 3–15.
6. Donabedian, A. *The Definition of Quality and Approaches to its Assessment.* Vol. 1. Ann Arbor, Mich.: Health Administration Press, 1980.
7. Newhouse, J.P., et al. "Some Interim Results from a Controlled Trial of Cost Sharing in Health Insurance." *New England Journal of Medicine* 301 (1981): 1501–07.
8. Tarlov, A.R., et al. "The Medical Outcomes Study: An Application of Methods for Monitoring the Results of Medical Care." *JAMA* 262 (1989): 925–30.
9. Ware, J.E., Jr., and Hays, R. "Methods for Measuring Patient Satisfaction with Specific Medical Encounters." *Medical Care* 26 (1988): 393–402.
10. Davies, A.R., and Ware, J.E., Jr. *GHAA Consumer Satisfaction Survey.* Washington, D.C.: Group Health Association of America, Department of Research and Analysis, 1988.
11. Meterko, M., Nelson, E.C., and Rubin, H.R., eds. "Patient Judgments of Hospital Quality: Report of a Pilot Study." *Medical Care,* suppl. (September 1990): S1–S56.
12. Nelson, E.C., et al. "The Patient Judgment System: Reliability and Validity." *Quality Review Bulletin* 15, no. 6 (1989): 185–91.
13. Cleary, P.D., et al. "Patients Evaluate Their Hospital Care: A National Survey." *Health Affairs* 10 (1991): 254–67.
14. Bergner, M., et al. "The Sickness Impact Profile: Conceptual Formulation and Methodology for the Development of a Health Status Measure." *International Journal Health Services* 6 (1976): 393–402.
15. Fanshel, S., and Bush, J.W. "A Health-Status Index and Its Application to Health-Services Outcomes." *Operations Research* 18 (1970): 1021–33.
16. Ware, J.E., Jr., and Sherbourne, C.D. "The MOS 36-Item Short-Form Health Survey (SF-36): I. Conceptual Framework and Item Selection." *Medical Care* 30 (1992): 473–83.

17. Nelson, E.C., et al. "The Functional Status of Patients: How Can It Be Measured in Physicians' Offices?" *Medical Care* 28 (1990): 1111–26.

18. Albrecht, K., and Zemke, R. *Service America! Doing Business in the New Economy.* New York, N.Y.: Warner Books, 1990.

19. Maskell, B.H. *Performance Measurement for World Class Manufacturing: A Model for American Companies.* Cambridge, Mass.: Productivity Press, 1991.

20. Goldratt, E.M. *The Haystack Syndrome: Sifting Information out of the Data Ocean.* Croton-on-Hudson, N.Y.: North River Press, 1990.

21. Keller, E.F. *A Feeling for the Organism: The Life and Work of Barbara McClintock.* New York, N.Y.: W.H. Freeman, 1983.

22. Carmines, E.G., and Zeller, R.A. *Reliability and Validity Assessment.* Quantitative Applications in the Social Sciences Series, Vol. 17. Beverly Hills, Calif.: Sage Publications, 1979.

23. Moen, R.D., Nolan, T.W., and Provost, L.P. *Improving Quality through Planned Experimentation.* New York, N.Y.: McGraw-Hill, 1991.

24. Nelson, E.C., et al. "Gaining Customer Knowledge: Obtaining and Using Customer Judgments for Hospitalwide Quality Improvement." *Topics in Health Record Management* 11, no. 3 (1991): 13–26.

25. Deming, W.E. *The New Economics for Industry, Government, Education.* Cambridge, Mass.: M.I.T. Press, 1993.

26. Kaplan, R.S., and Norton, D.P. "The Balanced Scorecard: Measures That Drive Performance." *Harvard Business Review* (January–February 1992): 71–79.

27. Tufte, E.R. *The Visual Display of Quantitative Information.* Cheshire, Conn.: Graphics Press, 1983.

28. Batalden, P.B., and Nolan, T.W. "Knowledge for the Leadership of Continual Improvement of Health Care." In *Manual of Health Services Management,* edited by R.J. Taylor. Gaithersburg, Md.: Aspen Publishers, 1993.

29. Nelson, E.C., et al. "Do Patient Perceptions of Quality Relate to Hospital Financial Performance?" *Journal of Health Care Marketing* 12, no. 4 (1992): 6–13.

30. Batalden, P.B., and Nelson, E.C. "Hospital Quality: Patient, Physician and Employee Judgments." *International Journal of Health Care Quality Assurance* 3, no. 4 (1990): 7–17.

21

The Measurement of Physician Performance

Nicholas A. Hanchak and Neil Schlackman

There is growing interest in information concerning the performance of physicians. This is hardly surprising—health care is important to those who receive it, those who provide it, and those who pay for it. There are, however, a number of issues raised by the measurement of physician performance, including such basic questions as how to do it, who should do it, and who should have access to the results. In 1990, U.S. Healthcare (USHC) formed a subsidiary, U.S. Quality Algorithms (USQA), to assist in the development and application of health care performance measures.

USQA's work has been performed in the context of USHC's medical delivery system. USHC is an independent contract model managed care organization with about 9,000 primary care physicians (PCPs), over 30,000 specialists, and approximately 400 hospitals. It is not a direct provider of health care services, and the providers with which it contracts also provide health care services to the members of other managed care organizations and to traditionally insured patients. For example, in the case of primary care, USHC members might represent less than 5 percent of a practice to over 50 percent. One consequence is that the information available to evaluate a provider is often restricted to the data generated in the care of USHC patients. However, in certain circumstances USHC has a more complete dataset from which to derive performance information.

USQA has been a leader in the developing population-based measures of health plan performance. It has developed and applied measures in assessing the performance of all key providers within the medical delivery system: PCPs, specialists, and hospitals (Figure 21–1). USHC uses performance information for

peer comparison, to set benchmarks for attainable performance, and to stimulate providers to continuously improve their performance. It rarely, if ever, uses such information in determining which physicians should be removed from the network. The focus of this article is on the measurement of the performance of physicians. USHC's quality-based compensation model, in which the measurement of performance is linked to compensation, is also described.

Overview of Performance Measures

There are a number of different classification schemes that can be used to categorize performance measures. Donabedian's well-known framework of structure, process, and outcomes provides a useful starting point for analysis. A related framework employed by USHC includes

- access to care (the availability of doctors and other health care providers, facilities, and services necessary to meet the health needs of an identified population),
- capability to provide care (the degree to which a health care provider's formal training and practical experience support the delivery of care and the likely achievement of desired outcomes),
- aspects of technical performance (attributes of tests and procedures, such as the clarity and completeness of diagnostic imaging studies, that maximize the likelihood of successful diagnosis and treatment),
- aspects of cognitive performance (aspects of mental activities that influence patient management decisions [e.g., the correctness of the interpretation of imaging studies and laboratory tests]),
- appropriateness of care (the correctness of decisions concerning the diagnosis and treatment of patients in relationship to the recommendations

Quality Management in Health Care 1995; 4(1): 1–12

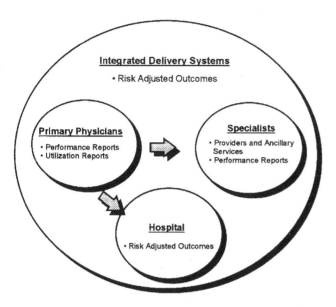

Figure 21–1. U.S. Healthcare measures the performance of each of the key providers in its medical delivery system.

in well-constructed, evidence-based practice policies),

- patient satisfaction with care (patients' perceptions of their experiences with the health care system in the context of their expectations),
- outcomes of care (direct and proxy measures for the current and future health status and well-being of patients), and
- costs of care (direct costs [consumed in the context of patient care] and indirect costs [e.g., lost productivity of workers, lost school days] related to health care and disease).

These items are what USHC would like to measure routinely when managed care members interact with the health care delivery system. Due to limitations in the methods and data available to assess performance, measures are often selected that approximate the items.

There are two key attributes of a measure: its literal value (e.g., 64 percent of the diabetics in practice X received a dilated retinal exam) and its meaning (e.g., a 64-percent dilated retinal exam rate is two standard deviations above the average for a particular health care system as a whole and is considered a "good" rate). The metrics used to impart meaning to performance measures can be derived from a number of different sources. They may be based on standards of care (e.g., all diabetics should receive annual dilated

retinal exams) or experience (e.g., in a particular health system, 45 percent of diabetics received a dilated retinal exam in the last year).

An overriding principle in the development of performance measures is that they must have the support and "buy-in" of those being measured. USHC has tried to develop and implement performance measures in a manner that relies on the input and support of those being measured. In general, the approach is to adopt a guideline issued by a nationally respected organization and to allow for modification based on local circumstances or new medical knowledge.[1–3] All of the work at USHC has benefited from the input of advisory committees composed of physicians who participate in its networks.

USHC's ability to measure performance is hindered by several factors. Process measures are indicators that measure what or how something is done, and their use is sometimes limited by the lack of evidence-based guidelines from which to derive performance measures. With regard to outcome measures, death and adverse events are often the only routinely collected relevant data, and the reliability of these items in available datasets is problematic. In addition, outcome measures generally require risk adjustment, which remains an incomplete science.

An additional limitation of performance measures is that they are only as good as the underlying data upon which they are based. USHC must weigh the feasibility of primary data collection against the accessibility of data in administrative datasets already collected for other purposes. Electronic medical records do not exist in most of the settings in which USHC members receive care. The raw material for performance measurement is mostly derived from administrative datasets. The nature of the data is related to the organization of the USHC medical delivery system. All primary care services are capitated and require submission of encounter forms. Most specialty and hospital care is paid for based on some form of fee schedule and the submission of claims is required for reimbursement. USHC also manages pharmacy benefits for the majority of its members and therefore has access to pharmacy claims information. Outpatient laboratory results data are available as well. USHC supplements these administrative data with primary data collected from providers and patients, including satisfaction and health status outcome information.[4–6]

The Evaluation of Primary Care Physician Performance

In USHC's managed care system, each member chooses a PCP who is expected to coordinate the member's care. The PCP is expected to focus on disease prevention, early identification of disease, and proper treatment of the member by the appropriate provider in the right setting. The fact that each PCP has responsibility for a defined group of enrollees allows for measures relating to health promotion activities. It also allows for the measurement of performance in caring for certain at-risk members with specific diseases. We describe below an example of USHC's work in evaluating physician performance in caring for diabetics. As a second example of the evaluation of PCP performance, we present the U.S. Healthcare Radiology Report, which provides baseline information about an individual provider's radiology utilization compared to practice-based norms. This gives providers insight into how their threshold for ordering radiologic studies compares to those of their peers. First, a brief overview of the PCP Quality Care Compensation System is presented, along with several examples in which tying compensation to performance has led to improved quality.

USHC's Primary Care Physician Quality Care Compensation System

USHC introduced the measurement of performance of PCPs into its compensation model in 1987. Since the introduction of this model, participating PCPs have had the opportunity to enhance their capitation and receive additional distributions based on their measured performance in providing quality care to USHC members. The PCP Quality Care Compensation System (QCCS) has gone through further development since its initial introduction and is currently in its third generation. As measures based on administrative data such as those in the diabetes and radiology reports are refined, they will likely be incorporated into future generations of the PCP QCCS model.[7,8]

The enhancement of capitation and the eligibility for additional distributions are dependent on a PCP office's overall Quality Factor. The Quality Factor for the office is derived from three components on a semiannual basis: Quality Review, Comprehensive Care, and Utilization (see Figure 21–2). Quality Review includes measures related to satisfaction (as indicated by member surveys), member transfer rates, focused medical chart reviews, and the PCP office's philosophy of managed care. Chart review includes measures related to compliance with health maintenance standards, such as compliance with the recommended provision of immunizations and cholesterol screening in the appropriate age

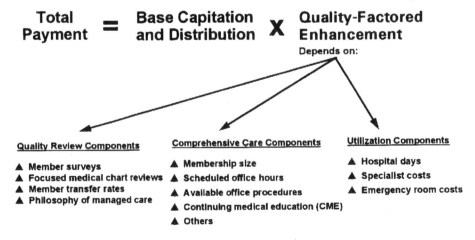

Figure 21–2. U.S. Healthcare's Primary Care Physician Quality Care Compensation System model.

groups. USHC has been able to achieve continued improvement in these audits because of the reinforcement of their importance by the professional service coordinators and medical directors servicing the offices, and because of their incorporation into the QCCS model (see Figure 21–3).[9]

The Comprehensive Care components are related to measures that enhance a PCP office's ability to succeed in a managed care system. They include the following measures: membership size, scheduled office hours, available office procedures, participation in USHC-sponsored continuing medical education, internal practice coverage, the care provided to catastrophic cases, participation in patient management, practice growth, and a computer link to USHC. The Utilization component includes the use of hospitals (as measured in bed days) and the use of specialist care and emergency rooms.

Each measure within each of the three components is given its own weight. Overall, the Quality Review and Comprehensive Care components account for 82 percent of the overall Quality Factor, while the Utilization component accounts for 18 percent. The Quality Factor may add as much as 29 percent to the capitation. The total compensation of the PCP office is composed of several components. The base capitation is dependent on the age and sex distribution of the capitated USHC

members. The enhancement to the capitation is based on the calculated Quality Factor. The base plus enhanced capitation payments are made twice a month. In addition to capitation, the office has the opportunity to receive monthly and annual distributions that are based on hospital, specialist, and emergency room costs and the office's Quality Factor. Finally, PCP offices that are open to new USHC members or open to existing patients converting to USHC insurance are eligible for semiannual "office status" payments.

The USHC Diabetes Performance Report

Diabetes mellitus is a chronic medical condition that, if not well managed, can lead to significant morbidity and mortality. The recently completed Diabetes Control and Complications Trial has demonstrated that aggressive glycemic control can delay and slow the progression of end-stage complications of diabetes.[10] Table 21–1 is the U.S. Healthcare Diabetes Performance Report that we mailed to all participating PCPs for educational purposes. We divided the report into process measures and outcome measures. The example shows a report for a sample family practice office in which we identified 165 members with diabetes, for an estimated office prevalence of 3.2 percent (the overall rate for USHC is 3.1 percent). We based the calculation of prevalence on a minimum

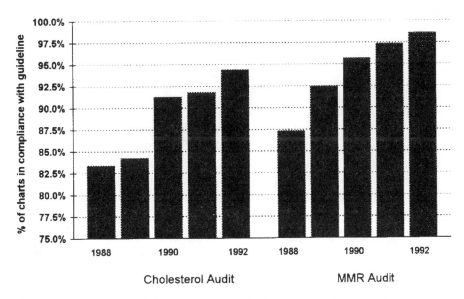

Figure 21–3. The chart audit measures of cholesterol and MMR immunization rates have seen yearly improvement since incorporation into the Primary Care Physician Quality Care Compensation System.

Table 21–1

U.S. Healthcare's Primary Care Physician Diabetes Performance Report

Practice Type: Family Practice
Office Address: Anytown, PA 19422
Number of Current USHC Members Identified with Diabetes: 165

Reporting Time Period: 07/01/93–06/30/94

	Office	USHC
Process measures		
1. Estimated overall prevalence of diabetes*	3.2%	3.1%
1a. Estimated overall prevalence of diabetes age 0–19*	0.6%	0.3%
1b. Estimated overall prevalence of diabetes age 20+*	3.8%	4.4%
2. Diabetics with pharmacy plan on insulin*	30.1%	25.1%
3. Average number of annual primary care visits per diabetic	7.1	4.0
4. Diabetics who visited their physician at least once during reporting period	93.3%	90.0%
5. Average number of annual glycated hemoglobin tests per diabetic	2.3	.8
6. Diabetics with at least 2 glycated hemoglobin tests during reporting period	58.8%	22.7%
7. Diabetics receiving retinal eye exams during reporting period	38.8%	30.4%
8. Diabetics receiving cholesterol screening during reporting period	67.9%	35.8%
9. Diabetics receiving microalbuminuria screening during reporting period	4.9%	2.8%
Outcome measures		
10. Emergency room visits specifically for diabetes/1000 diabetics/year		8.2
11. Total admissions (acute) specifically for diabetes/1000 diabetics/year		24.8
12. Admissions for ketoacidosis, hyperosmolar coma, or other coma/ 1000 diabetics/year		6.5
13. Admissions for hypoglycemia/1000 diabetics/year		3.0
14. Admissions for cellulitis/1000 diabetics/year		6.0
15. Prevalence of ischemic heart disease in diabetics		17.2%
16. Prevalence of end-stage renal disease in diabetics		1.5%
17. Prevalence of neuropathy in diabetics		0.6%
18. Prevalence of retinopathy in diabetics		13.7%
19. Annual incidence of lower extremity amputation in diabetics		0.2%

*Based on members who were in the health plan for the full 12 months.

membership of 12 months to allow for sufficient sensitivity in the detection of diabetes using administrative data.

The first step a health plan must take if it is to examine the quality of care provided to its diabetic members is to identify its diabetic members accurately. USHC has used administrative data selection criteria to identify members with 36 different chronic diseases and has profiled those members in a membership chronic disease database. The data used are different combinations of International Classification of Diseases, 9th Revision (ICD-9) diagnosis codes; Physicians' Current Procedural Terminology (CPT-4) procedure codes; NDC pharmacy codes; and laboratory criteria from the encoun-

ters, claims, pharmacy, and laboratory databases. We list the selection criteria used to identify diabetic members in Exhibit 21–1. The identification of members with diabetes and other chronic diseases allows for the evaluation of physician and health plan performance assessment in the care of these patients. Linking each PCP office's capitated membership with the dataset of all USHC diabetic members allows us to identify the office's diabetic members. This serves as the unit of analysis in measuring the performance of PCPs in providing care for their diabetic patients.[11]

We use practice guidelines developed by the American Diabetes Association as the basis for the process measures in the report. Physicians were provided

Exhibit 21–1 Diabetes Mellitus Selection Criteria

Diagnosis Criteria (ICD-9 Codes)
- 250-250.93 (diabetes mellitus with various manifestations)
- 357.2 (polyneuropathy in diabetes)
- 362.0 362.02 (diabetic retinopathy)
- 366.41 (diabetic cataract)

Procedure Criteria (CPT-4 Codes)
- C82985 (glycated protein) and/or C83036 (glycated hemoglobin) occurring twice in any 12 consecutive months, at least 90 days apart
- CJ1820 (diabetic injectable medications)
- CW0070 (oral hypoglycemic medications)
- CW0071 (antidiabetic products [miscellaneous])
- C5190D (registered nurse diabetic visit)
- C5205D (certified diabetes educator)
- C9890A (diabetes education program)
- CE0607 (home blood glucose monitor)

Pharmacy Criteria (NDC Codes)
- Insulin
- Sulfonylurea

Not Included (ICD-9 Codes)
- 648.8 (abnormal glucose tolerance test in pregnancy)
- 790.2 (abnormal glucose tolerance test)
- 962.3 (poisoning by insulin or antidiabetic agent)

with a reprint of these guidelines for educational purposes when they received their report.[12] One of the process measures is access to the PCP. We based this on the average number of annual primary care visits per diabetic (calculated using submissions of encounters). The premise is that the care of members with ongoing chronic conditions such as diabetes requires frequent contact (e.g., for glycemic control) and early detection of complications. We measured the attempt at glycemic control by calculating the average number of annual glycated hemoglobin tests per diabetic and the number of diabetics who had at least two glycated hemoglobin tests during the 12-month reporting period (indicated by CPT-4 codes 82985 [glycated protein] or 83036 [glycated hemoglobin]). We measured three further process measures from the claims and laboratory databases. These concerned compliance with standard screening for complications and in-

cluded members aged 31 and over receiving retinal eye exams by eye care specialists, cholesterol screening, and microalbuminuria testing during the 12-month reporting period. Because the chosen process performance measures were standard-based and represented good care for all diabetics regardless of the severity of their diabetes, these results were not risk adjusted.

Certain performance information does not occur with sufficient frequency to have meaning at the individual physician office level. These include outcome measures that allow for the health plan or a specific region to determine its performance and identify areas for quality improvement. Outcome measures derived from medical claims data reported for USHC overall include the following measures of morbidity or complications of diabetes: emergency room visits for diabetes, diabetic hospitalizations, hospitalizations for ketoacidosis or coma, and hospitalizations for cellulitis and hypoglycemia. In addition, we derived several prevalence statistics for important comorbidities and end-stage diabetic complications from an intersection of diabetes and several other diseases from the membership chronic disease database, including ischemic heart disease, end-stage renal disease, neuropathy, and retinopathy.

An important follow-up task will be to determine if measurement and peer comparison had any impact on performance. Although it is too early to tell, early anecdotes are encouraging. Some physicians pulled the charts of all their diabetic patients and called any who did not receive certain annual tests. One physician developed a standard adhesive-backed label listing guidelines for office visits for diabetic patients. Another physician commented that this was the first time she was able to see a list of her diabetic patients (limited to USHC members) for an internal office-wide quality improvement effort.

The USHC Radiology Performance Report

If they are to provide high-quality care, PCPs need to direct their attention to the cost-effectiveness of the tests they order. A fairly large portion of health care expenditures is devoted to the provision of medical care of uncertain or questionable effectiveness, which is inconsistent with the concept of value in health care. Ancillary services such as radiology have been frequently overutilized.[13,14] One of the first steps toward holding PCPs accountable for their use of medical resources is to measure the patterns of utilization within some framework that allows for comparison. It is difficult to identify a test as being appropriate or inappropriate unless the particulars of the clinical situation are known. There are no benchmarks available to determine what is the right "amount" of radiology utilization in caring for a defined patient population. Therefore, practice-based measures serve as the best means to gain insight into the patterns of radiologic test ordering by physicians.

The use of radiologic studies depends on the demographic and illness burden of a physician's population. In order to begin to address the differences in patients capitated to different PCP offices, we adjusted for the office type, age, and sex of the capitated population in our U.S. Healthcare Primary Care Physician Radiology Performance Report (Table 21–2). This accounts for an important component of the

Table 21–2

U.S. Healthcare's Primary Care Physician Radiology Performance Report

Practice Type: Family Practice
Office Address: Anytown, PA 19422
Average Number of USHC Members during This Reporting Period: 7,009
As of 12/01/94 your radiology services are capitated to:
Anytown Memorial Hospital for full X-ray services excluding MRI and OB Ultrasound.

Office Number: 00
Reporting Time Period: 7/1/93–6/30/94

	Office	USHC[†]
Overall measures		
1. Members age 20+ with at least 1 radiologic study	38.2%*	31.6%
2. Total number of studies/1000 members	633.2*	425.4
3. Relative Value Units of studies/1000 members	2,357.7*	1471.4
4. Studies not performed by capitated radiologist/1000 members	2.1%*	5.6%
5. Relative Value Units of studies not performed by capitated radiologist/1000 members	18.4*	60.5
Specific measures		
6. Chest X-rays/1000 members	76.3*	63.8
7. Abdominal X-rays/1000 members	7.7	6.4
8. Extremity X-rays/1000 members	113.7	104.8
9. Spine X-rays/1000 members	21.0*	28.2
10. Nonobstetric ultrasounds/1000 members	132.7*	62.9
11. CT scans/1000 members	80.7*	33.8
12. Head MRIs/1000 members	12.6*	8.1
13. Spine MRIs/1000 members	13.9	10.5
14. Upper GI series/1000 members	33.6*	15.2
15. Barium enemas/1000 members	15.1*	6.1
16. Bone scans/1000 members	13.5*	6.6
17. Cardiovascular nuclear medicine studies/1000 members	10.5*	15.5
Quality measures		
18. Head MRI and head CT scan occurring within 1 month of each other	2.0%	2.1%
19. Mammography rate for women aged 50–64	77.9%*	57.2%
20. Sinus X-rays (plain films and/or head CT with coronal images)/1000 members	4.9	7.2
21. Rib X-rays/1000 members	2.6	3.5
22. Skull X-rays/1000 members	0.0*	1.0

*Significant at $p < 0.05$.
[†]Adjusted for age, sex, and office type.

variation in radiology utilization. Furthermore, we identified those measures that were statistically different (at the $p < 0.05$ level) from the USHC adjusted averages. This allows physicians to know to what degree the statistical differences are possibly due to chance instead of representing true differences in practice patterns.

We divided the radiology report into three sections: global utilization measures, the use of specific tests and modalities, and quality measures. We measured only outpatient radiology utilization and excluded certain tests from the analysis, including the following: obstetric ultrasound, studies done in orthopedic and urologic offices, and studies performed at children's hospitals. The overall measures include the total number of studies and the RVUs (relative value units) of those studies as measures of global utilization patterns. Measures 4 and 5 represent process measures that identify how well the PCPs comply with USHC capitated relationships with radiology providers (referred to as leakage). Because USHC requires most PCPs to choose one capitated radiology provider, any studies referred to different radiologists are paid on a fee-for-service basis and thus are essentially paid for twice. It should be noted that because radiology services are capitated, we have removed any disincentive to refer.

The specific measures are the rates of performance of specific tests (e.g., chest X-rays and spine X-rays) or specific modalities (e.g., CT scans). These specific measures allow physicians to identify specific practice patterns that differ from those of their peers. The radiology report also includes quality measures such as mammography rates in women aged 50–64 and utilization of sinus films, rib films, and skull X-rays. We developed these procedures in conjunction with representatives from the Radiology Q/A Committee. We selected them based on a desire to maximize the use of mammography and eliminate the use of other studies that are of little value (e.g., skull radiographs) or have limited impact in the clinical management of the disease (e.g., sinus films for sinusitis or rib films in the evaluation of suspected rib fractures).

We mailed the radiology report to all PCP offices. In addition, we developed a desktop analytic tool with drill-down capabilities that allows USHC medical directors to evaluate regional differences at both the PCP office and radiology practice levels. We also mailed the reports to the PCPs' capitated radiologists. The report served as an objective tool to engage the radiologists in a discussion with PCPs regarding appropriateness of test-ordering patterns. Follow-up studies will help determine whether using the radiology report as a tool to feed back performance information to PCPs has any impact on their overall utilization of radiology services.

The Evaluation of Specialist Physician Performance

The evaluation of PCP performance can be population-based because of the defined capitated relationship between members and their PCPs. PCPs are responsible for most preventive services and much of the care in managing acute and chronic diseases for their patients. The evaluation of a specialist's performance must, however, be based on the population of patients that are referred to the specialist. Evaluation of the quality of care provided by specialists often focuses on their performance of diagnostic workups or of procedures. There is a greater need for severity adjustment in the measurement of a specialist's performance because of the differences in referral patterns between specialists. Some specialty providers may be especially qualified to provide care to particularly high-risk patients (e.g., perinatologists versus general obstetricians/gynecologists) or to perform particularly complicated surgical procedures (e.g., high-risk cardiac procedures). Below we demonstrate USQA's approach to the measurement of the performance of specialists by using USHC's Obstetrics/Gynecology Performance Report as an example. We also show how this measurement process has been incorporated into a QCCS model for obstetricians. Finally, we present an overview of a new initiative related to specialist performance measurement by USQA.

USHC Obstetrics/Gynecology Performance Report

The USHC Obstetrics/Gynecology Performance Report measures the quality of care provided by participating OB/GYN specialists. Specialist office results are compared to the results of their USHC peers on a regional basis. The C-section rate is one of the measures of effectiveness for obstetrical care. USHC has set the benchmark rate it hopes to achieve planwide at 20 percent. We based this on an analysis of our own

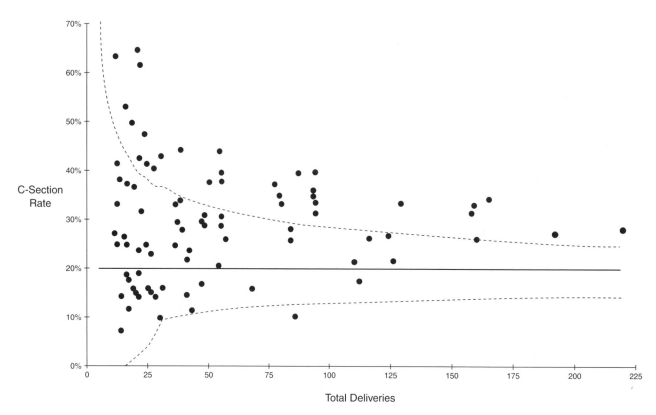

Figure 21–4. A USQA-developed funnel graph that displays the C-section rates of obstetrics/gynecology groups versus their case volumes.

data and a comparison with national standards. Figure 21–4 is a graphical display of the C-section rates for OB/GYN offices within a USHC region. Each point represents an individual OB/GYN office. The number of deliveries performed by an office is plotted against the C-section rate for the office. The horizontal line at 20 percent is the predetermined level of benchmark performance. The broken curved lines surrounding the horizontal benchmark line demarcate the 95-percent confidence intervals. Any rate falling within the confidence limits is not statistically different from the preset benchmark level of performance. Those rates falling above the upper confidence limit are significantly higher than benchmark, and those below the lower confidence limit are significantly lower than the benchmark. This graphical display allows physicians not only to identify their own performance but also to see how their performance compares with those of their peers in terms of volume and C-section rate.

We adopted the rate of performance of endometrial biopsy in the office setting as an appropriateness-of-site measure. The OB/GYN Q/A Committee adopted this from guidelines set forth by the American College of Obstetrics and Gynecology. This measure is the rate at which patients have an elective (nonemergency) endometrial biopsy, hysteroscopy, or dilation and curettage as the first procedure used to help determine the cause of abnormal uterine bleeding. We set a benchmark level just as we did for the C-section rate.

We measure the efficiency of OB/GYN care by a length-of-stay measure that is case-mix adjusted for the percentage of cases that are vaginal deliveries, cesarean deliveries, and hysterectomies.[15] Managed care philosophy is measured by the rate at which elective admissions to the hospital were precertified by the physician. The final measure of OB/GYN performance is member satisfaction. We surveyed all members who saw an OB/GYN specialist in the outpatient setting and used their overall satisfaction with the physician.

USHC's Specialist Quality Care Compensation System

In 1994, USHC instituted a quality care compensation system for participating OB/GYNs. First, the performance of each specialty office was determined and an ordinal rank was assigned based on whether the level of performance was as expected (2) or was statistically better (3) or worse (1) than expected (based on whether the performance was inside or outside of the 95-percent confidence intervals). Each measure was then differentially weighted, and based on the individual ordinal scores an overall Quality Factor was calculated.

Specialist care within USHC is typically paid for through some form of fee-for-service reimbursement. In the case of OB/GYN care, reimbursement is determined by a combination of case rates for pregnancy care and a fee-for-service REF schedule. Every participating OB/GYN specialist office that met certain minimum volume criteria was eligible for possible additional incentive distributions in 1994 for 1993 performance. Based on the office's Quality Factor and the number of unique USHC members seen, the office shared in a year-end budgeted distribution pool. Those OB/GYN providers who had higher Quality Factor scores earned a greater share of the distribution pool. Table 21–3 is a sample Obstetrics/Gynecology Performance Report for a USHC region.

USQA's Specialist Performance Measurement System

USHC has measured the performance of three other specialties by similar methods: general surgery, cardi-

ology, and orthopedic surgery. We are currently developing the USQA Specialist Performance Measurement System to measure the performance of all participating specialists (the top 10 specialties in 1995) in USHC's medical delivery system. The dimensions of quality to be measured are similar to those in the OB/GYN prototype: aspects of technical and cognitive performance, appropriateness of care, cost of care, satisfaction (of both the member and the PCP), and managed care philosophy.[16] We will not only case-mix adjust the measures but also use the U.S. Healthcare Membership Chronic Disease Database, along with important patient and practice variables, to severity adjust the results for the characteristics of the referred population and characteristics of the specialty groups.[17] We will incorporate new measures (e.g., mammography rate and VBAC [vaginal birth after C-section] success rate) in addition to detailed satisfaction information. We will then compare the actual performance of the office to the risk-adjusted mean and benchmark levels of performance.

• • •

We have described the methods of performance measurement at USHC through the use of measurement tools that have actually been developed and implemented. Physician performance measures typically evaluate the process and outcomes of care, can be practice-based or standards-based, and can measure quality along several different general dimensions. The ultimate goal of any measurement activity is to assess providers and provider education, thereby laying the foundation for improving quality.

Table 21–3

Sample Obstetrics/Gynecology Performance report for the top-ranked physicians in a USHC region

Practice	C-section rate	Office workup of abnormal uterine bleeding	Average length of stay	Member satisfaction	Precertification rate	Quality factor
Jones, Robert, M.D.	3	3	3	2	3	2.80
Smith, Jane, M.D.	3	2	3	2	3	2.70
Anytown OB/GYN Associates	3	2	3	2	3	2.70
Women's Health	2	2	3	2	3	2.55
Johnson, James, D.O.	2	3	3	2	3	2.55

We have described the differences in the measurement of the performance of PCPs and specialists. We measure all of them according to their ability to provide high-quality, cost-effective care, but they differ in regard to the primary roles they play in the health care delivery system. We measure the performance of PCPs using population-based measures, with an emphasis on risk factor screening, disease prevention, and management of acute and chronic disease. Using procedural-based quality measures, we measure the performance of specialists in their workups of specific conditions.

We have shown how baseline performance measurement can be the starting point for quality improvement through education, peer comparisons, feedback, and goal setting.[18,19] USHC has emphasized the importance of performance-based incentive systems in which quality of care is rewarded financially. In these systems, USHC pays providers for providing high-quality, cost-effective care that achieves good outcomes. This is in contrast to fee-for-service medicine, in which the amount of care drives reimbursement regardless of outcomes.

Performance measurement is sometimes limited by the statistical and clinical validity of the data. We need to recognize the value of performance information so that investments will be made in the continued development of clinical data systems. Our ability to leverage data collected in medical charts in a standardized format will be enhanced as medical records become automated and real-time transmission to centralized data repositories becomes standard. Information will be increasingly credible as data for valid clinical measures become more available and better adjustment for the severity of defined patient populations can be made.

There is also a need for educating practicing physicians on the importance of performance information. We need their involvement in the measurement process to continue to identify opportunities to improve the structures, processes, and outcomes of care.[20] Their participation in the measurement process will lead to greater expertise in applying the information to improve performance. We have come a long way in the measurement of performance, but its application in the quality improvement process has just begun.

REFERENCES

1. Brook, R. "Practice Guidelines and Practicing Medicine: Are They Compatible?" *JAMA* 262 (1989): 3027–3030.
2. Eddy, D. "Practice Policies: What Are They?" *JAMA* 263 (1990): 877–880.
3. Eddy, D. "Practice Policies: Where Do They Come From?" *JAMA* 263 (1990): 1265–1275.
4. Lasker, R.D., Shapiro, D.W., and Tucker, A.M. "Realizing the Potential of Practice Pattern Profiling." *Inquiry* 29 (1992): 287–297.
5. McNeil, B., Pederson, S., and Gatsonis, C. "Current Issues in Profiling Quality of Care." *Inquiry* 29 (1992): 298–307.
6. Garnick, D., et al. "Focus on Quality: Profiling Physicians' Practice Patterns." *Journal of Ambulatory Care Management* 17 (1994): 44–75.
7. Hurley, R., Freund, D., and Gage, B. "Gatekeeper Effects on Patterns of Physician Use." *Journal of Family Practice* 32 (1991): 167–174.
8. Schlackman, N. "Evolution of a Quality-based Compensation Model: The Third Generation." *American Journal of Medical Quality* 8 (Summer 1993): 103–110.
9. Morrow, R.W., Gooding, A.D., and Clark, C. "Improving Physicians' Preventive Health Care Behavior through Peer Review and Financial Incentives." *Archives of Family Medicine* 4 (1995): 165–169.
10. The Diabetes Control and Complications Trial Research Group. "The Effect of Intensive Treatment of Diabetes on the Development and Progression of Long-term Complications in Insulin-Dependent Diabetes Mellitus." *New England Journal of Medicine* 329 (1993): 977–986.
11. Weiner, J.P., et al. "A Claim-based Profile of Care Provided to Medicare Patients with Diabetes." *JAMA* 273 (1995): 1503–1508.
12. American Diabetes Association. "Standards of Medical Care for Patients with Diabetes Mellitus." *Diabetes Care* 17 (1994): 616–623.
13. Tierney, W., Miller, M., and McDonald, C. "The Effect on Test Ordering of Informing Physicians of the Charges for Outpatient Diagnostic Tests." *New England Journal of Medicine* 322 (1990): 1499–1504.
14. Hillman, B., et al. "Frequency and Costs of Diagnostic Imaging in Office Practice: A Comparison of Self-referring and Radiologist-referring Physicians." *New England Journal of Medicine* 323 (1990): 1604–1608.
15. Salem-Schatz, S., et al. "The Case for Case-Mix Adjustment in Practice Profiling." *JAMA* 272 (1994): 871–874.
16. Ramsey, P., et al. "Use of Peer Ratings To Evaluate Physician Performance." *JAMA* 269 (1993): 1655–1660.
17. Feinglass, J., Handler, I., and Hughes, R. "Using Severity-adjusted Physician Practice Profiles To Identify Cost-effective Care." *NLM Publications* 20 (1987): 99–122.
18. Greco, P., and Eisenberg, J. "Changing Physicians' Practices." *New England Journal of Medicine* 329 (1993): 1271–1274.
19. Tanenbaum, S. "What Physicians Know." *New England Journal of Medicine* 329 (1993): 1268–1270.
20. Brook, R. "Quality of Care: Do We Care?" *Annals of Internal Medicine* 115 (1991): 486–490.

Part V

Health Plan
Operational Management

22

Health Data Analysis and Reporting: Organization and System Strategies

Thomas D. Gotowka, Mark Jackson, and David Aquilina

The pivotal challenge in managed care today is to truly manage care. To balance cost and quality effectively, managed care organizations (MCOs) must systematically measure, monitor, and manage the basic dimensions of medical care delivery.

Three interrelated objectives are paramount. First, MCOs must identify specific medical management problems in order to target priority opportunities to improve the delivery of care as well as contain costs. Second, MCOs must evaluate the programs they have put in place to manage care (e.g., primary care gatekeepers, prior authorization, high-cost case management) in order to assess their effectiveness, determine essential program modifications, and ascertain how individual components of managed care can best be integrated to boost overall performance. Third, MCOs must profile individual providers and provider groups and help them improve their performance and thereby enhance the delivery of cost-effective, quality medical care.

Role of Decision Support

To meet the challenge of managed care, MCOs require comprehensive organizational and system strategies for decision support. Decision support encompasses computer systems and personnel resources to produce the information required to guide medical management planning, inform medical management decisions, and assess medical management initiatives. In most MCOs, however, investing in decision support capabilities for such intensive health data analysis and reporting has not been a top management priority.

Within the management information systems (MIS) departments of MCOs, the main emphasis has been on operational support and management control. That is, the focus has been on the organizational structure and computer systems for core processing to administer the basic, day-to-day operations of managed care (e.g., enrolling members, paying claims).

During the 1980s, as managed care companies built and acquired health maintenance organizations (HMOs), different plans often had different computer systems for basic administrative functions. Running and maintaining multiple administrative software systems, as well as migrating to common systems for plan operations, posed the most pressing and difficult MIS problems. As MCOs began to venture into new product offerings (such as open-ended plans and preferred provider organizations), another high priority for MIS departments emerged: ensuring that new and different managed care plan permutations could be managed. MIS departments had to adapt existing administrative software systems to challenging new operational requirements. Adapting traditional software systems to the increasingly complex managed care industry demanded management attention and commanded considerable MIS resources because overall system conversions are daunting endeavors requiring intensive organizational commitment and effort.

Major adaptations in existing systems and new computer systems involved modifications to accommodate fee discounts and an array of other new payment incentive arrangements in provider contracts. In addition, system changes were required to enable flexibility to administer increasingly complex benefit plans with more numerous variations in coverage provisions and consumer cost sharing. Furthermore, entirely new capabilities for medical management were introduced including software modules to support inpatient preadmission authorization.

Managed Care Quarterly 1993; 1(3): 26–34

In view of these difficult demands, decision support for health data analysis and reporting has not been a true top priority in managed care. To meet the current challenges of managed care, MCOs must develop innovative decision support strategies and systems that enable them to use data analysis to improve performance. That is, the key to truly managing care is the development of data analysis capabilities through decision support strategies and systems to measure and monitor the delivery of medical care.

Decision Support for Medical Management: The Focus of Health Data Analysis

What are the most important decision support requirements in managed care? Medical managers (including medical directors, provider relations coordinators, and network managers) must have high-level, executive information on the following core dimensions of medical care financing and delivery: price and payment, overall utilization efficiency, medical appropriateness, medical effectiveness, and conformance to standards (see Exhibit 22–1).

Price and payment

The price and payment dimension of managed care is focused on the impact of provider payment policies. Common questions for medical managers include: Which primary care physician (PCP) gatekeepers have higher than expected per member per month (PMPM) costs, and why? Based on prevailing hospital reimbursement policies, what are a plan's payments versus billed charges?

Overall utilization efficiency

Overall utilization efficiency centers on overall use and cost rates. Medical managers need answers to questions such as: What is the overall rate of inpatient

Exhibit 22–1 Core Dimensions of Managed Care

Price and payment
Overall utilization efficiency
Medical appropriateness
Medical effectiveness
Conformance to standards

days per 1,000 members, and how does a plan's performance compare versus relevant norms and standards? What is the overall rate of physician encounters per member per year, and how does a plan compare to norms and standards?

Medical appropriateness

Medical appropriateness encompasses the medical necessity of care, the applicability of specific services, the proper location of care, and the acceptable duration of care. Relevant analyses are aimed at questions such as: What is the average length of stay for maternity cases? What is the cesarean section rate, and how does this rate compare to the rate for other HMOs? Are questionable inpatient admissions for typically outpatient surgical procedures a problem in a health plan? Medical managers need the flexibility to profile performance on such measures for entire plans, provider groups, and individual physicians and hospitals.

Medical effectiveness

The medical effectiveness dimension includes two components: technical effectiveness and perceived effectiveness. Technical effectiveness refers to clinical outcomes. Perceived effectiveness relates to patients' perceptions of the results of treatment. While systematic measurement, monitoring, and management of effectiveness are still in a developmental stage, effectiveness will undoubtedly become an increasingly prominent dimension of managed care through the 1990s. Thus, medical managers are striving to answer questions such as: What are the differences in total costs and patients' perceptions of functional status (i.e., their ability to perform daily tasks) for members with back pain problems who are treated on an outpatient versus inpatient basis?

Conformance to standards

Measuring effectiveness is on the frontier of medical management and health data analysis. Managing care according to standards and measuring conformance to standards are requirements of successful managed care. Typical questions include: What is the mammography rate for women age 50 years and above, and how does this performance compare to other health plans?

In sum, for MCOs to meet the challenge of putting the "managed" into managed care, decision support for medical management is essential to provide the basis for health data analysis and reporting. MCOs must have the capability to undertake data analysis on the central dimensions of medical care, monitor conformance to standards, profile individual providers, target opportunities to improve performance, and evaluate actions taken to manage the efficiency, appropriateness, and effectiveness of care.

System Obstacles to Decision Support

Within most MCOs, however, the medical management professionals who need to turn data into information to measure, monitor, and manage performance confront obstacles to data analysis for high-level decision support. These barriers are rooted in the basic purpose and design of existing computer systems in managed care.

These systems are built to support operational tasks, not to provide data analysis for medical management and employer reporting. Administrative systems are designed for high-speed processing of large volumes of routine transactions. Health data analysis and reporting for decision support, in contrast, require large database storage and retrieval. From a technical perspective, these are fundamentally different purposes with distinctly different system requirements. Computer systems designed for high-speed processing of large numbers of small administrative tasks are simply different in function from those designed for storing large volumes of historical data.

Consequently, data analysts and data users in MCOs typically confront troublesome obstacles when they attempt to use administrative systems for decision support (see Exhibit 22–2). Typical problems include data element limitations, data quality issues, data integration difficulty, data quantity limitations, and data reporting inflexibility.

Data element limitations

The data in administrative systems are transactional. Data are created in the process of routine, administrative transactions within a plan (for instance, enrolling a member or paying a claim). Within such systems, only those data fields and actual data that are essential for specific operational tasks (e.g., the member identification number when an individual enrolls in a health plan) are generally included

Exhibit 22–2 System Obstacles to Decision Support

Data element limitations
Data quality issues
Data integration difficulty
Data quantity limitations
Data reporting inflexibility

in the software and retained in the system. Incorporation of fields beyond those necessary for administrative functions slows system performance, impedes administrative efficiency, and requires additional resources to maintain.

For data analysts and users, however, carefully selected additional fields and data make analysis more meaningful and the resulting information more useful. For instance, to evaluate the occurrence of adverse selection, it is beneficial to add a "flag" within membership and service files when services are delivered within a set number of days from a member's date of enrollment. Because such a flag is not necessary for the actual enrollment of members, however, core software systems for plan administration typically do not include a field for such flags.

Another common example relates to distinguishing claims for mothers versus babies in maternity cases. Designating which claims relate to the mother and which to the baby is not necessary to pay the claims. It is helpful to add such a designation, however, if the claims data are used to profile patterns of maternity care utilization and costs.

Data quality issues

Because administrative processing places a premium on speed for administrative efficiency, the data often have errors. Key stroke errors in claims entry, for example, can turn a $1,000 charge into a $10,000 charge. Without a systematic effort to detect and correct such common errors, the data may not adequately support valid and useful analysis.

Data integration difficulty

It is common for enrollment, encounter, claims, pharmacy, and other data to be generated and stored separately within an administrative system, or even on completely different systems. Analysts and users, however, frequently want information based on analyses that integrate data. Comparing physician office visit use and cost rates between providers or employer groups on an age- and sex-adjusted basis, for example, requires the ability to link demographic data from membership with utilization and cost data from encounters. Difficulty in integrating data from distinct modules within a system, or in linking data from different systems, hampers data analysts and users.

Data quantity limitations

Data analysts and users of information for medical management decision support want access to historical data for trend analysis. Analysts and users frequently ask questions that require 18 to 24 months of data, or more. For example, to assess mammography rates, a health plan may want to begin by identifying female members over the age of 49 years who have been continuously enrolled for at least 12 or 18 months in order to ensure the validity of the analysis. Administrative systems, however, are not designed to store large quantities of historical data.

Data reporting inflexibility

Administrative software systems typically have a reporting module and report writer features. Standard data reporting capabilities are generally adequate for operational decision support (e.g., ascertaining which members are in the hospital on any given day) and management control (i.e., primarily financial reporting). They lack the flexibility necessary for undertaking the complex analyses that data analysts and users require for high-level decision support, however. In addition, special reporting systems in many MCOs still require comparatively high levels of computer literacy (and even actual programming skills) and are often not accessible to the typical managed care professional.

Challenges for AETNA Health Plans

Aetna Health Plans (AHP) owns or manages a total of 24 HMOs across the country, serving over a million members. These plans offer traditional HMO products plus "Managed Choice" (Aetna's point-of-service product that enables members to use non-HMO providers). The plans vary in model type and size, ranging from 5,000 to 250,000 members.

The plans use 7 different systems for administrative transaction processing, and Aetna is in the midst of changing to a common computer system. In addition, some of the HMOs must collect data from over 100 different provider panels with different computer systems.

Thus, Aetna faces difficult problems in bringing health data analysis and reporting capabilities for decision support to the medical managers in its HMOs. In tackling these problems, AHP guided organizational and system planning and implementation by focusing on three key objectives:

1. empowering medical managers,
2. managing toward data consistency, and
3. achieving rapid implementation.

Empowering medical managers

AHP determined that to be successful, its decision support strategy had to be aimed at empowering local managers at the individual HMO level. To truly measure, monitor, and manage care, it was felt that these local HMO professionals on the "front lines" of managed care needed the capability to do data analysis themselves in order to produce information to improve managed care and make performance efficient and effective. Thus, a key goal was to put accessible data analysis capabilities in the hands of the local managers who need information to identify, track, and solve medical management problems. Thus, a computerized system for health data analysis and reporting that gives managers direct access to the data they need was a top priority.

Managing toward data consistency

AHP determined that data consistency across HMOs, managed care products, and computer systems was essential. Therefore, Aetna focused on integrating data for traditional HMO and "Managed Choice" products and standardizing data from all its plans. Standardization and consistency enable HMOs to compare performance and facilitate analysis by Aetna corporate staff to assess relative performance by region of the country as well as by HMO.

Achieving rapid implementation

The top leadership of Aetna Health Plans clearly saw that the pressures to improve managed care performance required a rapid response with implementation in 1992. The decision was made to move quickly in bringing a new data analysis system for medical management decision support to the HMOs.

The AETNA Experience: Critical Success Factors

In early 1992, AHP chose a system (MEDSYTE from O'PIN Systems, Inc., Bloomington, Minnesota) to meet its decision support objectives for medical management. As of May 1993, the new decision support system had been installed at 22 HMOs and several corporate locations. Complete implementation is scheduled for mid-1993.

Based on Aetna's experience, three sets of critical success factors (CSFs) were integral to bringing advanced health data analysis and reporting capabilities to MCOs. These sets of CSFs involved the following:
1. decision support database,
2. decision support system and software, and
3. organizational support for decision support.

Decision support database

Five CSFs were seen to comprise the overall set of CSFs related to the decision support database (see Exhibit 22–3). They are discussed individually in the text that follows.

CSF 1: Data error correction

Data from managed care transactions frequently contain errors that can and should be corrected in constructing a database for analysis and reporting. Therefore, extensive data edits are essential in building a decision support database from managed care transaction data.

CSF 2: Data source integration

The design of the database must allow for the integration of data from separate parts of administra-

Exhibit 22–3 CSFs: Decision Support Database

> Data error correction
> Data source integration
> Data format standardization
> Data element enhancement
> Database validation

tive systems, or from entirely different systems, if necessary. To provide a comprehensive resource for decision support, Aetna required the integration of membership, claims, encounter, authorization, provider, and employer group data.

CSF 3: Data format standardization

The administrative systems from which data are extracted are dynamic and constantly changing in response to operational requirements in managed care. For instance, in order to administer a new benefit plan for a new employer group, modifications to cost sharing provisions may be essential and must be accounted for in claims payment.

As noted previously, HMOs in Aetna Health Plans have different core computer systems. Therefore, the process to build and maintain databases for decision support had to include technical procedures for standardizing the data. This requirement was satisfied by translating the data to a common format in order to maintain consistency and comparability over time. Standardization is essential for retrospective analysis of historical data and trend reporting, particularly when data are derived from multiple system sources. Thus, if changes in a plan's claims paying policies result in changes in the way an inpatient hospital day is defined and measured, the process of building the decision support database must account for such a change in order to provide consistency in counting numbers of inpatient days over time.

CSF 4: Data element enhancement

Analytical enhancements are difficult to incorporate in operating systems, especially in the context of multiple systems. They are both possible and essential in dedicated reporting systems.

Enhancements in the system for Aetna include items such as flags for high-cost cases and members with chronic conditions and the construction of medical events (i.e., summaries of all the claims that logically belong to and define a single facility-based episode of care). These enhancements to the raw data add tools for more medically meaningful health data analysis and reporting.

CSF 5: Database validation

Analytical databases constructed for decision support must be validated against the systems from which they are derived. For instance, comparing membership counts to those on routine operational reports and tying paid amounts to plan financial reports should be standard steps to ensure the validity of the dedicated database.

Decision support system and software

Six CSFs comprise this set (see Exhibit 22–4). They are discussed in the text that follows.

CSF 1: Direct data access

The system must enable the local user to have direct access to the data needed to ask and answer specific questions for medical management. Managed care professionals must be able to do analysis themselves without having to go through the MIS department or using a computer programmer. Direct access for managed care professionals is required to give them the ability to transform data into information for decision making. Without direct access, managed care professionals encounter too many barriers to decision support.

CSF 2: Rapid access and response

The system should provide rapid access and response time. Rapid access and response time are essential to support the interactive and iterative nature of data analysis. Because the process of data analysis is essentially one of trial and error (i.e., asking a question, getting an answer, reformulating the question or probing for more detail), users must get rapid responses to queries so that the analysis process is not impeded or disrupted. Thus, users must be able to ask questions, get data to answer them, and then refine their questions without excessive waiting that breaks the continuity of analysis efforts or causes delays in decision making.

Exhibit 22–4 CSFs: System Software

Direct data access
Rapid access and response time
User flexibility
Standard medical management data views
Integration with standard personal computer tools
Incorporation of advanced analytical tools

CSF 3: User flexibility

Nontechnical users (e.g., senior executives, medical directors, network managers, customer relations managers) must be able to use the system readily to query data and produce useful, meaningful information rapidly. Yet, the system should also have flexibility for more technically adept data analysts who may have experience with databases requiring some level of computer programming skills. Neither the nontechnical user nor the seasoned data analyst should be forced to rely on programmers to get information from the system.

CSF 4: Standard views of the data and medical management

While flexibility for ad hoc reporting is critical, it is also important that the system provide a set of common views of the data for medical management. Thus, Aetna's implementation features an entire set of routinely updated standard reports that is available online to the users via electronic report distribution and retrieval. The library of standard reports gives all users within AHP a consistent way to examine and track basic medical care use and cost trends and establishes a shared starting point for further analysis.

CSF 5: Integration with existing tools

Increasing numbers of professionals within MCOs (such as AHP) are becoming comfortable with various personal computer software applications (especially spreadsheet programs). Thus, the system software must allow rapid downloads of reports or selected data files to such tools. Because certain applications are already part of Aetna's consistent office requirements, the system enables people to use the standard software tools with which they are familiar.

CSF 6: Incorporation of advanced analytical tools

Innovative tools are now available that may add value to the data and analysis and reporting for high-level decision support. Such tools include inpatient case mix grouping methodologies (e.g., inpatient severity measurement and adjustment methods) as well as standard diagnosis related groups and major diagnostic categories, newly developing ambulatory case groupings (e.g., ambulatory care groups from Johns Hopkins University), a variety of utilization and cost norms, and medical practice guidelines and standards.

Organizational support

Aetna found that three CSFs were especially important for organizational support for a new health data analysis system (see Exhibit 22–5). They are outlined in the following text.

CSF 1: Vendor partnership

Aetna deemed it advantageous to establish a partnership with a vendor of data analysis software and services. By so doing, Aetna has been able to achieve rapid implementation. Moreover, Aetna felt that a firm focused on health data analysis and reporting was more apt to keep pace with changes in managed care, advances in data analysis techniques, and computer technology. Thus a specialized vendor was selected. This vendor has responsibility for the mainframe hardware and system necessary for database storage and support for all the plans.

CSF 2: Basic training

Training is essential. AHP determined that training on the new system for three to five users from each key location would be critical to the successful integration of the new data analysis and reporting capabilities. A standard two-day training program for AHP users was conducted during the summer and fall of 1992 as part of the system implementation.

CSF 3: Ongoing user support

Continuing user support is another important factor. A toll-free telephone hotline for user technical support is maintained. AHP is also undertaking user surveys to track their experience and identify necessary improvements in the software and data services. Aetna's medical information management department provides analysis assistance to local HMO users and is developing advanced user training to continue to strengthen the data analysis skills of local HMO managers.

Exhibit 22–5 CSFs: Organizational Support

Vendor partnership
Basic training
Ongoing user support

The AETNA Experience: Turning Data into Information

AHP staff members are starting to make use of the system to transform data into information for medical management. One of the highest priority uses to date has been to assess the relative experience of PCP gatekeepers.

Standard reports within the system compare PMPMs by PCP with and without various types of case exclusions (obstetrics, gynecology, mental health, or high-cost cases). Perhaps the most frequently used analysis is the one that calculates and compares actual versus expected costs of PCPs with controls for differences in the age and sex compositions of the physicians' patient panels. Users often turn the actual or expected cost ratio into a graph (see Figure 22–1) to illustrate and highlight PCPs with markedly higher than expected costs PMPM. This technique enables the plans to identify and track the PCPs who may not be efficiently managing care for their patients.

Users are exploring and pinpointing the specific areas of utilization and costs that underlie the basic patterns. For instance, at one AHP plan, the system was used to identify higher office visit use for a particular PCP (see Figure 22–2).

Users are also producing reports by specialist. Some are analyzing data by employer group to support rating analyses by examining the variation between premium revenue and medical expenses.

The AETNA Experience: Lessons Learned

To truly manage utilization and costs, managed care organizations must improve their ability to provide high-level decision support for medical management. This objective requires a dedicated computer system for analysis and reporting that enables managed care professionals to access data to create the information they need to plan and evaluate medical management efforts.

Aetna intends to continue to develop its reporting capabilities and evolve toward a single data analysis system across its entire health insurance product line. This evolutionary approach is deliberately incremental and driven by the requirement to continue to meet the changing decision support needs of medical managers. Aetna anticipates continued exploration of the

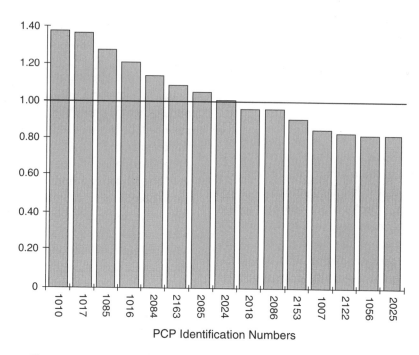

Figure 22–1. Primary care physicians: Actual to expected ratios.

incorporation of advanced analysis tools and clinical logic systems to increase the ability of MCOs to spot trends and medical management problems. Aetna's ongoing goal will remain to provide information to identify opportunities to improve the actual management of patient care.

Three aspects of Aetna's experience to date seem especially important. The first lesson revolves around ease of use of the system and meaningfulness of the data. Knowledge workers in managed care (i.e., especially medical directors and those who support them in medical management efforts) will actively and effectively use a decision support system if the use of the system software is intuitive and if they have confidence in the validity of the data and meaningfulness of the analytical tools. Aetna has found that medical directors have invested the time to learn its new system and that many use it on a daily basis in their work.

The second lesson focuses on the value of a dedicated decision support system. The ability to undertake health data analysis and reporting to turn data into information has a profound impact on managed care performance. Within Aetna Health Plans, the

new system is helping managers evaluate providers and improve provider network selection. Enhanced decision support capabilities assist Aetna in communicating with its providers and also help demonstrate AHP's managed care effectiveness to employers and their consultants.

The third lesson involves the value of a specialized vendor. Aetna has concluded that involving a specialized vendor of decision support software and services in its efforts was a positive move. Specialized expertise has proven to be an important asset and has enabled AHP to move forward quickly to provide new analysis tools to its health plans. The understanding and support of senior management are essential in establishing a good relationship with a third party vendor of data analysis software and services.

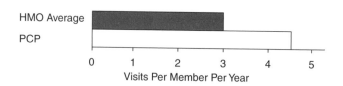

Figure 22–2. Primary care visits: PCP versus HMO average.

Finally, based on Aetna's experience thus far, one other significant lesson is clear. Advancing decision support for medical management certainly does require a dedicated computer system for health data analysis and reporting to transform data into information. But, the critical link is to then turn information into action. This step requires medical management leadership—especially local medical directors—who are able and willing to use data to work directly with physicians to improve the management of care.

23

Where Are the Data?

Stephen F. Coady

I t is increasingly common for managers of self-insured benefit programs to study claims and eligibility data. The purposes of such studies include:

- producing descriptive statistics,
- modeling plan design changes,
- identifying and valuating potential interventions,
- auditing vendor performance,
- evaluating effectiveness of existing interventions,
- measuring appropriateness of services, and
- profiling providers.

The last two elements are especially exciting. They promise the tools and techniques with which to manage managed care.

Nevertheless, many firms are stalled and frustrated, unable to manage health care plans because claims data are unavailable or of inadequate quality. Some of the problems, and insights on how they can be avoided, are presented in the text that follows.

Why Important Data May Be Missing

One cannot manage what one cannot measure. Any hope of better management of benefit programs is predicated on a minimum quantity and quality of data being captured.

The data studies that are being performed now (and in the future) all use the data that are being collected today—so corrective action, if required, ought not be delayed. Why might corrective action be required? Unfortunately, fewer data are required to adjudicate a claim than to statistically review a benefits program. Claims adjudication is a labor-intensive business. Every key stroke costs money.

Unless one assures that more than minimal data are collected, the requisite data elements may not be

available for study, because there is no economic incentive for a third party administrator (TPA) or an insurance company processing claims to capture more than the minimum dataset.

It is therefore recommended that contracts with TPAs or with carriers working in an administrative services only (ASO) mode should:

- specify the data to be captured,
- clarify "ownership" of the data, and
- provide for "exportation" of the data.

Specify the Minimum Quantity and Quality of Data

Quantity

Some claims processors do not use ICD-9 diagnosis codes. Instead they employ a "home-grown" system. Others use three-digit (instead of five-digit) ICD-9 codes, or only use diagnosis codes for inpatient claims, or only enter procedural codes (CPT-4) for surgical claims, or code physicians by telephone numbers instead of individual tax identification numbers. The list seems endless. Even simple logic is often not invoked. For example, some claims tapes still show vaginal deliveries by males.

Consider the following example demonstrating the value of information. If a plan costs $300 per employee per month, and is growing at a rate of 20 percent per year, and better management of the plan can reduce the trend rate to 10 percent, then better management is worth $30 per employee per month. That figure is a 10 to 1 return, direct to the bottom line. But, the better management is dependent on better information.

Some carriers appreciate that the value of the information derived from claims processing is higher than the cost of the incremental keypunching. This appreciation is especially evident in managed care plans and plans in which the carrier has some risk. One

Managed Care Quarterly 1993; 1(3): 40–44
© 1993 Aspen Publishers, Inc.

should, however, be wary of claims processing organizations whose compensation is never tied to changes in per capita cost or utilization.

How does one check the extent of a plan's current data holdings? Exhibits 23–1 and 23–2 list data elements that should be collected and available. Those lists are practical ones, not wish lists. These data are needed to review and manage a plan. Every element on these lists is required by at least one of the "standard" reports

Exhibit 23–1 Demographics

Employee or insured demographic information
  Name
  Identification number (Social Security number)
  Street address
  City
  State
  Zip code
  Telephone number
  Hire date
  Termination date
  Years of service
  Employment status (active, retired, continuation, COBRA)

Covered individual (including employee or insured) demographic information
  Name
  Identification number
  Date of birth
  Relationship to employee or insured
  Gender
  Marital status
  Zip code
  Employment status
  Other coverage indicator

Coverage information
  Benefit plan identifier (plan number)
  Plan type (medical, dental, vision)
  Coverage type (employee only, employee plus spouse, etc.)
  Accounting codes (division, department, etc.)
  Coverage effective date
  Coverage termination date
  Premium (or pseudo premium)—employer and employee
  Employee or insured contribution to premium

produced by the current major vendors of health care data products and analytical services (e.g., Medstat, CHS [Corporate Health Strategies], CCM [Corporate Cost Management], VHIS [Value Health Information Services]). No element on these lists should elicit the comment, "That's ridiculous. No one collects that!" from any competent claims processor. In fact, any such articulation should be interpreted as clear call for an audit.

How can problems be avoided? There are many claims processing organizations that can capture these data but will do so only if the client insists. Toward that encouragement, these lists (or something like them) can be incorporated as an appendix to the claims processing agreement. Develop performance standards that go beyond the usual turnaround time and accuracy minimums and specify exactly what needs be keypunched. Then develop a mechanism to measure compliance with those standards. Finally, reward such compliance, thereby fundamentally altering the economic incentives operating on the claims processor.

Quality: Garbage in, garbage out

All of the preceding steps secure the quantity of data. But what of the quality? To guarantee quality, insist that claims processors operate (integral to their system) a set of logical rules that screen obvious and subtle problems. One such test is for unbundled charges, illustrated by Dr. B's misrepresentation of the same task rendered by Dr. A:

Dr. A	Hysterectomy	$2,600
Dr. B	Exploratory surgery	$1,500
	Excision of scar tissue	$1,500
	Removal of ovaries	$2,500
	Removal of uterus	$2,500

Other integral checks include misuse of assistant surgeons, payments for cosmetic procedures, procedure diagnosis mismatch, and age, sex, or diagnosis mismatches. More sophisticated systems flag things like questionable practices and outcomes, inappropriate visit levels, and excessive tests and procedures.

This level of functionality not only improves the quality of data available for analysis, but represents significant savings for the payor compared to a less well-equipped claims processing system. Savings can be on the order of 1 percent to 4 percent of claims paid.

Exhibit 23–2 Claim Detail

Employee or insured demographic information
  Name
  Identification number (Social Security number)
  Street address
  City
  State
  Zip code

Covered individual (including employee or insured)
    demographic information
  Name
  Identification number
  Date of birth
  Relationship to employee or insured
  Gender
  Marital status

Accounting and reporting information
  Benefit plan identifier (plan number)
  Coverage type (employee only, employee plus
    spouse, etc.)
  Accounting codes (division, department, etc.)

Provider information
  Name
  Identification number (tax identification)
  Street address
  City
  State
  Zip code
  Telephone number
  Preferred provider organization indicator
  Specialty
  Type (physician, hospital, clinic, etc.)
  Primary care physician (if available)
    Name
    Identification number
  Referring physician (if available)
    Name
    Identification number

Claim-specific information
  Accident indicator
  Accident date
  Unique claim number
  Date claim received
  Date claim was processed
  Date claim was paid
  Claim status indicator (initial payment,
    adjustment to prior claim)
  Patient discharge status
  Precertification indicator
  Number of days precertified

Claim line-item–specific information
  Date services provided from
  Date services provided to
  Primary diagnosis (ICD-9 code)
  Secondary diagnosis (ICD-9 code)
  Third diagnosis (ICD-9 code)
  Fourth diagnosis (ICD-9 code)
  Fifth diagnosis (ICD-9 code)
  Primary procedure (CPT-4 code)
  Secondary procedure (CPT-4 code)
  Third procedure (CPT-4 code)
  Fourth procedure (CPT-4 code)
  Fifth procedure (CPT-4 code)
  Diagnosis related group (DRG)
  Major diagnostic category (MDC)
  Type of service
  Place of service
  Number of services (counter)
  National drug code (NDC)
  Billed amount
  Disallowed amount
  Disallow reason (Medicare carve-out penalty,
    reasonable and customary [R&C] cutback, not
    covered, etc.)
  Allowed amount (coordination of benefits [COB])
  Amount paid by other payor
  Amount applied to deductible
  Employee or insured copayment amount
  Amount paid by the plan

Clarify Ownership of the Data

Some claims processors assert ownership of the keypunched data. They argue that data belong to the claims processor and not the plan or the plan's spon-sor. The latter is supposedly entitled only to the deliverables (e.g., reports and graphics) specified in the TPA or ASO agreement. Such argument is usually raised when the plan's manager expresses surprise and dismay at the proposed charges for a special data extraction. The problem is easily avoided by addressing and clarifying ownership of data as part of the claims processing agreement.

Provide for "Exportation" of the Data

It is important to assure exportation of the data, which may be defined broadly as the ability to move claims data from whatever computer is used to process claims into whatever computer is used for analysis.

Just as the universal medium for communication among microcomputers is the modem, so the universal medium for exchange of data between and among large computers is magnetic tape (containing standard fixed-record-length flat files). Tape often comes in cartridges; consider the terms tape, reel, and cartridge as synonyms. The physical media are not important.

Contracts with claims processors must provide that the TPA or the carrier will provide a fixed-format tape with at least those data elements specified in the boxes and will provide such tapes on a timely basis. By the 10th day of the month, data regarding claims paid or adjusted during the prior month should be available. It should also be relatively easy for the claims processor to provide a magnetic tape containing the eligibility records used during the preceding month at this time.

That provision begs the question about the availability of eligibility information for dependents for whom claims have not been submitted. For example, no one can report if the rate of eating disorders in a covered population is within the range of expectations unless the number of 17-year-old females covered under the plan is known. If such "active enrollment" has not been done and the eligibility files only contain information on employees, correcting that deficiency is the first order of business. The savings from reduced fraud and abuse will likely surpass the cost of the enrollment.

The claims processor should deliver a copy of its processing procedure manual. The claims processor should also identify an individual to answer questions regarding how the system handles exceptions, corrections, adjustments, overpayments, and other atypical situations. Such a resource is invaluable during data interpretation.

Collect the tapes each month and, if nothing else, place them in a vault to be stored for that future day

when someone wants to study claims and eligibility data. Many firms must be doing just this because the aggregate revenues of current vendors of data products and analytical services suggest that less than 20 percent of their potential market is being addressed.

Those firms that have not looked at their data are in for a pleasant surprise. The savings associated with first efforts to describe and manage a benefits plan statistically are dramatic. Indemnity and preferred provider organization (PPO) trend rates in the single digits are typical.

What Comes Next?

What happens to those firms who have been doing this analysis for a while? In many instances, their learning curve has outgrown the product development curve of most vendors of information products and services. This situation is understandable. If a market is not saturated, one strategy is to sell existing products and services to new clients rather than expend research and development resources to continue to support long-term clients who have exhausted the utility of those products and services.

What comes next? Guidelines and protocols.

> Among the technical requisites that will lead to reform, none will prove to be more consequential than the implementation of practice guidelines or practice parameters. We are in the very early stages of guideline science and should not underestimate the power of the tool. In the past four years, the potential impact of practice patterns has become clear to everyone who has a stake in the cost and quality of medical care.[1(p.9)]

It is too soon to talk about practical overall measurements of quality. Even "outcomes analyses" are still too primitive and misleading. But there are proven and practical tools, metrics, and techniques available for measuring appropriateness and for profiling providers—activities that support and improve network management.

The continuum can be represented as follows:

Descriptive statistics → Analytic studies → Clinical profiling

Profiling is a management tool that sheds light on the provider community by evaluating individual and aggregate practice patterns. Profiling highlights "styles of practice." Profiling systems support provider recruitment, provider credentialing, provider privileging, network management, reimbursement methodology changes, focused physician review, and better risk rating. Profiling enables more focused physician review and increased credibility within the provider community.

The good news is that systems that profile physicians and measure appropriateness are driven by the same claims data used for descriptive statistics and analytical studies. The datasets created from claims and eligibility data in preparation for management decision support reports and graphs are the same datasets that drive the next generation of data applications. This fact is not surprising. Research scientists doubtless wanted more and different data, but realized that what were available comes from claims processing and contemporary eligibility systems.

Over time the amount and type of data will improve. In many hospitals much of the medical record is already on-line. But getting the data from the provider to the analyst is where the flow breaks down. While the industry appears committed to eventual electronic data interchange (EDI), keypunching is the norm and remains the bottleneck. It is worth noting that with EDI, not only does the cost of collecting data go down, but also the quality of the data increases.

Data from indemnity plans and PPOs are more readily available than data from health maintenance organizations (HMOs) and point-of-service (POS) plans. One argument is that in a capitated environment the purchaser has "passed off" the risk and has little incentive to review the data. But the counterargument is that the HMO data are needed to paint the complete picture for the plan's management, to provide comparison for the other plans offered, and to allow quality to be monitored. HMOs in the western United States are responding to demands of large employers for more and better data exportation. The rest of the country should be strident with similar demands.

Data from other sources, such as workers' compensation programs, should also be sought and incorporated to complete the picture. Tremendous economies can be achieved through pooling descriptive and analytical activities.

•   •   •

As benefit plan managers approach the problems of health care cost in a more businesslike manner, the need for accurate, timely, and complete information will increase dramatically. Those data needs should encourage every plan administrator to assure that the requisite quantity and quality of data are being collected and made available. In the future, it will be considered a dereliction of duty to stop there without assuring that the data are being studied and used to better manage the plan. The absence of such decision support virtually guarantees waste of plan assets.

REFERENCE

1. Filerman, G.L. "In Due Time." *Health Management Quarterly* 14, no. 4 (1992).

24

Information and Decision Support in Managed Care

Robyn Rontal

Health care purchasers today are confronted with unpredictable risks, poorly documented quality, and relentless cost increases. Many employers are adopting a managed care strategy, hoping to control risk, improve quality, and contain costs. To be effective in the long run, managed care decisions at each stage in the process (i.e., plan design, network selection, implementation, performance monitoring, and quality improvement) should be driven by reliable information that will successfully guide management actions.

Decision support information is critical to a managed care program's sustained success. Many managed care programs are effective in controlling costs in the first year. Some employers have seen their cost trends reduced significantly in the first year following introduction of managed care, but in subsequent years the rate of health care inflation has increased. The initial impact can be attributed primarily to greater provider discounts or to increases in employee cost sharing through out-of-network penalties. Providers can readily offset discounts to one purchaser with higher charges to others. But in the long run, as more employers in an area move to managed care, discounts become meaningless.

There are many sources of data available to support decision making. This article describes the application of claims data, integrated with other data on utilization and quality, in a decision support model that demonstrates how key management actions are aided by appropriate data and analyses.

Managed Care Decision Support Model

Health care purchasing decisions require reliable information to pinpoint "best-buy" options consis-

tent with a company's objectives, including cost, utilization, quality of care, and treatment outcomes. These decisions are made even if supporting information is not available. To improve the odds of success and increase the predictability of future trends in cost and use, a decision support information system (including reliable data, reporting and analysis tools, and relevant expertise) is a necessary investment.

The development of this decision support information system is based on "reverse engineering." The design starts with a thorough consideration of the immediate and ongoing decisions and management actions required for continued improvement of the managed care program. Exhibit 24–1 illustrates this model and provides a framework for discussing the application of this concept to several specific examples. Having identified the management actions required and the types of decisions, specific decision support information needs can be addressed. Decision support needs could be for short-term special studies or for routine performance monitoring. Guided by these needs, the resulting data and analysis capability will have the necessary characteristics to support management actions.

The decision support model can be successfully applied to improve management actions. Two examples of applying this model include evaluating managed care networks and setting performance targets.

Evaluating Managed Care Networks

The initial selection and subsequent monitoring of managed care networks are critical components of a successful managed care program. Table 24–1 summarizes the application of the decision support model to the selection of a managed care provider network.

Prior to implementation, it is important to understand some of the factors that may affect employee decisions to enroll in a managed care program and

Managed Care Quarterly 1993; 1(3): 3–14

Exhibit 24–1 Decision Support Model

Management action	Decision support needs	Data or analysis requirements
Specific decision required:	Comparative data	Data sources
• timing	Key indicators	Analytical capabilities
• impact	Modeling future scenarios	Reporting capabilities
• value	Financial forecasts	Level of detail
• objectives		Timeliness
		Data quality

attempt to maximize enrollment by altering the plan design, identifying the extent to which network providers already serve employees, and modifying existing networks by adding or excluding providers.

For many people, the most important issue is whether or not their current physician is in the network. This issue is most important to women with respect to their gynecologist. Men are generally less averse to switching physicians. Plan design changes can significantly alter these decisions. A woman, for example, may be allowed to pick a primary care physician and a gynecologist to whom she could go without a referral. Alternatively, a company with multiple health plan options may increase the cost differential between its managed care plan and its indemnity plan. Experience shows that the majority of people will switch plans if they face a material difference (25 percent to 30 percent) in out-of-pocket cost.

To determine the degree of overlap between current provider utilization and the proposed provider network, historical claims can be matched to the managed care organization's provider list. In addition to evaluating the overlap, it is important to determine whether the majority of current low-cost, high-volume, high-quality providers are included in the network. Access for employees who must switch physicians should also be evaluated by setting access criteria and comparing geographic locations of employees and primary care

Table 24–1

Managed Care Network Evaluation

Management action	Decision support needs	Data or analysis requirements
Select a managed care network that will provide high-quality, cost-effective care for employees	1. Extent of overlap between current providers and network providers. Who are the current high-volume, high-quality, low-cost providers and are they in the proposed network?	1. Company's health care claims data; cost and use by provider. Directory of network providers
	2. Are employee access criteria met by the network?	2. Employee and provider geographic locations
	3. How do the hospitals and physicians in the network perform compared to norms?	3. Comparative data on provider performance*
	4. Do network hospitals provide a comprehensive range of services?	4. American Hospital Association and managed care organization information

*MEDSTAT Systems, Inc., MarketScan$_{SM}$ norms.

providers. Access criteria will vary by geographic location and urban or rural setting. Such criteria may include a minimum number of primary care physicians by type within a specified distance or travel time from employees' residences.

Hospital and physician profiles can be prepared to evaluate pricing, discounts, quality of care, and outcomes (i.e., complications or severity-adjusted mortality) of proposed network providers. The range of services offered by network hospitals should be reviewed for comprehensiveness and access to high-technology services when necessary, using sources such as the annual survey published by the American Hospital Association that reports all major services and technologies offered by hospitals, or state health department surveys that may provide both an inventory of services and annual volume statistics.

Once a managed care program has been implemented, routine monitoring should be in place even where the plan is held accountable through such means as caps on annual cost increases. Otherwise, the opportunity to identify problems and make incremental adjustments may not occur in a timely manner, and costs in subsequent years will escalate. Changes may include additions or deletions from the provider network and the introduction of new programs to meet the employer's unique needs.

Performance measured against targets differentiates successful components of the program from those that require fine-tuning.

Setting Performance Targets

Meaningful performance measurement and target setting involve a partnership with the managed care plan. The plan must be able to collect, extract, and document the data elements needed for ongoing analysis. The plan must also be flexible and willing to make changes based on the results. The employer should understand that performance targets are screening tools that will focus more in-depth analysis on areas that may need improvement. They serve to clarify expectations for the plan and provide the basis for performance incentives. In summary, performance targets need to be:

- measurable,
- focused on areas of greatest impact,
- achievable, and
- mutually acceptable.

The application of the decision support model to the setting of performance targets is summarized in Table 24–2.

Performance targets may be established by modeling the employer's historical claims experience. The past experience of the managed care plan may be helpful to consider (e.g., utilization rates and cost per enrollee over time). Normative data may also be useful as a benchmark. Industry-specific norms within a geographic region enable an employer to compare itself to other employers with similar benefit packages and employee populations. For example, a company

Table 24–2

Performance Targets

Management action	Decision support needs	Data or analysis requirements
Establish annual performance targets to be used in contract negotiations with managed care organizations that are measurable and mutually acceptable	1. Historical patterns and trends	1. Company's health care claims data: cost, use, quality, outcome
	2. Industry-specific and regional data to set achievable trend	2. Comparative data to demonstrate validity of proposed performance targets*
	3. Model financial impact of performance targets. If targets are achieved, what happens to overall cost?	3. Modeling capability
	4. Baseline employee satisfaction	4. Employee satisfaction survey

*MEDSTAT Systems, Inc., MarketScan$_{SM}$ norms.

within the manufacturing sector typically has a "richer" benefit package than a firm within the service sector, and it may have a greater percentage of older male employees. The incentives to use discretionary services and the population's health care needs (e.g., cardiac care versus obstetrical care) may differ markedly. Industry-specific norms help control for these differences.

Realistic performance targets can be set in the following areas:

- quality of care,
- utilization,
- employee satisfaction, and
- financial.

Quality of care

Quality of care is multifaceted and can be quantified. Claims-based performance measures can be used as performance screens. Other types of measures based on employee-reported satisfaction and functional outcome following encounters with health care providers are necessary to document more fully quality of care. In areas where performance screens are not met, further investigation may be warranted. The plan should be committed to quality improvement and be an active participant in the change process.

An examination of quality of care measures is needed to assess whether or not a plan's provider network provides "good" quality care reliably and also whether aspects of the plan design adversely affect quality. Exhibit 24–2 provides a general summary of areas in

Exhibit 24–2 Quality of Care

Inpatient	Outpatient
Discretionary surgical admissions	Preventive care
Discretionary medical admissions	Chronic illness management
Cesarean-section deliveries	Health care education
Complications of treatment	Patient satisfaction
Infection rates	Functional assessment
Readmissions	Long-term and short-term disability
Mortality (in-hospital)	Adverse outcomes or complications
Sentinel events	

which inpatient and outpatient quality of care performance targets may be established.

Utilization

Utilization performance targets are the most commonly used indicators of "best practice" in the managed care industry. In addition to a variety of utilization performance measures (e.g., admissions or days per 1,000 population, outpatient encounters per capita), an assessment of network versus out-of-network experience and referral activity may be important when evaluating managed care. Examples of performance targets include the following:

- utilization per 1,000 enrollees by various provider and service categories;
- in- versus out-of-network utilization, including opt-out distinction with point-of-service (POS) plan; and
- referrals per capita, by service and provider type and whether they were in- or out-of-network.

An assessment of network versus out-of-network utilization may reveal that out-of-network care is predominantly emergency services, which would be appropriate unless the emergency department is used excessively due to lack of access to physician services. Conversely, such an assessment may point to heavily used out-of-network specialty areas, either referred or self-selected, indicating an inadequacy within the network.

Employee satisfaction

Performance measures should include an assessment of employee satisfaction with the managed care plan. Measures of dissatisfaction such as failure to retain employees at renewal and use of nonnetwork providers instead of network providers can be evaluated with existing claims and eligibility data. An eligibility database that includes enrollment detail by carrier for all employees permits the tracking of plan enrollment or disenrollment over time. Adverse selection (the enrollment of a disproportionate share of healthy or low-utilizing employees in one plan option) can be evaluated by modeling the impact of historical claims experience and demographic characteristics of managed care versus indemnity enrollees.

Employee satisfaction surveys should be administered to identify and correct problems before they become critical. Well-designed surveys are an indispensable tool to complement quality measurement efforts. For example, if an analysis of claims data reveals that a large percentage of employees are using out-of-network providers, a subsequent employee satisfaction survey may help explain why this pattern is occurring.

Financial

Financial performance targets are essential because they represent the net result of all the management controls a managed care plan has at its disposal. Several of these measures include:

- general financial—net pay per employee by various service and provider types. Includes fee-for-service claims and monthly capitation premium amounts, where applicable;
- employee costs—out-of-pocket employee payments;
- pricing—net pay per unit of service by various service categories; and
- discounts—by inpatient hospital, outpatient hospital, and physician.

Benefits and outcomes

An employer and its managed care plan should have clearly defined performance targets that are mutually acceptable and have been included in the contract. Periodic management reports will be prepared for ongoing monitoring and quality improvement. Quality improvement is a function of the man-

aged care organization's direct control over its internal operations and indirect control of its suppliers (hospitals, physicians, and other ancillary health care services). It is important to note that performance targets should be dynamic. Periodic assessment may indicate a need for revision. Table 24–3 presents examples of several performance targets.

Case Study

ABC Company has a POS managed care plan and three health maintenance organizations (HMOs) that had been effective in controlling health care expenses to the target rate during the previous year. The trend rate during the most recent year, however, was an increase in net payments per employee of 12 percent compared to a target rate of 9.5 percent (see Figure 24–1). Senior management is concerned about this change in trend. They had been convinced to pursue a managed care strategy primarily to contain rising health care costs. They challenge their human resources management to identify the underlying causes and submit an action plan to improve the trend.

ABC Company has a transaction level claims database for its POS plan and its largest HMO. This database contains records for all inpatient and outpatient services provided to ABC Company employees. The claims database includes detailed financial, clinical, provider, and enrollee information. Information unique to managed care is also included, such as primary care physi-

Table 24–3

Selected Performance Targets

	Previous year	Current year	Target
Quality of care			
Cesarean section rate (percent)	30	25	18–20
Pediatric immunizations (percent)	90	96	100
Utilization			
Hospital admissions per 1,000	90	82	60–70
Outpatient encounters per capita	5.5	4.8	4.5–5.0
Employee satisfaction			
Retention rate (percent)	86	91	90–95
General satisfaction survey score (percent)	65	72	70–80
Financial			
Net payment increase per enrollee (percent)	9.5	12	9.5
Net payments in-network (percent)	80	70	85

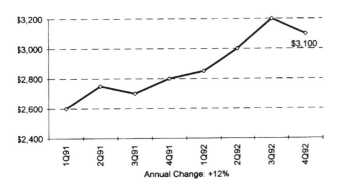

Figure 24–1. Net payments per employee (annualized).

cian (PCP) identification, referral indicators by type of referral, out-of-plan utilization and payment flags, and withhold amounts. Encounter records, for services provided under capitation agreements with providers, are integrated with the claims database to enable the analysis of total utilization. Capitation premium amounts are also integrated with the claims and encounter data to provide a complete picture of plan experience.

This type of database is appropriate when there is sufficient enrollment and the plan has the capability to report good quality data (i.e., minimum criteria for clinical coding and nonmissing values have been met). If a plan provides services under a capitation arrangement with its providers, then encounter records for those services should be included in the database.

Summary databases are available for ABC Company's two HMOs with lower enrollment, enabling the analyst to evaluate the company's complete health care experience. The HMO summary database loads ABC Company's HMO data into a personal computer to support quarterly performance reporting and graphics that profile each HMO and compare them to age- and sex-adjusted HMO and company-specific norms. The database format is based on the Group Health Association of America (GHAA) reporting guidelines with enhancements based in part on the HMO Employer Data and Information Set (HEDIS), developed by a business and health care consortium. These enhancements include premium amounts, more detailed clinical and financial information, and quality-of-care indicators.

ABC Company's analyst begins by evaluating performance across several broad service categories (Figure 24–2) and comparing these trends to targets (Figure 24–3). Figure 24–2 shows that in 1992 the aggregate

change in net payment per enrollee was 12 percent. Mental health and substance abuse (MH/SA) costs increased most sharply at 25 percent. Figure 24–3 shows that total costs were 2.5 percent above the targeted rate for 1992. MH/SA costs were 15 percent above the targeted rate of 10 percent for 1992.

Further analysis reveals that the percentage of net payments in-network has been declining over the past four quarters. As of fourth quarter 1992, only 65 percent of net payments are for in-network providers compared to a target set at 85 percent (see Figure 24–4).

Selected key indicators are shown in Exhibit 24–3. For each key indicator, data are reported quarterly and compared to annual targets, where applicable. Additional analysis is performed using the HMO summary database to compare the performance of all three HMOs and the POS plan. Table 24–4 shows each HMO's inpatient admissions per 1,000 population, including age- and sex-adjusted comparisons. Based on this and other summary utilization and financial measures (e.g., days and encounters per 1,000 population and payments per enrollee), it appears that there may be selection bias toward one of the HMOs.

The findings, which call for a more detailed analysis, include the following:

- MH/SA costs are increasing at a greater rate than other services.
- Out-of-network referrals in the POS plan are increasing, resulting in an in-network payment percentage (70 percent) that is significantly less than the target (85 percent).
- Possible selection bias exists for one of the HMOs.

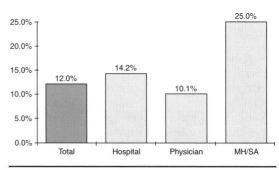

MH/SA = mental health/substance abuse

Figure 24–2. Percent change in net payments per enrollee 1991–1992. MH/SA = mental health/substance abuse.

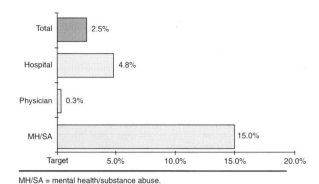

MH/SA = mental health/substance abuse.

Figure 24–3. Percent change in net payments per enrollee compared to targeted rate 1991–1992. MH/SA = mental health/substance abuse.

Mental health and substance abuse costs

To further evaluate escalating MH/SA costs, the analyst isolates all MH/SA claims and conducts a more detailed review of costs and utilization. The aggregate change in net payment per enrollee for MH/SA between 1991 and 1992 was 25 percent, ranging from 15 percent to 30 percent across the company's plans. This change compares to an overall rate of increase of 12 percent noted previously. Further analysis reveals that the dramatic increase in MH/SA costs was driven by increases in both price and utilization, and a 45 percent out-of-network use rate in the POS plan. Figure 24–5 displays the component changes in MH/SA payments. Clearly, out-of-network price is the most significant factor explaining the aggregate change in net payment. Figure 24–6 further explains the component changes in out-of-network payments, identifying inpatient price as the factor that explains the greatest portion of the overall payment increase.

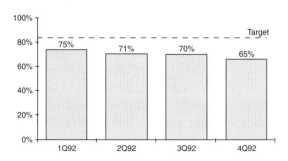

Figure 24–4. Percent of net payments in-network January–December 1992.

ABC Company had previously considered carving out MH/SA services to be managed separately but had delayed initiating any changes until the managed care program was well established. During the initial assessment of the managed care networks, the experience of inpatient MH/SA providers had been identified as a weakness. The analyst recommends that ABC Company first work with the various managed care plans to determine how costs can be controlled more effectively. Then, if the results are not adequate, ABC Company should reconsider a MH/SA carve-out, either in partnership with one or more of the plans or with a separate vendor.

Centers of excellence

A detailed analysis of out-of-network referrals in the POS plan, which increased from 15 percent of total payments to 22 percent since the previous year, indicates that the majority of the payment increase represents referrals for patients with cardiac conditions. Discussions of these findings with the POS plan reveals that their major cardiovascular physician group stopped participating in the plan earlier in the year and is now affiliated with a nonparticipating hospital, yet continues to receive new referrals and follow patients from the previous year.

The analyst recommends supporting the plan's efforts to negotiate a contract with one of the four hospitals in the community that performs open heart surgery. The hospital selected would be designated as

Exhibit 24–3 Key Indicators

Network performance
Percent of payments in-network
    Primary care provider
    Referral
Percentage of payments out-of-network
    Referral
    Out-of-area
    Opt-out
Admissions out-of-network by admission type
    (e.g., medical, surgical, psychiatric or substance abuse, obstetric)
Discounts in-network
    Hospital
    Physician

Table 24–4

ABC Company HMO Performance Comparison

HMOs	Admissions per 1,000	HMO total*		Aggregate HMO norm†		Point-of-service plan‡	
		Admissions per 1,000	Percent difference	Admissions per 1,000	Percent difference	Admissions per 1,000	Percent difference
HMO 1	71	85	−16.5	87	−18.4	90	−21.1
HMO 2	62	77	−19.5	85	−27.1	81	−23.5
HMO 3	97	89	9.0	95	2.1	96	1.0

*HMOs 1 through 3 ABC Company enrollees, age and sex adjusted.
†HMOs 1 through 3 aggregate book of business, age and sex adjusted.
‡ABC Company's point-of-service plan, age and sex adjusted.

the "Center of Excellence" and incentives would be created to funnel patients to the selected hospital. The hospital would be required to offer a service package that would include both facility and physician fees. If the plan cannot successfully initiate this program, then ABC Company may pursue direct contracting with providers for open heart surgery.

Adverse selection

Adverse selection occurs when one plan enrolls a disproportionate share of healthy or low-utilizing employees. This enrollment pattern usually increases an employer's costs because the cost of plans with adverse selection increases, while the plans with favorable selection do not pass their "selection savings" on to the employer.

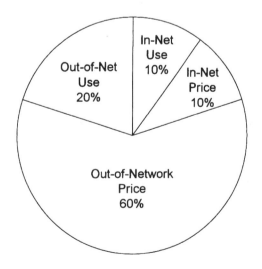

Figure 24–5. Component changes in mental health/substance abuse payments.

For ABC Company, one of their HMOs has a younger, healthier population with low utilization. The company employs age and sex adjustment and modeling to document that premiums should be lower than the current community rating to more realistically reflect actual use.

The HMO and POS rates are modeled based on the claims experience of the large HMO and the POS plan included in the transactions level database. The model is developed by extracting data for a demographically similar group of employees as compared to the two HMOs for which detailed data are not available. The measures created are age and sex specific but do not reflect possible behavioral differences between the plans. Modeled costs are consistently below the POS rates for one of the HMOs, indicating that there was favorable selection toward this HMO during the time period reviewed. The analyst recommends renegotiating the contract based on an adjusted community rating instead of the current rating structure.

Results

Access to meaningful health care data has supported the following management actions by ABC Company:

- Working with each managed care plan to revise targets and develop action plans to control MH/SA costs. If the results are found to be adequate within a specified period of time, then the company should pursue a carve-out for MH/SA, either in partnership with one or more of the plans or with a separate vendor.

- Supporting the POS plan's efforts to negotiate contracts with selected hospitals—Centers of Ex-

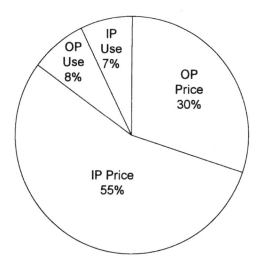

Figure 24-6. Component changes in out-of-network mental health/substance abuse payments. OP = outpatient; IP = inpatient.

cellence for specific conditions—that will significantly reduce the company's costs for these cases. If the plan cannot successfully initiate this program, then the company may pursue direct contracting with providers to manage these uncontrolled costs.

- Renegotiating rates with the HMO whose enrollees are younger and less costly based on age- and sex-adjusted comparisons with other plans.

Data Quality

The diverse financial and risk-sharing arrangements that managed care plans have with their providers continue to create a complex array of seemingly disjointed data. A plan may have different contractual arrangements with physician groups within the same plan. Some may be paid on a discounted fee-for-service basis while others may be capitated for a variety of services. In addition, managed care information systems were not originally intended to collect data requested by external organizations for performance evaluation. Working in partnership, employers and managed care plans are beginning to define standardized reporting formats and definitions.

Several years ago, GHAA and the Washington Business Group on Health developed a standard set of forms for reporting enrollment and utilization statistics by HMOs. Most HMOs are capable of completing the majority of the summary statistics requested on these forms. The majority of those who are unable to comply with this type of data request currently are upgrading their systems to allow them to do external reporting.

More recently, a business and health care industry coalition has expanded on the original GHAA format to develop a standardized reporting format called the HEDIS. The coalition involved in developing common performance measures includes 4 trade associations, 10 employers, and 30 managed care companies. HEDIS can be described as a set of guidelines designed to assist employers in reviewing and assessing HMO value. It includes aggregate reporting of membership and utilization statistics, summary financial information, quality-of-care performance indicators, and structural elements related to the HMO's ability to provide appropriate and high-quality care.

Many POS plans and HMOs are able to extract claims or encounter level records from their information systems for employers who choose to have a detailed transaction level database. Some of the data may be incomplete because these organizations often have information systems designed for internal management and claims processing that are limited in their ability to report data to their employer clients, either in standardized aggregate formats or claims-level detail.

The quality and specificity of financial data will continue to be a limitation for many managed care plans, particularly for plans with capitation arrangements. Capitation premium amounts, representing multiple services, may be loaded into a database at several levels of aggregation, such as the individual enrollee, the PCP, or the medical group.

The completeness of the data needed to create utilization performance measures may be lacking for plans with provider capitation arrangements. Encounter records should be generated for services provided under capitation arrangements. These records are similar to fee-for-service claims, but do not include net payments. The availability of encounter records is directly correlated with the stringency of the plan's reporting requirements. In the past, encounter data for HMOs were not required for internal analysis because they were community rated and patient management (frequency of visits and other services covered by capitation) was assumed to be self-regulating because the provider was getting a fixed fee. As employers began to request more detailed performance data, HMOs and other managed care providers began requiring their providers to submit encounter records as well as fee-for-service claims.

Data quality may also be an issue with referral identification. If a physician or group is capitated for both primary and specialty care services, the referral to a specialty provider may not be reliably reported as a referred encounter. When specialty providers are paid on a discounted fee-for-service basis, the claim is more reliably reported.

The information required to evaluate the performance of a managed care plan depends on the financial and risk-sharing arrangements it has with its providers. For example, a plan that reimburses its providers on a discounted fee-for-service basis may also include a withhold or escrow risk-sharing arrangement. In this situation a percentage of the approved payment for a service is withheld from the provider payment and placed in a risk-sharing pool for later distribution based on plan and provider performance. If a plan capitates its providers for selected services then both the capitation premium amounts and the encounter records for these services are needed to evaluate overall performance. An encounter record is most meaningful if it includes similar clinical and demographic data for a fee-for-service claim. Some plans are also able to report a fee-for-service equivalent charge or payment for services provided under capitation arrangements. This feature is useful both for the plan's internal management and for estimating what costs would have been under a fee-for-service arrangement. Table 24–5 summarizes the data elements needed for a thorough performance evaluation.

Different financial and risk-sharing arrangements also affect the focus of analysis for decision support. Positive and negative incentives are created that impact utilization, cost, and quality. For example, capitation arrangements create incentives to reduce inappropriate care by rewarding the conservative use of services. This arrangement may result in a reduction in unnecessary costs and an improvement in the quality of care provided to enrollees by not exposing them to certain tests, procedures, or hospitalizations that were unnecessary. Conversely, these arrangements may result in a reduction of appropriate and

Table 24–5

Data Elements for Performance Evaluation

Data elements	Provider financial arrangements	
	Discounted fee-for-service	Capitation
Clinical	X	X
Demographic	X	X
Financial		
Service level detail	X	
Aggregate capitation amounts		X
Fee-for-service equivalents on encounter records		X
Withhold amounts	X	

necessary care. It is essential that accurate information and analytical tools to manipulate and summarize claims data be employed to make this determination during a performance evaluation.

Information Sources

Decision support information can be derived from many sources. Suggested information sources related to quality and outcomes of care are summarized in Table 24–6.

Future Directions

A successful managed care program requires more of a partnership between the employer, the managed care organization, and its providers than did the basic indemnity plan. From the initial contract negotiations, which may have included risk-sharing arrangements and performance targets, to routine performance monitoring and quality improvement, all stakeholders must continue learning about what works best and how to do it better. They also must be cognizant of new approaches to measuring outcomes, quality, and best practices and adopt those best suited to their environment. Several enhancements to the performance evaluation process are described in the paragraphs that follow.

Table 24-6

Information Sources

	Employee			Claims data	
	Health risk appraisal	Outcomes survey	Satisfaction survey	Individual company	Normative comparisons
Quality of care					
Inappropriate utilization					
Place of service				X	X
Specific procedures				X	X
Preventive care	X			X	X
Cost effectiveness		X		X	X
Patient satisfaction			X	X	
Chronic illness management	X	X		X	
Access to care			X	X	
Patient education					
Outcomes of care					
Mortality				X	X
Morbidity	X	X		X	X
Complications		X		X	X
Readmissions				X	X
Quality of life		X			
Disability	X	X		X	

Severity adjustment

Disease severity can be defined as the likelihood of death or residual impairment as a result of disease. The measurement of disease severity greatly enhances analyses of hospital efficiency and effectiveness because severity directly affects the timing of hospitalization, treatment decisions, and intensity of care. Disease staging is a clinically based measure of disease severity that has been widely used in hospital management, quality assurance, reimbursement applications, and the measurement of quality in ambulatory care.

Adjustment for disease severity using disease staging can support the employer's comparison of managed care networks during the initial selection process or a managed care plan's contract negotiations with prospective hospital providers. Disease staging has been used in the comparison of hospitals competing for designation as Center of Excellence for selected procedures. An individual employer can compare its employees' severity-adjusted inpatient experience to norms for resource use (cost), length of stay, and mortality. Opportunities to improve the quality and efficiency of care can be enhanced by applying severity adjustment.

Outcomes assessment

Outcomes research focuses on assessing the long- and short-term benefits and risks of medical intervention. There is an increasing interest in outcomes research and the data it can provide. The Outcomes Management System, supported by the Health Outcomes Institute (HOI), is being tested by a consortium of 24 employers and managed care organizations. This research is based on patients' perceptions and descriptions of their own health and capabilities combined with physicians' descriptions of the medical intervention being provided. This study attempts to determine the medical interventions that provide the best patient outcomes by identifying outcome variations among similar patient populations.

Surveys have been designed to collect information from employees about their perceptions of their own health status. The survey instruments used by the HOI consortium include the Health Status Questionnaire and condition-specific surveys referred to as TyPE specifications. The resulting information can be consolidated into a database with linkages to an employer's claims database. This consolidation enables the employer to develop a comprehensive picture of the care delivered in response to a specific medical condition and to assess the risks and benefits of alternative treatments for these conditions.

Health risk appraisal

A number of employers are administering health risk appraisal surveys to employees and their spouses. The information gathered from these surveys, which document life-style habits (e.g., smoking), chronic illness, and functional and emotional well-being, supports the following objectives, when linked to medical claims data:

- reduction of health care costs and improvement of employee wellness through risk reduction and early detection programs,
- determination of more effective health plan design to influence life-style change, and
- implementation of specific programs targeted at high-risk people and that track the results over time.

Commonly used survey instruments include the Carter Center of Emory University and the U.S. Cen-

ters for Disease Control (CDC) questionnaire and a modified version of the original CDC questionnaire developed by Johnson & Johnson. The results from these surveys are loaded into a database and linked to medical claims data to evaluate program effectiveness and to quantify the relationship between risk factors and medical expenses.

•   •   •

Employers are increasingly purchasing health care benefits based on value, as it relates to both current and future needs, and they are seeking managed care partners who are committed to continuous quality improvement. They realize that meaningful health care information provides an essential foundation to support the development and implementation of future strategies, rather than allowing change to occur by chance. The success of a managed care strategy depends on the employer's ability to monitor plan performance routinely and target opportunities for improvement; the managed care organization's commitment to maintain cost-effective, quality-conscious provider networks; and the providers' willingness to change their practice patterns to improve quality and outcomes.

25

Managed Care and Health Information Networks

Caron Primas Brennan

In a managed care environment, the focus is on delivering value by providing consumers access to high quality health care at reasonable cost. The use of a health information network in the managed care system, linking all the related entities, improves the quality of health care by allowing access to critical data on demand and decreases the cost of the delivery by enhancing communications between the managed care providers.

The Environment

The health care industry is rapidly changing. The use of managed care is increasing and changing the look of the continuum of care. Traditional providers are becoming payers by creating or aligning with insurance plans. Payers are entering the provider business by buying practices. The primary care physician is becoming a focal point and a facilitator of health care. There is overcapacity in the hospitals as the trend moves toward ambulatory and alternative delivery of care. Home health care is taking its place as a major player in health care delivery. While legislation and regulation create obstacles from outside the industry, outcome measurements, guidelines, and protocols are being proposed inside. There is a movement toward clinical repositories and electronic medical records, which will require a reengineering of the workflow in the physician office. Documentation of procedures with a clear audit trail is becoming a requirement. The rate and span of adoption of technology by the physician community is varied: from physicians who are not interested in dealing with computers to younger physicians who used computers in school and are anxious to try all the new developments, including pen-based and voice recognition solutions.

The adoption of information technology by the health care field has lagged behind that of many other business industries. Hospitals and large health care systems have established proprietary information networks (such as those linking physicians to their hospitals and hospitals to payers), each requiring unique hardware and software to access the proprietary network. These multiple networks create data and infrastructure redundancy, which inflates health care costs, and compounds individual training and support requirements. Large physician practices and associations have begun adopting the available technologies, but generally primary care physicians have been out of the loop. With the increase in managed care, the role of the primary care physician is increasingly important, especially as a facilitator of care delivery. The health information network opens up these existing systems to the primary care physician by taking advantage of in-place technology. As the gatekeepers in managed care, the primary care physician is a key benefactor of regional health information networks.

What Is a Health Information Network?

A health information network (HIN) is an integrated collection of computer and telecommunications capabilities that facilitate the exchange of patient, clinical, and financial information among physicians, hospitals, payers, employers, pharmacies, and related health care entities within a geographical region. Each HIN is unique due to demographic and participation variables. These variables include ownership, the number of participants, transaction volume, the level of integration with internal and external systems, and the range of applications. Basic or initial connections usually include hospitals and their physicians, payer

J Health Care Financ 1995; 21(4): 1–5
© 1995 Aspen Publishers, Inc.

linkage offering electronic data interchange, and insurance eligibility information.

A managed care organization (MCO) can take advantage of the benefits of a network by establishing an enterprisewide HIN with full or partial ownership or by being a participant in an existing regional or community HIN.

How the HIN Works

The underlying technology is software that rides on the physical network establishing transparent connectivity and interaction between owners and users of data. Health Network Ventures (HNV) has developed state-of-the-art software to help establish HINs through on-line connectivity and a full function common user interface. HNVnet is the only proven HIN product. It is a comprehensive on-line transaction processing system that allows authorized participants in a health care network to access clinical, financial, and administrative information from participating hospitals, clinics, physicians, payers, pharmacies, laboratories, home health agencies, and other health-care-related entities (Figure 25–1). HNVnet's distributed architecture allows the system to be grown in small increments to meet the changing volume of users, transactions, and applications on the network. Transaction processing software provides a standardized interface for data exchange between subscribers. A simple, menu-driven system and a common user interface allow new users a quick start in navigating the system. Information may be requested on demand, ensuring that valuable data are available when they are needed most. With HNVnet, different levels of automation can coexist in the same environment or clinic without diluting the benefits of the information technology. Data can be shared on an "as needed" basis over a network while protecting ownership rights to individual databases and confidentiality of medical records.

HNVnet is a sophisticated communication and translation system designed to protect receivers and senders from unauthorized access. All databases reside at the providers' and payers' systems, remaining under institutional control. Organizations retain their capital investment in their information systems, because HNVnet supports transaction execution without requiring replacement of the host systems. HNVnet strictly adheres to industry computing standards,

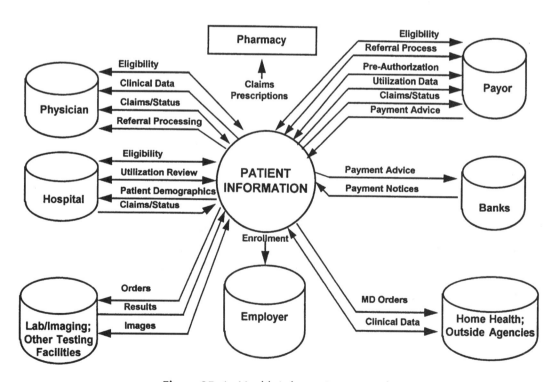

Figure 25–1. Health information network.

providing excellent portability characteristics, a smooth growth path, and the most cost-effective solution available.

Current Networks

Currently, HNVnet is being used by telecommunications companies in the United States and Canada for their regional and community HINs. This system has also attracted the interest of health insurers, managed care companies, hospital systems, and physician organizations looking for solutions to their network problems. HNVnet is the infrastructure of networks located in Milwaukee, Wisconsin; Indianapolis and Fort Wayne, Indiana; Louisville, Kentucky; Nashville, Tennessee; Cleveland and Cincinnati, Ohio; and Calgary, Alberta, Canada.

Current users of the HINs are physicians, nurses, medical records personnel, and other health care providers. Potential network users could be governmental agencies, employers, patients, research and/or educational bodies, accreditation agents, and regulators.

Through the HIN, users connect directly to host database systems to retrieve data. Connecting to hospital systems results in access to patient census, medical records abstracts, lab results, transcriptions (consults, history, and physicals, etc.), and radiology reports. Connections to MCO/payer systems allow access to patient eligibility, benefit plan detail, plan provider directories (physician and nonphysician), on-line referral processing, and utilization management information. Also available are on-line connections to pharmacies, home health agencies, and other ancillary providers. A "pass-through" capability allows connection to reference databases, other on-line services, and installed legacy systems.

The Impact on MCOs

Managed care is a system of health care delivery that influences utilization of services and costs of services and measures performance. MCOs need definitive, complete information about patient care, yet the data reside in multiple disparate computer systems among numerous organizations. As part of a HIN, the MCO can receive or retrieve information it needs from physicians, payers, or other health care providers. It can also provide on-line guidelines,

protocols, and formularies in support of its managed care contracts.

In the managed care environment, the emphasis is on delivering high quality health care. The delivery of the care (what was done) needs to be documented and the quality of care (how it was done) needs to be demonstrable and measurable through that documentation. To accomplish this, the primary care physician (in fact, all caregivers) must move from brief documentation on paper medical records to more comprehensive electronic medical records. By installing the information network technology and electronic medical record in the primary care physician office setting, the physician achieves greater productivity with improved outcomes while reducing overhead costs.

Benefits for a MCO Participating in a HIN

For the MCO, participating in a HIN can result in improved customer service and lower costs of care. Specific benefits are reduced administrative costs, electronic claims acceptance and repricing, on-line preauthorization and precertification, electronic transfer to mail-order pharmacy programs, improved credentialing, on-line, up-to-date physician and provider directories, and on-line case management and utilization review.

Provider Benefits

The physician connected to the HIN is able to provide a higher quality of care and support timely diagnoses and continuity of care while lowering the cost of providing the care. The physician benefits include reduction of duplicate testing, access to treatment-related medical information at the hospital(s), reduction of office paperwork; reduction of isolation of rural physicians; reduction of exposure to litigation through improved documentation; and electronic signature for electronic documents.

Patient and Employer Benefits

The patient benefits indirectly from the efficiencies in the HIN by a reduction in redundancy of forms, exams, and tests; greater continuity of care; better data for informed decision making; and lowered cost of care. When the employer is included on the HIN it facilitates on-line member registration and enrollment, on-line confirmation of eligibility, reduction in erroneous claims, reduction in costs of health benefits, and improved employer/employee satisfaction with MCOs and providers.

•   •   •

Communication and data exchange between existing health information systems is becoming increasingly important as the industry moves toward managed care. The technology available to connect all the systems is currently available and being utilized in HINs. MCOs can take advantage of the benefits of a HIN through ownership or participation. As HINs proliferate, there will be a migration from proprietary systems to communitywide open systems. The HIN infrastructure aids in this evolution by allowing different levels of automation and systems to coexist in the same environment. It also allows electronic data exchange between organizations that currently have only manual connections, thus saving time and money.

MCOs require information from multiple disparate information systems representing different modes of health care delivery. HIN connections allow access and data retrieval on an "as needed" or on-line basis or through batch file transmission. Participation in a HIN allows MCOs to reduce administrative costs and improve customer service. The improved efficiencies received through the MCO's participation in a HIN result in benefits to all their "customers" (members, physicians, and preferred providers), as well as their own organization.

Part VI
Public Sector Managed Care

26

Pursuing Value in Medicaid Managed Care: Access to Care and Enrollee Information Management

John D. Klein and James Chase

Health Plan Value in the Context of Medicaid

Pursuing value in managed care purchasing is challenging for employers; for Medicaid programs, it is doubly so. Compared with employee groups, Medicaid enrollees require a wider variety of health services, remain covered for a shorter time, and are dispersed across a much wider area:

- While employees are generally in good health, many people qualify for Medicaid because of pregnancy, disability, or acute health care needs. Many people entering publicly funded programs have been uninsured for a period of time, and have significant health care needs in the first months of enrollment. For these reasons, the "managed" in managed care is even more important for Medicaid enrollees than for the traditional insured population.

- While most employees remain with an employer for several years, the average Medicaid enrollee stays less than two years. It is also common for enrollees to have a change in the basis of their eligibility over the course of any given year. Although some enrollees who leave Medicaid continue with the same health care providers, high turnover adds to the challenge of Medicaid managed care.

- And while most employee groups are concentrated in a single area, Medicaid enrollees live in every city and town. Many of these areas have historically had low access to certain types of health care services. The special needs of enrollees in public programs also require a wider variety of providers to be available. For these reasons,

meeting the managed care needs of Medicaid enrollees requires arrangements with multiple health plans with combined networks covering the entire state.

Medicaid programs have tremendous potential leverage in the marketplace because of their very large enrollments. In Minnesota, the Medicaid agency covers about 13 percent of the population, or more than one of every eight persons. Size can be a disadvantage, however, since actions by Medicaid affect so many stakeholders, and any major change is accompanied by concerns. As a public program sponsored by federal and state government, the operating issues and constraints faced by Medicaid are very different from the issues faced by an employee benefits program.

Despite these differences, the fundamental challenge of pursuing value in managed care purchasing is the same for Medicaid and commercial purchasers: how to obtain high-quality, accessible health care in the most efficient way. This article examines two specific challenges faced by Medicaid and other low-income health care programs: (1) how to develop, evaluate, and communicate access to care; and (2) how to transfer enrollee eligibility and health status information to the health plans and their providers.

Medicaid and Managed Care in Minnesota

In Minnesota, health coverage for low-income persons is administered through the Department of Human Services (DHS). DHS administers three distinct but closely related programs: (1) Medical Assistance, the state's Medicaid program; (2) General Assistance Medical Care (GAMC); and (3) MinnesotaCare.

Medicaid is jointly funded by the state and federal governments, and serves low-income families, the elderly, and the disabled. Medicaid is the largest single purchaser of health services in Minnesota,

Managed Care Quarterly 1997; 5(1): 42–50

covering 421,000 people. GAMC is state funded and covers 42,000 people, mainly those who have Medicaid-level incomes but do not meet federal eligibility categories. MinnesotaCare is also state funded and covers 94,000 people who have incomes above the Medicaid and GAMC levels, and do not have access to other insurance. Medicaid and GAMC clients receive comprehensive coverage and do not pay a premium. By contrast, MinnesotaCare coverage is less comprehensive, and clients pay a sliding-scale premium based on income. The combined Medicaid, GAMC, and MinnesotaCare enrollment at any point in time is approximately 557,000.

Until recently, DHS operated all three programs primarily on a fee-for-service basis. In 1985, DHS began converting Medicaid to managed care in three counties under a federal demonstration program. Since 1993, an additional 13 counties have been converted to managed care, and the department plans to expand managed care for Medicaid and GAMC to all 87 counties in the next few years. However, the MinnesotaCare program is the first to move to statewide managed care. Since its creation in 1992, MinnesotaCare has been operated on a strictly fee-for-service basis. But from July through November, 1996, the program is being converted entirely to managed care contracts.

The conversion to managed care for all three programs has been facilitated by "waivers," or permission granted by the federal government to allow the state greater flexibility in health coverage administration. The state's goals under the waiver are: (1) to make it easier and more seamless for enrollees to move among Medicaid, GAMC, and MinnesotaCare as their eligibility status changes, with the ultimate goal of merging the programs; (2) to improve access to care; (3) to improve service quality, coordination, and outcomes; and (4) to increase the efficiency of care by drawing upon the expertise of the state's health maintenance organizations (HMOs) and managed care organizations, and on competition among them to serve DHS clients.

Access to Care as a Determinant of Health Plan Value

Although access to care has generally been good under fee-for-service, problems have occasionally arisen for some regions and some classes of health care providers. One objective of moving to managed care is to transfer "front-line" responsibility for access from DHS to the health plans. Health plans have expertise in the development and maintenance of provider networks, and in setting provider reimbursement at levels appropriate to market conditions. Under managed care, access becomes a key determinant of health plan value.

Access for Medicaid programs means more than just having enough primary care physicians and hospitals. Compared with an employee population, a Medicaid population is likely to have higher requirements for various medical specialties, disability management and rehabilitation, mental health and chemical dependency care, interpreters and culturally competent care, transportation assistance, and other specialized services. Medicaid enrollees are also more likely to receive public health and social services that support or complement primary medical services. All of these services are important facets of a comprehensive definition of accessible care for a Medicaid population. Coordinating these services is one of the principal access challenges facing managed care organizations serving Medicaid clients.

Market Challenges in Developing Access

Because Medicaid programs must serve the entire state, one of the common problems faced is developing managed care networks in areas with little or no managed care presence. While Minnesota is known for its history of HMOs and managed competition, there remain areas of the state that have few managed care options. As a large purchaser, Medicaid programs can directly facilitate the development of managed care in new areas.

One of the challenges in the initial transition to managed care is the chicken-and-egg problem that some health plans face. If a health plan has a client base in a given area, it is in a much stronger position to obtain contracts with clinics and hospitals. But the health plan cannot attract the new Medicaid client base until it has a provider network. As the purchaser, DHS has received HMO proposals for "conditional" provider networks, which may progress to completion only after a Medicaid contract is awarded. But there is always the possibility that final agreement may not be reached with a specific clinic or hospital, resulting in a gap in the health plan's provider network.

There is no easy solution to this problem. To meet program deadlines, DHS must determine a final, or snapshot, date for evaluating a health plan's provider network, and make judgments about the likelihood of any networks still in development becoming reality. Even in established provider networks there is always a degree of turnover, and the occasional necessity of special arrangements to ensure that adequate access is maintained. But at the time of initial conversion from fee-for-service to managed care, network evaluation can prove to be an especially inexact science.

Although it is in the purchaser's interest to maintain opportunities for new health plans and provider networks to be developed, it is not in the interests of Medicaid clients to have constantly changing health plan options, or to lose access to well-established networks. This creates a challenge for DHS to strike the right balance between the arms-length role of purchaser, evaluator, and promoter of competition, and the need to work with health plans as partners. Medicaid managed care remains a new and evolving field, and both purchasers and health plans have distinct expertise and resources necessary for success.

For access to care, this means that if obstacles arise in network development, especially in new areas of the state, DHS and the health plans may need to work together on a creative solution. The department hopes that most of its health plan relationships will be long-term. With this in mind, success in maintaining good access to care during the transition from fee-for-service provides a sound foundation for the future. For example, if a health plan with a generally good network in one region has an access "hole" for a specific type of specialty care, it will usually be better for DHS to work out a solution with that plan than to reject the plan's bid as unsatisfactory.

Another set of access problems can arise in connection with plan/provider disagreements about network opportunities. This can work in two ways:

- Providers "want in" to a health plan that may not want them.
- And at the other extreme, "key" or dominant providers in a given area may be resistant to managed care overtures, and use their market power as leverage to obtain higher fees.

While these are normally issues that plans and providers would work out amongst themselves, the purchaser cannot avoid at least some involvement in connection with the initial statewide conversion from fee-for-service to managed care.

Regarding the provider entree issue, with public programs such as Medicaid, GAMC, and MinnesotaCare, it is important that health care providers have a reasonable opportunity to participate in health plans that will be the new vehicles for providing coverage in their area. Adding to this expectation of opportunity in Minnesota is the fact that MinnesotaCare is funded in part by a two percent tax on all health care services. Providers who pay the tax understandably believe they should have the opportunity to participate in the program funded by the tax. Local politicians sometimes become involved in supporting the interests of specific health care providers. Government purchasers must respond to the needs of many stakeholders, and all of these factors must be taken into account in determining how to respond on a case-by-case basis.

In general, health plans moving into a new area are looking to expand their networks, and tend to be open to new relationships with health care providers. However, the opportunity for participation cannot become a guarantee or mandate. Ultimately, plan/provider contracts must be freely entered into, with mutual agreement on the financial and care management terms. DHS cannot act as a board of appeal for unsatisfactory plan/provider negotiations, although it can play a limited role to ensure that plans are being fair and reasonable in their overall approach to network development.

The issue of managed care network development can be especially sensitive for county governments, which in Minnesota play a dual role of handling eligibility and enrollment for Medicaid and GAMC, and providing a variety of social services, public health services, and (in some cases) medical services for program clients. Some of these services fall in the gray area of responsibility between managed care and local public services. DHS is currently studying this issue and working with county governments to ensure that, as the conversion to managed care occurs, mutually satisfactory arrangements are made to coordinate care with county services and to make good use of county resources and expertise.

The other type of plan/provider disagreement involves providers who are key or dominant in a given market area, and who are less than enthusiastic about participating in managed care in general, or Medicaid in particular. Minnesota has addressed the latter issue by requiring that health care providers who serve public employees also serve Medicaid clients. This "carrot" approach can be supplemented, if necessary, with the "stick" of direct licensure requirements.

DHS encountered the issue of key providers in some regions in the course of the statewide conversion of MinnesotaCare from fee-for-service to managed care. Ideally, the department would prefer not only that managed care be available in every county, but that enrollees have a choice among at least two health plans. Although DHS has not yet reached that goal, the department has done reasonably well, given the large number of rural counties in the state with few local providers. At present, managed care plans will serve every county, 61 of the state's 87 counties will offer enrollees a choice of plans, and 19 counties will have 3 or more plans available. The counties that will initially have a single plan are, in many cases, served by two or more licensed HMOs, and the department expects that plan choice will continue to improve.

For some sparsely populated rural areas to be served by two plans, some network overlap must occur at the primary care clinic level. Although overlapping networks limit to some degree the meaningfulness of plan choices, there can still be substantial differences in specialty care, referral arrangements, and other facets of managed care among HMOs with some primary care clinics in common. Given that many enrollees choose to travel to larger cities for specialty care, and that services other than primary care account for the majority of health care expenditures, the goal of encouraging health plan choice in every county remains meaningful and worthwhile.

There may always be a few regions that are effectively served by only one health plan, just as under the fee-for-service system these areas are served by only one group of primary care providers. These providers may choose to contract with only one health plan to increase administrative efficiency and continuity of care. In these areas, the state's role will not be to force a choice of plans, but to ensure that new plans can obtain contracts if they offer additional service advantages to the enrollees.

Technical Challenges in Evaluating Access

It is one thing to desire a choice of health plans that offer good access to care, and another thing to evaluate whether access is, in fact, "good" for a specific plan in a specific region. While HMOs are licensed to serve specific areas of the state, the access needs of Medicaid programs are more complex than the standards contained in licensure requirements. And since the conversion from fee-for-service to managed care results in new networks being formed, the established record of service area approvals may not be a sufficient tool for decision making. Since improved access is one of the goals of moving to managed care, it is incumbent upon DHS to confirm that this objective is being achieved.

DHS is working with a geographic analysis consultant to facilitate evaluation of the new managed care networks. For the purposes of the initial evaluation, analysis was limited to primary care clinics and hospitals. In subsequent iterations it will be extended to include other providers important to Medicaid populations.

One of the basic technical challenges to geographic analysis is collecting and compiling information about the networks of each health plan responding to the department's request for proposals (RFP). This seemingly straightforward task necessitated overcoming a variety of obstacles. The following are a sample of database issues we faced:

- The RFP asked bidders to submit provider network information in a specific database format. For some plans, it was difficult to comply with this requirement for the requested classes of primary care providers, either following the specified format or any alternative format.
- Several plans do not maintain physician license numbers in their databases. This omission increased the difficulty of creating a consolidated database, since many health plans used different spellings or arrangements of the provider's name or address.
- Other data quality issues included numerous duplicate entries within a specific plan's database, inclusion of first name and middle initial in the last name field, and mismatching of hospital names and addresses.

While DHS expects some of these problems to be resolved in future rounds of plan proposals, purchasers faced with conducting a geographic analysis of provider networks should appreciate the types of database issues they may encounter.

Once a consolidated provider database was created, including provider affiliations with all bidding health plans, the information was plotted or "geocoded" to a map of the state, using a street address level of specificity. The same was done for the database of program enrollees. This information was then used to create maps and tables analyzing health plan accessibility using a 10-mile, 30-mile, and 60-mile standard of accessibility. The use of alternative mileage standards allows for judgments to be made about a reasonable standard of access in different areas of the state. In areas with low population and relatively few health care providers, the "community standard" for travel time is different than in more densely populated areas.

Figure 26–1 is a sample of the type of map used to facilitate the geographic analysis. Large, color wall maps were prepared to illustrate areas of potential weakness in the networks of bidding health plans, with separate maps for each plan. The wall maps showed: (1) all hospital and clinic locations, (2) the number of physicians at each clinic, (3) the locations of all program enrollees, (4) boundary lines showing access at alternative mileage standards, and (5) the counties for which the health plan was bidding. By listing the number of physicians practicing at each clinic, the maps make it easier to judge at a glance the "weight" of the clinic in terms of providing access to an area. Separate tables show the exact number of enrollees with access at the alternative mileage standards for each county in the plan's bid proposal.

The maps are useful exhibits for negotiation meetings with health plans, as well as for objective evalu-

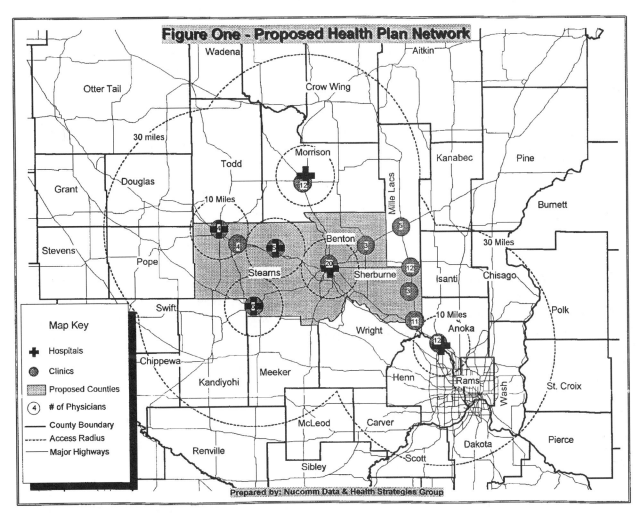

Figure 26–1. Proposed health plan network. *Source:* Nucomm Data and Health Strategies Group, St. Paul, Minnesota.

ation and network scoring. The database on which the plan-specific maps and tables are based also allows DHS to conduct other specialized analyses that may be required in the course of final negotiations or network development.

A number of technical refinements will be considered for future geographic analyses. The most important refinement will be adding classes of providers to the analysis to ensure that large gaps do not exist which would require unreasonable travel time for various types of specialty care. For some types of specialty care (e.g., chiropractic services), access standards comparable to primary medical care may be appropriate, while for other less common services, a longer travel time is the effective community standard.

Additional refinement is also possible at the primary care level. Different health plans define primary care in different ways. For example, some may use obstetrician/gynecologists and pediatricians as primary care providers for the purposes of referral authority and care management responsibilities, while other plans use only family practice, internal medicine, and osteopath practitioners. Some plans also make greater use of advance practice nurses, physician assistants, and other nonphysician providers to enhance access to primary care. Such practitioners can be an especially important tier of access in rural areas that face ongoing physician recruitment challenges. Capturing these types of distinctions allows for a more complete and accurate analysis of primary care access across different health plans.

Another important feature of evaluating access in rural areas is the "circuit rider" phenomenon, where a physician practice site represents less than a full-time practice. For example, a small-town clinic may be staffed on Tuesdays, Wednesdays, and Fridays, while another town's clinic is staffed on Mondays and Thursdays. Ideally, these types of practice arrangements should be incorporated in an analysis of primary care access. Failure to do so may lead to an analysis that understates or overstates the actual degree of access in a given area, depending on how the circuit rider physicians are counted and mapped. Unfortunately, such information is not generally available from health plan databases, which will simply list the same physician's name at two, three, or more separate locations. Health plans also do not usually

have current information about a clinic's capacity to accept new patients, although it is rare for a clinic to be completely closed to new patients.

Communicating Access Information

A key feature of a competitive health system is the ability of patients to select a care provider who best meets their individual needs. For patients to make these judgments, the purchaser must communicate the necessary information about providers and plan affiliations. Most managed care enrollees will have a choice of health plans, and access to specific providers is commonly a key factor, or the single most important factor, in a person's choice. What is the best way to inform Medicaid, GAMC, and MinnesotaCare clients about the provider networks and other access-related information for the health plans available to them?

Employee benefits managers have an advantage in communicating access information because the employees are generally in one place (at least part of the time), open enrollment presentations can be made available at convenient times, and health plan information can be distributed at the worksite. By comparison, the clients of DHS programs are more widely dispersed, and for many it is much less convenient to attend a centralized meeting.

At present, DHS handles access and health plan communications differently depending on how eligibility and enrollment intake are handled. For Medicaid and GAMC, counties determine eligibility and counsel clients through the enrollment procedures. This includes explaining the available health plan choices, supplying directories and other information describing the provider networks, and directing enrollees to sources for additional information. For clients with a chronic health condition and established and complex patterns of provider relationships, choosing a health plan can be an especially difficult decision.

For MinnesotaCare, eligibility and enrollment are handled directly by DHS through the mail, and in-person counseling is not feasible. The statewide conversion of MinnesotaCare from fee-for-service to managed care is being handled through a combination of mailed information and a telephone hotline. Clients are sent information about the health plan choices available in their area, and a 21-minute video explaining enrollment options and procedures. Clients are advised to follow up with the health plans and health care providers they are interested in, to confirm the current status of the network.

To date, DHS and the participating counties have been quite successful in assisting clients to reach a voluntary health plan choice. For health plans, few things are worse than having an enrollee involuntarily assigned to a plan that they may not understand or accept—not a good foundation for managing care. In some states, rates of involuntary assignment to a health plan have been fairly high, and assignments have even been used as an incentive for lower-premium health plans. Minnesota is striving to achieve a rate of voluntary health plan choice as close to 100 percent as possible.

In the future, DHS intends to explore a number of options for better communicating access information to enrollees. Although it is challenging to keep health plan network information up-to-date, it may be practical to do so at several intervals over the course of each year. This information could be made available to county intake staff and directly to enrollees through telephone hotlines or a variety of other means.

Software now exists that allows for easy preparation of provider directories that are tailored to specific regions, allowing for mailings that are cost-effective and more useful than receiving a large, statewide directory. It is also possible to prepare client-specific listings of the clinics, hospitals, and other key providers within a specific radius of the client's home, and the health plan affiliations of each provider. This approach has the advantage of allowing enrollees to locate their providers and then identify plan affiliation, rather than having to search through several provider directories to find the same information.

Another communication technique in keeping with the information age would be to make provider network information available through the Internet, or through kiosks or terminals placed at locations convenient to DHS clients. Again, the challenge will be to keep the information current and accurate, and available in a format that is simple and easy to use. Over the coming years, the department may very well use a combination of all of these communication tools.

Moving Enrollee Information from Purchaser to Health Plan

Just as it is important for Medicaid enrollees to have good information about health plans, it is essential for the health plans to have good information about their enrollees. While this may seem a self-evident truism, like so much in managed care purchasing, the details in this area can be especially devilish, and even more so for Medicaid.

In employment settings, new employees usually face a waiting period before health coverage is effective. This period allows ample time to provide information about health plan choices, to choose a plan, to communicate the choice to the health plan, and for the chosen health plan to mail the employee a membership card and new member packet. In Medicaid settings, these timelines are usually compressed, and the information transfer challenges are correspondingly greater. Once eligibility has been established, clients do not generally face a waiting period, and in most cases coverage is effective immediately. And at the other end of the cycle, under program eligibility rules, coverage terminations may occur under DHS programs with less advance notice than normally occurs in employment settings.

As discussed earlier, the average length of enrollment under DHS programs is less than under employment-based programs, and the Medicaid population requires more health care, on average. For these reasons, it is especially important that health plans have the opportunity to begin "managing" care right away. For example, plans would benefit from learning which new enrollees are pregnant, so they can encourage them to receive prenatal care as soon as possible. Any confusion about when a new enrollment began, the enrollee's choice of primary clinic or care system, or the enrollee's own responsibilities as a member of the newly chosen health plan, can substantially diminish the HMO's opportunity to manage care well—and increase the potential for misunderstandings, denials, complaints, and other counterproductive activity.

Like most large managed care purchasers, DHS maintains a complex internal database for tracking eligibility and enrollment information. Information is gathered at the time the county or state makes an initial eligibility determination and the client chooses a health plan, and is updated as the client's circumstances change. DHS transfers this information to health plans at regular intervals by magnetic tape. The department has the capability for electronic data interchange (EDI), but no health plan is currently using this method.

Unfortunately, both tape and EDI methods for transferring enrollee information carry a number of important shortcomings. No two health plans have the same internal database structure, software, or data transfer methods. In each case, they must translate DHS's data into their own internal format. While this translation is now fairly routine, errors of translation occasionally occur. Delays are a more common issue, given the time that passes from when data are entered into DHS's system, deposited to tape, transferred to the plans, and finally translated into their internal systems.

None of these "data movement" issues are unique to DHS, Medicaid agencies, or managed care purchasers in general. They are of concern, however, since they limit the potential effectiveness of managed care, especially in a Medicaid environment. DHS would prefer to concentrate more efforts on outcomes, access, and service improvements, and less on ongoing reconciliations of DHS and health plan enrollment and premium payment records.

DHS is exploring a number of options for streamlining the movement of enrollee information from the department to the health plans. Ideally, a system would be accurate, comprehensive, and efficient, moving information immediately from DHS's data base to a client's chosen health plan. It would not be necessary to move through the intermediate stage of tape transfers and data translation. Instead, data would be "mapped" and moved directly into the appropriate field of the recipient health plan's information system. Once such a system was in place and its accuracy verified, reconciliations should become a rarity instead of a regularity, and payments would generally require few subsequent adjustments.

In addition to transmitting "name, rank, and serial number" information, the goal would be to include information about an enrollee's health status, estab-

lished relationships with public health or social service providers, and other special needs information that would facilitate effective case management. Not all of this information is currently available through the state and county intake procedures, but collecting such information and sharing it with health plans is one way DHS can contribute to the success of managed care. Such information may also provide a necessary foundation for evaluating the relative costliness of different plans' enrollee groups, and making appropriate risk adjustments to DHS payments.

A data transfer system with all of these capabilities may seem far-fetched, but we believe it may be feasible in the fairly near future. A number of initiatives are under way in state government and the private sector to streamline and standardize information movement for claims and provider payments. The same types of improvements can be applied to health plan enrollee information, as well, and some vendors are beginning to develop expertise in this area. Five years ago, *world wide web* was not a part of the common vocabulary. Five years from now, or perhaps sooner, we believe that methods will be in place to use the web or equivalent means to move enrollee information much more effectively. By then, enrollment transfers via magnetic tape may have gone the way of the rotary phone.

•   •   •

As publicly funded health care programs continue to move from fee-for-service to managed care, purchasing methods, strategies, and administrative systems must continue to evolve and improve. Managed care is viewed by many as the panacea for controlling costs, improving access, and ensuring quality for Medicaid programs. These hopes can only be fulfilled if managed care purchasers, providers, and clients become sophisticated and effective in working with the new information this system requires. Sophistication in evaluating and communicating access to care, and managing the transfer of enrollee information, are important factors in realizing that goal.

27

Can Managed Care Save Medicare? Achieving High Quality and Low Costs Through Managed Care

Robert Giffin

Congress is looking for ways to drastically reduce Medicare expenditures. Part of this is driven by deficit reduction policies. But part stems from the growth trajectory of Medicare costs themselves. Private sector health care costs have moderated; average 1994 health costs for firms surveyed by Foster Higgins fell by 1.1 percent, as a result of major shifts in enrollment to managed care plans. In addition, 1995 premiums declined, as indicated in a Towers Perrin survey of employers showing a 2 percent decline for 1995 and a Group Health Association of America (GHAA) survey of health maintenance organizations (HMOs) reporting a reduction in 1995 premiums of 1.2 percent.[1] But Medicare costs have continued to increase unabated. Medicare costs "have been growing at least 50 percent faster than the private sector since 1990."[2]

The Medicare Risk program has been highly successful in bringing high-quality and low-cost care to millions of Medicare beneficiaries. But the program remains small: 2.3 million enrollees, or 7 percent of the total Medicare population. This compares with 23.7 percent of the non-Medicare insured population enrolled in HMOs at year-end 1993.[3] Many question whether expanding the Risk program can result in the kind of savings needed to rescue Medicare.

The central question for policy makers is, how much can HMOs really save? The research literature on the savings ability of HMOs is unambiguous: substantial HMO savings, with no adverse effect on quality and satisfaction, have been demonstrated through a wide variety of studies over many years. But general agreement on the magnitude, sources, and sustainability of these savings has been elusive.

Furthermore, in spite of this remarkably positive record of savings, Congress has been presented with conflicting information on this point. The Congressional Budget Office (CBO) has consistently credited HMOs with very limited average savings rates. The Medicare Risk Evaluation indicates that the program cost Medicare more money than it has saved. And in the public discourse, even acknowledged savings are often dismissed by critics with a variety of arguments: the savings are just "one-time" savings; they result from risk selection, or cream-skimming healthy enrollees; they are achieved by shifting costs to other payers; or savings are achieved by cutting back on necessary care.

The research studies supporting these arguments, however, typically describe a marketplace that existed five to ten years ago, at best. They are today widely believed to be obsolete myths with little or no basis in evidence. Their obsolescence results from the dramatic changes that have occurred in the managed care industry over the last decade, and the availability of recent data that reveal these changes.

For example, the widely accepted notion that independent practice association (IPA) model HMOs save little in comparison to staff and group model HMOs has only been shattered within the last two years in light of new studies and data. The notion was based partly on limitations in the data that were available to resolve the question, and partly on the real differences that probably did exist earlier in the evolution of HMOs. Another longstanding industry tenet that has recently been challenged is that HMOs systematically experience substantial favorable selection. Recent data disputing this selection bias reflect fundamental changes in the HMO industry, such as HMO popula-

Managed Care Quarterly 1996; 4(4): 12–29
© 1995 AMCRA Foundation

This article, in part, was previously published in R. Giffin, *Managed Care Can Save Medicare.* [Report]. Washington, DC: AMCRA Foundation, June 1995.

tions aging into established plans, benefit managers beginning to exercise control over risk selection, and increasing levels of adverse selection into HMOs as a result of benefits and out-of-pocket costs that encourage chronically ill patients to enroll in HMOs.

Even more revealing are recent returns from state and local initiatives that are yielding unprecedented savings as a result of: HMO penetration achieving "critical mass" in certain markets; employee benefit design innovations that empower the consumer to make choices based on efficiency; and purchasing groups exploiting their pooling opportunities and market power.

To the researcher, the HMO marketplace presents a moving target, which can be exciting but unnerving, as the gap between current trends and available data is often painfully apparent. While relying on the published record alone would present a misleading picture of HMOs today, to rely on anecdotal evidence and less rigorous studies contains inherent dangers. In presenting a snapshot of this changing industry, this article strikes a balance between these competing interests by first considering published literature, and filling the gaps by drawing on a variety of industry information, case studies, and inferential secondary data.

The article tackles the broad questions that currently engage policy makers grappling with Medicare managed care: quality, satisfaction, selection bias, disenrollment trends, cost savings, and the full savings potential of HMOs. HMOs have been shown to perform well in both the private sector and the Medicare Risk program on all of these dimensions, although the Risk program's flawed payment methodology limits the overall cost savings to Medicare. While the article stops short of suggesting specific approaches for expanding the Risk program, it presents evidence supporting the value of using HMOs to substantially reduce Medicare expenditures without cutting benefits or reducing quality. In addition, it considers how the highest levels of savings that have been observed in the private sector can be transferred to the Medicare Risk program.

Evaluating Quality

Superiority of HMO quality to fee-for-service

Virtually every study demonstrates that the technical quality delivered by HMOs is as good as or better than fee-for-service, after controlling for selection bias.[4] For example, in a study of hypertensive patients, HMO patients were found to have better hypertension con-

trol, and received better preventive services, including colon and breast cancer screening: "In the type of network model HMO we studied, the quality and quantity of ambulatory care for HMO patients was equal to or better than that for fee-for-service patients."[5]

Further, in a study of treatments and outcomes of myocardial infarction, Carlisle and colleagues found no difference in mortality, but HMO compliance with process indicators was superior. They concluded "HMO patients received hospital care that was generally better in terms of process than that received by patients in a national fee-for-service sample."[6]

Parity between Medicare and non-Medicare enrollees

The evidence of HMO quality of care is based on both Medicare and non-Medicare studies. There is no apparent difference in the care delivered in Medicare or non-Medicare settings. In a Health Care Financing Administration (HCFA) study of inpatient care for Medicare beneficiaries admitted for cerebrovascular accident (CVA) and colon cancer, the authors conclude:

> The results demonstrate that, overall, the medical care for CVAs and colon cancer delivered in Medicare Risk plans is both reasonable and efficient compared to the care rendered in the fee-for-service sector. . . . Although close monitoring of patient outcomes should continue for the TEFRA HMO program, these results should be reassuring to advocates of managed care for the elderly.[7]

In addition, Medicare HMOs have certain clear quality advantages. For example, 90 percent of HMOs with Medicare Risk contracts included preventive benefits. Most preventive screening services are not covered under Medicare fee-for-service, nor under supplemental Medigap policies. Studies have shown that the HMO coverage and promotion of preventive screening result in more screening services and better outcomes than for fee-for-service enrollees. For example, a recent study of Medicare Risk enrollees shows that HMO preventive screening results in significantly earlier diagnosis than fee-for-service for cancers that are susceptible to routine screening procedures: breast, cervix, colon, and melanoma.[8]

Accountability for quality

Systems of accountability for quality are more developed and stronger in HMOs than in fee-for-service.

Unlike fee-for-service, HMOs have clearly defined, manageable enrollee populations and provider networks, which present opportunities to measure and manage care for the population.

While medical care in all settings is subject to myriad medical licensure, regulatory, and quality assurance mechanisms, HMOs are additionally accountable for the quality of care they provide through multiple levels of regulation at the state and federal levels. The movement for accountability in terms of both price and quality, through such mechanisms as NCQA's HEDIS (The National Committee for Quality Assurance's Health Plan Employer Data and Information Set), assures that competition is based on quality, not just price. When held accountable for both cost and quality, HMOs have incentives to excel at both.

As competition increases, future HMO quality is unlikely to be adversely affected for various reasons: (1) there is a high degree of inefficiency yet in the system (as indicated by the degree of excess hospital capacity); (2) increased cost pressure will eventually slow the medical input prices, reduce technological costs, and arrest the medical inflationary cycle by forcing companies to provide technology that is cost effective, rather than simply providing marginal enhancements for enormous costs.

Comparing Satisfaction

HMO enrollees more satisfied

Managed care enrollees consistently rate satisfaction with their health plan higher than fee-for-service enrollees in surveys. Among these examples are recent surveys by the Sachs Group, which included 12,300 HMO members in five cities, in which HMO enrollees rated their satisfaction with their health coverage higher (82 percent) than fee-for-service enrollees (72 percent), and the National Research Corporation, which surveyed 10,000 health plan participants in 1994 and found that 66 percent of HMO enrollees were "very satisfied" or "somewhat satisfied" with their health plan, versus 57 percent of fee-for-service enrollees.[9,10] In addition, the *AMCRA/ Gallup Managed Care/Fee-for-Service Satisfaction Survey*, a random sample of 1,402 consumers in seven geographic markets, found that respondents in both managed care and traditional fee-for-service plans were equally satisfied. There was no difference in satisfaction on 10 of the 12 individual items rated. On the remaining two (cost and convenience), managed care scored higher.

Satisfaction levels in less healthy populations

There was no difference overall between HMO and fee-for-service satisfaction among chronically ill patients in an analysis conducted as part of the Medical Outcomes Study (MOS). Across 349 practices in three cities, 17,671 patients were surveyed.[11] Among subgroups of HMO enrollees in this study, however, there was significant variation, with IPA enrollees significantly more satisfied than group/staff enrollees.

Satisfaction high among Medicare Risk HMO enrollees

A recent study found that 95 percent of enrollees were satisfied with their ability to receive the care they felt they required, and most reported timely physician appointments for primary and specialty care.[12] Medicare enrollees with no HMO experience, however, were more critical of their HMOs.

A recent Kaiser Foundation focus group study of Medicare beneficiaries found that "Medicare beneficiaries currently in managed care plans are generally satisfied with their HMOs and say they would recommend their plans to friends." Enrollees cited lower out-of-pocket costs, quality of care, and convenience among the benefits of belonging to an HMO, with the most common complaint reported being delay in getting an appointment.

In contrast to enrollees, the study found that "those with fee-for-service coverage are uninformed or have mixed feelings about managed care."[13] Furthermore, Medicare beneficiaries are still generally uninformed about the advantages of managed care. According to the study, "when presented with basic information about HMO coverage under Medicare, many of these seniors expressed disbelief that managed care could provide full, quality coverage for nominal co-payments."

Dispelling Selection Bias Myths

HMOs do enroll chronically ill populations

Risk selection poses difficult problems for benefit design, and presents particular problems for researchers in comparing populations. Selection effects will always occur in multiple-option health plans to some degree. The longstanding assumption, however, that selection is always favorable for HMOs is seriously undermined by recent events and new evidence. Studies of selection have tended to show that HMOs have favorable selection relative to fee-for-service, although these studies have used data from the early to mid-1980s, and have been based on prior use models, which may bias HMO health risk downward.[14,15]

- One recent study found that HMOs are just as likely to have chronically ill patients as indemnity plans, and found no systematic selection favorable or adverse to HMOs.[16]
- Selection to HMOs is often adverse, because they typically offer better benefits at lower costs to the beneficiary (for example, full coverage of pregnancy and prescription drugs), as well as the absence of exclusions or waiting periods for pre-existing conditions.
- A recent CBO report confirmed substantial adverse selection to HMOs due to enrollment by women anticipating childbirth. Controlling for childbirth substantially altered the results of their regression model. The magnitude of the selection effect is obviously quite large, as eliminating the variable that controls for childbirth results in less than half the HMO savings when it is included.[17]

Selection has changed

The selection picture has changed dramatically since the 1970s and 1980s because the industry itself has undergone dramatic change. For example, populations have aged into HMOs. Once-favorable populations have aged within established HMOs, resulting in populations that look more like the general fee-for-service population. Further, as HMO penetration rates in some markets have climbed into the 20 to 50 percent ranges, resistance to HMOs by both patients and physicians has declined, eliminating a major cause of selection.

IPA and point-of-service (POS) plans experience less selection than group and staff model HMOs, since they are less restrictive and often do not require patients to terminate a longstanding provider relationship.[18] As the IPA and POS proportion of total HMO enrollment has increased, IPA and POS enrollment together represented 48.3 percent of HMO enrollment in 1990, and 54.0 percent of enrollment just one year later,[19] the "average" degree of selection bias has declined.

High employer managed care enrollments also reduce selection opportunities. Like a small but grow-

ing number of employers, Pacific Bell has removed the traditional indemnity option completely. KPMG Peat Marwick reported that the percentage of workers with the option of enrolling in a conventional fee-for-service plan dropped from 65 percent in 1993 to 51 percent in 1994.[20] Other employers have adopted premium contribution methods that provide strong incentives to employees to join managed care plans.[21]

Adverse selection for Medicare Risk HMOs

It has been argued that selection among Medicare beneficiaries will be greater than among other populations. The Medicare population is thought to be more likely than others to have established provider relationships and to be familiar with the fee-for-service delivery system. While plausible, there is no evidence that this is the case. On the contrary, there are some reasons to suspect that there may be considerably more adverse selection to HMOs by the Medicare population. For example:

- As beneficiaries age and their health declines, their health care utilization will increase, resulting in a greater proportion of income and assets going to health care supplemental coverage, co-payments, and other costs. HMOs with their comprehensive coverage, low premiums, and low copayments will be increasingly attractive to these beneficiaries.
- HMO coverage of prescription drugs is particularly likely to attract adverse risk selection among chronically ill patients who have high drug costs.
- Adverse selection may result from the continuous open enrollment provision of the Medicare Risk program. Enrollees can shift in to get specific benefits when needed, and then disenroll with ease to return to their regular physician.
- Finally, even when selection does occur, it is already partially controlled for in the age-sex risk adjustment.

HMOs still more cost-effective than fee-for-service

Even when selection occurs, HMOs are more efficient (i.e., even if the average HMO enrollee were healthier, the care given to an HMO patient and a fee-for-service patient in exactly the same health would cost less in the HMO; this is what most studies that "control" for selection or health status have found). Medicare Risk HMOs are 10.7 percent more efficient on average than fee-for-service,[22] and reductions in hospital utilization (admissions and average lengths of stay [ALOS]) and costs are 20 percent to 30 percent, after controlling for selection.[23]

Monitoring and controlling risk selection

Finally, when risk selection does occur, it can be controlled by various methods, including: eliminating multiple choice options by mandating one plan (obviously the most powerful option, and one that has been used by various organizations recently); basing employee choice of health plan on the relative efficiency of plans, by making the consumer pay the difference; and by requiring less healthy employees who may still self-select to higher cost plans (for example, to maintain a physician relationship) to pay a higher price to do so. In addition, monitoring plans to identify risk-segmentation practices, such as providing certain drugs but not others (e.g., insulin) enables employers to directly regulate risk-segmentation activities.

Another powerful approach is standardization, especially of benefits. This eliminates all benefits-based risk segmentation and selection caused by heavy marketing of marginal benefit differences. The provision of accurate, user-friendly information on benefits and plans facilitates choice based on efficiency and quality. In addition to benefits, standardizing the access design of a plan further reduces segmentation. Access design refers to network location and availability (accepting new enrollees), geographic coverage, controls on specialists, special services (e.g., mental health), and so on.

Accurate risk adjustment of premiums compensates for selection that has already occurred, and reduces subsequent selection by eliminating the advantages of risk segmentation. While a perfect risk adjustment mechanism has not been devised, several health status indicators show considerable promise.[24]

Analyzing Disenrollment

Among older and sicker individuals

Older and sicker individuals in HMO risk plans do not have higher rates of disenrollment than healthier enrollees. There is some historical evidence of favorable disenrollment, based on health risk and pre-disenrollment utilization.[25] There is only limited re-

cent evidence to support this view, and it is challenged by some recent trends and data.

- Older enrollees disenroll less than younger enrollees. According to HCFA data, enrollees aged 75 and older represent 42.4 percent of all enrollees, but only 38.2 percent of disenrollees.[26,27]
- Data supplied to the AMCRA Foundation by a major Risk contractor indicated that the proportion of enrollees aged 75 or older is increasing substantially.
- A recent study by the Department of Health and Human Services (DHHS) Office of Inspector General found that while self-reported health status is lower among disenrollees, their actual health as indicated by the number and severity of acute/chronic conditions was no different. In fact, 14 percent fewer disenrollees than enrollees reported being admitted to a hospital.[28]

Medicare Risk disenrollment no higher

There is some historical evidence showing that Medicare disenrollments were higher than private sector disenrollments. A 1990 HCFA study indicated that one third of enrollees disenrolled annually between 1985 and 1987. But this is based on old data from the Risk program's early years of operation. Medicare Risk plan total and voluntary disenrollment rates for 1994 are 18.2 percent and 10.4 percent.[29] This compares favorably with the average "total" disenrollment rate of 23 percent for the 21 HEDIS Report Card Project health plans. Plans providing disenrollment data for this study reported an average "total" disenrollment rate of 12.9 percent and an average voluntary rate of 6.8 percent. (Five Risk plans, representing 690,000 Medicare enrollees in 1994, reported Medicare Risk disenrollment information to the AMCRA Foundation for this study.)

Disenrollment not an indicator of problems in the Risk program

The continuous "open season" aspect of the Medicare Risk program makes disenrollment easy in that a Medicare enrollee can disenroll at any time, without waiting for an annual open enrollment period. Given the ease of enrolling and disenrolling, it is surprising that voluntary disenrollment is not even higher. Furthermore, as many as half of all voluntary disenrollees switch to another HMO, indicating that the system of care itself was not problematic; HCFA reports that 49 percent switched to another HMO.[30] Plan switching reflects highly competitive markets, and the high availability of benefit and plan choices for Medicare beneficiaries. Enrollees in these markets can switch fluidly from plan to plan, lured by competing HMOs offering better and less expensive benefit programs, service improvements, and wider provider networks. This view is borne out in a non-Medicare study that shows that "disenrollments are largely a function of economic factors. Disenrollments rise significantly with increases in both relative premiums and in the number of plan choices available to consumers."[31] Another study confirms this by following enrollees of an HMO that severed its contract with their physician. The study showed that "beneficiaries demonstrated considerable loyalty to their providers; nearly 60 percent switched to the competing HMO."[32] Such switching behavior will only be magnified in Medicare because of the continuous open enrollment provision. Another indicator of the positive nature of disenrollment is that 25 percent of disenrollment occurs in the first six months of enrollment,[33] possibly indicating search behavior on the part of beneficiaries.

More than half of voluntary disenrollment is due to beneficiary, provider, or benefit changes that are not considered problematic to HCFA. The most important reasons for disenrollment are related to lock-in features, lack of access to specialty providers, and difficulties obtaining desired treatments. These access issues, while not to be dismissed, are fairly typical for populations unused to managed care. The Inspector General report found that "Disenrollees without prior HMO experience were more critical of their HMOs than those with prior experience; however, the majority of both groups joined another HMO upon leaving."[34]

Comparing Cost Savings

Substantial HMO cost savings

Extensive research literature dating to the 1950s has consistently demonstrated substantial HMO cost savings, after controlling for selection bias. This literature was reviewed in detail in an earlier AMCRA Foundation report, *Managed Care Cost Containment: A Review and Reassessment, November 1, 1993,* and is updated here.[35] On average, HMOs have reduced utilization by

between 20 and 30 percent from fee-for-service levels. These reductions resulted from reduced hospital admissions and inpatient length of stay, offset partially by a small increase in ambulatory utilization. These results do not include the additional effects of provider discounts negotiated by HMOs.

Although representative of only one HMO, the RAND Health Insurance Experiment provided early evidence of the magnitude of these savings.[36] Using data from the late 1970s, the study found that both hospital admissions and days were 40 percent less for the HMO population, and total expenditures were 25 percent less.

More recent controlled studies have also identified substantial reductions in utilization. For example:

- The MOS found a 34 percent drop in admissions for HMO enrollees.[37]
- ICU lengths of stay were reduced by 38 percent in a Massachusetts hospital.[38]
- Four Medicare studies showed reductions in length of stay of between 17 percent and 25 percent.[39–42]

"One-time" savings?

Critics have argued that the modest differences in premiums demonstrate that enrollment in managed care may result in one-time savings, but that the rate of growth of costs is unchanged. There is no recent evidence of this, however. The two primary studies supporting this view are based on data no later than 1981, and relied largely on premium data, which is an unreliable indicator of efficiency.[43,44]

In addition, the ability of HMOs to find savings appears not to have diminished, in light of recent findings (e.g., the MOS) that are comparable to those found in the RAND study, and in the early literature.[45] Considering the lack of controls for favorable selection in many early studies, one could make a case that actual savings have increased. In addition, recent studies reveal substantial reductions in hospital length of stay not evident in early studies, which found savings influenced mainly by lower admissions.

All HMO payers save

Evidence of reduced medical cost inflation as a result of HMOs has been mixed, with some studies documenting reductions in hospital cost inflation and others showing no or negative effects, mostly using data from the mid-1980s.[46] The lack of consistent effect may result from the absence of a "critical mass" of HMO penetration, which may be required in order for HMOs to exert a strong effect on practice patterns and prices. There is emerging evidence of system-wide savings in very high penetration markets such as California and Minnesota, and recent studies have documented significant hospital cost reductions as a result of managed care.

- A recent study showed that between 1982 and 1990, selective contracting in California (which enables managed care plans to contract with selected providers) has resulted in hospital cost reductions of 13 percent in markets with significant hospital competition. HMOs would have maximum effect in competitive markets; in monopoly markets, HMOs would have limited negotiating power given the lack of ability to divert patients to competing institutions.[47]
- A study by the Florida Health Care Cost Containment Board found that for each 1 percent increase in managed care admissions, hospital revenues declined by $16.00 per admission. Furthermore, in high penetration counties, the revenue per admission is hundreds of dollars less than the state average. The study, using 1990 data, was based on an examination of 1.5 million patient records at 201 hospitals throughout the state.[48]
- A study comparing costs and utilization of Medicare fee-for-service and risk-HMO patients found lower ALOS for all major diagnostic categories and DRGs, in all Southern California hospitals.[49]
- A report from the Tax Equity and Fiscal Responsibility Act (TEFRA) Risk Evaluation found that increasing managed care penetration has a strong effect on Medicare fee-for-service costs. The study showed that a 10 percentage point increase in HMO risk penetration results in a 5 percent decrease in fee-for-service costs.[50]
- A recent study of 1,300 U.S. hospitals by KPMG Peat Marwick shows that high managed care penetration reduces lengths of stay, costs, and mortality rates. The study, based on 1993 HCFA data, showed that discretionary hospital costs (those not related to severity or cost of living) were 11.5 percent lower than the national average in high managed care markets. Lengths of stay

were 16.9 percent less than expected (adjusted for severity in these markets), versus 17.5 percent higher in low managed care markets. Mortality rates in high managed care markets were 8 percent lower than expected.[51]

Recent innovations achieve dramatic savings

- The Minneapolis-based Business Health Care Action Group has used an open-ended HMO program to reduce premium growth to nearly 50 percent of the average premium growth in that market.[52]
- The Cleveland Council of Smaller Enterprises' (COSE) use of HMOs reduced small employer premiums by 35 to 50 percent, and lowered cost increases to 25 percent of market levels.[53]
- The Health Insurance Plan of California (HIPC), a government-sponsored small group purchasing pool using HMOs, reduced premiums by 6 percent in 1994.[54]
- States have achieved enormous savings by enrolling Medicaid populations in HMOs. Hawaii was able to reduce medical care costs for chronic care by 28–47 percent. Arizona reduced the trend in per capita costs to 7 percent from 10 percent annually. A review of 25 state program evaluations found that managed care resulted in savings of between 5 and 15 percent.[55]

Medicare Risk HMOs more cost-effective

Results from the TEFRA evaluation demonstrated that Medicare Risk HMOs reduced hospital length of stay by about 17 percent, and were on average 10.7 percent more efficient than fee-for-service, based on reduced admissions.[56] (For unexplained reasons, this study was unique among recent studies in finding an effect from reduced admissions but not length of stay.) These savings do not take into account additional savings resulting from provider discounts, use of less expensive providers (e.g., fewer specialists), or less intensive use of services during encounters.

Further, while the evaluation showed that Medicare paid 5.7 percent more for Risk enrollees than it would have paid for the same enrollees under fee-for-service, this added cost is clearly unrelated to the efficiency of Risk HMOs. It has only to do with a fee-for-service–based payment methodology that is defective but that can be fixed.

Medicare Risk enrollees share in cost savings

Beneficiary out-of-pocket costs are far less in HMOs since the premiums and cost-sharing of HMOs are, on average, far less. This results from both competition among plans for enrollees, and statutory requirements that Risk HMOs return Medicare revenues in excess of their adjusted community rates (ACRs, rates they would have received for Medicare enrollees at market premium rates) in the form of increased benefits or reduced premiums. Nearly 10 percent of payments to Risk HMOs are used to provide additional benefits to enrollees.[57] According to HCFA, "[A]s of 1993, nearly 50 percent of all Medicare Risk HMO enrollees were enrolled in zero-premium plans offering outpatient prescription drugs."[58] Other additional benefits are even more prevalent. For example, 95 percent of Risk plans offer annual physicals, 88 percent provide free eye exams, and 86 percent provide immunization benefits.[59]

The out-of-pocket cost savings to beneficiaries can be substantial. For example, in a comparison of five cities constructed by HCFA, the lowest cost Medigap coverage (with limited benefits, no balance billing protection, and no prescription drug coverage) averaged 4.6 times more expensive than the highest cost HMO coverage, an average difference of $447 annually (calculated by author, based on data in HCFA's report).[60]

CBO underestimates HMO savings

The CBO has complicated the discussion of managed care solutions to the Medicare crisis by publishing a series of studies "scoring" the savings that can be expected through managed care. While methodologically weak, these studies are typically given strong weight on Capitol Hill. The CBO's estimates have changed frequently, as indicated in Table 27–1, further complicating the issue. While the CBO scores group and staff model HMOs highly, most HMOs are of the IPA model type. The CBO's low savings estimate for these models results in a low total HMO savings estimate. A recent CBO study attributes utilization-based savings of 19.6 percent to group and staff models, while crediting IPAs with only 0.8 percent savings, and HMOs overall with average savings of 7.8 percent, considerably below most independent esti-

mates. The CBO's changing savings assumptions (in terms of reduced utilization, not prices) are summarized in Table 27–1.

The CBO studies

The CBO's managed care savings assumptions are based on an in-house, unpublished study using data from the 1992 National Health Interview Survey (NHIS) and reported in *The Effects of Managed Care and Managed Competition*.[61] This report updates the CBO's findings reported in March 1994,[62] which were also based on the 1989 NHIS. This research contains some potentially serious flaws.

One flaw is that the CBO eliminated approximately twenty thousand observations because the respondent could not identify type of insurance.[63] This probably results in sample selection against low utilizing IPA members. IPA model HMOs are more like PPOs (preferred provider organizations) than are group and staff models, and therefore IPA respondents are less likely to be sure which HMO model type they are enrolled in. The low utilizers among them (those who have less contact with the plan) are even less likely to be sure of the type of plan. Thus, there is likely an important bias toward high utilizing IPA members in the sample. Because only 37 percent of the original sample was used, the magnitude of this bias should be enormous. Even though there was some adjustment for health status, in a linear regression, the absence of

Table 27–1

CBO's Average Managed Care Savings Assumptions (Percent of Savings)

	June 1992 %	August 1992 %	July 1993 %	March 1994 %	Feb. 1995 %
Staff and group model HMOs	>25	15	7.5	9–12	20
IPA network model HMOs	0	1	7.5	0–3	<1
Point-of-service plans	0	1	7.5	—	—
PPOs	0	1	—	2–4	2–4
Utilization review	4–8	2.5	—	2–4	—
HMO average	—	—	—	3.9	7.8

observations in the low-utilizer category could seriously bias the results.

Another problem is that the large number of terms (variables), many of which are likely to be related, suggest the possibility of substantial multicollinearity. (Multicollinearity is a situation in which strong inter-relationships between independent variables make it difficult to disentangle their separate effects on the dependent variable.) Such a model may yield reasonable predictive value, assuming that the independent variables are properly specified. But such an approach has very limited explanatory value for specific terms. The coefficients in models with substantial multicollinearity can be extremely biased and frequently have inverted signs.[64] Consequently, the reliability of the coefficients on the "insurance type" variable is low.

Furthermore, these results deal solely with the effects of managed care on utilization. By ignoring managed care discounts, the study ignores an area with the greatest potential for managed care savings: downward pressure on market prices. These effects are just beginning to be felt in certain highly penetrated markets, such as Minneapolis, San Francisco, and San Diego.

In addition, the CBO's pronouncements that IPAs save less than other types of HMOs are simply contradicted by a large body of highly credible evidence.[65] Consequently, until the CBO's research can be replicated by more rigorous research methods, it does not represent credible evidence on savings, or lack thereof.

IPA, staff, and group model HMOs equally cost-effective

HMO savings do not differ substantially by model type. Substantial IPA model savings were demonstrated through a variety of high-quality studies. For example, the TEFRA Risk evaluation found that staff model HMOs utilized more resources than IPA and group model HMOs for physician services, nursing home days, and home health visits, while IPA model HMOs had higher utilization of skilled nursing facilities.[66] The MOS found that all types of HMOs reduced admissions rates substantially (between 29 and 39 percent), with staff and IPA models at the low end of the range, and group models at the top of the range.[67] There is some limited evidence that POS plans, or open-ended HMOs, can also be cost-effective, although the evidence to date is inconclusive.

Realizing Managed Care's Cost-Saving Potential

Private employers

Employers began offering HMOs in the 1970s and 1980s as part of multiple-option plans, in hopes of substantial savings or reduced growth of health plan costs. While most employers have generally experienced lower premiums for HMOs, their total benefit costs in many cases continue to grow unabated. This results from the combined phenomena of favorable selection into HMOs and shadow pricing of premiums by those HMOs. As healthier employees move into HMOs, costs and premiums in the less healthy fee-for-service pool increase. By following a once common practice of pricing just below fee-for-service premiums, HMOs actually can drive total benefit costs higher than they would have been without the option.

The reasons for employer disappointment are easily understood. Between 1986 and 1994, despite the rapid expansion of managed care, premiums grew 3.5 times faster than corporate profits, and five times faster than wages.[68] In addition, although HMO premiums consistently grow at a lower rate than fee-for-service rates, the differences are modest, averaging two percentage points between 1988 and 1993 (11.6 percent for HMOs, versus 13.4 percent for fee-for-service).[69] Larger differentials have been reported, but are based on less reliable data; most employer surveys are not based on representative or random samples of employers. Also some calculate premiums in unreliable ways, for example, dividing total benefit costs by active employees (rather than active and retired). Consequently, the results vary substantially. KPMG Peat Marwick's survey has greater reliability than most because it is based on a random sample of employers.

The disappointing experience of employers over time is also reflected in opinions of benefit managers. For example, according to KPMG Peat Marwick, 17 percent of respondents stated that their HMOs did not save money, while 44 percent said they saved "a little."

Case studies of individual employers also reflect these general results, even for the large and "sophisticated" employers. Within the last two to three years, however, employers have begun to make specific changes to their benefit plans that appear to have resulted in substantial improvements in overall performance. Several cases are described below for which published information was available.

Pacific Bell

During the 1980s, Pacific Bell experienced health benefit premium increases of between 13 and 15 percent each year for its four indemnity plans, and 23 HMOs spread out over multiple regions.[70] The company did little to manage risk or improve competition between plans during this period. In the late 1980s, however, the company shifted all employees into managed care (HMO or PPO) with no pure fee-for-service alternative.

Savings: Following this change, the cost trend declined from 10 percent a year during the 1987 to 1990 period, to 4 percent from 1991 to 1992. The company estimated that it saved $15 million per year. Also, both inpatient and outpatient utilization declined. Inpatient days per thousand declined from around 450 in 1988 to 350 in 1992. This utilization trend partly reflects national trends, but is still significant. Unlike national trends, outpatient utilization did decline.

Xerox

Xerox was, in 1991, one of the first large companies to establish aggressive management of its HMO plans through its HealthLink program.[71] An essential element was the benchmarking of premium contributions to low-cost health plans. This increases price competition between plans by forcing consumers to pay the difference between the benchmark premium and the more costly plan's premium. Xerox had enrolled 40 percent of employees in HMOs by 1989. After HealthLink this increased to 62 percent in 1993, and was targeted for 80 percent in 1995. With such high participation in managed care, the company has greater leverage with health plans, as well as reduced opportunities for cream-skimming by health plans.

Savings: HMO premiums that had increased on average 12 percent a year through the 1980s had remained only a percentage point or two behind fee-for-service, and well above inflation. This continued even after more than half of Xerox employees had joined network plans. However, in 1991, the year the

HealthLink program began, HMO premiums were 9.5 percent versus 14.6 percent indemnity plans, and the company saved an estimated $1,000 per employee in HealthLink.

Other companies, such as American Express, have attempted to encourage both efficiency and quality by benchmarking premium contributions to the low-cost plan, and by further reducing employee contributions for high-performing plans based on employee satisfaction ratings.[72]

Many more companies, however, have yet to begin benchmarking low-cost plans, and even fewer have dealt with selection problems. Without controlling selection, the benchmarking strategy can eliminate shadow pricing, but may exacerbate the escalation of indemnity premiums because of adverse selection into these plans, and may still increase overall health benefit costs, at least until penetration in the managed care plans becomes sufficiently high to more than compensate for the higher indemnity premiums. Enrolling all employees in managed care is one of the best ways to deal with selection problems. Other solutions, such as risk adjusting premiums, are much more difficult. A number of employers have fostered close partnerships with their health plans to better monitor and manage care to their employees.

Public and private purchasing cooperatives

Business coalition purchasing cooperatives

A number of business coalitions have established purchasing cooperatives, which have launched some of the most comprehensive approaches to cost containment.

Minneapolis/St. Paul Business Health Care Action Group

This group of self-insured employers established an exclusive contracting arrangement with a consortium of providers in the Twin Cities (the "GroupCare Consortium," which includes HealthPartners, Mayo Clinic, and Park Nicolette Medical Center).[73] The cooperative provides members with a single POS plan, that has 90,000 enrollees (40 percent of those eligible). The coop is distinguished by the degree of involvement with the health plan and its providers. For example, it is involved in setting standards for necessity and effectiveness of treatments.

Savings: The per member plan costs increased 4 to 5 percent between 1992 and 1993, versus 7 to 8 percent for the Twin Cities.

Cleveland Chamber of Commerce's Council of Smaller Enterprises (COSE)

This coalition has established substantial purchasing power by enrolling 200,000 members.[74] The plan offers one fee-for-service plan, two PPOs, one POS plan, and two HMOs. All of the options are provided by Kaiser and Blue Cross, to provide volume and ensure leverage. Only 21 percent have enrolled in the HMOs, but enrollment is increasing rapidly.[75] Despite the purchasing power, the coalition's plan is somewhat traditional, in that it includes multiple choice with a fee-for-service option, allows restricted underwriting, and does not benchmark low-cost premiums.

Savings: The plan nevertheless claims cost reductions of 35 to 50 percent below the previous, conventional plan rates paid by the members. The program's cost increase was only 6 percent in 1992 versus the local trend of 22 percent and 4 percent in 1993 versus the local trend of 18.5 percent.

Other examples include the Employer Association Buyers' Coalition (Minneapolis/St. Paul), a small business coalition of 100 small firms; the Central Florida Health Care Coalition, which achieved relatively flat premiums for 1995 in a high-cost market; and the Massachusetts Health Care Purchasers Group, a coalition of large employers and state agencies that experienced 1994 premium increases of only 3.2 percent.

Publicly sponsored employer purchasing pools

There are a number of purchasing pools that are sponsored by state governments for private employers. Unlike the private coalitions, which restrict the number of plans, these pools tend to allow any plan to participate. Because these are voluntary, a key issue is how to avoid attracting high-risk groups only. An example is the Health Insurance Plan of California (HIPC). In 1992, it was the first government-sponsored voluntary small employer purchasing pool. By March 1994, there were 2,500 firms with 44,000 workers, offering 15 HMOs and 3 PPOs. As for savings, in the first year, premiums were 15 percent below market rates, and in the second year, there was a 6 percent premium decline.

Other examples include the Public Employees Insurance Plan and the Minnesota Employers Health Program, two Minnesota-based plans for local governments and for all private employers, respectively. Both plans follow a managed competition model.

State employer purchasing groups

The most aggressive and comprehensive health plan management has come from state employer purchasing groups. Like state-sponsored coalitions, these tend to include all plans that want to participate.

Minnesota Employee Group Insurance Program

This plan has used a managed competition model for five years.[76] The program serves 144,000 beneficiaries with two PPOs (one state funded), four HMOs, and no fee-for-service plan. (There are, in addition, a local government pool and a private sector pool with slightly different configurations.) The program has negotiated rates since 1989; negotiations include actuarial review of plan data to develop target premiums.

The managed competition features of the program include: standard (although not identical) benefits; premium contribution benchmarked to the lowest cost plan (which resulted in low-cost Group Health enrollment increasing from 27 to 51 percent of Twin Cities market share between 1989 and 1993); and controls on selection bias, such as standardizing *access* to all benefits and providers, monitoring of satisfaction and disenrollment, and providing accurate information on plans.

Savings: Before the managed competition model went into effect, the state experienced significant shadow pricing in its multiple choice (MC) plan, with MC and fee-for-service premiums clustered closely together. But with the advent of managed competition in 1990, cost increases moderated steadily. Costs increased 14 percent in 1991, 10 percent in 1992, and 6 percent in 1993. Rates were at least 2 percent lower than market levels between 1991 and 1993. Fee-for-service and HMO premiums no longer cluster together, and according to an internal analysis, selection effects have been minimal. The state calculates realized program savings of $23 million over a three-year period.

CalPERS

CalPERS serves 930,000 California state and local employees, retirees, and dependents, through 23 HMOs and four PPOs.[77] The program has standard benefits, flat dollar premium contribution, and, since the legislature froze state contributions to premiums, has employed aggressive negotiations based on health plan utilization and cost data.

Savings: Premiums have shown declines in each of the last three years, in a high-cost market. Premiums declined 0.2 percent in 1993 (compared to a 15.4 percent overall increase in California), declined by 1.1 percent in 1994, and declined by 5.2 percent in 1995.

State Medicaid HMO programs

Managed care is being used increasingly by the states as a way to control rising Medicaid costs and to extend coverage to previously uninsured populations. HCFA data show that enrollment in some type of managed care program soared 60 percent in 1994 to 8 million people (25 percent of the Medicaid population). Nearly every state now has developed or is developing managed care arrangements to provide care to part or all of the Medicaid program. While many of these primarily involved primary care case management programs, rather than HMOs. Twenty-two states now utilize HMOs as central components of their managed Medicaid programs.

Information on Medicaid managed care savings derives from waiver evaluations, other state studies, and reviews. Hurley et al. reviewed 25 program evaluations, finding calculated savings of between 5 and 15 percent.[78] Most states show substantial savings, but the methodologies employed limit their value for our purposes. Arizona, for example, has no comparison group, and must compare its experience to fee-for-service Medicaid in "like" states. States typically institute other confounding reforms concurrent with the HMO Medicaid programs. And most studies do not consider population differences. In fact, most states do not collect data on HMO experience, but simply calculate savings by comparing capitation rates to previous per capita costs. Thus, the results could be subject to selection effects that are not accounted for.

Two states that have attempted to measure HMO results explicitly include Hawaii and Arizona.

Hawaii

Based on a randomized, prospective design with Medicaid enrollees, managed mental health treatment reduced medical services and costs by 23 to 40 percent relative to control groups. For chronic medi-cal diagnoses, costs were reduced by 28 to 47 percent, while fee-for-service costs increased by 17 percent. Medical outpatient utilization increased threefold, but still cost 20 percent less.[79]

Arizona

From 1983 to 1991, the Arizona Health Care Cost Containment System calculated savings of $103 million over what traditional Medicaid would have cost (for acute, not long-term, care). The rate of growth was also substantially below the trend in traditional Medicaid (7 percent versus 10 percent for traditional Medicaid), and savings are accelerating over time. On the other hand, administrative costs were as much as double traditional Medicaid costs. Without these higher administrative costs, savings would have been $173 million.[80]

Medicaid programs can be either voluntary or, given proper waiver authority from HCFA, mandatory. Mandatory enrollment minimizes problems related to selection and risk segmentation. In some states, low payment rates have deterred plan participation. But the enormity of the program size and the opportunity to capture huge memberships have overcome much reticence. Also, while Medicaid fee-for-service rates are low, much Medicaid care is typically so inefficient that fully capitated programs are able to do quite well even with modest capitation rates.

Federal Employee Health Benefits Program (FEHBP)

The FEHBP Program enables unusually wide choice among plans during an annual open season, and pays a percentage of premium (typically 75 percent) up to a maximum amount. This should encourage use of efficient plans, but the maximum is set high, which effectively eliminates competition among lower-cost HMOs. FEHBP is a good example of apparent competition in health care undermined by selection. This can be corrected, however, by using standard benefits, flat rate (or risk-adjusted) contribution, separating risk pools, and better monitoring of selection practices. Also, FEHBP does nothing to take advantage of the enormous group purchasing power that it represents.[81]

Savings: There have been documented cost savings for FEHBP, but they have been minimal. Between 1987 and 1991, FEHBP per capita spending increased

16 percent, versus 14 percent for health benefits nationally, although for some time spans, FEHBP has performed slightly better than private sector.

The Medicare Risk program

The Medicare Risk program currently enrolls about 2.3 million enrollees, or 7 percent of the Medicare population. Risk plans are paid a rate equal to 95 percent of the fee-for-service costs in each county. Incentives for competition among plans are complicated by the payment rules. There is some degree of competition in the Risk program, mainly through increasing coverage. While there is a minimum benefit, plans are free to offer additional benefits and waive cost-sharing for enrollees. The competition, however, is limited by the fee-for-service–based capitation rate, the lack of high-quality comparative information on plans, and the opportunities for risk segmentation and selection through benefit design.

Savings: The TEFRA evaluation showed Medicare Risk HMOs to be 10.7 percent more efficient than fee-for-service Medicare, although these savings were not captured by the program due to the fee-for-service–based payment system.

Conclusions: Realizing Medicare Savings

HMOs have proven their ability to achieve large savings and high quality

HMOs have inherent efficiencies that can result in significant and sustainable savings. Savings relative to fee-for-service have not diminished, even as hospital utilization has become compressed and fee-for-service has become increasingly managed. In fact, the long-run potential of managed care may just be emerging as penetration rates reach "critical mass" in certain markets, and competitive market reforms encourage real competition among plans. These changes are likely to have long-run impacts on medical input prices that have the potential to substantially arrest the medical inflation spiral. In particular, cost competition will likely shift the technological mix toward innovations that reduce costs, and away from the current focus on marginal improvements at any cost.

HMOs could produce greater savings

HMOs have the potential to produce far greater savings for Medicare if enrollment in Risk plans is substantially increased, and if the Medicare Risk payment system is modified. Capitation in the Risk program provides incentives for HMO efficiency, and competition among plans improves the costs and benefits to beneficiaries. Increasing enrollment in Risk plans has the potential to result in immediate savings to Medicare by reducing the average per capita cost. While selection will probably reduce these savings somewhat, there are indications that selection is less problematic than it once was. Therefore, increasing enrollment in the Risk program, along with modifications to the payment system, could enable Medicare to realize real savings from the inherent efficiency of HMOs in the Risk program, rather than increasing its total expenditures, as in past years. However, as long as the Medicare payment system is linked to fee-for-service prices, HMOs do not need to reduce premiums, or improve their own baseline efficiency, in order to survive.

Borrowing strategies

Strategies that borrow successful innovations from the private sector, such as premium contributions benchmarked to low-cost plans, standardized benefits, and high-quality information, will yield the greatest savings. Medicare can achieve significant savings, and can actually reduce expenditures, not just growth of expenditures, by applying models of managed care that are economically rational and competitive. In a well-designed, competitive environment, there is no reason that Medicare HMOs could not save at least as much as the private sector, which saw premium reductions for many efficient benefit plans in 1994. Applied to the entire Medicare system, this would result in savings that could be applied directly to federal deficit reduction.

Approaches that can yield significant savings for Medicare are essentially similar to those in the private sector, although there are some differences. For example, the purchasing power of the federal government is far larger than any state or business coalition could imagine. On the other hand, the political problems associated with certain approaches make them less tenable in the public sector.

Several approaches are likely to result in Medicare savings.

• Benchmarking premium contributions to low-cost plans within market areas. Under one approach,

HCFA would define a benefit package that would serve as the basis for bidding among different plans. The low-cost plan would be free to beneficiaries, while higher-cost plans would require enrollees to pay the difference out-of-pocket. Since Part A premiums are currently covered in full by Medicare, the benchmark could either apply to supplemental coverage, or to the entire premium, by introducing cost-sharing into Part A.

• Developing a standard benefits package. In the case of Medicare, this requires eliminating the wide array of Medigap policies.

• Improve the quality of information on HMOs available to beneficiaries in HMOs. This will reduce selection problems and facilitate selection of health plans based on efficiency and high quality.

• Purchasing power/competitive bidding. The federal government should exploit its enormous purchasing power in both structuring competitive bid situations, and negotiating rates directly. As of this article's date, HCFA has announced its intentions to develop competitive bidding demonstration projects.

• Establish effective local program management. Because of the diversity of local markets, beneficiary populations and plans, Medicare must tailor programs to some degree and manage the programs locally. It should consider building in local monitoring and controls on risk selection, network access, and quality measures and controls. It can thus avoid the problems experienced by FEHBP and many private employers that offered numerous managed care options with little effect on costs. Because this may increase administrative costs, it should be conducted initially in markets with substantial Medicare Risk penetration where the likelihood of compensating cost savings is high.

Point-of-service options

POS options represent an increasingly popular and feasible approach to increasing managed care enrollment. POS plans have gained wide acceptance in the private market, and represent the fastest-growing segment of the managed care industry today. POS plans have grown to 15 percent of insured employees (in mid-sized and large companies) in 1994, from only 3 percent in 1991.[82] Because enrollees can go outside of the network at any time, for a price, they help to

overcome a real psychological barrier for the segment of the population that feels claustrophobic about being "locked in" to a panel of physicians. There is clearly a high demand for POS products.

The efficiency of POS plans has not been conclusively demonstrated. One study suggested that POS may be similar to HMO savings, but the findings are inconclusive.[83] Because POS plans have less control over the utilization by their enrollees, and the rates they pay to providers, they tend to be the most expensive network model in the private sector. POS premiums usually lie between conventional indemnity and HMO rates. However, in 1994, POS plans had the lowest rate of growth in premiums.[84] Furthermore, a report by Johnson and Higgins found that POS plans were the most effective of the three managed care choices, averaging $2,423 per employee in 1994, versus $3,063 and $3,062 for PPOs and HMOs, respectively.[85] (This experience, however, is not necessarily representative of the average employer.) Because POS plans typically experience adverse selection relative to HMOs, the differential cannot easily be explained by selection. On the other hand, administrative costs may also be higher for POS plans. There are yet unresolved issues surrounding POS plans regarding the fairness of placing capitated primary care physicians at risk for out-of-network use, as well as general coordination of care issues.[86]

The early experience with POS plans seems to indicate that the incidence of people going outside the network is small.[87] According to AMCRA Foundation data, out-of-network claims represented 12 percent of total medical expenses in 1993, based on 86 plans with an open-ended option that responded to the question. Out-of-network utilization occurs primarily in OB/GYN and mental health. A lower incidence of OB/GYN utilization in the Medicare population may minimize the out-of-network use problem in the Risk program.

Implementation also presents certain challenges. Premiums could be higher than in the private sector, since few plans have experience with out-of-plan use for this population. If POS and standard HMOs are both used, selection between them must be monitored and controlled. The option may be mainly attractive to "snowbirds" (who are healthier) and retiree groups—people that typically move out of the network area for extended periods. Also, to make the POS option attractive to HMOs, to consumers, and to Medicare, it will require some restructuring of the payment methodology to ensure that the premium required to cover deductibles and copayments, and the exposure faced by individual enrollees, is not higher than under current supplemental policies. Despite these concerns, the POS option represents a viable approach for Medicare and a highly desirable option for Medicare beneficiaries.

ENDNOTES

1. Group Health Association of America, 1994 Market Position Report. Washington, DC: GHAA.
2. Wilensky, G. "Incremental Health System Reform: Where Medicare Fits In." *Health Affairs* 14(1) (Spring 1995): 173–181.
3. Health Care Financing Administration, *Medicare: A Profile,* February 1995; AMCRA Foundation, *1994–95 Managed Health Care Overview;* U.S. Bureau of the Census Statistical Brief, *Health Insurance Coverage—1993.* Washington, DC.
4. AMCRA Foundation report, *Managed Care Quality: Evidence and Issues* (March 1994). Washington, DC: American Managed Care and Review Association.
5. Udvarhelyi, I., et al. "Comparison of the Quality of Ambulatory Care for Fee-for-Service and Pre-Paid Patients." *Annals of Internal Medicine* 115(5) (September, 1991): 394–400.
6. Carlisle, D., et al. "HMO Feast. Fee-for-Service Care of Older Persons with Acute Myocardial Infarction." *American Journal of Public Health* 82(12) (December, 1992): 1626–1630.
7. Retchin, S., et al. *The Quality of Care in TEFRA HMOs/CMPs.* Princeton, NJ: Mathematica Policy Research, Inc., June 15, 1992.
8. Riley G., et al. "Stage of Cancer at Diagnosis for Medicare HMO and Fee-for-Service Enrollees." *American Journal of Public Health* 84(10) (October, 1994): 1598–1604.
9. "Three Studies Show HMOs Offer Superior Care." *Business and Health* (December 1994):12.
10. "How Patients Rate Health Plans." *Business and Health* (December, 1994):16.
11. Rubin, H., et al. "Patients' Ratings of Outpatient Visits in Different Practice Settings: Results from the Medical Outcomes Study." *Journal of the American Medical Association* 270(7) (August 1993): 835–840.
12. Department of Health and Human Services (DHHS)/Office of Inspector General. *Beneficiary Perspectives of Medicare Risk HMOs.* Washington, DC: Government Printing Office, March 1995.
13. The Henry Kaiser Family Foundation, "Medicare and Managed Care," May 2, 1995.
14. Studies of selection have tended to show that HMOs have favorable selection relative to fee-for-service, although these studies have used data from the early to mid-1980s, and have been based on prior use models, which may bias HMO health risk downward. Kravitz, R., et al. "Differences in the Mix of Patients and Systems of Care: Results from the Medical Outcomes Study." *Journal of the American Medical Association* 267(12) (March 25, 1992): 1617–1623.
15. Hill, J. *Biased Selection in the TEFRA HMO/CMP Program.* Princeton, NJ: Mathematica Policy Research, Inc., 1990.
16. Fama, T., et al. "Do HMOs Care for the Chronically Ill?" *Health Affairs* 14(1) (Spring 1995): 234–243.
17. *The Effects of Managed Care and Managed Competition.* Washington, D.C.: Congressional Budget Office, February 1995.
18. Hill, J., and Brown, R. *Biased Selection in the TEFRA HMO/CMP Program: Final Report.* Princeton, NJ: Mathematica Policy Research, September 21, 1990.
19. IPA and POS enrollment together represented 48.3 percent of HMO enrollment in 1990, and 54.0 percent of enrollment just one year later. AMCRA Foundation Managed Healthcare Database. 1993–1994 and 1994–1995.
20. KPMG Peat Marwick. Health Benefits in 1994. October 1994, p. 28.
21. Xerox, for example, pegs the premium contribution to the lowest cost plan in each market. To join a more expensive plan, the employee must pay the additional premium out-of-pocket. See *The Health Reform Challenge: Employers Lead the Way.* Washington, D.C.: Washington Business Group on Health, May 1993.
22. Hill, J., et al. *The Impact of the Medicare Risk Program on the Use of Services and Costs to Medicare: Final Version.* Princeton, NJ: Mathematica Policy Research, December 3, 1992.
23. "Managed Care Cost Containment: A Review and Reassessment." AMCRA Foundation, 1993.
24. *Medicare: Changes to HMO Rate Setting Method Are Needed to Reduce Program Costs.* General Accounting Office (GAO). September 1994.
25. Porell, F., et al. *Factors Associated with Disenrollment from Medicare HMOs: Findings from a Survey of Disenrollees.* Boston, MA: Brandeis University, July 1992.
26. Health Care Financing Administration (HCFA). *Monthly Disenrollment Patterns for December 1994,* and Risk program data from the *Market Penetration Survey for January 1994.* Washington, DC: OPMCOO, February 2, 1995, and April 19, 1995.
27. HCFA. *Market Penetration Survey for January 1994* (February 2, 1995).
28. Department of Health and Human Services (DHHS). Office of Inspector General. *Beneficiary Perspectives of Medicare Risk HMOs.* Washington, DC: Government Printing Office, March 1995.
29. HCFA. *Disenrollment Rates Report for 1994.*
30. HCFA. *Disenrollment Rates Report for 1994.*
31. Long, S., et al. "Employee Premiums, Availability of Alternative Plans, and HMO Disenrollment." *Medical Care* 26(10) (October 1988): 927–938.
32. Sofaer, S., and Hurwicz, M. "When Medical Group and HMO Part Company: Disenrollment Decisions in Medicare HMOs." *Medical Care* 31(9) (1993): 808–821.
33. HCFA. *Monthly Disenrollment Patterns for December 1994.*
34. DHHS/ Office of Inspector General. *Beneficiary Perspectives.*
35. This literature was reviewed in detail in an earlier AMCRA Foundation report, *Managed Care Cost Containment: A Review and Reassessment, November 1, 1993,* and is updated here. See also Miller, R., and Luft, H. "Managed Care Plan Performance Since 1980." *Journal of the American Medical Association* 271(19) (May 18, 1994): 1512–1519.
36. Manning, W., et al. "A Controlled Trial of the Effect of a Prepaid Group Practice on Use of Services." *New England Journal of Medicine* 310 (1984): 1505–1510.
37. Greenfield, N., et al. "Variations in Resource Utilization Among Medical Specialties and Systems of Care: Results from the

Medical Outcomes Study." *Journal of the American Medical Association* 267(12) (March 25, 1992): 1624–1630.

38. Rapoport, J. "Resource Utilization Among Intensive Care Patients." *Archives of Internal Medicine* 152 (November 1992): 2207–2212.

39. Brown, R., et al. "Does Model Type Play a Role in the Extent of HMO Effectiveness in Controlling the Utilization of Services?" Princeton, NJ: Mathematica Policy Research, Inc., May 10, 1993.

40. Bradbury, R., et al. "Effect of an IPA HMO on Hospital Resource Use for Elderly Medicare Patients." *Medical Interface* 5(7) (July 1992): 20–22, 25.

41. Hill, J., et al. "The Impact of the Medicare Risk Program on the Use of Services and Cost to Medicare." Princeton, NJ: Mathematica Policy Research, Inc., December 1992.

42. Retchin, S., et al. "The Quality of Care in TEFRA HMOs/CMPs."

43. Luft, H. "Trends in Medical Care Costs: Do HMOs Lower the Rate of Growth?" *Medical Care* 18(1) (January 1980): 1–13.

44. Newhouse, et al. "Are Fee-for-Service Costs Increasing Faster than HMO's Costs?" *Medical Care* 23 (August 1985): 960–966.

45. Miller, R., and Luft, H. "Managed Care Plan Performance Since 1980."

46. *Managed Care Cost Containment: A Review and Reassessment.* AMCRA Foundation, November 1, 1993. Washington, DC: American Managed Care and Review Association.

47. Zwanziger, J., et al. "Costs and Price Competition in California Hospitals." *Health Affairs* 13(4) (Fall 1994): 118–126. HMOs would have maximum effect in competitive markets; in monopoly markets, HMOs would have limited negotiating power given the lack of ability to divert patients to competing institutions.

48. Kenkel, P. "Latest Study a Boost for 'Managed Competition.'" *Modern Healthcare* (April 13, 1992): 76. The study, using 1990 data, was based on an examination of 1.5 million patient records at 201 hospitals throughout the state.

49. *The Medicare Risk Program in Southern California: An Evaluation Using PDS Data.* Special Report Series, vol. 1, no. 1. DATIS Corporation, Fall 1994.

50. Clement, D., et al. *The Effects of Risk Contract HMO Market Penetration on Medicare Fee-for-Service Costs.* Richmond, VA: Williamson Institute for Health Studies, December 18, 1992.

51. Kertesz, L. "Managed Care Cuts Costs, Mortality-Study." *Modern Healthcare* 25(23) (June 5, 1995): 6–8.

52. GAO. *Access to Health Insurance: Public and Private Employers' Experience with Purchasing Cooperatives.* May 1994. Washington, DC: Washington Business Group on Health, 1993.

53. *The Evolution of Managed Care: A Comparative Regional Analysis.* Washington, DC: New Directions for Policy, March 25, 1994.

54. GAO, Access to Health Insurance, 1994.

55. Hurley, R., et al. *Managed Care in Medicaid: Lessons for Policy and Program Design.* Ann Arbor, MI: Health Administration Press, 1993.

56. Hill, J., et al. *The Impact of the Medicare Risk Program on the Use of Services and Costs to Medicare.* Princeton, NJ: Mathematica Policy Research, December 1992. (For unexplained reasons, this study was unique among recent studies in finding an effect from reduced admissions but not length of stay.)

57. Health Care Financing Administration, *Medicare: A Profile.* Washington, DC: February 1995.

58. Ibid.

59. Henry Kaiser Family Foundation. *Medicare and Managed Care,* May 1995.

60. *Medicare: A Profile.* Health Care Financing Administration, February 1995, Chart MC–8.

61. Congressional Budget Office memorandum. *The Effects of Managed Care and Managed Competition.* February 1995.

62. Congressional Budget Office memorandum. *The Effects of Managed Care: An Update.* March 1994. Washington, DC: Government Printing Office.

63. Personal Communication between the author and Sandra Christensen, Health and Human Services Division, the Congressional Budget Office, April 14, 1995. (Multicollinearity is a situation in which strong interrelationships between independent variables make it difficult to disentangle their separate effects on the dependent variable.)

64. Maddala, G.S., *Econometrics.* New York: McGraw-Hill, 1977.

65. AMCRA Foundation, *Medicare Cost Containment,* 1993.

66. Brown, R., et al. "Does Model Type Play a Role. . . ?"

67. Greenfield, N., et al. "Variations in Resource Utilization." As healthier employees move into HMOs, costs and premiums in the less healthy fee-for-service pool increase. By following a once common practice of pricing just below fee-for-service premiums, HMOs actually can drive total benefit costs higher than they would have been without the HMO option.

68. KPMG, *Health Benefits in 1994.*

69. *Trends in Health Insurance: HMOs Experience Lower Rates of Increase than Other Plans.* Washington, DC: KPMG Peat Marwick, December 1993. Most employer surveys are not based on representative or random samples of employers. Also some calculate premiums in unreliable ways, for example, dividing total benefit costs by active employees (rather than active and retired). Consequently, the results vary substantially. KPMG Peat Marwick's survey has greater reliability than most because it is based on a random sample of employers.

70. Austin, N. "Pacific Bell's Evolution to Managed Care." *Managed Care Quarterly* 1(4) (1993): 12–19. Inpatient days per thousand declined from around 450 in 1988 to 350 in 1992. This utilization trend partly reflects national trends, but is still significant. Unlike national trends, outpatient utilization did decline.

71. Day, K. "Putting a Realistic Price on Cost of HMO Care." *The Washington Post,* August 30, 1993, p. A1, A10.

72. Tweed, V. "Making HMOs Compete." *Business and Health* (October 1994): 27–38.

73. GAO. *Access to Health Insurance: Public and Private Employers' Experience with Purchasing Cooperatives.* May 1994; Washington Business Group on Health, 1993.

74. Ibid.

75. *The Evolution of Managed Care: A Comparative Regional Analysis.* Washington, DC: New Directions for Policy. March 25, 1994.

76. Klein, J., and Cooley, R. "Managed Competition in Minnesota." *Managed Care Quarterly* 1(4) (Autumn 1993): 58–67.

77. GAO. *Access to Health Insurance.*

78. Hurley, R., et al. *Managed Care in Medicaid: Lessons for Policy and Program Design.* Ann Arbor, MI: Health Administration Press, 1993.

79. Pallak, M.S., et al. "Medical Costs, Medicaid, and Managed Mental Health Treatment: The Hawaii Study." *Managed Care Quarterly* 2(2) (Spring 1994): 64–70.

80. McCall, N., et al. "Managed Medicaid Cost Savings: The Arizona

Experience." *Health Affairs* 13(2) (Spring 1994): 234–245.

81. Enthoven, A. "Effective Management of Competition in the FEHBP." *Health Affairs* (Fall 1989): 33–50.

82. POS plans have grown to 15 percent of insured employees (in mid-sized and large companies) in 1994, from only 3 percent in 1991. KPMG, *Health Benefits in 1994.*

83. Goetzel, R., et al. "Behind the Scenes of a POS Program." *Journal of Health Care Benefits* (March/April 1992): 33–37.

84. KPMG, *Health Benefits in 1994.*

85. Schwartz, M. "More Mid-Sized Companies Are Shifting to Managed Care." *National Underwriter* (September 5, 1993): 70.

86. Christianson, J., et al. "Open-Ended Options in Medicare Risk Contracts with HMOs." *Managed Care Quarterly* 3(1) (Winter 1995): 47–55.

87. Freudenheim, M. "H.M.O.s Offering a Choice Are Gaining in Popularity." *The New York Times,* February 7, 1994, p. D1.

Appendix 27–1

Selected Readings

AMCRA Foundation. *Managed Care Cost Containment: A Review and Reassessment*. November 1, 1993.

AMCRA Foundation. *Managed Care Quality: Evidence and Issues*. March 1994.

Department of Health and Human Services, Office of Inspector General. *Beneficiary Perspectives of Medicare Risk HMOs*. March 1995.

Fama, T., et al. "Do HMOs Care for the Chronically Ill?" *Health Affairs* 14(1) (Spring 1995): 234–243.

General Accounting Office. *Access to Health Insurance: Public and Private Employers' Experience with Purchasing Cooperatives*. May 1994.

General Accounting Office. *Medicare: Changes to HMO Rate Setting Method Are Needed to Reduce Program Costs*. September 1994.

Greenfield, N., et al. "Variations in Resource Utilization Among Medical Specialties and Systems of Care: Results from the Medical Outcomes Study." *Journal of the American Medical Association* 267(12) (March 25, 1992): 1624–1630.

Hill, J., et al. *The Impact of the Medicare Risk Program on the Use of Services and Cost to Medicare*. Princeton, NJ: Mathematica Policy Research, Inc., December 1992.

Retchin, S., et al. The Quality of Care in TEFRA HMOs/CMPs. Final version. Princeton, NJ: Mathematica Policy Research, Inc., June 15, 1992.

Riley, G., et al. "Stage of Cancer at Diagnosis for Medicare HMO and Fee-for-Service Enrollees." *American Journal of Public Health* 84(10) (October 1994): 1598–1604.

Rubin, H., et al. "Patients' Ratings of Outpatient Visits in Different Practice Settings: Results from the Medical Outcomes Study." *Journal of the American Medical Association* 270(7) (August 1993): 835–840.

28

Using Research for Successful Medicare and Medicaid Risk Marketing

Sheila Jacobs, Anne-Marie Nelson, and Steven D. Wood

Headlines about "the fastest growing market in health care" tout the profitability of Medicare and Medicaid risk products, and managed care organizations have jumped on the bandwagon. The soaring number of health maintenance organization (HMO) Medicare and Medicaid contracts and members seems to confirm this: nearly 30 percent of HMOs had contracts for one or both groups by the end of 1993, according to the Group Health Association of America. Seventy percent offered a Medicare risk product,[1] and the number of Medicare beneficiaries covered under prepaid contracts with the Health Care Financing Administration (HCFA) grew from 2 million in 1991 to 3.9 million by the end of 1995.[2] Nearly one fourth of the nation's 32 million Medicaid recipients in 42 states are enrolled in managed care programs—double the level since June 1993, reports the National Institute for Healthcare Management.

Government programs offer a significant growth and profit opportunity for managed care organizations with a quality product. However, strategic marketing of these government risk products is the challenge that accompanies the opportunity for most organizations. Early entry into new markets and aggressive participation in existing markets are essential to meet competitive pressures. And once the contract is won, the managed care organization must continually define and refine the marketing strategies and tactics in order to achieve member acquisition and retention goals. These activities are not unusual for any new venture. The difficulty lies in the uniqueness of the Medicare and Medicaid risk products themselves, the regulations and restrictions that go hand in hand with marketing them, and the specific characteristics and needs of the consumers who make up the prospective members of the risk product.

An experienced and informed team is more likely to develop valid data, assumptions, and strategies that will achieve defined goals. This team of marketing, sales, and research personnel should be backed by resource staff with clinical understanding of the target markets. The task of the team is to gather sufficient data to understand the current situation, learn the needs and perceptions of the target markets as well as the providers and staff who will serve them, review membership and revenue objectives for each Medicare or Medicaid product, assess the competition, and develop and continually adjust marketing plans.

While there are similarities between Medicare and Medicaid risk contracts, each has unique research requirements as well as specific regulatory issues that affect development and implementation of a marketing plan. This article looks at each government program individually.

Understanding Medicare

Medicare has been in existence for nearly 30 years. According to the U.S. Department of Health and Human Services:

- Medicare is the world's largest health insurance program and by many measures one of the most successful.
- It began in 1966 as a federal health insurance program for the elderly, and was expanded in 1972 to cover individuals with disabilities and those with end stage renal disease (ESRD).
- It was established because these vulnerable populations had difficulty obtaining private health insurance coverage.
- In 1994, Medicare served almost 36 million persons: 32 million aged beneficiaries, 3.6 million persons with disabilities, and 77,000 with ESRD.

Managed Care Quarterly 1996; 4(4): 30–38
© 1996 Aspen Publishers, Inc.

249

- It is the single largest payer of older persons' health care expenses, accounting for 45 percent of all spending on seniors.
- Relatively few Medicare beneficiaries can be considered financially well off. In 1992, about 83 percent of program spending was for beneficiaries with incomes below $25,000, and more than 60 percent was for those with incomes below $15,000.
- Currently, 20 percent of beneficiaries are seniors 85 and older, most of whom are women or individuals with disabilities, including ESRD.
- Per capita health care spending for aged beneficiaries is four times the average for the under-65 population.
- Medicare beneficiaries express a high degree of satisfaction with the program.

In 1995, the U.S. Department of Health and Human Services committed to extending the managed care choices available so that beneficiaries would have the full range of managed care options, similar to those available to the general insured population. The cornerstone of the government's Medicare policy is informed choice in a fair marketplace, in which beneficiaries have full and objective information and are not discriminated against on the basis of relative need. Today, any discussion of measures to enhance the cost effectiveness as well as the accessibility of quality medical care for Medicare beneficiaries must include a discussion of managed care.

Managed care is not a new concept for the Medicare program. Since its inception in 1966, a portion of Medicare beneficiaries has received care through managed care arrangements. However, 1995 saw impressive growth in Medicare managed care, as the number of Medicare beneficiaries enrolled in HMOs grew 20 percent over the previous year, to 3.9 million. Continued strong growth is anticipated as familiarity with managed care expands through strong word of mouth among seniors and new 65-year-old beneficiaries moving from commercial HMOs to Medicare. The number of managed care plans offering Medicare HMO products will also affect future enrollment growth, for as Medicare HMOs proliferate, they will become more accepted among Medicare beneficiaries. In 1995, the number of plans offering a Medicare managed care product increased by 12 percent, for a total of 276 products in 31 states.[3] Many of these new contracts are in regions that traditionally have not had a strong Medicare managed care presence, such as Columbus, Ohio, and St. Louis, Missouri.

Medicare HMO enrollees approach or top 50 percent in some areas of the United States. In Mesa, Colorado, Columbia, Oregon, and Carver, Minnesota, 41 percent of Medicare recipients are in managed care programs, while 50 percent are covered by HMOs in Multnomah County and Clackamas County, Oregon and in Riverside and San Bernardino, California.[4]

Overall plan enrollment is growing as well. In mid-1996, PacifiCare reported 398,953 participants in its Secure Horizons HMO; FHP International had 331,823 Senior Care members; Kaiser Permanente's Senior Advantage had 425,507 enrollees; and the small but mighty Oxford Health Plan had 110,012 Medicare Advantage participants in three eastern states.[5] Health plans that are most successful with their HMO Medicare product learn quickly that success demands rapid growth to reach critical mass. A 1994 Mathematica Policy Research Inc. study found that a minimum of 20,000 enrollees is necessary for economic efficiency. Mathematica also found that at least 10 to 15 percent of an HMO's total membership should consist of Medicare risk members, to ensure adequate resources and attention to procedures and cost controls.

Research Reveals Biggest Concern of Seniors

Health plans intent on success in government risk programs should conduct research to learn the medical needs of the seniors in the geographic area they serve, as well as their psychographic and demographic characteristics. They should talk to seniors individually and in focus groups to learn how the 65-plus market views managed care in general, competitor plans, and to learn which benefits are most important to them and why they stay with or depart from a plan. One of the first things these HMOs are likely to learn is that the biggest concern of seniors—and the primary reason they may avoid an HMO, no matter how appealing its benefits and monthly premium—is the fear they will not be able to remain with the physician they have trusted for years. Another deterrent: seniors who have retirement insurance usually cannot go back once they switch to a

Medicare HMO plan. They would rather stay than switch, even if the new plan seems far better.

Managed care organizations that are successful in Medicare risk product marketing realize that it requires sales and communication techniques much different than those used to reach the blue-collar worker, the white-collar professional, baby-boomers, or any other market niche. A 1995 study for the Kaiser Family Foundation found that Medicare HMO members are generally satisfied with the quality of care and lower out-of-pocket costs. A quality product coupled with superior marketing encourages seniors to enthusiastically convey their satisfaction to their friends, for this is the most persuasive marketing the plan can get.

FHP International (recently acquired by PacifiCare) is the largest and oldest health plan in the Arizona Medicare managed care market, with 87,555 Medicare HMO members. The company did not reach its market size by accident. FHP never stops analyzing its product and measuring member service satisfaction and perceptions. The difference between FHP and other health plans is in FHP's study methodologies and its use of the data. FHP's director of marketing, Sandy Karkos, expands the tried and true market research methods (patient satisfaction surveys, focus groups, and the like) to gain critical market and competitive data with out-of-the-box approaches. One of these innovative market studies for which FHP engaged The HSM Group led to findings about the impact of provider quality and location, promotional strategies and plan benefits, and competitor offerings. The variety of ongoing research FHP engages in ensures consistent and accurate understanding of senior wants and needs, competitor activities, acquisition costs, and enrollment and disenrollment incentives.

Results from FHP's 1995 focus groups with seniors led to development of a Medicare-risk product offering self-referred chiropractic care among other benefits. The menu of benefits as well as the premium amount were arrived at through regression analysis of the focus group "wish list" of benefits and values they assigned to them. An investigation of the range of charges for Medicare supplement premiums confirmed that a zero-premium product would be regarded by Arizona's seniors with suspicion, even though zero premium options are the most appealing to seniors in other geographic areas.

FHP gathers unique competitor intelligence by monitoring all available state and federal agency reports, research, documents, and data. The data are categorized and charted in trend lines. FHP marketing and operations staff use the knowledge they gather about the success of competitor products, premiums, and benefits to plan and adjust their own. One-on-one research is also highly regarded. Marketing department staff are encouraged to ride along with FHP's Medicare sales personnel on visits to seniors to gain a real-life understanding of the market they serve. "You learn more when you sit across the table from your customers and listen to them tell you why they like their doctor than you can from reading a stack of reports," according to FHP's president Steve Lindstrom.

Innovative research is the norm for FHP's marketing department, but traditional research is not forgotten. The HSM Group conducts periodic disenrollment surveys and patient satisfaction studies for FHP. The data as well as recommendations for improvement are given to each FHP provider and clinic location. According to Marketing Director Karkos, "Research is not merely for management information, but for management action." She believes strongly in "doing the right research," then sharing results across a wide audience. Patient satisfaction survey results go to every FHP department; in addition, they are distributed in a computer file accessible to all employees in the region. Employee response to this open sharing of survey results, especially from front-line staff, has been extremely favorable.

Satisfaction survey summaries are sent to FHP members as well. There is a threefold benefit: the intended one of reinforcing for members the wisdom of choosing FHP as their Medicare HMO; and the more subtle benefit of encouraging positive performance by providers and employees, who know that members will not only rate them, but also eventually see the aggregate results. In addition, very favorable survey outcomes give FHP members "bragging rights" to friends, thus increasing referral potential. A colorful card boasting of FHP's high satisfaction rating was mailed to its senior members in late 1995, encouraging them to refer friends. The card generated significant leads, and while the conversion rate was high, the idea will be modified for future marketing efforts. "Our goal is to turn a cost center (research) into a potential profit center," Karkos said.

She encourages marketers to think creatively in seeking data for the Medicare and Medicaid risk market, and to be equally creative in sharing and using the data. Measuring every aspect is important too. "FHP has been able to develop new products and benefits that no one else offers. They are a direct result of using a variety of traditional and unstructured research techniques," she said. "We obtain information that wouldn't be available otherwise at much lower cost."

Another Potential Entrant in a Highly Penetrated Market

Blue Cross and Blue Shield of Arizona, the largest health insurer in Arizona, entered the Medicare risk market in 1995. Arizona is one of the most HMO-penetrated markets in the country, and there are numerous competitors with similar products. So when Blue Cross and Blue Shield decided to create a risk product, market research was considered essential to find the right niche for the organization. The survey size and sampling techniques were constructed to yield findings that could be generalized to the overall older population in Arizona.

Blue Cross and Blue Shield considers telephone surveys an excellent way to obtain valuable information about the mature market's needs and concerns. Its marketing vice president believes the costs are minimal in relation to the volume of useful and reliable data received.

While primary research is vital to localize characteristics to each market segment or geographic area, it is also wise to take advantage of secondary and syndicated research, from which a wealth of information can be extracted. Studies are published by government agencies such as HCFA, trade and professional organizations, academic institutions, marketing research firms, and senior organizations.

Setting Objectives

Entrants to the Medicare HMO field should adapt comprehensive objectives in developing and marketing their risk product. The following objectives can serve as a guide:
- Determine the market potential of the prospective Medicare HMO product.
- Describe the needs of the specific geographic market being targeted.
- Establish the most important benefits to include in the Medicare HMO product.
- Evaluate the product in relation to competitor products.
- Develop meaningful "value-added" elements not covered by Medicare to separate the product from others in the marketplace. One study by HSM found that prescription coverage and annual physicals were of greatest importance to the 65-plus group in the Arizona market.
- Test the product for benefit value and price sensitivity.

When objectives have been met, continued growth results from analyzing and refining the product continually; listening to members, providers, and staff; learning from research; and revising objectives and strategies as research outcomes dictate. Continuous review of the product, providers, and plan members is critical, not only for statistical evidence, but also to document quality. The HCFA and the Health and Human Services Office of the Inspector General (IG) regularly monitor health plans to ensure that Medicare HMO services are on a par with commercial services. The IG focus for 1995 included scrutiny of ratios of specialists to primary care physicians and waiting times for physician appointments, and reviews of Medicare beneficiary grievance procedures and HMO financial safeguards.

CIGNA Enters the Field

CIGNA HealthCare of Arizona, a recent entrant to the government programs field, is the oldest and largest HMO in Arizona, with one in every nine Arizonans as a member. Like FHP and Blue Cross and Blue Shield, CIGNA learned that marketplace numbers do not tell the whole story. For example:
- The 325,000 individuals who make up the 65-plus population of Maricopa County in Arizona may yield as few as 70,000 net eligibles when seniors who have employer retirement health plans, the working aged, and other categories are eliminated.
- Nearly 44 percent of the residents of Sun City and Sun City West, large retirement communities in Maricopa county, have retirement health plans.

These seniors are highly adverse to switching, because traditionally employers pay all or most of the cost of the benefit.

However, this is changing. One third of companies offering health care benefits increased premiums or copays for retirees in 1992 and 1993. H. J. Heinz Co. told retirees in 1994 that from then on, all nonunion and salaried employees would have to pay 20 percent of the cost of coverage, with their share rising to 100 percent in 1998.[6] Despite increasing employer efforts to shift upward the retiree's portion of the cost of retirement health care, many health plans have found that converting these seniors to Medicare risk products is fruitless. Thus many HMOs put this group last (or not at all) on their list of target markets.

When CIGNA HealthCare of Arizona ventured into the Medicare risk market in 1993, its goal was to convert 14,000 Medicare members from the cost contract through which CIGNA was a subcontracted provider to CIGNA's new Medicare risk product. To gain a realistic view of the mature market in Arizona, CIGNA conducted an extensive series of original studies to learn the following information: purchasing habits, media use, health status and utilization, demographic characteristics and brand perceptions, and historical events of the 1920s to 1940s that influence seniors' attitudes and beliefs today.

Patient Questionnaires Improve Care Quality

Original, market-specific research such as this yields critical marketing and clinical data that can be used to improve care and member satisfaction and retention. Sentara Health System in Norfolk, Virginia, mails health status questionnaires to all of its Medicare HMO enrollees, then sends the information to the member's physician as advance notice of health problems to be addressed proactively. Friendly Hills Health Care Network in La Habra, California, uses patient assessment information from the HMOs it contracts with to identify high-risk patients who need special attention to maintain their health.

CIGNA's intensive effort using original qualitative and quantitative research to understand the market potential and the values, concerns, and needs of prospective Medicare risk members yielded results. CIGNA converted 100 percent of its 14,000 Medicare

cost contract members and became the Medicare risk provider in the Phoenix market.

Sophisticated Seniors Need On-target Message

As seniors become more familiar with Medicare risk plans—the benefits and services they offer (or do not offer), the advantages and restrictions—the promotional message must change to reflect this customer's increasing sophistication. Seniors in mature HMO markets already understand the concept of HMOs. They are much more serious today than they were even six months ago about comparing the pros and cons of individual plans. Some of these 65-plus customers speak the managed care lingo as well as the marketing representatives trying to sell their product to them. As a result, managed care plans need to hone their message to define their product and emphasize the advantages of their product over other Medicare risk HMOs in their market. Since most plans look alike in their fundamental offerings, the most effective messages call attention to the size and geographic scope of the provider network and the quality of physicians in the network.

At the same time, it is important *not* to assume that a message or positioning tactic that worked in Kalamazoo, Michigan, will be equally effective in Kerrville, Texas. The HSM Group's research and experience have proven that local health care markets are just that—local and unique. It is critical to know the customer's expectations and concerns before creating a "me-too" message for it, yet across the United States, this is one of the biggest failings of managed care plans promoting their Medicare risk products.

Retention Drives Profitability

The second biggest failing of managed care plans, HSM's research has found, is failure to develop strategies to make senior customers *loyal* customers who stay with the HMO for an extended period and encourage their friends to join them. With Medicare risk plans in particular, retention drives profitability. Retention should be a significant component of the acquisition strategy, built in from the beginning rather than hurriedly tacked on when senior members begin to drift away. While enticing seniors to enroll in a Medicare HMO is certainly a critical concern of managed care organizations, keeping the seniors in the plan over time may be even more important.

To understand why retention is so important, one need only consider the high cost of attracting seniors. Advertising, public relations, sales, and administrative costs for signing up the average enrollee can amount to $500 to $600 (and as much as $1,000 in some high-cost, very competitive markets). Given that profits do not flow in until the senior has been with the HMO for a significant period of time, and that seniors can switch from one Medicare risk plan to another every 30 days, this creates an enormous challenge for the organization.

Ensuring that seniors are satisfied with the HMO is no longer enough. Satisfied consumers leave plans all the time. It is more important to seek out and learn from the *dissatisfied* patients. Dissatisfied customers reveal what is wrong, and therefore what needs to be fixed. Managed care organizations with Medicare risk plans must understand what seniors want from a plan, why they choose their particular HMO, what causes them to disenroll (or think about leaving), and what changes would encourage them to stay. Ideally, this information is gathered and then acted on through ongoing and distinct research with current members and disenrollees.

AHCCCS: Reaching Out to the Indigent Population

As of December 1995, 48 states had been approved or had approval pending to establish at least one Medicaid managed care organization. The number of Medicaid participants in managed care programs has steadily climbed, from 2.7 million, or 9.5 percent in 1991, to 7.8 million, or 23.2 percent in 1994.[7] Tennessee has the highest number of Medicaid HMO enrollees with 458,812 participants, but every state is pushing hard for privatization of the welfare health care system.[8] Economics is the driving force leading HCFA to encourage states to pursue this trend: state and federal governments spent $125.8 billion on aid to the indigent in 1993, up from $69 billion in 1990, and expenditures were projected to soar to $137.5 billion in 1994. Projected 1995 Medicaid expenditures were $148 billion.[9] By the year 2000, federal payments alone for Medicaid are expected to total $133 billion— more than the combined total budgets of the Departments of Agriculture, Commerce, Education, Energy,

Interior, Justice, and State. And, unless policies change radically, nearly one third of that Medicaid budget will be spent on long-term care.

In 1982, Arizona became the last state to establish a Medicaid program. It examined the experience of other states and chose to create a very different system based entirely on prepaid managed care. In effect, the Arizona Health Care Cost Containment System (AHCCCS) works like a giant HMO that is capitated by the federal government. In turn, AHCCCS capitates various health plans to deliver services to the entire eligible population of about 460,000 around the state. The result has been an overall savings of 7 percent over the estimated cost of a fee-for-service Medicaid program like that in other states, and improved access and quality of care for recipients.

A 1993 RAND Corporation study gave the Arizona program high marks, and this encouraged other states to step into the Medicaid capitation pool. The comment has been made that if Medicaid were invented today, it would probably look a lot like AHCCCS.

While AHCCCS has in general achieved its financial and medical care objectives (although not without some struggle), AHCCCS provider organizations such as Phoenix Health Plan (PHP) have discovered that participation in the program is not an easy ride. PHP found that comprehensive market research is a critical resource in developing marketing and educational programs that avoid misconceptions and stereotypes about the Medicaid population. Since beneficiaries are a culturally diverse group, physicians can be a primary source of information during reenrollment or open enrollment as long as they are knowledgeable about this population and attuned to their cultural needs.

Physicians and staff often need to be educated about being sensitive to issues that have broad impact on medical treatment and outcome. For example, ethnic, cultural, and socioeconomic factors can inhibit patients from disclosing their symptoms or make them less aware of the benefits of treatments considered standard in the Anglo culture. Ethnic or cultural influences can make patients less compliant due to doubts about the benefits of a medication regimen, or more likely to miss appointments because of a different perspective of the time than clock-conscious North Americans.

The Medicaid population covers a wide spectrum. The AHCCCS market in Arizona consists of the following categories: Aid to Families with Dependent

Children (AFDC), 49 percent; Supplemental Security Income (SSI), 16 percent; the medically indigent and medically needy (MI/MN), 7 percent; Eligible Assistance Children (EAC) and Eligible Low Income Children (ELIC), 26 percent; and women who qualify for other reasons, 2 percent.

The target audience consists of eligible children plus adults age 18 to 54, many (but not all) of whom live in low-income households and may have only a high school education or less. Seventy percent of this group are women (many of them single parents) with children. A secondary target is the medically needy—those disabled by an injury or disease and unable to work, thus qualifying for assistance from AHCCCS.

Strict Rules and Regulations

Managed care organizations investigating this market quickly learn that each state imposes its own restrictions, requirements, and regulations, some of them extremely stringent, on marketing and sales efforts of HMOs seeking to reach prospective enrollees. They also discover that the characteristics of the lower income population limit the use or effectiveness of marketing strategies traditionally used with commercial groups. Example: no telephone numbers are listed for many in this group. The reason is simple: many have no phone. Lists of AHCCCS eligibles often have a high address error rate. Frequent moves and job changes result in relatively short eligibility spans and constant turnover of this highly mobile population.

The literacy rate for the indigent population is lower than for commercial members, and a relatively high number speak little or no English or speak English as a second rather than a primary language in the home. Because of the high number of English-as-a-second language AHCCCS eligibles, Arizona regulations require that all AHCCCS educational or marketing materials be in English and Spanish.

Because of these challenges, working with state regulatory officials in a coordinated manner for marketing and clinical outreach was the most effective way to implement activities without facing regulatory roadblocks. For example, state regulations prohibit giving "incentives" to AHCCCS members or prospects. But working with state officials allowed the PHP to develop a program to increase prenatal visits by pregnant women by providing them with a free infant car seat if they completed a certain number of visits as certified by their obstetrician. "Working with the state allowed us to offer wellness-related incentives," according to the health plan's vice president.

PHP has a very strong emphasis on quality, as proven by its recent accreditation by the National Committee for Quality Assurance. PHP is the first HMO in Arizona and the first Medicaid HMO in the United States to receive this recognition. Activities such as credentialing of physicians, annual surveys of members and physicians, tracking of 17 different quality indicators by a committee of physicians and administrators, and medical record audits to ensure that preventive and primary care services are not underutilized are all steps in the plan's total quality management process.

These activities not only improve medical care, but also help attract providers to the PHP network. Providers play an important role in marketing a Medicaid HMO. It is important to physicians to understand the plan's philosophy of care so that they will be proponents to their patients. Providers who are aligned with the HMO's philosophy are more likely to allow enrollment brochures and information to be distributed in their offices; this helps during open enrollment periods where every communication opportunity is important.

PHP and other AHCCCS HMOs in Arizona learned that the single most effective method for letting prospective members know what their plan has to offer is to reach out to them in their community with face-to-face group educational programs. Presentations for churches, community action groups, school nurses, and Head Start programs are highly effective. Working closely with the Women, Infants, and Children (WIC) program and Planned Parenthood and other social service agencies and participation in or sponsorship of health fairs and community outreach events are important ways to reach this audience.

A successful AHCCCS marketing strategy requires awareness and acceptance of the target group by commercial members. Focus groups with plan members can help to surface the perceptions, stereotypes, and beliefs of the commercial customer toward the indigent population as well as attitudes toward a plan's efforts to solicit this group. The results can help in forming the marketing strategy and positioning of the HMO for prospective Medicaid members as well as commercial members.

Word-of-Mouth Advertising

Like the Medicaid population, the AHCCCS market is culturally diverse, consisting of Latinos, African-Americans, Anglos, and Asians. They have close ties to their community and are likely to listen to and heed their neighbors' experiences and recommendations. Although unpredictable and unmanageable, word of mouth is the most successful form of advertising.

The target for advertising a Medicaid HMO typically is the female head of the family, who makes health care decisions in almost all cases, whether indigent or wealthy. No matter what their economic status, these individuals want to be treated with the same empathy and skill as anyone else. The drawback is that they may not be medically knowledgeable or highly educated. Because of this and a lower literacy rate, Arizona requires that all marketing and educational materials be written at the fourth grade level. Television advertising is not permitted in Arizona, although radio and outdoor media are approved. Direct mail is allowed but has limitations because of the tendency of the target group to change addresses often (30 percent of mail is returned as undeliverable). Bus shelters and bus cards as well as posters in areas frequented by this population are effective.

PHP, which currently has 22,000 members, has found that besides community outreach activities such as health fairs, telemarketing, and mailing of enrollment materials or a member newsletter can generate new members or reenrollees. Telemarketing and mail can be a challenge because telephone numbers and addresses are likely to have changed or be difficult to find, but if the plan can work through these barriers, these forms of contact get results in an enrollment campaign.

Lessons and Learnings

The philosophy for health plans trying to communicate about their Medicaid managed care product should be to market at the grass roots level. A managed Medicaid plan must become a good neighbor, meeting people face to face, using culturally appropriate messages in all communications, and emphasizing community education. Becoming involved in the community the plan serves and matching its needs are crucial success steps. Outreach coordinators should go to the neighborhoods, to the welfare offices, and to the churches to meet the people.

Advertising follows the same philosophy, targeting precisely the population the plan serves. Radio and outdoor media focus on specific communities. Advertising is always backed with aggressive community outreach efforts. Health education seminars and screenings should be held at schools, churches, and public housing projects.

Demand management is becoming increasingly important to the profitability of a managed care organization involved in government contracts, especially as reductions in capitation are being discussed at the federal level. A demand management effort serves member needs well, and is absolutely essential in serving the Medicaid population. With a well-designed program, members learn to understand and deal with chronic medical conditions as well as acute problems in ways that minimize problem flare-ups, reduce emergency visits and calls, and promote healthier living. And, as PHP's experience demonstrates, demand management for Medicaid HMO members may be as much a question of too little use of routine or preventive care services, or inappropriate use of emergency facilities, as it is overuse. PHP addresses these issues with an integrated health care delivery system involving ambulatory centers, providers, and Phoenix Memorial Hospital; active case management; and by using a multidepartmental approach to identify and educate patients who use the emergency department rather than its after-hours urgent care.

Managed care organizations (MCOs) would be wise to seek a partnership or strategic alliance for developing programs for member satisfaction, demand management, and clinical outcomes improvement and evaluation. Pharmaceutical firms are eager to ally with MCOs in these areas, and the pharmaceutical firms can bring resources, technology, and research that may not be available to or affordable by the MCO. For example, Searle announced in late 1994 that it would spend $30 million to $50 million over the next three to five years to help MCOs improve care and services to older members in Medicare risk contracts. Searle is a sponsor of the Alliance for Healthy Aging, a group of 55 MCOs banded together to provide educational forums, consultation, and patient education materials to seniors.

Monitoring Success

Member satisfaction surveys are as routine for most health care providers today as patient charts and billing procedures. But for health plans offering Medicare or Medicaid products, they are a "risk prevention" strategy. Regular evaluation of member satisfaction can reveal potential or actual problems while they are small and manageable rather than pervasive and impossible to correct. However, if the member satisfaction survey is not accompanied by a "service recovery" strategy, asking members for their opinions will accomplish little except to raise expectations.

Member retention strategies are absolutely critical for managed care organizations, regardless of the lines of business. With Medicare in particular, seniors are free to disenroll and join another HMO provider each month. Therefore, understanding the satisfiers and dissatisfiers is as important as learning why they leave. Focus group research, ongoing member surveys, periodic review of the database to create senior member profiles, and encouraging physicians and staff to report comments and suggestions from senior members are all methods that can be used to gather information regarding services and features important to Medicare members.

To some people, surveys of members who have voluntarily left a health plan (as opposed to those who switch because they moved or their employer changed plans) might be considered similar to closing the barn door after the horses gallop away. However, disenrollment surveys provide valuable information that can shape retention strategies, improve member satisfaction, and prevent future disenrollment.

Disenrollment studies and focus groups provide invaluable information on the importance of new member orientation. Orientation sessions can help ensure better understanding by members of how to use the system, and can correct any unrealistic expectations created by overexuberant testimonials from friends, or inaccurate interpretation of benefits by new members. Admittedly, orientation can be a difficult task for some groups, especially Medicaid. Their first contact with the system is usually to schedule an appointment for an acute or chronic problem. Thus orientation may need to occur during that first visit.

•   •   •

There are many lessons to be learned from the experience of marketing government HMO products. But one lesson clearly predominates: Nothing is as important as collecting *and using* highly detailed and intelligent data. Comprehensive, insightful research that is interpreted by knowledgeable experts permits astute decisions and logical strategies. It guides marketers and advertisers as they chart a course in marketing communication and new product development for managed care organizations.

REFERENCES

1. Cerne, F. "Rehabbing Medicare: Is Managed Care a Cure-All or Just a Crutch?" *Hospitals & Health Networks* 69(8) (April 20, 1995): 22.
2. Suber, R. "ABC$ of Medicare HMOs." *Managed Care & Aging* 3(2) (Summer 1996): 3.
3. Ibid.
4. Anders, A., and McGinley, L. "Managed Eldercare, HMOs Are Signing Up New Class of Member: The Group in Medicare." *The Wall Street Journal* 225 (82) (April 27, 1995): A1, A8.
5. HCFA. *Monthly Report: Medicare Managed Care Plans.* Baltimore, MD: Health Care Financing Administration Office of Managed Care, August 1996.
6. Miller, J. "Managed Care Lowers Retiree Benefits Costs." *Managed Healthcare* (March 1995): 40.
7. "Managing Medicaid." *American Medical News* (December 19, 1994): 11–14.
8. "Medicaid Managed Care Enrollees Up 60% in 1994." *Managed Care Outlook* 7(243) (October 7, 1994): 2.
9. *Monthly Report Medicare Managed Care Plans.*

29

A Medicaid Mental Health Carve-Out Program: The Massachusetts Experience

Christopher W. Counihan, Deborah Nelson, and Elizabeth Pattullo

In the late 1980s and early 1990s the Medicaid program in Massachusetts had become derisively referred to as a "budget buster" expense item that state government officials of both Democratic and Republican administrations found difficult to control. These rising costs were fueled by the rate of inflation in health care and the unlimited and unmanaged benefit of the Medicaid program.

Several factors contributed to rising costs. First, payments for Medicaid reimbursable services were negotiated on a fee-for-service basis. These rates, established by an independent state agency, reflected that organization's policies of cost accounting principles that governed most of the hospitals and clinics that delivered mental health care to Medicaid recipients. "Class rates" were eventually established for the outpatient services provided by community mental health centers, and only minimal utilization review was conducted for inpatient and outpatient care. Moreover, the rate-setting process for hospital-based services was conducted separately for each provider, and hospital administrators identified inpatient mental health care as one of the primary means of increasing hospital revenue. Sophisticated lawyers and accountants who were hired by hospitals to negotiate these rates easily dominated the state regulators, who did not have the resources to match these experts.

A second, and perhaps most disturbing, factor was the lack of available data. Government public policy managers had few answers when asked what services the state was buying with its Medicaid dollars and what quality indicators, if any, were being measured. In short, little accountability existed for a growing public sector program for some of the state's neediest residents.

Managed Care Quarterly 1996; 4(3): 85–92

Third, Medicaid recipients' access to inpatient mental health care was uneven. Hospitals had sole discretion over admissions; difficult clients could be denied admission at one after another private hospital and ultimately sent to state-funded community mental health centers and hospitals. A few hospitals marketed their programs to attract a high volume of Medicaid recipients. While access was high for most recipients, attention to quality was often lacking. These hospitals were criticized for overmedicating unruly recipients, discharging the homeless to shelters, and letting others leave despite active symptoms. These hospitals became known as "Medicaid mills."

A fourth factor for rising Medicaid costs was the reduction in federal funding under the Community Mental Health Center Act. These funds, administered by the Massachusetts Department of Mental Health (DMH), covered acute inpatient and outpatient mental health services for uninsured residents, intermediate and long-term hospital care, and rehabilitation services for residents of the state with a major mental illness. DMH sought to make up for federal reductions by directing its case managers to enroll uninsured individuals into Medicaid and requiring its emergency screening teams to refer any clients in need of acute care who had insurance to be treated at private hospitals so that use of state-funded facilities could be reduced.

Finally, many private insurance companies had begun to experiment with firms that specialized in capitated risk-based mental health "carve-outs." These firms were paid a flat fee on a per-member per-month basis and in turn agreed to manage the mental health benefit with an incentive to earn a profit if they spent less than their flat fee. The management involved a review of level of care decisions made by providers. However, "managed care" was not universally accepted by providers, researchers, or advocates. In fact, it was labeled as "managing cost, not care," and several respected authors raised very fundamental questions about the ability of managed care organizations to accomplish cost savings without reducing quality and access.[1,2]

Choosing Managed Mental Health

In 1990 the Medicaid director at that time, Bruce Bullen, proposed applying private sector managed care to the Medicaid program to resolve these issues. With support from the governor and human services policy makers, Bullen applied for and eventually obtained a Section 1915 demonstration waiver from the Health Care Financing Administration (HCFA) to implement a Medicaid mental health managed care program.

After the review process, Mental Health Management of America (MHMA), a small Nashville, Tennessee–based company, was selected as the contracting managed care organization. The firm had experience in utilization review for state Medicaid departments. The company's founder, the late Richard Sivley, had been the commissioner of mental health in Tennessee.

Under the terms of the mental health carve-out contract between MHMA and Medicaid, a "cap" was established for the benefit that was paid out to MHMA on a per-member per-month basis. If the cost of services exceeded the cap, the contractor was obligated to pay eight cents on each dollar spent above the cap up to a maximum risk of $2 million. Savings generated below the cap accrued to the contractor along the same formula.

This capitated managed care program was the first example of a statewide capitation for mental health and substance abuse services applied to a Medicaid population. Still, MHMA faced numerous challenges during the program's development:

- Establishing clinical protocols that met the needs of a population more chronically ill than populations previously served by managed care.
- Managing the cost without limiting the benefit or shifting it to a delivery system run by the state.
- Improving access and quality for the individual without increasing cost.
- Developing a network of services that could provide quality and access at a reasonable price.
- Implementing managed care in partnership with other state agencies that provided vital services for many of the Medicaid recipients.

- Building support among individuals and potential partners who were skeptical about the viability of the project serving such a vulnerable population.
- Measuring and improving the processes and outcomes of service delivery so that the Division of Medical Assistance and the public could be satisfied with quality, access, and outcomes of the program.

From the beginning, MHMA and Medicaid made clear that managing costs by reducing or limiting benefits would not be acceptable. As a result, a utilization review (UR) process was created and communicated to all MHMA staff and network providers; all UR decisions would be based solely on clinical appropriateness. Inpatient providers would be required to initiate active and timely discharge plans from the time of admission, while at the same time payment would only be denied for clinical reasons. This combination of a drive for aggressive discharge planning and a strict adherence to clinical levels of care was designed to ensure that patients received necessary, but not excessive, inpatient care.

MHMA clinical managers and mental health experts convened and developed an extensive provider manual clearly spelling out these principles as well as the level of care criteria that would guide the managed care contractor and their providers in making clinical decisions. Two strongly emphasized themes were that chronic mental illness required ongoing treatment and that recipient benefits would not be arbitrarily capped.

Provider contracts also required that access to health care services be direct, open, timely, and universal for Medicaid recipients. This provision assured that individuals would have the same type of access to any private hospital as recipients of private insurance policies, a situation that many managed care critics often noted was lacking.

To prevent cost shifting to the public sector, which historically occurred when private benefits ran out, MHMA developed a working agreement with the Massachusetts DMH that addressed two principles: (1) clinical criteria govern the responsibilities of each entity and (2) lines of direct communication among MHMA, Medicaid, and DMH were to be created at all levels. An interagency agreement addressed continuity of care: MHMA agreed to provide the acute mental health services, including inpatient, outpatient, and other alternative services; DMH agreed to provide intermediate and long-term inpatient care and rehabilitative services for DMH clients whose mental health benefits were managed by MHMA.

Clinical protocols were then developed to ensure that acute care patients could be easily transferred from the MHMA network hospitals into intermediate care facilities run by DMH. These protocols established clinical care criteria, pathways to evaluation, review and decision making, and avenues for higher level appeal, all steps created to further the goal of continuity of care between MHMA and DMH.

Creating the Network

MHMA adopted three strategies for a timely and cost-effective development of a service network. The first strategy was to make provider contracting an open and competitive bidding process for inpatient care. The provider network would be limited to hospitals that could meet service needs in terms of quality and cost, reflecting the view that not all of the 76 hospitals licensed to provide inpatient mental health care were equally capable of providing high-quality care, nor were all necessary to meet the network's capacity needs. Moreover, this competitive process would allow MHMA to be an aggressive purchaser that could bargain with providers based on quality and price.

Network management staff sought input from inpatient providers in designing the network application and selection criteria. Staff also visited applicant hospitals, reviewed sample records, and checked the hospital's track record with the chronically mentally ill.

The second contracting decision was to develop alternative and diversionary levels of care that had not been previously available to Medicaid recipients:

- mental health acute residential treatment programs for children and adolescents
- acute residential programs for substance abusers, including people with chronic mental illness and substance abuse
- crisis stabilization programs
- extended assessment observation and holding beds
- partial hospitalization
- intensive clinical management and community support programs.

The third contracting decision was to allow all existing outpatient providers to become part of the network without a competitive bid process, in contrast with the inpatient process. This decision was made due to the recognition that the community mental health centers had a long and credible history of serving many of the uninsured and poor chronically mentally ill. Community providers had become skilled in the important art of linking these individuals to rehabilitative and support services, working with them in a variety of crises, and being accessible to violent, noncompliant, and high-risk cases. Including all of the community health centers in the early years of the program would help promote access to the least restrictive level of care and maintain continuity of care by keeping patients with their same providers, avoiding confusion and chaos.

Network management staff with experience in mental health services in Massachusetts were recruited. These individuals brought a great degree of credibility to MHMA, as an out-of-state managed care organization. Key managers with experience serving Medicaid recipients with chronic mental illness were also recruited. They included community mental health center providers; administrators from state departments of mental health, social services, and youth services; and community advocates, who were somewhat skeptical of applying managed care principles to the Medicaid population.

Addressing Barriers

Several factors posed potential barriers to successful implementation of the managed mental health and substance abuse program in Massachusetts. First, private managed care organizations had a negative reputation. They were seen as single-mindedly focusing on reduced rates of admission and shorter lengths of stay that would reduce costs but also neglect quality. Second, difficult-to-treat clients were often discharged quickly into the community with no discharge planning and readmitted within days, often to another hospital, and thus "bounced around" the mental health system. Third, managed care clients who were ready to leave the hospital generally languished as inpatients because community or long-term inpatient resources were not readily available. Finally, lack of service and cost data left administrators with no means of tracking quality, cost, and outcomes.

According to critics, applying managed care UR to these already existing problems would only exacerbate these conditions. Hospitals, they noted, would admit only cooperative individuals and avoid disruptive clients who might require more staff resources during the course of treatment and extend beyond the average length of stay, thus limiting access. Moreover, UR, they said, did not take into consideration the complex mental and social conditions of these patients.

MHMA sought to address the barriers to smooth and successful implementation by including an assessment of the inpatient recipients' level of functioning during routine utilization review. Additional care was approved if it was shown that a patient was not yet stabilized and if further specific inpatient interventions and treatment were necessary.

As clinicians conducting UR for MHMA gained more experience, they realized that stabilization of psychiatric symptoms was not the only goal of inpatient hospitalization for the chronically mentally ill recipient. Addressing homelessness, transiency, and diverse chronic conditions influenced how inpatient social workers developed a sound discharge plan. Resolving these issues would increase or maximize the benefits of inpatient treatment, increase continuity into the community, and potentially prevent or reduce subsequent hospitalizations.

UR staff turned to the network department and the regionally based treatment services specialists for assistance in addressing these psychosocial stressors. This collaboration resulted in a more thorough discharge plan for the patient's return to the community. Moreover, managed care gained more credibility among its initial skeptics, especially those who experienced first-hand the attention to enhanced linkages that MHMA facilitated.

In time, an "alert" system was created among network providers via computer, whereby client-specific crisis plans were developed. These alerts enabled any user of the system to coordinate services for an individual and to collect individual case data into an aggregated form to highlight broader systems issues around access to other types of care within the MHMA network or the DMH service system.

Staff were also encouraged to forward to MHMA and DMH relevant patterns and trends that affected lengths of stay in the organization. The nature of the risk-based contract and the freedom from bureaucratic constraints contained in state agency procedures enhanced this organizational decision making process within MHMA.

Measures of Success

Some of the Medicaid program results to date show positive results with respect to the goals of the Medicaid waiver: improved access and quality and reduced costs. Others address the process of care: the development and use of a broader continuum of care for chronically mentally ill adults resulting in more effective interventions; utilization review decision making; the relationship among the managed care partners (i.e., MHMA, DMH, providers, Medicaid recipients, and advocates); and collection and use of the data gathered to improve care.

A final issue addresses the actual management of the mental health and substance abuse care that was received by recipients: identifying, measuring, and improving quality with data generated from the managed care reporting mechanisms.

The findings are drawn mostly from an external evaluation of the first and second years of the program that was conducted by Brandeis University.[3] Other sources include another independent study of the third program year by Suffolk University and data generated by MHMA, principally a client satisfaction survey and level of functioning data.[4]

According to the Brandeis study, in terms of access, the number of Medicaid recipients being served in outpatient services per 1,000 recipients increased from 118.5 to 131.2, or 10.6 percent. Clinic medication use, which is one measure of illness severity, increased from 24.7 recipients per 1,000 to 31.9, or 29.1 percent. Penetration, defined as the number of recipients using any of the mental health or substance abuse services per 1,000 recipients, increased from 212.7 in 1992 to 222.6 in 1993. The number of Medicaid recipients using inpatient services per 1,000 recipients declined from 16.5 to 16.1, less than 3 percent.

Contrary to the fear that the managed care company would use denials and diversions as a primary means to save money, the Brandeis researchers found that diversions and denials "generally declined." The MHMA service network also expanded the range of programs to include partial hospitalization, community support, and structured outpatient addictions, none of which were available to individuals under the traditional Medicaid benefit. The Brandeis team concluded that access had increased slightly.

Another measure of access is the severity of the population served. The Brandeis study found that the clients served by the program had more severe problems than the clients served before the project started. The expected cost shift of difficult clients to DMH programs was not documented, and the trend toward treatment of a more severely disabled population continued in the third year.[5,6]

In terms of quality, in the areas of treatment recommendations, aftercare plans, length of stay, and "settings decisions" (i.e., level of care), providers reported slight increases in quality along some dimensions and equal outcomes along others. The Brandeis researchers concluded that quality was "about the same" as before managed care. The Brandeis report also examined the readmission rate as a measure of quality and found a slight drop despite a shorter length of stay. The Brandeis study reports that the readmission rate for the population of Medicaid recipients who were disabled was reduced from 25.8 percent to 22.5 percent.

In September 1995 MHMA completed a pilot project with six hospitals to reduce the readmission rate. A team at MHMA had determined that 72 percent of all adult readmissions were made up of recipients in the disabled aid categories who had a diagnosis of psychotic or affective disorder. The goal of the pilot intervention was to provide enhanced services to link these patients with their respective hospital's outpatient programs. These enhanced services included holding an outpatient meeting on the unit before discharge and making available a community support worker to assist the client in obtaining clinical, self-help, and rehabilitation services in the community after discharge. The statistical analysis identified the individual hospital to which the recipient was admitted as the best predictor of reducing readmission in the pilot project. Three hospitals had dramatically reduced readmission rates. When hospitals were interviewed about their implementation of the pilot, the following factors were associated with the hospitals that had reduced readmissions rates during the pilot: lower patient to social work staff ratios, broader integration of the pilot from line staff to management, and greater experience of staff in continuous quality improvement projects.

The second best predictor of readmission was a shorter length of stay. There was a significant difference between the lengths of stay of readmitted recipients and non-readmitted recipients. The overall readmission rate during the pilot was 16.7 percent, down from 19.6 percent for the same population in the previous year, a reduction in the rate of 25 percent.

Another measure of quality and of outcome is client satisfaction. MHMA completed a client satisfaction survey of recipients in outpatient care and found the following:

- 3,000 surveys were mailed, out of which 29 percent were completed. If those surveys returned as undeliverable were omitted (a common problem with this population) the resulting response rate rose to 38 percent.
- The majority of persons (85 percent) reported satisfaction with their outpatient treatment, and noted that their day-to-day functioning improved.
- The most important predictors of satisfaction were the respect shown for patients by the therapist and agency and the self-confidence gained from participation in therapy. Staff communication with the client about the treatment options and not being disappointed with the clinic were important, but less so.
- The strongest predictors of quality were client respect and staff communication.
- Being friendly and courteous is the single most important way a clinic can improve satisfaction, followed by staff working together in partnership with a client, and the clinic being clean, answering the phone on time, and having appointments begin and end on time.
- No differences existed along gender lines or by race group on overall satisfaction.
- The six sampled clinics varied in their satisfaction ratings. The clinic with best overall satisfaction and best access rating also operated within the outpatient utilization parameters that were established by MHMA.

In terms of cost savings, the Brandeis team found the following results:

- The projected 1993 cost without managed care was estimated to be $209 million. Under managed care the total costs were $162.7 million, with $10 million in administrative cost and the balance in direct care services.

- The net cost of direct care services in the program was $184.5 million in 1992 and $151.7 million in 1993, resulting in a savings of $33.8 million, or 18.3 percent.
- Because enrollment increased from 1992 to 1993, the cost per enrollee was reduced from $488 to $402, or 17.6 percent.
- Inpatient care costs fell from $76.8 million in 1992 to $60.0 million in 1993, or 24.5 percent, and outpatient mental health was reduced from $79.1 million to $76.9 million, or 2.7 percent.

Inpatient cost savings were generated by a combination of shorter lengths of stay in 24-hour care, reductions in the per diem costs negotiated between MHMA and its inpatient provider network, and shifts from inpatient substance abuse to detoxification programs. The reduction in outpatient cost occurred because MHMA eliminated the practice of physicians billing for services to inpatients as an outpatient expense. The doctors' fees were instead included in the per diem rates.

Program Progress

The Massachusetts Medicaid managed care program for mental health and substance abuse had other success factors. First, only a private organization could have prompted such far-reaching changes in so short a period of time. Unsaddled by politics, MHMA was accountable for and was able to: contract at favorable rates for services in a competitive environment; respond to financial incentives for meeting deadlines for creating a provider network; publish a provider manual; and establish a computerized clinical case management system. The financial targets in the capitated contract also provided the momentum to make decisions on programming and policy quickly.

Second, an emphasis on collaborations among program participants, and hiring key staff with experience in the Massachusetts mental health system were critical strategies that allowed an out-of-state company to be accepted in a skeptical and resistant environment. Third, making providers the primary clinical decision makers for developing UR clinical protocols enhanced the ability of clinicians to treat and place individuals with especially complex cases into the most appropriate treatment settings.

Fourth, because of the federal waiver, existing services were added to better meet program participants'

needs, including partial hospitalization, crisis stabilization, 24-hour observation beds, acute residential treatment for substance abuse, and mental health acute residential treatment programs for children and adolescents.

Fifth, claims data were used to give providers information on basic measures such as length of stay and on more sophisticated measures, such as length of time to outpatient care after inpatient discharge and 30-day readmission rate. Sharing these measures with providers has helped expand MHMA's quality improvement plan to include such measures.

Still, challenges remain in a program targeting a chronically mentally ill Medicaid population. For example, while providers were included in the design of the inpatient selection document, they were not included in all of the changes made in billing formats, reporting forms, and program specifications. Moreover, initial telephone system problems made it difficult for providers to call in to the clinical department for approvals for urgent care and review of ongoing cases.

MHMA's system of payment to providers went smoothly in the initial stages of the program. However, as the volume and complexity of the program grew, significant delays arose, confusing providers and payers. In addition, entering and retrieving data in the MHMA computerized case management system was sometimes cumbersome and time-consuming.

Numerous Medicaid policies and procedural issues beyond the control of MHMA also had an impact on the care patients received. For example, all providers were required to determine a person's MHMA Medicaid eligibility in order to get authorization and payment for services. Yet, because of the complex nature of the methods in which individuals qualified for disability and AFDC benefits, the eligibility status for the benefit managed by MHMA sometimes changed without any prior notification to MHMA, the provider, or Medicaid recipient.

Applying the Model

The MHMA program indicates the potential of managed care applied to a Medicaid population with chronic mental illness, particularly where UR standards for hospital care are designed to promote thorough discharge planning to move clients to the most appropriate level of care on a timely basis. In addition, it has demonstrated that specialized interventions for individual recipients using a provider network and assistance by network staff to hold hospitals accountable to certain care standards enhance the continuity of care.

Over time, for example, providers and staff made more use of the collected data. Individual providers received data on cost per case and length of stay. Quality issues such as the rate of readmission within 30 days were calculated for each provider and across levels of care. The availability of objective information allowed providers to be held accountable for their performance and to compete among themselves.

By requiring its contractor to report this information, the Division of Medical Assistance identified areas of improvement in both the process and outcomes of care. The division worked with MHMA to develop the principles of continuous quality improvement (CQI) in its management and problem-solving functions. Eight quality improvement teams within MHMA are using the information to improve care. Introducing the concept of managing with such data represented a major cultural shift in the delivery of mental health care to the chronically mentally ill for all parties.

Can the Massachusetts model be applied in other states? The model may be adapted, but several key conditions for success must be present. States and private managed mental health care companies must be as committed to the needs of Medicaid recipients as they are to managing costs. They must also ensure that individuals retain some choice of provider and geographic access, while closely managing a provider network for quality care. In addition, states and their partners must be able to handle crises and stresses within the public policy arena, with the managed care organization including community providers and policy makers in problem-solving. They must also collect and use claims data to help identify and solve problems such as how to treat the clients who are high users of service, and to improve overall administrative and clinical processes.

Industry observers will be watching the outcome of similar programs in Iowa, Colorado, and Ohio. If Medicaid directors can implement programs despite numerous legal, procedural, political, and bureaucratic pitfalls and are able to measure the quality and outcomes of mental health projects, a mental health carve-out for Medicaid has a potential future for any number of states.

REFERENCES

1. Dorwart, R. "Managed Mental Health Care: Myths and Realities in the 1990s." *Hospital and Community Psychiatry* 10 (October 1990):1087–1091.
2. Edinburg, G., and Cottler, J. "Implications of Managed Care for Social Work in Psychiatric Hospitals." *Hospital and Community Psychiatry* 10 (October 1990):1063–1064.
3. Callahan, J., et al. *Evaluation of the Massachusetts Medicaid Mental Health/Substance Abuse Program.* Heller School for Advanced Studies in Social Welfare, Brandeis University. January 1994.
4. Beinecke, R.H., et al. *An Assessment of the Massachusetts Managed Mental Health/Substance Abuse Program: Year Three.* New York, NY: Suffolk University, May 1995.
5. Ibid.
6. Callahan et al., *Evaluation.*

30

Success of Medicaid Managed Care Using a Public-Private Sector Model

Charlette L. Beyerl

After 11 years of experience with some Wisconsin counties under Medicaid managed care programs and others under fee-for-service, the State of Wisconsin has determined that the public-private sector model used in their Medicaid Managed Care Program has been successful in improving health outcomes of Medicaid recipients while reducing medical costs. This overview explains the use of private sector providers, how health care delivery was streamlined, special programs that were implemented, and statistics that document the success of the Medicaid Managed Care Initiative.

In the summer of 1984, operating under a Section 1915(b) federal waiver, Wisconsin mandated that all AFDC (Aid for Families with Dependent Children) recipients in Milwaukee and Dane counties receive their Medicaid benefits through health maintenance organizations (HMOs). The AFDC population represented roughly 97 percent of the Medicaid population in these counties with approximately 120,000 recipients located in Milwaukee County. The next 11 years served as the building blocks of listening, learning, changing, and expanding that created the successful public-private sector program that serves Medicaid recipients through the Medicaid HMO Initiative in Milwaukee County.

Annual bids are requested from the HMOs by the state for Medicaid contracts. The HMOs must meet certain contract specifications that require the HMO at a minimum to

- use only state licensed or certified Medicaid providers
- show capacity to provide all Medicaid covered services
- provide for a grievance procedure and appeal process
- meet data reporting requirements
- maintain an internal quality assurance program
- demonstrate a savings over fee-for-service in an amount predetermined by the state.

The providers of service in the Milwaukee HMO Initiative include physicians in solo practice, multiple specialty clinics, academics in hospital-based clinics, and community health centers. Eighteen local area hospitals are included in the provider network as well as nurse practitioners and nurse midwives if used in conjunction with physician. Free-standing medical entities such as imaging, laboratory, and therapy centers; dental, vision, and mental health networks; and urgent care centers complete the provider network. The services are arranged and coordinated through subcontracts with the HMOs. It is the responsibility of the HMOs to manage the care through the HMO or through subcontracts with other organizations such as Wisconsin Independent Physicians Group (WIPG).

WIPG is a managed medical provider network (MMPN) with more than 900 physicians who utilize 18 of Milwaukee's hospitals and provide service to almost 50 percent of the Medicaid recipients in Milwaukee County. This group is unique in that it is a fully integrated medical delivery system that manages all medical care for its enrollees utilizing the primary care physician gatekeeper model of medical care. WIPG is the most successful network in Milwaukee not only from a quality and access to care standpoint, but also in its ability to identify and address the special needs of Medicaid recipients and to implement nontraditional programs that serve to improve the health and outcomes of the population while reducing costs.

One such program was WIPG's Prenatal Support Program (PSP). Following a June 1987 study of prema-

Managed Care Quarterly 1996; 4(1): 13–23
© 1996 Aspen Publishers, Inc.

ture and low birthweight infants during the preceding two years, WIPG developed and implemented the PSP, which would help decrease the premature and low birthweight rates for WIPG enrollees. Policy objectives of the program included the goals of promoting early identification of high-risk members, promoting early prenatal education, and providing an aggressive follow-up for those members missing prenatal appointments. PSP nurses performed home visits during which they obtained risk information determined by the enrollee's family history, health history, current pregnancy, and socioeconomic status. Educational materials regarding the importance of good prenatal care, pregnancy, nutrition, childcare, and parenting were provided to and reviewed with the enrollee. The risk information collected by the PSP nurses was assessed and the obstetrical provider was notified of the care expected for the enrollee based on her risk. Providers were encouraged to report enrollees for follow-up by the PSP nurses when appointments were missed or the enrollee did not obtain medical tests prescribed by her physician. Rather than duplicating services available from other local community agencies or grant funded programs, WIPG formed a collaborative effort with these agencies and programs to refer enrollees and assist them in accessing these community programs.

A detailed and lengthy analysis of this program determined that the PSP nurse's social intervention

had the following positive impact on WIPG enrollees who were participants in the PSP:

- PSP enrollees had fewer premature infants (over 20 weeks and under 36 weeks of gestation) than non-PSP enrollees (Figure 30–1).
- PSP enrollees had a higher number of prenatal visits to their primary care physician than non-PSP enrollees (Figure 30–2).
- PSP enrollees had a higher number of antepartum hospital days than non-PSP enrollees (Figure 30–3). This number is a plus for the program since it shows that more women agreed to bed rest or other hospitalizations that prevented premature births.
- Lengths of stay in the hospital for both mothers and infants were lower on the average for enrollees in the PSP (Figure 30–4).
- The infant mortality rate is lower for PSP enrollees than non-PSP enrollees (Figure 30–5).

The success of WIPG's PSP was shared with the state, which has since implemented a statewide Prenatal Care Coordination Program available to all Medicaid recipients in Wisconsin regardless of whether they are enrolled in an HMO or fee-for-service. WIPG has seen a reduction in neonatal intensive care (NICU) days from 151 days per 1,000 in 1990 to 75 days per 1,000 in 1994. Although the savings in the reduction of bed days is easily calculated, there are significant additional medical cost savings in the first years of life

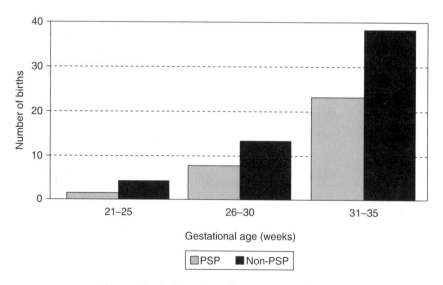

Figure 30–1. Number of premature infants.

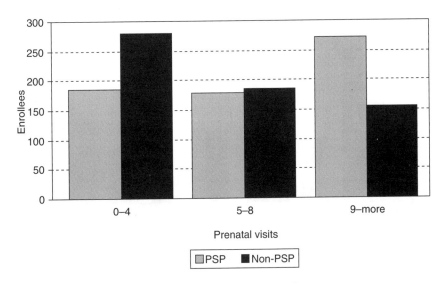

Figure 30–2. Number of prenatal visits.

for infants who are healthier from birth. There may also be savings in social services and educational services for these children.

Early Periodic Screening, Development, and Testing (EPSDT) screenings, called HealthChecks in Wisconsin, are required for all Medicaid children under the age of 21. WIPG addressed the challenge of encouraging and training member physicians to perform HealthChecks by developing forms that made the record-keeping task as simple as possible for physicians. A separate check-off type form was developed for each age for which a HealthCheck is required (Figure 30–6).

The forms are maintained in the enrollee's medical chart and reviewed by WIPG during the physician's annual site visit and audit. The forms systematically list all testing to be performed during each visit to assure that a complete HealthCheck is performed. The combination of the simple recording form and the higher payment for performing HealthChecks dramatically increased WIPG's percentage of screenings.

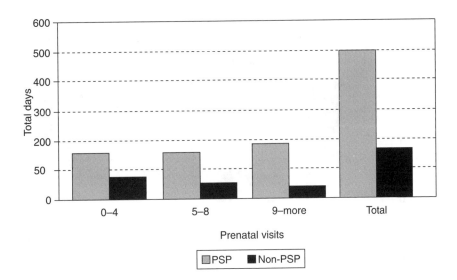

Figure 30–3. Antepartum hospital days.

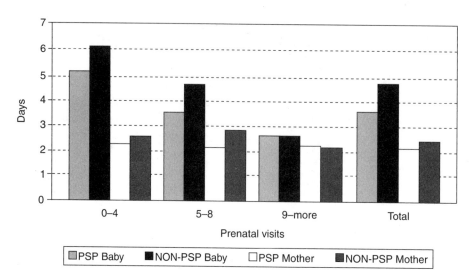

Figure 30–4. Length of stay related to prenatal care.

WIPG additionally monitors physicians to assure HealthChecks are completed at every opportunity. For instance, if a child presents for a medical reason that would not prohibit performance of a HealthCheck, WIPG member physicians are expected to perform a HealthCheck on that child. In addition, WIPG does not permit payment to WIPG member physicians for well child visits unless all required HealthChecks have been completed for the child.

The state comparison of HMO services to fee-for-service shows that a greater percentage of children in the HMOs received HealthChecks than children under fee-for-service. In fact, almost twice as many children in HMOs received HealthChecks for the 1992 and 1993 years reported in the study (Figure 30–7).

In addition to its special programs for Medicaid recipients, WIPG has developed a medical management model for managing its 800 member physicians. Since WIPG is a physician managed and controlled entity, member physicians are managed by their peers through close scrutiny of utilization and health outcomes. Physicians are paid on a fee-for-service basis,

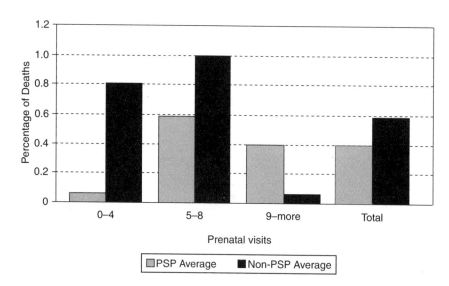

Figure 30–5. Length of stay related to infant mortality rate.

WIPG HEALTHCHECK & WELL CHILD VISITS
6, 7, 8, 9, 10, 11, 12 (CIRCLE AGE)
YEAR VISIT—ALLERGIES _____

Name: _____

Parental Concerns: _____
_____

Name of School: _____
Name of Teacher: _____
Interval History

1. Allergy _____
_____

2. Illness—Accidents _____
_____

3. Diet—Appetite, Stool, Stomach or Headache _____
_____

4. Sexual Development—Breast, Testicular, P. Hair _____
_____

5. Weight Gain _____ Loss_____
Weight _____ **Height**_____
T_____ P_____ R_____ B/P_____ (mandatory)
         (optional)

Physical Exam:

Check appropriate box (X = Normal, O = Abnormal).
Document all abnormal findings.

RESULTS	
General app	
Skin	
Head	
Breasts	
*EENT	
Lungs	
Heart	
Abd	
Ext genitalia	
*Vision	
*Hearing	
Back	
Extremities	
Neurologic	

Date of Visit: _____

Growth & Development: (Check to indicate if item was discussed)
_____ Tanner classification
_____ Achievement
_____ Sports
_____ Peer relationship
_____ Attendance

Education: (Check to indicate if item was discussed)
_____ School
_____ Correct diet
_____ Bed time
_____ Discipline
_____ Puberty progress (menstruation)
_____ Early sex education
_____ Smoking, alcohol, marijuana
_____ Discipline questions, abuse concerns
_____ Dental referral needed?

Immunizations

(Details in chart or immunization record)

COMMENTS (Must include Dx and Rx)

*Puretone audiometric screen to be done with referral to audiologist if patient fails. Vision charts to be used age 3–20 years.

List any referrals: _____ Next visit: _____

Physician signature: _____

PERMANENT RECORD   **Turn over for additional notes** [ ]

Figure 30–6. Sample HealthCheck form.

PERCENT RECEIVING PER ELIGIBLE YEAR

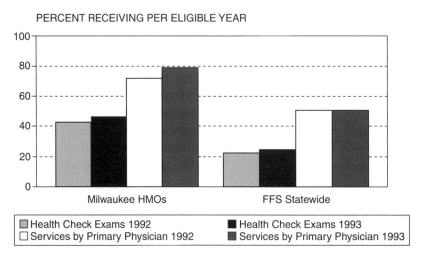

Figure 30–7. HMO/fee-for-service comparisons.

so there is no incentive to reduce the amount of care provided as there might be under a capitation arrangement. WIPG has detailed reports to monitor all services provided to an enrollee, to a group of enrollees, to a physician, or to a group of physicians. This enables WIPG to compare, for instance, all pediatricians to determine where they each rank in a group of their peers. The more detailed reports allow WIPG to determine high-cost patients or patterns of "creative" billing.

It is WIPG's philosophy to educate its member physicians as opposed to terminating them. WIPG contracts with free-standing centers, such as imaging, laboratory, surgery, and therapy centers, and encour-

ages use of these centers by educating WIPG member physicians of the cost savings compared to similar services in hospital settings. The enrollees also prefer these centers because of the ease of access and friendly, prompt service received at these sites. The quality of care at these sites is equal to or better than that provided in hospitals because of the competitive nature of the centers.

WIPG also believes that the only reason to capitate for services is if the management organization is unable to manage its providers. Capitation serves to guarantee the expenses and profits of the organization paying the capitation since the organization has no

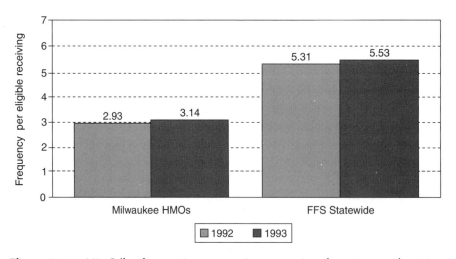

Figure 30–8. HMO/fee-for-service comparisons: services by primary physician.

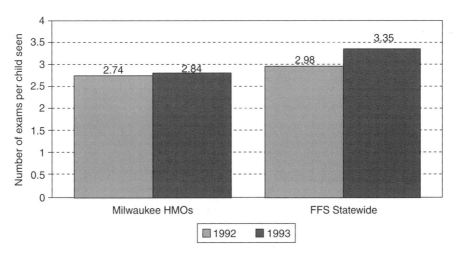

Figure 30–9. HMO/fee-for-service comparisons: non-HealthCheck child visits (sick visits).

risk and can identify, in advance, their cost for these services. Capitation also discourages the provision of services by the capitated group because every service provided lowers the profits of the group. If a group is well managed the providers can be paid on a fee-for-service basis since the management organization will monitor all services provided to assure medical necessity. Monitoring and fee-for-service payments also eliminate the incentive to not provide medically necessary services since the providers know they will be paid for each service provided.

WIPG's administrative staff participate on many local community committees, which address proposed or ongoing community programs and problems. Many of these committees address community problems that may not be directly related to Medicaid recipients; however, WIPG feels it is important to work with community groups to assure that they are not spending grant or fund dollars on issues that could be more easily handled through a group like WIPG. For instance, a group may feel the need to contact or educate Milwaukee area physicians regarding a specific health issue. Since WIPG is in constant contact with its member physicians, WIPG can easily add the committee information when visiting physician offices. This collaborative effort reduces costs and provides for an effective method to share information that benefits Medicaid recipients and other patients who may also be seen in WIPG member physician offices.

Another program that has been in place for several years was initiated by the state to better address the concerns of HMOs, providers, Medicaid recipients, and community advocates regarding the Milwaukee Medicaid HMO Initiative. This program, the Milwaukee Managed Care Forum, was designed to allow all public, private, or individual parties the opportunity to voice concerns, request changes, review audit and statistical information, and make recommendations for future audits regarding the Milwaukee Medicaid HMO Initiative. The meetings that began as HMO bashing sessions took a quick turn toward cooperative, productive, brainstorming sessions when the state shared with the community the low level of capitation that the HMOs received compared to the expansive services that the HMOs must provide. The HMOs had the opportunity to hear from community advocates concerns that they and their clients had regarding medical care, access, and the special needs of the Medicaid population. This provided the HMOs with information that enabled them to better target the medical care and provided the advocates with a mechanism to provide input into how medical care would be delivered in the inner city.

Forum participants have the opportunity to recommend changes in the contract between the state and the HMOs and to recommend the type and extent of monitoring performed by the state regarding the HMOs and the delivery of health care under the HMO initiative. Audits requested and performed over the past few years included those on the number of EPSDT screens, mental health services, number and location of providers in underserved areas, dental care services, and transportation.

On an annual basis, the state prepares a report comparing the services provided to the AFDC population in the HMO initiative and those under fee-for-service. The purpose is to report utilization patterns, health outcomes, and quality issues, which serve as a basis for continual evaluation and improvement of the program. The reporting categories are targeted at care of women and children, which is representative of the Medicaid AFDC recipients. The report also cautions the reader that all information is related to Medicaid recipients and should not be compared to commercial insurance populations because of their very different health problems and general demographics of the group.

A reduction in the number of inpatient hospital days per thousand enrollees in the HMO initiative has been significant. At the inception of the initiative in 1984, Milwaukee County Medicaid recipients utilized more than 1,200 days per thousand. WIPG's 1994 days were reported at 377 days per thousand. But the state report goes far beyond hospital days in proving the value of the Wisconsin Medicaid HMO Initiative.

Medical care is most effective when the patient develops a personal relationship with his or her primary care physician. Medicaid managed care programs develop this physician-patient relationship, which serves to improve the overall health of the recipient through continuity of care, but also results in a reduction of emergency room care for urgent and less-than-urgent medical care. Wisconsin reports that a higher number of recipients in the HMOs receive care from their primary care physician than those in fee-for-service, and that the frequency of visits is much lower in HMOs than under fee-for-service. In addition, there were fewer children seen for "sick" visits in physicians' offices, which we assume is a direct result of these children receiving more preventive care through their primary care physician than the children in the fee-for-service environment (Figures 30–8 and 30–9).

A reduction in the use of emergency rooms and ambulance services for recipients in HMOs compared to those in fee-for-service was also reported by the state. Since emergency room services are more expensive than those in a physician's office, the savings from this reduction were significant (Figure 30–10).

Immunizations is another area of preventive medicine that attracted national attention to Milwaukee because of the 1989 measles epidemic. Since 1989, HMOs have consistently reported a higher immunization rate than their fee-for-service counterparts. This is particularly significant since Wisconsin requires all school-age children to be fully immunized. The higher HMO rate of immunization indicates that children below school age and those beyond school age receive

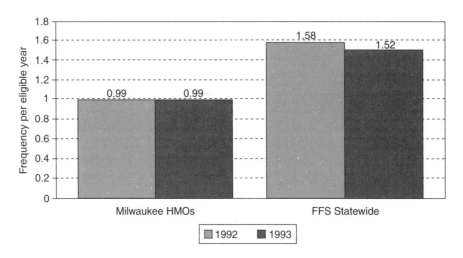

Figure 30–10. HMO/fee-for-service comparisons: use of emergency rooms, ambulance, or specialized motor vehicles (SMV).

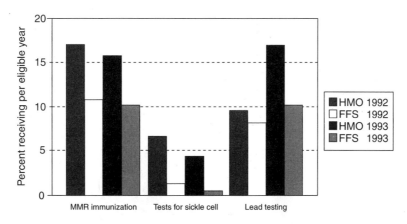

Figure 30–11. HMO/fee-for-service comparisons: children's services.

more immunizations in the HMO managed care setting (Figure 30–11). Lead testing and tests for sickle cell in children were also performed at a higher level for recipients in HMOs than those under fee-for-service (Figure 30–11).

Although the AFDC population is primarily children, women make up the majority of the balance; therefore it is important to review the results of preventive medicine for Medicaid women. The state reported that Medicaid enrollees in HMOs had a higher number of pap smears and mammograms than enrollees in fee-for-service. It was also reported that the cesarean delivery rate was several percentage points lower for HMO enrollees than fee-for-service. The trend toward preventive medicine under the HMO managed care program has improved the overall health of women and children in Milwaukee (Figure 30–12).

In addition to higher numbers of preventive services being provided through the state HMO initiative and the resulting improved health outcomes, there is significant savings to the state by using mandated managed care for Medicaid recipients. Not only does the state save a minimum of 10 percent of total medical costs, the HMOs are required to perform a higher level of administrative service such as reporting, quality assurance programs, and arranging for transportation, as well as being required to have Medicaid enrollee advocates on staff at the HMOs.

The additional benefit is the special programs, such as the ones developed by WIPG described earlier, that

serve to improve health outcomes through creative programs targeted toward the special needs of the Medicaid population. In most cases these programs add a social intervention to encourage and assist Medicaid recipients to obtain health care that has been made available for them.

The providers in groups such as WIPG have also benefited. Their managed care efforts have reduced unnecessary services and shifted services to free-standing, less costly but high-quality providers such as imaging centers, rather than hospitals. Before contracting with a free-standing provider, WIPG enlists the assistance of its member physicians to review the quality of these providers to assure that the quality meets the needs and requirements of WIPG member physicians. This has resulted in the ability to pay higher fees to physicians for services that are medically appropriate.

Many lessons have been learned from the Wisconsin Medicaid HMO Initiative during the program's 11 years of operation:

Special programs, such as WIPG's Prenatal Support Program, which add a social service component to traditional medical care, improve health outcomes. There was no additional cost for providing the combined social/medical services due to the reduction of related medical costs.

An unexpected benefit of community cooperation of the private and public sectors was accomplished as a result of the State Managed Care Forum meetings. This resulted in an improved health system for Med-

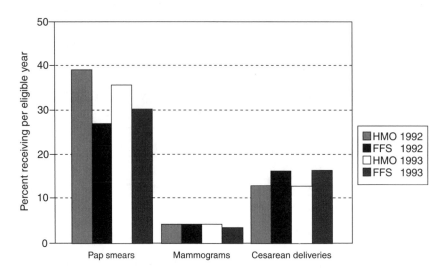

Figure 30–12. HMO/fee-for-service comparisons: women's services.

icaid recipients due to the opportunity of forum participants to voice concerns and work cooperatively to arrive at solutions.

Mandating participation of Medicaid recipients in the HMO initiative required the recipients to select a primary care physician who would manage their medical care. The relationships between these patients and their primary care physician improved the overall health of the recipients due to continuity of care.

Physicians and other providers are paid on a fee-for-service basis, which encourages them to provide medical care. The management organization, utilizing physician peers, monitors the providers to assure quality care is provided without over- or underutilization. The physicians benefit from the provision of quality, cost-effective medical care, resulting in improved health outcomes, by receiving higher payments if the group performs well. There is satisfaction among the physicians that all members of the group have the same goal: to provide quality care or be removed from the group.

Accomplishing the shift from high-cost medical care (such as emergency visits and seeking care from a specialist) to receiving preventive medical care from a primary care physician results in improved health outcomes, a healthier population, and reduced medical cost. The savings from the reduction in medical costs can be used for additional programs that continue the cycle of increasing preventive care and improving health.

The conclusion to be drawn is that mandated Medicaid managed care programs increase preventive medical care through the use of primary care physicians, which results in improved health outcomes at a reduced cost. Unfortunately, managed care networks are not available in all areas. Each state and city has its own specific problems and needs based on population mix, geography, and access to medical care. What works in one part of the country may not work in another; however, it is clear that managed care Medicaid programs such as Wisconsin's HMO Initiative can be very successful through a collaborative effort of the public and private sectors.

31

Medicare Managed Care and the Need for Quality Management

Nicholas A. Hanchak, Sandra R. Harmon-Weiss, Patricia D. McDermott, Alex Hirsch, and Neil Schlackman

Currently, approximately nine percent of Medicare's 33 million beneficiaries are enrolled in HMO plans.[1] The Medicare segment of U.S. Healthcare's business is one of the fastest-growing areas, and its growth is gaining momentum (see Figure 31–1). The quality of care delivered under managed care versus traditional indemnity insurance has been highlighted regarding the transition of Medicare beneficiaries and Medicaid recipients into managed care. Because of the lack of comparable data in the fee-for-service sector, little direct comparison can be made; however, as the growth of Medicare managed care continues, methods to evaluate the quality of care delivered will become increasingly important.

In creating the Health Plan Employer Data and Information Set Version 2.5 (HEDIS 2.5), the National Committee for Quality Assurance (NCQA) has taken the lead in developing a standardized tool for health plan performance measurement. HEDIS 2.5, however, focuses only on the commercial population up to age 65 and includes measures such as childhood immunization and prenatal care.[2] The Medicare population, with multiple chronic diseases, is much different from the commercial population: it has many special needs. To address this, the Health Care Financing Administration (HCFA) and the Kaiser Family Foundation have initiated the development of a standardized Medicare Report Card based on the HEDIS model. This project remains in the planning phase. HCFA, through a contract with the Delmarva Foundation, has recently begun the pilot phase of a project to gather data on quality indicators in Medicare managed care. To fill the void in health plan performance measurement for its Medicare enrollees, U.S. Healthcare and U.S. Quality Algorithms, Inc. (USQA) have used their expertise in performance

measurement to develop the Medicare Quality Report Card. 1994 represents the second calendar year for which performance has been measured.

USQA developed the Medicare Quality Report Card to evaluate the quality of care provided to U.S. Healthcare members enrolled in the HMO plan. The USQA Medicare Quality Report Card is population-based and divided into several sections, including quality of care measures, access and satisfaction measures, and enrollment and utilization statistics. This article focuses on the quality of care, member access, and member satisfaction measures.

Although utilization statistics are part of both HEDIS 2.5 and the USQA Medicare Quality Report Card, this article describes the methodology and results of the quality, access, and satisfaction measures only. The measurement of baseline performance allows U.S. Healthcare to develop initiatives to improve the quality of the care delivered to its members. This article discusses the specific measures chosen to evaluate the quality of care provided to Medicare members, the methods used and specifications followed, and the results of the measures for 1994, including a description of how U.S. Healthcare uses these results to develop quality improvement programs.

Quality Indicators

USQA selected the quality of care measures based on process and outcome measures that are important to Medicare enrollees. Member access, which is a significant indicator of quality, is necessary in managing acute and chronic conditions and in providing the appropriate health maintenance and preventive services to maintain optimal health. Satisfaction measures reflect how well U.S. Healthcare and its participating providers meet the expectations of members.

A copy of the 1994 Medicare Quality Report Card for U.S. Healthcare is shown in Figure 31–2. The first

Managed Care Quarterly 1996; 4(1): 1–12

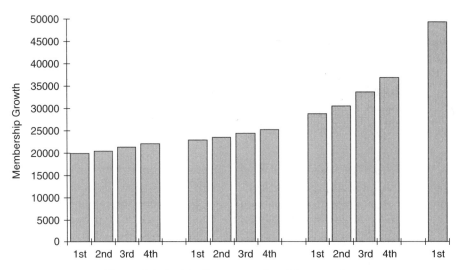

Figure 31–1. Medicare membership growth.

group of measures consists of preventive services. The three performance measures related to prevention in the Medicare population are the influenza vaccination rate, the biennial mammography screening rate, and the biennial eye examination rate.

Influenza virus infection leads to substantial morbidity and mortality, especially in the elderly population and in patients with chronic medical conditions. The cost of excess hospitalization from influenza-related illness for Medicare recipients has reached more than $1 billion annually during epidemic seasons and nearly $750 million during nonepidemic seasons.[3] There is substantial observational evidence that influenza vaccines are cost-effective in reducing serious complications of influenza infections and respiratory complications.[4] Yet despite this evidence, vaccination against influenza remains suboptimal. Reasons for low vaccination rates include provider and patient doubts about the vaccine effectiveness, patient fears of the vaccine side effects, and the lack of programs to promote the vaccine use.[5]

Killed influenza virus vaccines have been available for many years. For young adults, the vaccine has been shown to be 65 to 80 percent protective against illness caused by influenza viruses whose antigenic characteristics match those in the administered vaccine. Since 1964, the Advisory Committee on Immunization Practices has recommended influenza vaccination, based on the virus' devastating effects on morbidity and mortality and its demonstrated efficacy in young adults. The ability of a health plan to reach out

and encourage its at-risk patients to be appropriately immunized against influenza indicates the quality of its preventive services programs.

Mammography has been shown to be effective in the early detection of breast cancer, and has led to an improvement in breast cancer mortality in women screened. Although there is some disagreement about the effectiveness of mammography in women under age 50, its effectiveness in women 50 and older has been consistently proven.[6] Mammography screening leads to a downstaging of breast cancer at the time of diagnosis.[7] HMO enrollees have been shown to have their breast cancers detected at earlier stages as compared to fee-for-service patients, presumably because of a greater emphasis on outreach programs.[8] The ability to develop programs designed to promote eligible female members to have routine mammograms is an important indication of health plan quality.

Eye diseases are increasingly common as people age. In addition, general visual acuity has been identified as one of the most important senses that can lead to an improved sense of well-being and health status. Therefore, the provision of an eye care benefit and the health plan's ability to encourage its use are important indicators of quality. Routine eye care is important in the routine screening and early detection of prevalent eye diseases such as cataracts and glaucoma, the treatment of which can lead to improved functional status and prevention of progressive disability.

The management of chronic disease is an important aspect of providing quality care to a Medicare popu-

Quality of Care Measure	Description	USHC Overall 1994
PREVENTIVE SERVICES		
1. Influenza Vaccination Rate	members age 65 or older receiving an influenza vaccine based on patient's self-report	65.5%
2. Mammography Screening Every Two Years (age 65–75)	women age 65–75 who received a mammogram in previous 2 years	73.5%
3. Biennial Eye Examination	members receiving an eye exam in previous 2 years	65.6%
ACUTE and CHRONIC DISEASE		
4. Diabetics Receiving Hemoglobin A1 Test	members with diabetes who received an annual glycated hemoglobin test	72.5%
5. Diabetics Receiving Retinal Eye Examination	members with diabetes who received an annual retinal eye exam	53.7%
6. Chronic Obstructive Pulmonary Disease (COPD)		
a. COPD Admission Rate	members hospitalized for COPD	0.50%
b. COPD Readmission Rate	members hospitalized more than once for COPD	0.09%
c. COPD Readmission Rate Ratio	ratio of members hospitalized more than once for COPD compared to members admitted only once	0.185
7. Congestive Heart Failure (CHF)		
a. CHF Admission Rate	members hospitalized for CHF	1.18%
b. CHF Readmission Rate	members hospitalized more than once for CHF	0.24%
c. CHF Readmission Rate Ratio	ratio of members hospitalized more than once for CHF compared to members admitted only once	0.203
MENTAL HEALTH		
8. Ambulatory Follow-up after Hospitalization for Depression	ambulatory follow-up of members within 30 days of discharge after a hospitalization for depression	85.5%
MEMBER ACCESS and SATISFACTION		
9. Member Access	members who visited a USHC participating provider	95.8%
10. Satisfaction Measures		
a. Overall Medical Care	response of good or better to survey question concerning "overall medical care"	98.8%
b. Primary Care Physician	responded that would recommend their primary care physician to a family member	96.9%
c. U.S. Healthcare	responded that would recommend U.S. Healthcare to a family member	99.0%

Figure 31–2. U.S. Healthcare 1994 Medicare quality report card.

lation because of the increased prevalence of chronic conditions in this age group. USQA has developed a Membership Chronic Disease Database, in which administrative data is used to identify U.S. Healthcare members who have any of 36 individual chronic diseases. The identification criteria use the following

sources of data to identify members with specific chronic diseases:[9,10]

1. ICD-9 (International Classification of Diseases, Ninth Revision) codes from claims and encounter files
2. CPT-4 (Current Procedural Terminology, Fourth

Edition) codes from claims and encounter files

3. Medispan® Generic Product Identifier pharmacy codes (Medispan® is a proprietary grouping system that maps all National Drug Classification (NDC) codes into similar drug classes)
4. utilization patterns of certain laboratory tests
5. patient demographic data

An example of the administrative data selection criteria used to identify diabetic members is shown in Exhibit 31–1. Similar criteria have been developed for each of the 35 other diseases profiled. The intent of the Membership Chronic Disease Database is to profile members within the health plan who have certain diseases that are chronic in nature. Managed care organization members suffering from chronic diseases will most likely require ongoing medical care for the management of their condition and can be identified for further intervention. Diseases were selected based on the ability of an improvement in their processes of care to lead to better outcomes.

The three most important diseases in the elderly population are diabetes mellitus, chronic obstructive pulmonary disease (COPD), and congestive heart failure (CHF). These diseases are prevalent in this population and account for substantial morbidity.[11] An estimate of the prevalence statistics has been calculated for the U.S. Healthcare Medicare population using administrative data selection criteria as profiled in the U.S. Healthcare Membership Chronic Disease Database (see Exhibit 31–2).

The two process measures related to the care of diabetic patients are the annual rate of hemoglobin $A1_c$ testing and the annual rate of retinal eye exams. The American Diabetes Association has recommended both measures as part of good diabetic care.[12] Based on the recently completed Diabetes Control and Complications Trial, there is good evidence that tight glycemic control can retard the progression of diabetic complications.[13] Observing hemoglobin $A1_c$ values can be helpful in monitoring glycemic control. The measure incorporated into the USQA Medicare Quality Report Card evaluates the percentage of diabetic members who receive a hemoglobin $A1_c$ test on at least an annual basis. Early detection and treatment of diabetic retinopathy can retard progressive eye disease related to diabetes.[14] The measure used in the Medicare Quality Report Card is the rate at which an annual retinal exam is performed by an eye care professional, which follows the HEDIS 2.5 criteria for the commercial population.

COPD and CHF are two of the most common chronic conditions in the elderly population. To measure the successful ambulatory treatment of these conditions, USQA evaluated the rate at which Medicare members were admitted to acute care with these diagnoses. In addition, USQA measured the admission rate of multiple admissions for the same condition (identified as readmission rates to reflect HEDIS 2.5 nomenclature).[15]

A key determinant in the optimal management of depressed patients is how closely they are followed up after an inpatient hospitalization for their illness.[16] Following similar but not the same specifications as those used in HEDIS 2.5, the appropriate ambulatory follow-up of patients following an admission for depression was evaluated by the rate at which they were

Exhibit 31–1 USQA Administrative Selection Criteria

Diagnosis Criteria (ICD-9 codes)
- 250–250.93 (diabetes mellitus with various manifestations)
- 357.2 (polyneuropathy in diabetes)
- 362.0–362.02 (diabetic retinopathy)
- 366.41 (diabetic cataract)

Procedure Criteria (CPT-4 codes)
- 5190D (registered nurse diabetic visit)
- 5205D (certified diabetes educator)
- 9890A (diabetes education program)
- E0607 (home blood glucose monitor)
- J1820 (diabetic injectable medications)
- W0070 (oral hypoglycemic medications)
- W0071 (antidiabetic products, miscellaneous)

Not Included (ICD-9 codes)
- 790.2 (abnormal glucose tolerance test)
- 962.3 (poisoning by insulin or antidiabetic agent)

Exhibit 31–2 USHC Estimated Prevalence Statistics for Certain Chronic Diseases

Chronic Disease	Estimated Prevalence (%)
Diabetes mellitus	15.5
Chronic obstructive pulmonary disease	5.1
Congestive heart failure	6.1

seen by a mental health provider, primary care physician, or visiting nurse within 30 days of the discharge from the hospital.

As people age, the prevalence of chronic disease and burden of morbidity increases. There is also an increased need for screening for major causes of mortality, especially heart disease and cancer. Therefore, an important determinant of health plan quality is the ability to provide access to appropriate health care providers for the geriatric population. This is measured by the rate at which members saw any U.S. Healthcare provider during the year. This is a more aggressive measure than that used in the commercial population in HEDIS 2.5, which evaluates the visits to a health plan provider within a three-year period, as opposed to one year.

The satisfaction of members with the health plan is an important determinant of how well the expectations are being met by the health plan and its providers. To this end, the USQA Medicare Quality Report Card has incorporated three measures of member satisfaction: satisfaction with the overall medical care, satisfaction with the primary care physicians, and satisfaction with U.S. Healthcare.

Methodology and Specifications for Measures

The measures included in the U.S. Healthcare Medicare Quality Report Card have been calculated using data from various sources. The Medicare population has been defined from the enrollment file. Only Medicare members active for the entire calendar year 1994 have been included in the calculation of the quality of care measures (except for the influenza vaccination rate, which required enrollment for the entire 1994–1995 influenza season, and the biennial mammography rate and biennial eye examination rate, which required two years of active enrollment). Calculations have been made by merging the clinical information from the encounters, claims, and U.S. Healthcare Check™ databases. In addition, member satisfaction data and data on self-reported influenza immunizations were utilized. The measures have been calculated for U.S. Healthcare Medicare enrollees and include all age groups, unless otherwise noted.

The U.S. Healthcare Medicare Quality Report Card has been developed using administrative data and patient-supplied data, including vaccination questionnaires and satisfaction surveys. Only evidence of actually having received the indicated test or service was included as a positive response. Referrals for a test or service without objective evidence of its completion were included in the calculations as a negative response (i.e., included in the denominator but not in the numerator of the calculation of the measure). The administrative data were not supplemented with medical chart review. Because of the sole reliance on administrative data without the addition of medical chart review, and the strict criteria for a "positive," the measures reported are very conservative estimates of actual performance. In most cases, they likely underestimate the true level of performance.

The influenza vaccination rate denominator consisted of all U.S. Healthcare Medicare members at least age 65 enrolled in U.S. Healthcare from September 1, 1994, to March 31, 1995. This represents the time from the generation of the vaccine reminder and survey that went to all U.S. Healthcare Medicare members through the end of the 1994–1995 influenza season. The numerator was the sum of all those patients from the denominator who have evidence of a self-report for having received an influenza vaccine during the 1994–1995 influenza season (based on the flu vaccine database) and all those without self-report evidence who have an encounter or claim indicating administration of influenza vaccine based on the CPT-4 code 90724.

The biennial mammography screening rate evaluated the 65–75 age group. The denominator included all U.S. Healthcare female Medicare members who turned age 65–75 during 1994 and were continuously enrolled in U.S. Healthcare from January 1, 1993 to December 31, 1994. The numerator was made up of all members from the denominator who had evidence of receiving a mammogram during 1993 or 1994 based on a CPT-4 code 76090 through 76093 from the radiology encounters database, U.S. Healthcare Check, or claims databases.

The biennial eye examination rate denominator was made up of all U.S. Healthcare Medicare members continuously enrolled in U.S. Healthcare from January 1, 1993 to December 31, 1994. The numerator was all members from the denominator who have evidence of an ophthalmology visit during calendar year 1993 or 1994 based on a series of CPT-4 codes that were derived from the USQA proprietary grouping system, the USQA Clinical Groups Procedure Category 1030 Eye Procedures, which includes the following procedure groups: Cataract Procedures, Other Eye Procedures, Glaucoma Procedures, Refraction-Routine Eye Exams, Retinal Procedures, Cornea Procedures, and Strabismus Procedures. Essentially, any claim that had a CPT-4 procedure code indicating a visit or a procedure by an eye care professional was accepted as evidence that the members had access to the appropriate eye care.

The two process measures related to diabetes first required the identification of U.S. Healthcare Medicare members with diabetes. The selection criteria used to identify a diabetic member is shown in the first box. In addition, USQA has conducted research into the sensitivity and specificity of various selection criteria used in the identification of members with diabetes. Based on the confirmation of a sample of 4,172 diabetics by their capitated primary care physicians, the use of any one ICD-9 diagnosis code, CPT-4 procedure code, or NDC pharmacy code led to a sensitivity of 97.3 percent, but a positive predictive value of 84.2 percent. In addition, when a diabetic member was identified by only one database by any of the above criteria, the positive predictive value ranged from 43 percent to 58 percent, depending on the database from which the member was identified. In order to improve the specificity of the selection of diabetic members for the purposes of health plan performance measurement, the selection of diabetic members for the Medicare Quality Report Card selected only diabetic members identified by at least 2 different databases, which has been shown to have a sensitivity of 74 percent while having a much improved positive predictive value of 95 percent.

The measure of diabetics receiving at least an annual hemoglobin A1$_c$ test had as its denominator all U.S. Healthcare Medicare members continuously enrolled in U.S. Healthcare from January 1, 1994 to December 31, 1994 who have been identified as a diabetic at any time from January 1, 1990 to present according to USQA administrative selection criteria profiled in the U.S. Healthcare Membership Chronic Disease Database for diabetes on at least two separate occasions from two separate databases. The numerator included all diabetic members from the denominator who have any evidence for a glycated hemoglobin CPT-4 code 83036 or glycated protein CPT-4 code 82985 during 1994. The annual retinal eye exam rate used the same denominator. The numerator included all diabetic members identified from the denominator who had evidence of a retinal eye exam by an eye care professional (following HEDIS 2.5 standards) based on the following codes:

- 92002 Ophthalmic services, intermediate, new patient
- 92004 Ophthalmic services, comprehensive, new patient
- 92012 Ophthalmic services, intermediate, established new patient
- 92014 Ophthalmic services, comprehensive, established patient
- 92018 Ophthalmic exam, general anesthesia, complete
- 92019 Ophthalmic exam, general anesthesia, limited
- 92225 Ophthalmoscopy, extended, initial
- 92226 Ophthalmoscopy, extended, subsequent
- EY001 Routine eye care visit (eyeglass wearer)
- EY002 Routine eye care visit (non–eyeglass wearer)
- 92235 Ophthalmoscopy, with medical diagnostics evaluation
- 92250 Ophthalmoscopy, with medical diagnostics evaluation

The admission and readmission rates due to chronic obstructive pulmonary disease (COPD) and congestive heart failure (CHF) are both measured in terms of rates per the entire eligible population, as opposed to only the members with these diseases. This measure is very similar to the asthma admission rate and readmission rate as reported in HEDIS 2.5. The denominators for both measures consist of all U.S. Healthcare Medicare members continuously enrolled in U.S. Healthcare from January 1, 1994 to December 31, 1994. The COPD admission rate numerator includes members from the denominator who have evidence of one or more acute care admissions for COPD in 1994 based on a principal diagnosis ICD-9 code from the facility bill within the USQA Diagnosis Group COPD from the USQA Clinical Groups (see Figure 31–3). The CHF admission rate numerator includes members from the denominator who have evidence of one or more acute care admissions for CHF based on a principal diagnosis ICD-9 code from the facility bill within the USQA Diagnosis Group CHF (see Figure 31–3). The readmission rate for each uses the same denominator as the admission rate. The

6. COPD

Diagnosis Group	Description	ICD9	ICD9 Description
176	Chronic Obstructive Pulmonary Disease	491	Chronic Bronchitis
176	Chronic Obstructive Pulmonary Disease	491.0	Simple Chronic Bronchitis
176	Chronic Obstructive Pulmonary Disease	491.1	Mucopurulent Chronic Bronchitis
176	Chronic Obstructive Pulmonary Disease	491.2	Obstructive Chronic Bronchitis
176	Chronic Obstructive Pulmonary Disease	491.20	Obstructive Chronic Bronchitis, Without Mention Of
176	Chronic Obstructive Pulmonary Disease	491.21	Obstructive Chronic Bronchitis, With Acute
176	Chronic Obstructive Pulmonary Disease	491.8	Other Chronic Bronchitis
176	Chronic Obstructive Pulmonary Disease	491.9	Unspecified Chronic Bronchitis
176	Chronic Obstructive Pulmonary Disease	492	Emphysema
176	Chronic Obstructive Pulmonary Disease	492.0	Emphysematous Bleb
176	Chronic Obstructive Pulmonary Disease	492.8	Other Emphysema
176	Chronic Obstructive Pulmonary Disease	494	Bronchiectasis
176	Chronic Obstructive Pulmonary Disease	496	Chronic Airway Obstruction, Not Elsewhere
176	Chronic Obstructive Pulmonary Disease	506.4	Chronic Respiratory Conditions Due To Fumes And
176	Chronic Obstructive Pulmonary Disease	506.9	Unspecified Respiratory Conditions Due To Fumes
176	Chronic Obstructive Pulmonary Disease	748.61	Congenital Bronchiectasis

7. Congestive Heart Failure

Diagnosis Group	Description	ICD9	ICD9 Description
8	Congestive Heart Failure	398.91	Rheumatic Heart Failure (congestive)
8	Congestive Heart Failure	425	Cardiomyopathy
8	Congestive Heart Failure	425.1	Hypertrophic Obstructive Cardiomyopathy
8	Congestive Heart Failure	425.2	Obscure Cardiomyopathy Of Africa
8	Congestive Heart Failure	425.4	Other Primary Cardiomyopathies
8	Congestive Heart Failure	425.5	Alcoholic Cardiomyopathy
8	Congestive Heart Failure	425.7	Nutritional And Metabolic Cardiomyopathy
8	Congestive Heart Failure	425.8	Cardiomyopathy In Other Diseases Classified
8	Congestive Heart Failure	425.9	Secondary Cardiomyopathy, Unspecified
8	Congestive Heart Failure	428	Heart Failure
8	Congestive Heart Failure	428.0	Congestive Heart Failure
8	Congestive Heart Failure	428.1	Left Heart Failure
8	Congestive Heart Failure	428.9	Heart Failure, Unspecified
8	Congestive Heart Failure	429.3	Cardiomegaly

8. Depression

Diagnosis Group	Description	ICD9	ICD9 Description
160	Depressive Disorders	296.2	Major Depressive Disorder, Single Episode
160	Depressive Disorders	296.20	Major Depressive Disorder, Single Episode, Nos
160	Depressive Disorders	296.21	Major Depressive Disorder, Single Episode, Mild
160	Depressive Disorders	296.22	Major Depressive Disorder, Single Episode,
160	Depressive Disorders	296.23	Major Depressive Disorder, Single Episode, Severe
160	Depressive Disorders	296.24	Major Depressive Disorder, Single Episode, Severe
160	Depressive Disorders	296.25	Major Depressive Disorder, Single Episode, In
160	Depressive Disorders	296.26	Major Depressive Disorder, Single Episode, In Full
160	Depressive Disorders	296.3	Major Depressive Disorder, Recurrent Episode
160	Depressive Disorders	296.30	Major Depressive Disorder, Recurrent Episode, Nos
160	Depressive Disorders	296.31	Major Depressive Disorder, Recurrent Episode, Mild
160	Depressive Disorders	296.32	Major Depressive Disorder, Recurrent Episode,
160	Depressive Disorders	296.33	Major Depressive Disorder, Recurrent Episode,
160	Depressive Disorders	296.34	Major Depressive Disorder, Recurrent Episode,
160	Depressive Disorders	296.35	Major Depressive Disorder, Recurrent Episode, In
160	Depressive Disorders	296.36	Major Depressive Disorder, Recurrent Episode, In
160	Depressive Disorders	300.4	Neurotic Depression
160	Depressive Disorders	311	Depressive Disorder, Not Elsewhere Classified

Figure 31–3. USQA diagnosis groups.

numerator for each measure includes members from the denominator who have evidence of two or more admissions meeting the same diagnostic criteria as the admission rate.

The readmission rate ratio is an indication of all members who were admitted for the condition of interest who had multiple admissions for that condition. The readmission rate ratio for both COPD and CHF uses the numerator from the admission rate measures. For example, the COPD readmission rate ratio's denominator consists of all U.S. Healthcare Medicare members continuously enrolled in U.S. Healthcare from January 1, 1994 to December 31, 1994 who had an acute care admission for COPD. The numerator for this measure is all members from the denominator who have evidence of two or more admissions for COPD in 1994. The same specifications are followed for calculating the CHF readmission rate ratio.

The measure ambulatory follow-up after hospitalization for depression has as its denominator all U.S. Healthcare Medicare members continuously enrolled in U.S. Healthcare from January 1, 1994 to December 31, 1994 who had an admission for depression during calendar year 1994 based on a principal diagnosis ICD-9 code from an inpatient facility claim that falls within the USQA Diagnosis Group Depression (see Figure 3). The numerator is all members in the denominator who had a visit with their primary care physician, mental health provider, or visiting nurse within 30 days after discharge from an admission for depression. Evidence of the visit was obtained from any visit recorded in the encounters (primary care or mental health provider) or claims files.

Member access was calculated using a denominator that consisted of all U.S. Healthcare Medicare members enrolled in U.S. Healthcare from January 1, 1994 to December 31, 1994. The numerator was all members in the denominator who had any evidence of an encounter with the health plan based on any episode in the claims or encounters databases.

The measurement of member satisfaction evaluated satisfaction from three different perspectives: overall medical care, satisfaction with the primary care physicians, and satisfaction with U.S. Healthcare. Only those U.S. Healthcare Medicare members continuously enrolled in U.S. Healthcare from January 1, 1994 to December 31, 1994 for whom there was a satisfaction survey completed during 1994, and who provided an answer to the indicated question, were included in the denominator of each measure. For the overall medical care measure the numerator consisted of all members from the denominator who recorded a "good," "very good," or "excellent" in response to the question rating "overall medical care." For the member satisfaction with primary care physician measure the numerator included all members from the denominator who responded that they would recommend their primary

care physician to a family member. For the member satisfaction with U.S. Healthcare measure the numerator consisted of all U.S. Healthcare members from the denominator who responded that they would recommend U.S. Healthcare to a family member.

The overall response rate was 67.1 percent, based on a total of 18,289 returned surveys out of a total of 27,253 surveys sent.

Results

USQA produced the first Medicare Quality Report Card in November 1994 for 1993 performance. Because of limited enrollment in other U.S. Healthcare regions, the 1993 Report Card was produced only for the Southeastern Pennsylvania region. Publicly released in April 1995, the 1994 Report Card was produced for all Medicare enrollees in U.S. Healthcare. The measure of annual diabetic retinal eye exams was added in 1994. USQA will make year-to-year comparisons, where possible, between the 1994 and 1993 report cards for the Southeastern Pennsylvania region. Exhibit 31–3 lists the numerators and denominators of all 1994 measures for U.S. Healthcare overall.

The influenza vaccination rate of 65.5 percent compares favorably to the HCFA reported rate of 38.0 percent for 1993 Medicare influenza immunizations in Pennsylvania, and to *Healthy People 2000's* target goal of 60 percent for the year 2000 (see Figure 31–4).[17] The 1994 rate for the Southeastern Pennsylvania region is 67.3 percent, which is an improvement over the 1993 rate of 63.2 percent for the same region. The continued superior performance in this measure is likely the result of U.S. Healthcare's influenza vaccine reminder program, which provided all Medicare enrollees and their primary care physicians with a series of postcard reminders during the fall of 1994 to encourage compliance with this recommendation. In a separate cost-effectiveness analysis, USQA determined that 144 admissions for chronic respiratory conditions had been averted.

U.S. Healthcare has developed the tracking program U.S. Healthcare Check to encourage screening for breast cancer at appropriate intervals. This program is responsible for the impressive 73.5 percent rate of mammography screening every two years for women aged 65 to 75. This percentage exceeds the *Healthy People 2000* goal of achieving a mammography rate of 60 percent for women aged 50 and older

Exhibit 31–3 Quality Indicator Results

Measure	Numerator	Denominator	Result (%)
Influenza vaccination rate	21,315	32,524	65.5
Mammography screening every two years (65–75 age group)	4,852	6,601	73.5
Biennial eye examination	12,362	18,844	65.6
Diabetics receiving hemoglobin A1$_c$ test	1,908	2,632	72.5
Diabetic retinal eye exam	1,446	2,695	53.7
Chronic obstructive pulmonary disease (COPD) admission rate	130	25,945	0.50
COPD readmission rate	24	25,945	0.09
COPD readmission rate ratio	24	130	0.185
Congestive heart failure (CHF) admission rate	305	25,945	1.18
CHF readmission rate	62	25,945	0.24
CHF readmission rate ratio	62	305	0.203
Ambulatory follow-up after hospitalization for depression	59	69	85.5
Member access	24,851	25,945	95.8
Member satisfaction with overall medical care	16,331	16,830	98.8
Member satisfaction with primary care physician	16,388	16,912	96.9
Member satisfaction with U.S. Healthcare	17,691	17,870	99.0

(see Figure 31–4). The 1994 rate of 73.8 percent for Southeastern Pennsylvania also surpassed the 1993 rate of 72.1 percent and is consistent with the trend of increasing mammography rates documented in the U.S. Healthcare commercial population.

Because of the U.S. Healthcare Medicare plan's generous program benefit for eye exams, a full 65.6 percent of eligible Medicare enrollees had biennial eye examinations in 1994. The Southeastern Pennsylvania U.S. Healthcare Medicare rate of 66.4 percent in 1994 exceeded the rate of 63.6 percent calculated for 1993. This improvement is attributable to the U.S. Healthcare member education efforts to encourage the use of benefits important for early disease detection and prevention.

In 1993, a rate of 50.3 percent was calculated for the annual glycosolated hemoglobin test in diabetic patients. Through its continued research efforts, USQA has determined that there is a 15.8 percent false positive rate in the use of selection criteria identifying a member as a diabetic. The false positive rate is much higher (on the order of 40 to 50 percent) when only one medical claim, pharmacy claim, or encounter meets the criteria. To improve the specificity of the identification of diabetic members and evaluate and hold

accountable performance of a specific measure only for true diabetics, the 1993 rate was recalculated based on the more specific selection criteria of two or more claims or encounters. This new rate for 1993 was 56.3 percent. The 1994 measure using the same specific selection criteria was 72.5 percent for all U.S. Healthcare regions, with 72.8 percent in Southeastern Pennsylvania. This marked year-to-year improvement is likely the result of a number of diabetic initiatives undertaken by U.S. Healthcare in 1994. These initiatives include providing primary care physicians a list of their patients whom USQA has identified with diabetes in June 1994. A repeat mailing that was sent in December 1994 included a Diabetes Performance Report, which profiled individual physicians on their use of hemoglobin A1$_c$ testing and identified the most recent glycosolated hemoglobin of each of their diabetic patients. The 1993 calculation of baseline performance provided a foundation upon which physicians were encouraged to improve the quality of care provided to their diabetic patients.

The diabetic retinal exam rate is another example of how the innovative quality improvement programs that U.S. Healthcare implements can improve performance. In July 1994, a letter was sent to diabetic

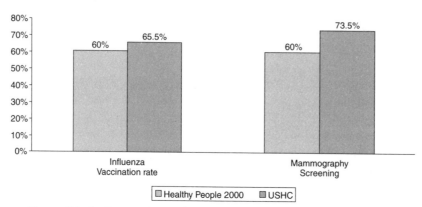

Figure 31–4. Comparison of USHC to *Healthy People 2000* goals.

members for whom a yearly retinal eye exam could not be identified. This letter stressed the importance of a yearly eye exam. Figure 31–5 shows the U.S. Healthcare results for its Medicare population for 1993 and 1994. As shown, the rate for U.S. Healthcare overall improved from 40.82 percent to 53.7 percent. Figure 31–6 shows the monthly rates that were annualized for all U.S. Healthcare members (commercial and Medicare; members may be counted in more than one month, thus accounting for the higher baseline rate than the annual rates). The baseline shows that the increase to 53.7 percent in 1994 can be temporally tied to the time of the letter given a flat baseline in the first six months of the year, but with a marked peak in July with a higher rate for several months afterward. Following the results out over 1995 will be important to determine whether the letter created a "Hawthorne effect" with a one-time increase without a lasting improvement, or whether a higher baseline will be achieved because of the one-time mailing. If the baseline falls back to the old baseline of approximately 40.8 percent, then an ongoing reminder program will be initiated to encourage USHC diabetic members to receive appropriate screening services.

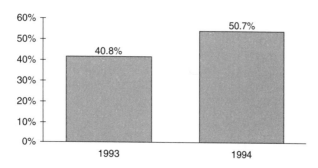

Figure 31–5. Impact of diabetes reminder program.

U.S. Healthcare has developed several Patient Management Programs that enable certain at-risk Medicare enrollees with chronic diseases to obtain additional medical service resources. COPD is a disabling chronic disease that leads to significant morbidity and mortality. Only 0.50 percent of U.S. Healthcare Medicare members were admitted to acute care during 1994 with COPD, and of those admitted, one in five COPD patients was admitted more than once during the 12-month reporting period.

U.S. Healthcare has developed a CHF Patient Management Program that provides additional resources to members with CHF to improve their health status and prevent acute exacerbations of their illness. During 1994, 1.18 percent of U.S. Healthcare members were admitted for CHF, and approximately one in five of those admitted for CHF were admitted more than once during the 12-month period. Although these statistics are good, it is hoped that the continued development of the CHF Patient Management Program will improve this rate.

The percent of members who had follow-up in the 30 days following a discharge from a hospitalization for depression increased in 1994 to 85.5 percent for U.S. Healthcare overall. The 86.7 percent rate for Southeastern Pennsylvania is increased from the 81.5 percent that was reported for 1993. This is a tribute to the continued success of the U.S. Mental Health Department at U.S. Healthcare, which continues to develop innovative programs to provide members with access to quality care for mental health conditions.

An impressive 95.8 percent of U.S. Healthcare Medicare enrollees visited a U.S. Healthcare provider sometime during 1994. The rate for Southeastern Pennsylvania was similar in 1993 (95.9 percent) and 1994

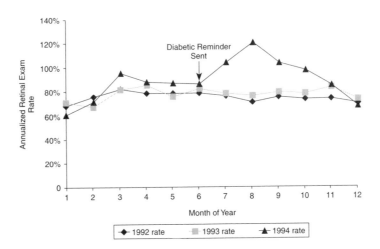

Figure 31–6. Impact of diabetes reminder programs for 1993 and 1994. Annualized monthly rates for all U.S. Healthcare members.

(96.2 percent). In 1993, 42.7 percent visited their primary care physician five or more times, and 34.4 percent visited their primary care physician three to four times in 1993.

The satisfaction level of Medicare enrollees continues to be exceptional. In 1994, 98.8 percent responded that they felt the overall medical care that they received was good, very good, or excellent. This was based on a high response rate of 67.1 percent to the survey. Furthermore, 96.9 percent of Medicare enrollees in U.S. Healthcare who responded said that they would recommend their primary care physician to a family member; 99.0 percent said that they would recommend U.S. Healthcare to a family member.

The development of the Medicare Quality Report Card is a tool that can be used by health plans to measure the quality of care to which its members have access, as well as their satisfaction with the plan. The report card rigorously measures health plan performance, and can be used to direct the development of programs to continuously improve performance.

REFERENCES

1. Iglehart, J.K. "Health Policy Report: Republicans and the New Politics of Health Care." *The New England Journal of Medicine* 332 (1995):972–975.
2. Health Plan Employer Data and Information Set Version 2.5, The National Committee for Quality Assurance.
3. McBean, A.M., Babish, J.D., and Warren J.L. "The Impact and Cost of Influenza in the Elderly." *Archives of Internal Medicine* 153 (1993):2105–2111.
4. Mullooly, J.P., et al. "Influenza Vaccination Programs for Elderly Persons: Cost-effectiveness in a Health Maintenance Organiza-

tion." *Annals of Internal Medicine* 121 (1994):947–952.
5. Govaert, E., et al. "The Efficacy of Influenza Vaccination in Elderly Individuals." *Journal of the American Medical Association* 272 (1994):1661–1665.
6. Kerlikowske, K., et al. "Efficacy of Screening Mammography: A Meta-analysis." *Journal of the American Medical Association* 273 (1995):149–154.
7. Solin, L.J., et al. "Downstaging of Breast Carcinomas Associated with Mammographic Screening." *Breast Disease* 8 (1995):45–56.
8. Riley, G.F., et al. "Stage of Cancer at Diagnosis for Medicare HMO and Fee-for-Service Enrollees." *American Journal of Public Health* 84 (1994):1598–1604.
9. *International Classification of Diseases, Ninth Revision, Clinical Modification.* Vols. 1–3. Baltimore, MD: HCIA, Inc., 1992.
10. *Current Procedural Terminology.* 4th ed. Chicago, Illinois: American Medical Association, 1994.
11. Rubin, R.J., Altman, W.M., and Mendelson, D.N. "Health Care Expenditures for People With Diabetes Mellitus." *Journal of Clinical Endocrinology and Metabolism* 199 (78) (1992):809A–809F.
12. American Diabetes Association. "Standards of Medical Care for Patients With Diabetes Mellitus." *Diabetes Care* 17 (1994):616–623.
13. The Diabetes Control and Complications Trial Research Group. "The Effect of Intensive Treatment of Diabetes on the Development and Progression of Long-Term Complications in Insulin-Dependent Diabetes Mellitus." *The New England Journal of Medicine* 329 (1993):977–986.
14. American College of Physicians, American Diabetes Association, and American Academy of Ophthalmology. "Screening Guidelines for Diabetic Retinopathy." *Annals of Internal Medicine* 116 (1992):683–685.
15. Ashton, C.M., et al. "The Association Between the Quality of Inpatient Care and Early Readmission." *Annals of Internal Medicine* 122 (1995):415–421.
16. NIH Consensus Development Panel on Depression in Late Life. "Diagnosis and Treatment of Depression in Late Life." *Journal of the American Medical Association* 268 (1992):1018–1024.
17. Public Health Service. *Healthy People 2000: National Health Promotion and Disease Prevention Objectives.* DHHS 91-50213. Washington, DC: Government Printing Office, 1990.

Part VII

Regulatory and Legal Issues

32

Legal Considerations in Managed Care Contracting

Wayne J. Miller

Health maintenance organizations (HMOs), preferred provider organizations (PPOs), and other managed or coordinated care organizations (MCOs) all generally have the same thing in common: their activities are in large part dictated by contractual arrangements with a number of different parties. This chapter will discuss basic terms of medical or hospital service contracts entered into with MCOs, and some of the negotiating strategies that often arise in connection with such agreements.

Types of Arrangements

A typical MCO, for example, an HMO, may have a number of basic contractual arrangements with different parties. These arrangements usually include the following six types:

1. Agreements with third party payers, including, without limitation, employers, trust funds, multiple employer groups, private insurers, and even other MCOs.
2. Health care providers, including, without limitation, hospitals, long-term care facilities, primary care physicians, and physician specialists.
3. Management and services agreements with nonphysician professionals, such as consultants, utilization review (UR) and quality assurance (QA) companies, and groups specializing in the administration of MCO contracting.
4. Agreements among shareholders or partners of the MCO pertaining to voting rights and distribution of profits.
5. Subcontracts with providers and others to fulfill obligations under contracts with payers that are not met by the MCO's main provider network,

such as highly specialized physician services, e.g., pediatric subspecialists.
6. Agreements with ancillary providers, such as, without limitation, laboratory, diagnostic facilities, pharmacies, home health agencies, and durable medical equipment.

Elements of MCO-Provider Contracts

In order to provide insight into the types of issues that can arise in MCO contracts, listed below are some of the usual substantive provisions found in agreements between MCOs and providers that are often at issue in negotiations. Of course, the following discussion is not exhaustive, and each contract should be reviewed on its own merits by the contracting parties and their counsel, as appropriate, to identify other issues that may be unique to each arrangement.

If the MCO is well established in managed care, it will usually offer a form provider agreement, personalized for the financial terms negotiated by the provider and the MCO. The MCO may desire that the agreement be accepted in nearly its original form, in order to maintain consistent terms among the various contracts with network providers and thereby reduce the administrative burdens of maintaining multiple contracts. However, providers often find that many terms in MCO form agreements are negotiable, so it is useful to become familiar with the basic contract terms and potential areas permitting further negotiation.

Preliminary provisions

These sections of a typical contract contain references to the parties to the contract and definitions of contract terms. From a provider's perspective, the named parties are important to know, since they may identify if the MCO is a separate entity from the payer for services and, if they are separate, whether both are directly contractually obligated to, or have "privity"

Top Health Care Financ 1993; 20(2): 17–25

with, the provider. From the MCO's or payer's perspectives, the person(s) defined as the provider identifies whether there is one or potentially several locations or groups of providers that are authorized to provide services under the terms of the contract.

The definition section, although often overlooked, should be carefully reviewed, since it normally includes key terms that dictate the scope of the services to be provided and the circumstances under which payment will be made. For example, this section usually includes definitions for such terms as "covered services," "emergency services," and "complete claim."

Covered services

Under the agreement, the provider agrees to provide "covered services" as part of a network of providers for patients of specified payers at a negotiated rate of payment, subject to certain conditions. The types of services that are "covered" are normally specified in greater detail in the body of the agreement or in an exhibit. From the MCO's and payer's perspectives, it is obviously desirable to define covered services as broadly as possible. From the provider's perspective, it is important to precisely define not only what is covered but what is not, since noncovered services are typically paid by the subscriber at ordinary and customary rates. Likewise, it is important to identify the services that are not available through the provider or its subcontractors; as to these services, the provider should not be required to provide or arrange for such services and these services should not be included in any all-inclusive payment rate, if applicable.

Contracts also normally specify the circumstances under which covered services are to be provided. This is also a key term for each party in determining their respective obligations to provide services and to pay for such services, as applicable. For example, as a condition of the MCO's or payer's obligations, the agreement may require a provider to obtain authorization to provide the service as well as verification of the patient's status as being covered to receive the service. On the other hand, the provider's obligation to provide services may be subject to the availability of beds, personnel, and the like. The provider may also seek to obtain a guarantee of payment from the MCO or payer if the provider complies with the authorization and verification procedures.

Another important aspect of defining covered services, especially in the hospital and skilled nursing facility setting, is identifying whether "ancillary services," such as laboratory, radiology, physical, and other therapies, are to be included within "covered services" and therefore are to be provided or subcontracted by the provider. As discussed further below, ancillary services may be included within an "all-inclusive" or other "at-risk" compensation rate paid for covered services.

Compensation provisions

The key compensation terms in a provider contract normally include rate, billing, and payment provisions.

Rate

The contract will identify the payment rate or formula for covered and, possibly, for noncovered services. In sophisticated managed care markets, the payment methodology may take a variety of forms and may include more than one type of formula. Traditional payment formulas include, for example, discounted fee for service, percentage of cost or charge, and fees based on relative value scales or diagnosis related groups.

Increasingly, however, there are more arrangements that place the provider "at risk" for extraordinary patient care costs, e.g., per diem, per service, and capitated rates. In capitated contracts, there is typically the potential for additional compensation out of "risk pools" maintained on behalf of hospital providers. Risk pools reward physicians and hospitals for utilization and costs under projected levels and penalize overutilization.

As noted above, where the payment formula places the provider "at risk," there is even greater incentive to ensure that the contract fully identifies which services are expected to be provided for the payment rate, as well as services that are paid separately under a different formula.

A provider may also desire to establish the payment rate for noncovered services under the contract, if not stated, preferably paid at the provider's usual and customary rates. The provider also may want to ensure that any separate copayment and deductible obligations of the patients are expressly stated.

Billing and payment

The contract will normally include procedures and billing for, and payment of, covered services. From the MCO's and payer's perspectives, these provisions typically specify the billing form to be used (e.g., UB-82) and also specify the period in which billings are to be submitted (e.g., 30 days). Payment is typically conditioned on providers submitting "complete" claims, which may or may not be defined in the agreement. The contract may also contain provisions specifying a penalty for late submission of billings, which providers typically seek to eliminate.

The payment provisions in the provider agreement typically identify the time period for payment of undisputed "complete" claims. In addition, payment procedures are often included for noncovered services and for copayments and deductibles, and these usually require direct billing of the patient. These provisions also usually contain coordination of benefits (COB) procedures (i.e., the payment priorities if the payer is primary or secondary, or if the subscriber may have a claim against a third party tort-feasor for the medical or hospital care). Often, COB provisions provide that if the payer is determined to be secondary to another payment source, its obligation to pay is delayed until the primary payer makes a final payment.

In addition to the timing of payments, these provisions often cause concern for providers because they typically limit the total reimbursement that may be received by providers from all payers for services to the contract rate; providers, on the other hand, may desire to collect up to their usual and customary charges from all payers, if possible.

Term and termination provisions

Form contracts prepared by MCOs or payers typically provide for an indefinite term or for automatic renewals. For instance, the contract may provide for a one year term, with an "evergreen clause" permitting automatic renewal unless one party gives written notice of termination prior to the renewal date. If a provider is unsure of the financial stability of the MCO or payer, or desires to revisit payment rates on a periodic basis, the provider may seek a short fixed term without renewals, requiring the parties to reach agreement first if the contract is to be renewed or extended. If a fixed term, no automatic renewal approach is followed, the parties need to consider whether they will agree to continue negotiations and their relationship if they are unable to reach a new agreement by the expiration date of the contract. An alternative approach that is sometimes utilized is to have a fixed contract term of several years, but to require renegotiation of rates annually. In this instance, the current rates would remain in effect until the parties reached agreement, with the new rates being effective retroactively to the commencement of the new term.

The form agreement usually permits termination without cause on notice by either party and may also allow termination for cause on shorter notice. Form termination provisions may specify in detail the events that constitute cause for the MCO or payer to terminate the contract, but may be less detailed or silent as to causes for termination by the provider. Often, the provider may seek rights to terminate the agreement upon, for example, failure to make payments; upon the dissolution or bankruptcy of the MCO or payer; or upon loss of any insurance, HMO, or other licensure.

Termination provisions often include postcontract obligations of the parties. These provisions typically mandate that the provider continue providing care to the covered subscribers at the contract rate for an often indefinite period following the termination or expiration of the contract. These provisions are important to MCOs and payers to ensure the continuity of care of their subscribers in their transition to new providers and to ensure that a provider completes a course of treatment that is in progress on the termination date. On the other hand, providers usually seek to limit the posttermination services period to a fixed length period (e.g., 60 to 90 days) and may demand their usual and customary charge if they are required to provide services beyond the initial period.

Utilization review and quality assurance

A key component in any managed care arrangement is the agreement by the provider to submit to the UR and QA procedures imposed by the MCO. Such procedures may provide for periodic reviews of cases, either on a retrospective, concurrent, or prospective basis, to evaluate the utilization and quality of services provided. They may provide utilization and quality guidelines and impose penalties for noncompliance with such guidelines, subject to appeal rights by the provider and the patient.

These procedures are usually to be attached as an exhibit to the contract, and may not be provided until the contract is signed. The contract may also enable the MCO or payer to unilaterally amend such procedures on notice. From the MCO's and payer's perspectives, such provisions may be justified on the basis that UR and QA procedures are considered proprietary and that they must remain uniform among a network of providers. On the other hand, providers usually seek to review the UR and QA procedures in advance of executing a contract to determine if they are reasonable and feasible. Likewise, they may seek rights to receive adequate notice before any procedures are amended and to terminate the contract if they do not accept any new procedure to be imposed.

Miscellaneous provisions

Form agreements often contain "boilerplate" provisions that may be presented as standard or nonnegotiable. Such provisions have legal implications for both parties, however, and deserve close review. They may include, for example:

- indemnification and malpractice insurance requirements;
- dispute resolution procedures (e.g., mediation or arbitration);
- ongoing disclosure or report obligations (e.g., the provider's licensing or accreditation survey reports are to be provided to the MCO or payer); and
- noncompetition, nonsolicitation, and geographic exclusivity covenants.

Precontracting Considerations

In the heat of working out a "deal," contracting MCOs, payers, and providers may neglect to do some background homework on the party (or parties) on the other side of the table. The instances of bankruptcies that have occurred among large HMO payers in recent years, and the increasing shakeout of contracting provider groups in states where managed care contracting has matured, underscore the need for both sides to a contract to conduct some basic due diligence to provide some assurance that the other party will be able to fully and properly perform its obligations during the entire term of the contract.

Review of MCO and payer

A contracting provider may find that it needs to investigate at least two parties, e.g., the MCO creating and administering the provider network and the payers responsible for paying claims. In actuality, an MCO may represent a *number* of payers, and the provider may find that, if it has limited resources or time, it may need to limit its review to the largest payers in terms of potential patient subscribers. In conducting its due diligence, the provider's main objectives are to establish whether the MCO and payer can deliver the business that has been promised, whether their financial health appears sound for the foreseeable future, and whether the financial arrangement is permissible under applicable laws, so that claims can be expected to be promptly paid upon submission and not disputed. The items that should be reviewed by providers include the following four:

1. *Financials.* Clearly, a review of current audited and unaudited financials of the MCO and the payer(s) should be conducted by persons knowledgeable about managed care. These documents should identify the total size and mix of the subscriber pool among the various plans offered, and the amount of business and revenues derived from among discounted fee-for-service, per diem, capitated, and other at-risk plans. This information may be used by the provider to more accurately project the types of patients and possible revenues that may be derived from the contractual relationship.

    The obligations identified in the MCO and payer financials should be closely reviewed by providers as well, since they may evidence potential problems that could affect cash flow available for paying claims and the future financial health of the organization. For example, if an HMO has usually high reserves for "incurred but not reported" liabilities, this may be a signal that it expects to pay large claims in the near future, which may affect its ability to meet its obligations to the contracting provider. Likewise, debt service obligations of MCOs and payers should be carefully reviewed to determine their impact on future cash flow. In addition, providers should review the terms of office or equipment lease, management, or other long-term obligations identified by the financials to estimate their ongoing impact on the profitability of the MCO and payers.

2. *Background review.* Contracting providers should contact other providers who are participating in the MCO's network to find out their satisfaction and potential problems that they have identified. Through these discussions and discussions with MCO and payer representatives, providers may want to review the recent operational history of the MCO and payers: e.g., whether actual performance met projections, whether claims are paid within contract deadlines or whether there is a high percentage of denials, whether the MCO is able to maintain long-standing relationships with payers and other contracting providers, and whether the MCO and payers have had extensive turnover of key management personnel.

3. *Network reputation.* New contracting providers should review the list of current providers of a network to evaluate their reputation in the community and quality of care, as well as the reputation and quality of the network itself among subscribers.

4. *Compliance review.* A quick review of actual or threatened lawsuits may provide insight into possible contingent liabilities of the MCO or payers. Further, if the MCO or the payer is a licensed entity, the provider could review their files at the licensing authority, which are typically open to the public, to ensure that they have complied with applicable legal requirements. The provider should also confirm that the MCO and payer maintain at least the minimum general and malpractice insurance coverage required by the agreement or by applicable law.

Review of new provider

If there is a choice of potential contracting providers in a particular geographical area, MCOs and payers are likely to also want to conduct a due diligence review in choosing among such providers. Such review is likely to encompass much of the same areas as noted above, including a review of financials, background, and reputation of each contracting provider. Above all, MCOs and payers will likely want assurances that each contracting physician network repre-

sents a fully organized group, individual practice association (IPA), or other association of sufficient size, experience, and, as applicable, affiliations to meet the primary care and specialist needs of subscribers in a managed care setting, and that each contracting hospital has accepted or intends to accept members of the applicable physician network on its medical staff.

In addition, MCOs and payers may request initial and ongoing information that they may use as measures to evaluate quality of participating providers. For example, for hospital providers, MCOs and payers may require evidence of licensure, accreditation and Medicare certification, as well as copies of facility surveys and notices of deficiency. Further, MCOs and payers may request that hospitals share with them outcome data that are compiled to fulfill accreditation and Medicare certification requirements. Physician providers may be requested to provide copies of any investigation or action by the state medical licensing agency or by governmental payers as well as notify payers of any pending disciplinary action of any facility. Likewise, MCOs and payers will monitor quality and utilization through the UR and QA program imposed under the payer agreements, as discussed above.

Negotiations with Provider Groups

As noted above, providers continue to form multiprovider groups in order to attract contracts with large MCOs and payers as well as obtain a stronger negotiating position. Although physicians, IPAs, and hospital networks are by now common in most parts of the country, in mature managed care markets, IPAs and networks are affiliating to create supergroups representing a multitude of providers covering large geographical areas. Among the legal issues that may arise in the formation of such groups, one concern is whether such groups may represent individual providers in contract negotiations with MCOs and payers in a manner that is consistent with federal and state antitrust laws.

Although a detailed discussion of antitrust laws is beyond the scope of this chapter, participants need to be aware that the organization and the collective negotiation by such provider groups on behalf of its members could be found to be concerted action of actual or potential competitors resulting in a violation of antitrust laws. Under federal law, for example, Sections 1 and 2 of the Sherman Act, dealing with monopolization and restraint of trade, may be enforced against providers by the federal government or may be asserted by private parties in a civil action. Under such laws, provider groups could be subject to essentially automatic antitrust liability if they engage in activities that constitute *per se* illegal price fixing, division of markets, and group boycotts, even if the groups do not command market power.

Prior to forming and operating such groups, providers should consult with qualified counsel to evaluate the potential antitrust risk. However, there are a number of considerations that may assist in reducing the potential risk, including the following three strategies:

1. *Noncompetitors.* Forming a contracting group of noncompetitors (e.g., due to geographical location) could reduce antitrust concerns. However, providers should be cautious before proceeding on this basis, and should confirm that members of their group do not constitute competitors for antitrust purposes.

2. *Financial integration.* To the extent that there is sufficient financial integration of group members, the arrangement may be deemed a joint venture for antitrust purposes and thereby reduce the risk of a *per se* violation. Financial integration may be demonstrated, for example, if the group enters into contract for capitated or other risk-sharing compensation, and if the group withholds member compensation in risk pools that may be distributed later based on the performance of the group or other criteria established by the group.

3. *Supermessenger.* The supermessenger model is relied upon in negotiating rates and other payment terms for provider contracts where there is insufficient financial integration of the members of a provider group. In this capacity, the group acts as a "messenger" between the MCO/payer and the individual members. Each member is polled separately as to their acceptable rates, which are communicated to the MCO/payer by the group, and the group notifies each provider of the MCO/payer response. Under this model, price and price terms are not collectively discussed or negotiated by the provider group.

In practice, provider groups have adopted mechanisms to streamline the process and reduce the potential administrative difficulties with the supermessenger model. One method is to have individual members identify a range of price and price terms that would be acceptable and to authorize the group in writing to adopt contracts whose terms fall within the acceptable ranges.

•   •   •

As both the managed care industry and providers become more experienced and sophisticated in contracting, it is clear that personnel participating in the process need to develop the expertise to recognize and address the various issues that can arise in a provider contract. The discussion above may be helpful to serve as a checklist for managers in their review of contracts and to alert them as to some to the areas that may be the subject of discussion and negotiation between the parties.

33

Legal Obstacles to Medical Communities' Full Participation in Managed Care

David W. Hilgers

The failure of the federal government to legislate a change in the health care industry has in no way slowed the health care revolution. Managed care has solidified its base in most major metropolitan areas and is now inexorably expanding from those centers into every nook and cranny of American medicine. If anything, the pace of expansion has increased in the last six months, and its impact is shaking the foundation of the health care industry. In all likelihood, before the revolution is complete, the structure of the health care industry will undergo a radical reformation unseen in medicine since the late 1800s.[1]

Presently, only the outline of this reformed structure is visible. No one can foresee the final result, or which of the present major players in the industry will remain standing in the end. Few doubt, however, that the final shape of the health care industry will be less fragmented with larger, consolidated providers and insurers.[1]

Physicians, as a group, are at a disadvantage in this reformation. Each of the other major players (government, employers, insurers, and hospitals) is far better suited to survive the consolidation, integration, and volatility. Although there are relative differences between these other major players, all have established histories of managerial experience, access to large amounts of capital, and far greater negotiating leverage in the health care market than physicians.

To compete with these relative behemoths and maintain some autonomy and control in the health care industry, physicians must consolidate and develop large physician-driven delivery systems. This is a monumental task. Physicians, in general, did not become doctors because they wanted to manage large organizations. They have not developed the skills or the knowledge required to operate large organizations. Additionally, they ordinarily do not have access to the capital that is necessary to create these organizations. Nevertheless, large physician-driven organizations have organized in various areas in the country. For example, there are numerous physician-driven organizations that have consolidated and maintained some control over the delivery of medicine in southern California, Houston, Texas, and New Mexico. It has been difficult in all parts of the country, however, for others to duplicate these examples.

This disadvantage for physicians may result in an inferior medical delivery system. There are many flaws in the American health care system, but the quality of its physicians is not one of them. Although this quality is not cost efficient, nor available to all U.S. citizens, the American physicians' demonstrated excellence in the practice of their profession is second to none. If the result of managed care is that physicians become merely employees of hospitals, insurers, large employers, or the government, then the quality of health care will suffer. Without substantial physician input into, and control of, the delivery of health care, the quality of health care must deteriorate.

This argument has frequently been made as a criticism of managed care. Change in the system of health care delivery is, however, both desirable and inevitable. Because of the excessive costs involved, the present system cannot continue. The market will not tolerate the excess costs created by the fee-for-service system. This does not mean that physicians and other providers should become merely fungible employees delivering a health care product without real autonomy and control. Instead, if the medical profession maintains a substantial voice in the manner in which health care is delivered in the new managed care system, then the health care product will be improved.

J Health Care Financ 1995; 21(3): 9–16

Unfortunately, natural market disadvantages are not the only obstacles to the development of physician-driven health care organizations. Natural market disadvantages have been exacerbated by a number of legal obstacles that block and restrain the development of physician-driven organizations. There are other less significant hurdles, but antitrust restrictions, antireferral statutes, insurance regulation, and malpractice liability risks each independently create substantial difficulties for consolidation by physicians. Additionally, the interplay between these four legal obstacles will continue to dramatically hamper consolidation of physicians in many market areas unless changes are made. This article describes these legal obstacles and their role in limiting physician consolidation.

Antitrust Restrictions

Because of fragmentation in the physician population, full consolidation of physicians cannot take place overnight. Most physicians do not have the management ability, the capital, or the desire to form large regional organizations to deliver care. Instead, physicians have come together in a variety of less-integrated forms such as preferred provider organizations (PPOs) and independent practice associations (IPAs), many of which defy clear categorization. They are mongrelized organizations—part corporate, part contractual, and part partnership. Even in the more sophisticated networks, there may not be full integration between primary care physicians, specialists, ancillary services, and hospitals. These partially integrated organizations are developed in order to provide the flexibility and cost management that is needed to deal with managed care, without establishing fully integrated corporate organizations. All of these partially integrated organizations must, upon formation, immediately be concerned with the potential effect of the Sherman Antitrust Act and its prohibitions against price fixing and restraint of trade.

Price fixing

The most obvious area of concern to partially integrated organizations is price fixing in the fee-for-service area. Any fully integrated group of physicians, such as a corporation or similar entity, is relatively free to negotiate fees as a group.[2] Any organization

that is not fully integrated, however, may not negotiate fees as a group. The group's lack of integration leads to its characterization as a conspiracy of competitors attempting to fix prices.

If groups of physicians cannot jointly negotiate fees, then they are helpless in the market of consolidated buyers. Employers are able to consolidate the demand of all employees for medical care and negotiate on behalf of employees reduced fee-for-service charges. Similarly, health maintenance organizations (HMOs) and other insurers are able to consolidate the demand of all their members and negotiate reduced fee-for-service charges. This enables employers, HMOs, and other insurers to easily play the fragmented physicians against one another, thereby reducing the physicians' status to the equivalent of an employee with no control over the delivery system. Only through group negotiations can physicians avoid total subservience to health care buyers.

A recent occurrence of such a phenomenon illustrates the arrogance with which HMOs treat physicians. A large HMO called all three cardiology groups competing in the market area to a meeting. When all parties were seated at the table, the HMO representative stated its demands, which included a low capitation rate, regional coverage, and a pediatric cardiologist, which none of the groups had available. When all three groups remarked about their inability to meet this demand, the HMO representative replied, "I guess you shouldn't have missed that day in medical school."

The antitrust restrictions allow HMOs and employers to shift all the risks in the provision of health care to physicians who are faced with take-it or leave-it decisions. Since physicians cannot negotiate prices as a group, they are defenseless. They must take the price offered or risk losing patients. Essentially, the entire health care system is placed at risk. HMOs and employers are free to lower prices at will. If a physician group is unscrupulous or guesses wrong, then the physician group may not be able to financially survive. If the group fails, it impacts not just the physicians, but the patients as well.

At present, any physicians operating a nonintegrated or partially integrated group, such as an IPA, must develop an elaborate "messenger" process in order to avoid price-fixing accusations. The messenger process requires each individual physician and physician group in the IPA to deliver their proposed fee schedule to an independent third party. Based on those fee schedules, the third party compiles a fee schedule that it then delivers to the IPA's management. By this method, the IPA's management has the ability to determine the level of fees at which it may market most of its physicians to HMOs and employers. The cumbersome process leaves much to be desired since negotiations with HMOs and employers often involve issues that the messenger process fails to address.

A more reasonable approach would be to place the price-fixing aspects of partially integrated organizations under the "Rule of Reason" antitrust doctrine. The real danger to the public of price fixing is the risk that all physicians in a particular specialty band together to jointly avoid price competition. As long as there are two or more delivery systems in any region, however, avoiding price competition would seem impossible to do. Therefore, there should be no prohibition against physician groups jointly negotiating prices so long as there is a least one or more other viable physician network or group in the market area able to compete in the specialty. Such relaxation of the antitrust rules would allow for the provision of quality health care by physician-driven groups, and at the same time protect consumers from price fixing.

Restraint of trade

The monopolization prohibitions of the Sherman Antitrust Act also create enormous problems for physicians attempting to consolidate.[3] In many small and even relatively large communities, it is difficult to assemble a physician organization without potentially running afoul of the monopolization prohibitions. For example, in a town of 100,000 to 200,000 people, it is not uncommon to have only half a dozen cardiologists. Often there may be only one group of cardiologists or obstetricians in an entire town. Therefore, a multispecialty physician organization could have in its organization 100 percent of the physicians practicing certain specialties.

Even a city of half a million or more people may have, for example, only 4 or 5 neurosurgeons, 15 or 16 gastroenterologists, 20 cardiologists, and 12 or 13 pulmonologists. Therefore, any substantial physician organization in the city will need in its organization over 50 percent of the members of a specialty in order to provide adequate coverage.

The Department of Justice and the Federal Trade Commission (FTC) have made efforts to help alleviate some of the antitrust uncertainties by publishing the *Statements of Enforcement Policy and Analytical Principles Relating to Health Care and Antitrust.*[4] Additionally, the FTC will issue advisory opinions upon submission of proper information. Even these efforts, however, do not resolve all of the uncertainties that face a physician organization attempting to consolidate. In a small city, it is almost impossible to fit within the safe harbors created by the Statements. Therefore, physicians must accept substantial risks when putting together a network since they may be subject to attack by the government. Additionally, the Statements give no protection against civil litigation by competitors, insurers, or other individuals in the market. This potential exposure is a significant concern for individual physicians. A large corporation can take some antitrust risks. If the corporation is found to be in violation of the antitrust laws, any damages will be assessed against the assets of the corporation. The individuals within the corporation have very little personal risk. On the other hand, when groups of individual physicians consolidate, they can be individually sued for violation of the antitrust laws and any damages will be assessed against their individual estates. Consequently, the antitrust laws are working in several ways to inhibit the development of a healthy counterbalance to the dominant influence of insurers and employers in the health care market.

Antireferral Statutes

The Stark statutes and the Medicare fraud and abuse statutes and regulations were, like many government regulations, adopted long after the need for reform had ended. Most of the damage to the cost structure of the health care industry from excessive referrals had been suffered long before any of these regulations began to impact the industry. In fact, the real impact of these regulations and statutes on health care costs will be insignificant when compared to the cost reductions caused by market-driven changes in physicians' incentives under the managed care revolution. With the advent of risk-sharing by physicians, the incentives to aggressively refer have effectively been eliminated. Incentives in the health care industry now work to create exactly the opposite risk. Now, the great fear is that, in order to enhance their income through cost savings, physicians will not adequately refer and will inappropriately ration care.

If this antireferral incentive is to be counterbalanced, it will be partially by physicians owning and having an interest in the ancillary services of their profession. Thus, the Stark statutes and the Medicare fraud and abuse statutes and regulations have created exactly the wrong prohibitions for the health care industry's new structure. For example, under many insurance plans, a physician is penalized for referrals to ancillary services. Thus, a physician sustains a loss in potential revenue when he or she refers to an imaging center, creating a great disincentive to make the referral. If the physician owns an interest in the imaging center, however, he or she will be much more likely to refer because the loss of revenue will not be as substantial. The physician will be receiving the premium for both the imaging center and his or her medical services and is therefore better able to manage the costs and reduce the disincentive for the referral. These government regulations now hamper the market development of a managed care system.

Presently, the Stark statutes and the Medicare fraud and abuse statutes and regulations are major obstacles to the creation of consolidated medical delivery systems by physicians. For example, a particular situation can arise when a community desires to establish a multispecialty IPA in which all the physicians own an interest in the IPA. If there is a cardiology group in the IPA that owns a catheter laboratory, then an IPA physician who refers to that catheter laboratory may be subject to the antireferral statutes because of the referring physician's and the cardiology group's ownership in the IPA. What if a physician group desires to develop an imaging center as a subsidiary of the holding corporation? Under the Stark statutes and the Medicare fraud and abuse statutes and regulations, the physician group cannot refer to that imaging center even though referral may be the best method of controlling costs.

This is a substantial problem despite the fact that a physician taking a capitation payment is not subject to the Stark statutes or the Medicare fraud and abuse statutes and regulations. There will be few groups that are willing to accept only a capitation payment during the early stages of consolidation. There will often be

contracts for fee-for-service payment, as well as contracts for capitation payment. Additionally, neither Medicare nor Medicaid have gone to total capitation payment. Therefore, any group attempting to consolidate is substantially limited in its ability to provide full health care services because of these antireferral statutes.

Further, a number of states have now adopted similar antireferral statutes. Unfortunately, most of the states have not enunciated the exceptions and safe harbors as clearly as those set forth in the Stark statutes and Medicare fraud and abuse statutes and regulations. Any organization attempting to consolidate, therefore, is at substantial risk of violating these state antireferral statutes. The best solution for this obstacle is to repeal these antireferral statutes and substitute risk arrangements for the delivery of Medicare and Medicaid services. This will allow the health care market to develop the systems it needs without antiquated regulations.

Insurance Regulation

Because of the enormous ramifications of managed care and capitation payments, most states are far behind in developing statutes and regulations that effectively protect the public while at the same time allowing for market flexibility. The entire concept of insurance has changed. Under the old system, insurance regulators could actuarially evaluate the risks taken on by an insurance company and require reserves sufficient to meet those risks. Under managed care, however, much of this risk is shifted to the providers. Insurance companies have effectively downloaded to providers substantial parts of the risks through capitation and risk contracts. The HMO statutes drafted in the late 1970s did not foresee the multiple ramifications of managed care. Therefore, many physician organizations that are trying to take risks and provide health care under this new system are uncertain as to the applicability of insurance regulations to them. For example, is a physician group without an HMO license permitted to contract directly with an employer on a capitated basis to provide health care services to the beneficiaries of the employer's benefit plan? Does ERISA preempt state regulation of this activity? Is a physician group permitted to subcapitate a hospital or a specialty group without being required to register as an HMO? The uncertainty makes it very difficult to determine exactly what a physician group is permitted to do in the health care market.

Because of this uncertainty, physicians attempting to provide managed care services in the health care market must take substantial risks. Recently, in Texas, the Department of Insurance determined that many physician groups presently providing services on a capitated basis are in violation of the Texas Health Maintenance Organization Act. In attempting to develop a reasonable method of regulating physician groups providing health care on a capitated basis, it seems reasonable to require a physician group to comply with regulations like those governing HMOs unless the physician group is providing strictly physician services.

Since physicians are always at risk, even when providing health care in a discounted fee-for-service system, there should be no substantial restrictions when a physician provides strictly physician services on a capitated basis. On the other hand, if the physician begins to provide hospital or other services for which he or she is not licensed to deliver, then HMO-like regulation is appropriate. Development of this system would enable physicians to market their services directly to employers without the prohibitive capital requirements necessitated by HMO regulations.

There is clearly a need to create rational regulation to protect consumers from failing delivery systems. If an HMO or an employer is obtaining 30 or 40 percent of its health care services from a physician group that subsequently fails, then the public is potentially at risk unless the insurance regulators have provided for such a circumstance. The insurance regulators should be cautious, however, that they do not overzealously protect the public from such risks to the detriment of development of the very systems that will cut costs and provide more cost-efficient care.

Some states have attempted to create new statutes to deal with the issues raised by the managed care revolution. Unfortunately, some of the statutes (like those in Minnesota) are so complex and create so much bureaucratic regulation that they stymie any creativity in the market. Simple statutes that allow physicians to develop delivery systems for their services with modest regulatory restrictions will serve both the consumer and the health care industry.

Malpractice Liability

A fourth major legal obstacle to the development of physician organizations in the managed care environment is the malpractice liability risk. The malpractice area has long been a source of great anger among physicians. Rightfully or wrongfully, physicians have felt that the courts have created an ad hoc welfare system for medical patients. A system that was intended to recompense plaintiffs for negligence has been converted into a system that recompenses patients for injury. The accuracy of this complaint, however, is not the issue for managed care.

Instead, it is a new phenomenon that creates the present problem. The plaintiffs' bar has long suspected that capitation and risk will substantially impair the quality of medicine. Therefore, it is not now uncommon to see a malpractice claim against a capitated physician include a count for intentional tort. The argument is consistently made that a physician has intentionally failed to perform a procedure, prescribe a medicine, or order a test, in order to save money and thereby increase the physician's compensation. This claim works against the concept of managed care. Society wants its medicine delivered at reduced cost. Therefore, it has created a capitation system to do just that. On the other hand, it does not want this incentive to produce reduced care. Thus, physicians are caught in an impossible situation. If they try to practice cost-efficient medicine, then they are subject to liability because of failure to order a test. On the other hand, society excoriated them for running up the costs by ordering tests that are later deemed to be unnecessary. Therefore, physicians organizing to deliver medicine in a managed care environment must weight the consequences of this liability issue. The greater the integration and, consequently, the more risks taken by the physician, the greater the potential for being sued because of "intentional" failure to render proper medical care. This intentional tort claim subjects the physician to liability that is not covered by insurance. Thus, the individual physician is again putting his or her estate at risk. In essence, the further a physician moves toward embracing managed care, the more personal risk he or she must have from the malpractice liability system.

The malpractice liability system serves a very useful purpose. There is a need to counterbalance a physician's tendency to reduce care in a managed care system. This potential liability, however, cannot be so great as to create unreasonable obstacles to the development of physician organizations. Therefore, substantial tort reform should be effectuated throughout the country. Mandatory arbitration and damage limitations should be implemented. The malpractice liability risk will still be sufficient to serve as a limiting factor on the physician's willingness to unnecessarily cut costs, while at the same time, it will not create unsurmountable obstacles to the development of an adequate managed care system.

•   •   •

The development of strong physician-driven delivery systems that can compete with HMOs and hospital-driven organizations is vital to the creation of a quality medical system for the United States. Unfortunately, the deck is already stacked against physicians by their fractionated position in the market today. If physicians are going to maintain a position in the market where they have substantial say in the manner in which medicine is delivered, then they will have to overcome perhaps insurmountable obstacles created by the economics that structure the system. When combined with the major legal obstacles to the formation of medical groups, the outlook is indeed bleak. The government needs to recognize the problems that federal and state laws have created for the development of physician groups. These laws can be relaxed without endangering the consumer to a great degree. The resulting benefit to the medical system will more than offset any potential risk of loss to the public.

REFERENCES

1. Starr, P. *The Social Transformation of American Medicine*. New York, N.Y.: Basic Books, 1982.
2. Thompson, M.J. "Integrated Delivery Systems—Antitrust Issues." Paper presented at the University of Texas School of Law 6th Annual Health Law Conference, Austin, Tex., 7 April 1994.
3. Sherman Antitrust Act, 15 U.S.C.A.§ 1(1973).
4. U.S. Department of Justice and the Federal Trade Commission. *Statements of Enforcement Policy and Analytical Principles Relating to Health Care and Antitrust.* 27 September 1994.

34

Miscellaneous Legal Issues Affecting Integrated Delivery Systems, Foundations, and Management Services Organizations

James F. Owens

In addition to those issues discussed in the preceding chapter, there are other legal issues that uniquely affect the formation or operations of an integrated delivery system (IDS), a foundation, or a management services organization (MSO). This chapter addresses some of the more significant legal issues involved.

Licensing Issues

IDS and foundation licensing issues

In order to provide services legally, an IDS or a foundation must either be licensed by the applicable state entity to provide the particular services being offered or fall within an exemption for licensure. Generally, hospital and other institutional-based services are required to be licensed, while many states allow exemptions from licensure for certain types of organizations providing physician services only. The rationale behind these exemptions is that there is sufficient control by licensed professional persons over the particular entity providing the services to ensure quality. Thus, a foundation, which only provides physician services, or an IDS which provides physician services exclusively, may fall within an exemption from licensure depending upon the licensure laws and regulations of the particular state.

An IDS or foundation failing to satisfy the applicable state requirements for either licensure or exemption from licensure could be subject to criminal and civil penalties. In addition, the improperly licensed or exempted IDS or foundation could be forced to return any payment for unlicensed services received from third party payers.

MSOs

An MSO is generally not required to be licensed as a professional or institutional entity nor must it satisfy requirements for licensure exemption since it generally only provides support services to physicians, physician groups, or hospitals, rather than professional health care services directly to patients.

Credentialing and Peer Review Issues

Selection and retention of a participating physician by an IDS or a foundation

A newly formed IDS or foundation must carefully establish criteria for deciding who becomes a participating physician and for monitoring the quality of care being provided on behalf of the IDS or foundation. Among other things, the failure to exercise reasonable care in screening and monitoring physicians could result in antitrust liability for improperly excluding a physician on theories of group boycott and monopolization.

For those arrangements where physicians provide professional services to an IDS or a foundation on an independent contractor basis rather than as an employee, the failure of the foundation or the IDS to exercise reasonable care in screening and monitoring physicians could also result in malpractice liability for claims arising out of alleged injuries to patients on a theory that the foundation or IDS negligently selected or retained the physician.

Establishing credentialing criteria

Noneconomic Criteria

The duty to credential participating physicians may be delegated to an organized committee of the

Top Health Care Financ 1994; 20(3): 61–69

foundation or the IDS, or even an MSO comprised of individuals with sufficient experience in such matters. Where the IDS or the foundation is affiliated with a hospital, it may choose to rely on the hospital's medical staff to credential the physician for participation in the IDS or foundation. The requirement of active staff privileges as one of the participation criteria ensures that the participants will be active practitioners or part of the local medical community, and known to their peers. It also provides assurance that the participants will pass the initial and ongoing scrutiny of the hospital credentialing and peer review process.

Where an IDS or foundation is interested in credentialing a physician who ordinarily does not have access to a hospital, such as a physician whose practice is simply outpatient or family practice, or specialists who may not have hospital privileges because of an exclusive arrangement between the hospital and another provider, it may be necessary to create special categories of physicians who may be exempt from the active medical staff requirement.

Economic Criteria

The criteria for obtaining medical staff appointments usually do not include factors such as a willingness to work toward minimum efficiency targets and other economic criteria because in most states economic credentialing by hospitals is illegal and against public policy. However, because these factors are crucial to success in the managed care setting, credentialing criteria should consist of certain business and economic factors in addition to active staff hospital privileges, provided that these criteria are developed in large part by the physician participants. Also, economic credentialing by a foundation or an IDS is less susceptible to a legal challenge because there is less opposition to credentialing based on economic concerns by a nonhospital provider than by a hospital medical staff.

Background Check

As with hospital medical staffs, during the credentialing process the IDS or foundation should consider state and federal laws that allow or require health care entities to query the National Practitioner Data Bank and the applicable state licensing board whether adverse action has occurred regarding a physician seeking to participate.

Conducting peer review

Peer review issues that should be addressed by the organizers of an IDS or a foundation include deciding who will be responsible for conducting peer review of participating physicians, and whether such peer review activities will be subject to any state or federal immunities.

Forming a Committee

As with deciding who will be responsible for credentialing physicians, participants in a foundation or an IDS should decide from the outset who shall be responsible for conducting peer review activities. In foundations, the responsibility for such activities should be expressly set out in the professional services agreement.

If the foundation or IDS is hospital based, it may be feasible to contract with the hospital to perform peer review activities. It is also possible to form a committee comprising members of the various organizations that constitute the IDS for conducting IDS peer review or members of the medical group and the foundation for conducting foundation peer review. It is conceivable, although not always advisable, that the committee responsible for credentialing physician participants could also be responsible for conducting peer review activities. In setting up the committee responsible for peer review, particular attention should be given to how the information is shared among affiliated organizations in order to ensure confidentiality.

Ensuring Peer Review Protections

Most states provide both evidentiary privileges for records and proceedings of peer review committees as well as immunity from liability for those individuals participating on such committees in good faith. Although those peer review protections may not expressly contemplate a foundation or an IDS, they may still be available to a committee of the foundation or IDS which is organized for the sole purpose of conducting peer review activities.

An IDS or foundation permitting economic considerations to enter credentialing or peer review deliberations may be sacrificing the legal protections granting them immunity for peer review activities. Under the federal Health Care Quality Improvement Act of 1986, specialty immunity from damage awards may be available for "conduct [that] affects or could affect adversely the health or welfare of a patient."[1] The Act states that its immunity provision "has no bearing on peer review of fees or utilization for cost containment purposes." Thus, the federal and state law immunities and privileges may not be available where the professional review action is based on concerns other than quality, such as economic considerations.

Providing due process protections to physicians excluded from IDS or foundation participation

Although the exclusion of a physician from the medical staff of a hospital has significant impact on his or her ability to practice medicine, the exclusion of a physician participating in an IDS or foundation may not. Therefore, in contrast to membership on the medical staff of a hospital, the current view is that physicians excluded from participation in an IDS or a foundation are generally *not* entitled to due process. Nonetheless, an IDS or foundation may decide to provide certain uniform due process protections.

Employee Benefit Plan Issues

Some of the more difficult issues that may confront an IDS, foundation, or MSO are how to ensure that (1) benefit plans offered by the particular entity will be "qualified" for purposes of the Employee Retirement Income Security Act of 1974 (ERISA) and (2) the existence of those plans will not jeopardize the qualification of existing plans of participants in the IDS, foundation, or MSO. Qualification of a benefit plan such as a pension plan, profit-sharing plan, or group health insurance plan is beneficial in that it allows an employer to deduct contributions and an employee to defer reporting the benefit and interest or earnings on the benefit as taxable income.

Requirements for qualification

The rules for qualifying as a benefit plan under ERISA are extremely complex and broad, and a detailed explanation of the rules is beyond the scope of this discussion. Basically, they include certain "non-discrimination" requirements which mandate that

highly compensated employees not receive a disproportionately greater amount of benefits than those received by other employees. They also include certain "coverage" requirements pertaining to benefit eligibility, vesting, contribution, and limits. Individuals forming an IDS, foundation, or MSO should consult with experienced legal counsel to determine how to structure the entity's benefit plan to ensure that it is ERISA qualified.

In addition, if an IDS is organized other than as a single organization, or is otherwise related to another organization, section 414 of the Internal Revenue Code may require the various employers comprising the IDS to be treated as a single employer for purposes of satisfying coverage, nondiscrimination, and other requirements for ERISA qualification. This is always a risk for foundations and MSOs, notwithstanding how they are organized. Separate benefit plans could lose their favorable tax treatment when analyzed together if they are offered by an IDS, a foundation, or MSO which satisfies certain tests under section 414, including the "controlled group" rules, the "affiliated service group" rules, and the "management organization" test.

The controlled group rules

The "controlled group" rules are prescribed under section 414(b) and (c) of the Internal Revenue Code. An IDS organized as a parent holding company system, a hospital-controlled system, a physician-controlled system, or an IDS/MSO affiliation may satisfy the controlled group rules. The controlled group rules specify that two or more organizations or persons will be treated as an employer for purposes of employee benefit analysis if (1) a parent company owns or controls 80 percent of the other organization or (2) a person or company owns an identical interest in two or more corporations or partnerships which is more than 50 percent of the total interest in each organization.

The affiliated service group rules

The "affiliated service group" rules are set forth at section 414(m) of the Internal Revenue Code. A service organization (the "first service organization") will be deemed part of an affiliated service group if, as defined under section 414(m), the other organization is deemed an "A" organization or a "B" organization with respect to the first organization. The affiliated service group rules are likely to be applicable to a professional medical corporation that has another professional corporation as its shareholder, a foundation, and the medical group contracting with the foundation for the provision of professional services, and to a typical MSO providing services to a medical group.

Management organization test

The "management organization" test or the "management functions" test is prescribed at section 414(m)(5) as another type of organization that will be aggregated with one or more related organizations for purposes of specified pension requirements. Under this test, an organization that has a principal business of performing management functions for one other organization (i.e., if those particular management services exceed 50 percent of the organization's business activities as a whole) will be aggregated with the organization that receives those services for ERISA qualification. For example, a typical MSO performing services for a medical group on a regular and continuous basis is likely to satisfy the management organization test.

It is important to note that the management organization test applies even if one organization does not have ownership of the other organization. Taken literally, the management organization test could classify a medical group that supplied a medical director to a foundation or an IDS as a management organization.

Recommended approaches

One possible approach to deal with this issue is to undertake an analysis of all the plans of all the aggregated entities in order to determine whether the coverage, discrimination, and other requirements are satisfied in the aggregate. If the plans do not meet the statutory requirements, the plans could be modified. Participants can determine whether the benefit plans of affiliated employers still qualify by conducting an actuarial study plan audit. However, conducting audits and modifying plans are likely to be expensive and extremely time consuming.

Probably the most widely accepted approach is to jointly adopt a single plan for the combined work force and to qualify the plan under ERISA qualification requirements. Existing plans may be terminated and rolled over to individual retirement accounts or to

the new plan. Another solution is to "freeze" a preexisting plan prior to affiliation. Although no additional contributions are made to frozen plans, they continue to exist and administrative expenses continue to accrue. Participants should be careful to consult with an ERISA expert to ensure compliance with all applicable laws if the participants decide to terminate or freeze an existing employee benefit plan.

Self-Referral Issues

Physician self-referral ban

An issue particularly relevant to an IDS organized other than as a single organization or a foundation is whether the organization being contemplated raises issues under the federal law banning physician self-referrals.

The law in its recently amended form provides that if a physician or a member of a physician's immediate family has a "financial relationship" with an entity, the physician may not refer patients to the entity for the furnishing of clinical laboratory or any other "designated health services" under the Medicare and Medicaid programs.[2] For referrals made on or after 31 December 1994, "designated health services" include the following ancillary services in addition to clinical laboratory services: physical therapy services, occupational therapy services, radiology and "other diagnostic services," radiation therapy services, the furnishing of durable medical equipment, parenteral and enteral nutrients, equipment and supplies, prosthetics, orthotics and prosthetic devices, home health services, outpatient prescription drugs, and last but especially not least, all "inpatient and outpatient services."

"Financial relationship" has been broadly interpreted to include almost any type of ownership interest held by the physician in the entity providing designated health services and any compensation arrangement between the physician and that entity. Certain express exceptions are provided for physician group practices, in-office ancillaries, prepaid plans, rural providers, personal service arrangements, bona fide employment, and other financial relationships. In addition to risking nonpayment for services rendered, sanctions for violating the federal self-referral ban include substantial civil monetary penalties and exclusion from the Medicare and Medicaid programs.

The federal self-referral ban is relevant when assessing whether an IDS or foundation can legally provide designated health services to patients of physicians who are associated with the IDS or foundation. For example, a medical group that has entered into a professional services agreement with a foundation would be considered to have a "financial relationship" with the foundation. Thus, any physician who is a shareholder or an employee of that medical group would be prohibited under the federal self-referral ban from referring Medicare or Medicaid patients to the foundation for designated health services such as clinical laboratory services. As a result, a medical group comprised of physicians who sold their clinical laboratories and other practice assets to a foundation would no longer be able to refer Medicare patients to those labs legally, even though the labs were formerly owned and operated by the medical group. The same would be true with regard to referrals to any additional designated health services occurring on or after 31 December 1994.

One school of thought is that referrals for designated health services between a medical group and the foundation with whom it contracts fall within the "group practice" exception to the federal self-referral ban. Under the group practice exception, physician services furnished on a referral basis are not prohibited if the services are furnished personally by another physician in the same group practice as the referring physician. The argument is that the foundation and the medical group make up a group practice in that they consist of "a group of two or more physicians legally organized as a . . . foundation."[3] However, this argument may not survive scrutiny because if the group of two or more physicians is contractually bound through their medical group to provide services to the foundation, they are actually organized as a partnership or professional corporation, and not as a foundation.

Beginning 31 December 1994, another possibility will be for foundations and the medical groups with whom they contract to satisfy the new exception under the federal self-referral ban for personal services arrangements. This exception, which also includes an exception for certain physician incentive plans, is expressly intended to apply to payments made by foundations under a contract with physicians to provide health care services. By ensuring that the professional services agreement meets the various criteria for that exception, the referrals will be permitted, notwithstanding the financial relationship that exists among the parties.

Therefore, organizers of an IDS or a foundation should carefully consider whether the IDS or foundation can legally provide clinical laboratory and other designated health services to Medicare and Medicaid patients referred by the medical group or physicians with which they contract in light of the federal self-referral ban and its exceptions.

Other self-referral bans

Both federal and state health care policy makers are paying considerable attention to recent studies showing that physicians who have ownership interest in freestanding ancillary health facilities have a financial incentive to refer their patients to such facilities, resulting in overutilization and corresponding increased and unnecessary costs. In addition, in December 1992, in the wake of the enactment of the federal self-referral ban, the American Medical Association adopted a resolution stating it is unethical for physicians to own centers used for self-referral unless it is necessary to meet a special medical need of the community or is the only way the particular center can be established. The result has been increased federal and state legislative focus on self-referral bans beyond both Medicare and clinical laboratories.

For example, the scope of the original federal prohibition was dramatically expanded through the recent passage of the Omnibus Reconciliation Act of 1993. Among other things, the amendments to the federal law extended the existing federal self-referral ban beyond clinical laboratory services to additional ancillary services or "designated health services," as previously discussed, while carving out more exceptions, such as the one for physician incentive plans. Proposals have also been made (e.g., the 1993 Health Security Act) to extend the existing ban to all public and private health care payers.

Momentum to ban physician ownership of health facilities is building in the states as well. During the early part of 1993, legislation had been introduced in over half of all the states curbing physician self-referral. As a result, organizers of an IDS or a foundation should be careful to comply with existing state self-referral bans and should structure their organizations with an eye toward being able to modify arrangements for providing ancillary services, as state and federal legislative bans become tougher.

Although early conflict-of-interest legislation by the states was largely concerned with ensuring that physician ownership interests in ancillary services were disclosed in conjunction with a patient referral, recently states have taken a more direct approach to prohibiting certain physician referrals. While the federal self-referral statute presently applies only to publicly funded health care systems such as Medicare and Medicaid, the numerous state laws addressing the issue apply more broadly to all third party payers. The types of health care entities and health care providers subject to the state law bans vary from state to state, and usually contain numerous exceptions. In certain instances, the state law may be much broader than the federal law. As a result, it is intended by Congress that federal law not preempt state laws that are more restrictive.

Law on Disclosure of Ownership and Control

An IDS or foundation that plans to be certified to provide Medicare services should ensure compliance with the federal requirements to disclose ownership and control information.[4] The rules are aimed at protecting the integrity of the Medicare program by disclosing ownership by physicians and other interested persons. Penalties for failure to comply with these rules could result in exclusion, termination, or suspension from the Medicare program.

The federal disclosure rules require a foundation, an IDS, and certain other health care providers that participate in the Medicare program to report any person who falls into one or more of the following four categories:

1. has a direct or indirect ownership interest totaling five percent or more in the disclosing entity;
2. owns an interest of five percent or more in any mortgage, deed of trust, note, or other obligation secured by the disclosing entity if that interest equals at least five percent of the value of the property or assets of the disclosing entity;
3. is an officer or director of a disclosing entity that is organized as a corporation; or

4. is a partner in a disclosing entity that is organized as a partnership.[5]

Among other things, these rules also require disclosure of the identity of any principals convicted of a Medicare-program-related crime as well as the disclosure of certain significant business transactions between the disclosing entity and any subcontractor. Reporting is required to the Health Care Financing Administration in some instances upon written request, while in other instances at the time the provider is surveyed by the state licensing agency or prior to the acceptance of a provider agreement by the program.

Additional federal reporting requirements pertaining to physician ownership require that an IDS, a foundation, and other entities that receive Medicare or Medicaid reimbursement must report the following: (1) all items and services provided by the entity that are covered by Medicare or Medicaid, and (2) the names and provider numbers of physicians who have a financial interest in the entity.[6] In addition, this law also requires referrals of clinical laboratory services under the Medicare program to be reported. The report entity is required to indicate whether the physician has an investment interest in the referral recipient. Currently, this is reportable to the Department of Health and Human Services upon changes of ownership, and as part of the routine certification and survey process conducted by state licensing agencies.

Some states have also enacted laws that require providers to disclose their financial relationships with other service providers to patients who refer to them. States differ as to the scope, requirements, and penalties of these laws. Accordingly, organizers of an IDS or a foundation should ensure policies are in place in order to comply with these laws and other reporting requirements upon the formation of the IDS or foundation.

Additional Issues

In addition to the issues discussed in this chapter and elsewhere in this issue, individuals involved in the planning and formation of an IDS, foundation, or MSO should review labor issues, such as issues arising under the Civil Rights Act, the National Labor Relations Act, and Occupational Safety & Health Act;

environmental issues; securities issues, such as requirements for registration and exemption from registration and disclosure; insurance issues; and certificate of need issues. Legal counsel should be consulted to ensure that these and other legal issues are considered in order to ensure compliance with any applicable federal or state laws or regulations.

REFERENCES

1. 42 U.S.C. §§ 11101, *et seq.*
2. 42 U.S.C. § 1395nn, as amended.
3. 42 U.S.C. § 1395nn(h)(4)(A), as amended.
4. 42 U.S.C. §§ 1320a-3; 1395nn(f).
5. 42 U.S.C. § 1320a-3.
6. 42 U.S.C. § 1395nn(f).

Index